WORLD RESCUE

March 2016

~

An Economics Built on what we Build

~

by Richard Register

For
Stella

ISBN-13: 978-0692659984

All drawings and photos by Richard Register

Book design and layout by Creative Juices: www.cjuices.com

Made available through Ecocity Builders, all contributions to that organization have helped make this book possible.

Books can be ordered there:
Ecocity Builders, 339 15th St., Oakland, California 94612, USA
More information from: www.ecocitybuilders.org

Contents

Our Ecocity Future – an economics built on what we build

Prelude

I was living in Los Angeles when it was the City of the Future. It was the car city world leader, the pace setter with its in-house #1 on the planet PR outfit called Hollywood and a steady supply line, direct from Detroit, of the tool for urban undoing. Already the Long Beach oil wells were drying up in the south part of the greater city and the source for the drug of choice, the energy it was running on, was switching over to the Middle East, as the city's parts scattered ever farther one from another, asphalt and acrid haze replacing fragrant citrus orchards and gorgeous views in winter to snow capped mountains. Remember the innocent, colorful, ever cheerful orange crate labels?

More for that story if you hang in here with me while I go from aspiring young sculptor living in Venice, California to doing my best to support the dream of the healthy, creativity-generating city, aka "sustainable," "resilient" or the truly lackluster "low-carbon" city. "Green" is a little better, being alive and given chlorophyll's role processing solar energy into the vast majority of nothing less than all of us Earthlings called the biosphere and our total economy. But I prefer "ecological" city, meaning guided by the principles of ecology, guided by life itself, with human economics a subset of the economics of nature. And why not the city supremely ecologically healthy and happy, congruent with the patterns of evolution here on this very particular planet?

My cities, infinitely varied versions of the ecocity, were more culturally exciting than just sustainable or resilient. Still are. *My* economics – the same for them. We can invest in and build a place where we all thrive, not just survive, and it – the city, town and village – can build soils and protect and restore biodiversity. The city can be a net contributor to culture, prosperity and nature too. It can restore dynamic climate stability and the happy snows of Kilimanjaro. Not by itself, but as part of a pattern of a six interrelated big solutions working together, a system we will discuss here later: the Six Big Ones of the economics to succeed as a species with our unique gifts, *with*, not apart from, all the other species. We can build soils using our organic "waste" and build biodiversity for healthy evolution – if by clear intent – on our fantastically beautiful planet. We can do all this only if cities roll back sprawl and provide the literal physical space to give nature a chance to work its magic and agriculture to feed its people.

We can coordinate city building, in economic strategy, with launching a world campaign to boost natural CO2 sequestration in forests, grasslands, agricultural soils, peatlands, mangroves, sea grasses and corals, and we can, to a large extent, roll back deserts. We can reverse global heating. How do we know we can't do that when we haven't even systematically tried?

We can match supply side renewable energy systems – solar and wind – with demand side city design and stringent recycling of materials to avoid producing excessive CO2 in the first place. Bhutan is CO2 negative, takes more carbon dioxide out of the air to place it in the soils of the country than it contributes to the planet's atmosphere. All countries could do that. Never have people had more tools, power and latent wisdom to do good and build the beautiful. But we need to summons our creativity and design and build things that way, make the decision and engage the enterprise with real resolve.

We need to face the fact that cities are the largest of human creations and they need to be confronted resolutely and changed from their currently immensely damaging form into forms and designs that can actually contribute to vitality of life systems on Earth. We need to do this as we go about converting sunlight and soil, through chemistry and energy, by way of plants and chlorophyll, into our products and services, largely embodied in and facilitated by the cities and towns we construct and inhabit: nature's economics transmuting into a nature/human combo, a total economics in a world that is both nature's and human's together at the same time.

These artifacts, the largest things humanity creates, not only shelter us but provide a context, a real physical lattice work that organizes – well or badly – our technologies and lifestyles – actually, life *ways*. It's that deep as well as practical in everyday delivery. When we speak in this book of building an economics on what we build, that includes building not just buildings and laying them out well as our cities, towns and villages, but also building the tools and the products and whatever makes them run.

In the city-form-and-design-first, then-fill-out-the-technologies approach, build a compact city, and then it works with and supports the technologies of transit, bicycles and pedestrians, which in turn support such a city. It's called a "whole system." Getting the form right and then the components that flesh out that form is part of what, later in these pages, I will call the "builders sequence." Build sprawl and only deserts of asphalt, endless swarms and clots of cars and lakes and rivers of gasoline can get people from point A to point B. But place those points close together and most of the intractable physical problems are solved.

For now, entertain this and hold it in the back of your mind: When I was in my 20s, we solved the smog problem in Los Angeles, a local atmospheric disaster – about 90% of said disaster – by fixing the car, by affixing the "smog device," not fixing the city. Now 50 years later, after showing the car could be a clean machine we have delivered of that leadership, with thousands of cities following LA's scatterizing example, a whole planet's atmosphere very significantly altered. And in the deal we now have a hotter planet and climate change for an entire world and all it's life forms including us humans. We've delivered even the rising of the level of the one great World Ocean and the shifting of its almost inconceivably vast currents. If that isn't an absolutely spectacular human failure requiring profound reassessment of human activity, what else could eclipse it? Maybe only and probably not quite, an all out nuclear war? We've paved over millions of acres of farmland and natural habitat, accelerated extinction of species world wide, and are accelerating toward, at some variously predicted date in a few decades, destruction of the economically available fossil chemical supply of organic origin that took the planet about 150 million years to create. This vast resource could be used as material feed stocks for making many things rather than just burning it up and transferring its carbon into the air.

Now my dream of the best possible cities – sculptures to live in that I imagined in my twenties – might turn out to be the lifeboats of my old age... maybe. They could be the vision of what to build for a deeply satisfying kind of prosperity. Though cars have taken over and distorted our cities radically since I first recognized something needed to be done about cities, we could still produce fabulous achievements for highest cultural expression as part of the human role in Earth's evolutionary adventure, create something still quite uplifting. Or, at this late hour it would be far easier to fail – or rather continue to fail – fail to heed the warnings and take up the positive challenge.

This book is about ecologically healthy cities – and quite a bit more that they are anchored in and profoundly influence. Such cities don't exist yet but some cities are improving fairly quickly now. It's also about a brand of economics only hinted at in a few other places and based on two things omitted or glossed over by conventional economics: nature's economics determining role in ours, and, what literally building has to do with building a better economics. Cities play a key role in this regard because they are by far the largest of human creations. Their impacts are stunning, not the least for changing the atmosphere of an entire planet, heating the whole thing and raising the seas, while not to be gainsaid in the slightest, while delivering cultural vitality and a certain kind of prosperity that could only be imagined with them operating like magnificent machines that crank out treasures and pleasures galore. I thought and still think there is no reason cities can't instead be helpful in every way – if conceived, designed, built and operated properly.

I have to admit my own work and that of those closest in thinking to mine amounts to something of a failure. Despite "green" features of cities being adopted in a scattershot kind of way everywhere around the world and getting better all the time, the general destructive impacts and continuing pattern of growth of the city of cars far outpaces urban contribution to environmental health, resources security and, eventually, social, cultural and economic peace, something I think of as a dynamic stability. It's not the kind of peace that sits placidly in a sunny, grassy field breathing in the fresh sun toasted afternoon smells, though nothing wrong with that once in a while, but a peace that goes out and builds a more exciting world even richer in experience, insight and fulfillment than we've ever seen before. That's the human creative enterprise, and it could be advanced with respect and compassion for all.

Perhaps, rather recently I thought, economics – which has some very curious and promising similarities to ecology and is similarly so all embracing – needs to be confronted with the insights and principles of the science of ecology. What we see now among "ecological economists" is the reverse: the effort to use the tools of economics to think through a better relationship to ecology. We need to emphasize the opposite: to use the insights and basic principles of ecology to transform economics.

For full understanding of complex living systems – and cities are complex living systems – long chains of cause and effect and broad networks of cross influence, the everyday stuff of ecology, have to be understood in the realm of politics and economics. The very creative and so-called whole systems thinking at the core of ecocity design holds profound insights.

Thus I began thinking of writing this book. Convinced as far back as I can remember that nature's economics are the basis of all life on Earth and from that basis, human economics too, and noticing mainstream economists seemed to have not the foggiest about such a connection, I began exploring the terrain of economics to see if something productive might appear. Some classic economic dogma struck me as close to insane, such as the notion that infinite growth in a finite world could ever be seriously entertained, much less seen as anything close to ideally "healthy." Also, how the dynamics of booms and busts could be meticulously observed and never learned from, as Alan Greenspan failed to do (or said he did) leading into the 2008 financial crisis.

Yet much in economics made sense to me, such as the relationship between supply and demand, the use of taxes and the power to loan on bank deposits not actually in the bank – fractional reserves – to supply money through government controlled interest rates, and so on. The market, at least if carefully regulated and mainly free, free among other things of false information about products and services and free of monopoly, looked very productive with reasonable delivery of prosperity to those contributing to useful and satisfying exchanges between participants in the market. Particular critiques such as those made about, I should say against, derivatives leading up to 2008 for example, made sense. But many financial services, such as simply providing loans at reasonable interest, obviously worked wonders. But at unreasonable interest, similar practices could abuse, even destroy broadly. These items of focus and many others are part of a pattern about which theories abound. But a great deal seemed to me to be missing if one were to take nature's systems seriously.

I began thinking an important key to a new economics was missing or glossed over: simply knowing what to build. Economists, politicians, developers, architects and environmentalists... none of them seemed to know what to build. During the Great Depression, and especially during the Second World War Franklin Roosevelt's administration had some powerfully effective ideas on that score, ideas for basic infrastructure and restoration of forests and soils. But shortly after the war we were all building for cars, not people, and building buildings, not cities, paving soils not enriching them. The disjointed and massive result now is well into degrading the world for all of us. We seemed to have forgotten something very important FDR's administration had begun exploring and literally building in both physical form and in finance structures and laws.

Along the way of my own education I noticed – it would be hard to miss if you set out on such a journey with such thinking – that reshaping cities for a more healthy and in fact sane economics was only a part, if a crucial and integral part, of the few major other "things" that had to be dealt with. Not surprisingly and true to our tendency to procrastinate and do the easy things first, the most consequential issues have been not only the hardest to confront but also the ones we have avoided most assiduously.

The "Big Ones" would be six in number,

#1 extremely high human population at the irreducible base of human numbers' needs and impacts on the planet, and...

#2 our environmentally destructive agricultural/diet nexus which for "food and fiber" has left practically no truly natural environment on the face of the planet, and, along with the effects of climate change, what's left changed and greatly reduced in biodiversity, natural biomass and fecundity.

#3 would be the built infrastructure of cities, towns and villages, the piece of the economics puzzle I will focus most directly upon herein.

#4 would be helping nature do what it normally does anyway. Given our current climate crisis – or catastrophe as it might turn out to be – that would be nature's role in sequestering carbon from the atmosphere. There are surprisingly easy tactics in a strategy I call natural carbon sequestration that can, first, get out of nature's way so it can work its normal mega magic on its vast global scale, the first and only real economic globalization that has been and always will be of energy and matter creating all life and even much of the geological substance of the Earth. Then, second, we humans can play a role of assistant to nature if we understand correctly how she works. We can function like a microscopic catalyst on Earth's surface, a kind of positive self-replicating workforce doing ever more of the right thing rather than a disease of the biosphere. We can tweak natural processes here and there boosting what nature does naturally in grasslands, forests, peatlands, shallow waters, open sea and coral reefs. We can get out of the way and help nature put in motion an impatient force like a wild mustang ready to charge forth, in this case the whole biosphere greedily sequestering carbon into its soils and sediments as new organic biomass and regenerated biodiversity in stunning vitality. Forget the massive, tricky, risky, untried terriforming technologies like filling the atmosphere full of sulfur compounds to try to darken the sky and cool the Earth, probably impossible anyway, as well as working against healthy solar electricity production, as well as *ugh-ly! That* part of the answer to oppose the problem is natural carbon sequestration, Big One #4.[1]

#5 is the first of the two non-physical big issues we need to confront first and all at once. It's generosity – which is the positive side of the coin whose negative side is greed and greed's low-powered cousin, lazy, easy, thoughtless, habit forming, lost in a fog comforts. Generosity's dimensions include giving from ourselves back to the Earth, repaying for the magnificent gift of our lives on this extravagantly varied and glorious planet. It's time for the good old sharing advocated yet largely ignored in action in all religions on Earth, and its time for an understanding of the "gift economics" at the values core of economic value that preceded capital economics all over the world. The "fundamentals" here are essential to understanding the links from nature's economics to human's economics. Now we need to give back, to invest in healthy *whatever it takes.* And that includes putting breaks on overconsumption, radically reducing over-exploitation, taxing the rich as if they had a warm philanthropic spot in their heart of hearts, which some do. Generosity means not stealing from others and ceasing to wage war, the ultimate opposite of generosity. Reinvest all that from the rich, from military budgets and from the wrong kind of infrastructure, which is car dominated… bring all that wealth to bear and rescue the world.

"Well, that certainly isn't about to happen!" Practical skeptics would say that immediately. But then if we actually can think it through, what are the chances that we could actually build genuinely and deeply healthy cities, begin reducing our population as if there were other living creatures with whom to share the planet's chlorophyll and basic biological product? (In some circles that's called ppp: primary photosynthetic product.) Could we come up with an agricultural/diet pattern that isn't based on massive inputs of fuel, fertilizer, irrigation and "fiduciary responsibility to investors profits only" corporate control?

It might be we need to reset our mind-set and start all over. Or maybe we just need to understand the connection between gift rconomics and capital economics (not capital"ist") when the kind of capital called money was invented to simplify the growing complexities of exchange as products and services proliferated. A little historic understanding often goes a long way. We definitely need the realization of just how high the stakes are, that a world cultural, biological and in fact evolutionary collapse is no longer just whispers on the fringes and in the nooks and crannies where cranky worry-warts lurk, but a state of things beginning to shake our state of being and the ground of consciousness like the early first waves of a colossal earthquake beginning to break loose.

In most basic terms, in this quest for finding solutions from a fresh look at economics, in taking ecology seriously and working with the design of cities, towns and villages from the neighborhood level to the whole potential "ecotropolis" level

[1] This line of thinking was launched for me by learning about the grassland restoring work of Alan Savory, Zimbabwe rancher and profound theoretician, with his animal grazing strategy as part of what he calls "holistic management." More on him later.

to the bioregional scale and finally the global... In all that, what I discovered was this: we need a short outline strategy to frankly and convincingly stated to rescue the world. It is not a new idea. Al Gore Suggested it in his book *Earth in the Balance* in 1992, calling for a "Global Marshall Plan," and Lester Brown called for something similar in his several *Plan B* books.

I need to emphasize at the outset that I'm not saying we need to rescue the geological, climatological and biological planet – and from ourselves. But we need to rescue all that *and* the whole world of society human beings have created with all our infrastructure, farming, happy filigrees of consciousness evolving, beautiful arts appearing and scientific exploration unfolding. We need to rescue all of both the natural and the people-created worlds. We need to rescue the "world" in that most inclusive sense, and a simple outline that gets its proportions of scale and importance right is the powerful good start to succeed.

It comes down to the "Six Big Ones." Population + agriculture + built environment + generosity + natural carbon sequestration + generosity and finally #6: simply education resolutely and energetically emphasizing the above five.

You might notice there is something different about this methodology than what our politicians say and business people sell. Their approach, beyond self-serving, with services of some sort to others, is rather random, piecemeal and lacks the order that makes much more sense. In many cases the short term apparent benefit promulgated "improves" something we shouldn't be involved with in the first place. You wouldn't want, for example, to improve a disease. Similarly, to improve the automobile is to assist in the spreading of suburbia out over farm and natural landscapes and encourage more car accidents and road kill, more commuting, less community face to face conviviality, more energy for transport and so on. The conventional approach to moving toward a hoped to be healthier, happier future is often tokenistic and may appear to help a little when what we really need is a massive improvement. On the theory that a little improvement here and there is all we can do, for example, no one has the courage to suggest we can actually reverse global heating if we get better organized, "get our act together."[2] Often little "improvements" are actually counterproductive, producing the illusion of improvement while diverting attention away from what will actually work.

Recently I've been pointing out this popular easy-things-first-approach is often called "picking the low hanging fruit." The idea: get people started on small steps in the right direction and then they will take longer more effective, more important steps later. Well then how come in the last 60 years better cars delivered us a scattered city with immense damage to nature, agriculture and society even to the point

2 Actually, James Hansen, long time head of the NASA Goddard Institute for Space Studies in New York City, and one of the most influential and earliest experts on climate change, has been bold enough to propose strong steps toward reversing global heating.

of changing climate and raising sea level? In fact, most people take a small step and – smug alert! – they become self-righteous about it, believe they are doing great already and resist further movement in the right direction. The low hanging fruit idea has failed badly.

Leave the low hanging fruit to the children. It's good they pick them and the starter exercise is thoroughly appropriate. But we who are past adolescence need to be adults now and step up to fight the difficult battle to rescue the world. How could it be easy? It will require profound change, and we will need to face those crucial issues head on. Maybe unfortunately, maybe for the best, it will be more like Winston Churchill's "blood, sweat and tears" during the Second World War, but also it would be our "finest hour."

A virtue of this set of major categories we need to deal with is its small number of categories, just six. (Some would say, "What about renewable energy with energy conservation and thorough recycling?" These apply to all the physical four and society has mostly understood this by now, if moving slowly and needing the direction provided by those first big four.) Another virtue is that our set of six categories insists on prioritization based on the proportionally more important things: no postponing. It provides a truly meaningful context and establishes a framework for seeing synergistic relationships. The ancient Chinese said wisdom begins with calling things by their right names. I would add: *and*, with getting those words well ordered in relation to other words in a clear language. Get the proportions right, get those big things clear, and their interrelationships take on meaning and we are well on our way.

Is the problem of doing all that at once absolutely insurmountable? Probably. Given the human propensity to make excuses in the face of difficult choices it will be an immense challenge. But what else might work? And down that path perhaps positive surprises that sometimes in history flare into brilliant progress will actually appear just around the corner. If we are on the right track and ready for such an opportunity we have a real chance for creating a far better world at the eleventh hour, averting collapse and striding into a creative, compassionate future. And that's the best hope and strategy I can try to offer.

2. Bell and airplane, ancient and modern – Kathmandu

These could be seen as symbols of time, space, speed, beautiful clear notes and a wide range of human experience. I imagine 200 people in the airplane, small we are in this picture, sailing along the face of the Himalaya Mountains needing to decide where we are all going and those looking up and wondering. Or just gazing.

Note on images in this book…

They are simply some of my favorite over the years, photos I took while traveling to speak at conferences and single person talks around the world. I use my drawings – some included here – as part of these talks I give. I also enjoy Photoshop. Warning: these images may or many not relate to the text.

Introduction

Gift of Life

Life starts with the ultimate gift, life itself. Then mother's milk gives more and baby's warmth gives back something wonderful beyond words, and, contained by memory, mother knows her own mother's gift to her as well – and her own happy obligation to the new child. Father protects, provides and receives. Both feel giving and receiving in the pleasures of sex, food, clothing, shelter, affection, comfort, profound unity or at least closeness, the irreducible community of 2 parents plus offspring, then cousins, uncles, aunts, friends cascading through the generations.

That was my first thought wondering where our economics comes from going back about as far as I thought made sense. I was contemplating writing a book on the economics of what we build, looking for a starting point for material exchanges among us people, including biological and ecological exchanges, even genetic. Guess what? The exchanges were emotional as well as material, perhaps eternally inextricably both physical and spiritual, genetic and created on the run for necessity and fun.

I was also wondering about economics because it seemed to me, as far back as I could remember working on ecological city projects and advocacy, something I've been doing for over forty years now, I'd seen few signs that those concerned with big investments and budgets – nations, states, cities, international corporations and big developers, the World Bank, Wall Street, even large NGOs (non-governmental organizations) – never seemed to get around to seriously addressing the design of cities, towns and villages. There was design for the elites, for the poor, for the car, for themselves (whoever was doing the designing and planning) but never getting around to the basic principles and dynamics you will see here in these pages. That seemed like a stunningly large omission considering the built environment we live in – our cities, towns and villages – constitutes the largest creation of our species. It was a puzzle and working it out might help me in my work on cities, maybe everyone else too since we all live in one or, one way or another, are profoundly affected by our built environment.

Another early thought in my growing interest in economics related to the idea I'd heard economists and investment managers repeat endlessly that all economics is strictly, with all pretense stripped away, about self-interest, pure and simple. Working on environmental issues for most of my life, usually connected to city design, this seemed true for some but very definitely false for many others, and in general I can think of few things "simple." If well ordered, complexity is certainly comprehensible with a little effort, but simple? Try a frontal lobotomy. You don't even *want* simple. Studying my own motivations and noticing the popularity of many things "green" and others "equitable" or "socially just" suggested there were millions of people primarily motivated by giving back to their world in one way or another. Certainly the old fable of King Midas turning his daughter to gold stood for a very real principle – there are few people quite so gold cold as to sacrifice their child for wealth. For most of us, loving our child gives mutual pleasure to both the parent and child. For most people, pleasure is much more than just for me alone. It tends to magnify when shared. That so much in economic theory and in the social sciences in general regarding human altruism and selfishness puts self-interest over all else seemed to me bizarrely out of touch. Something was profoundly wrong with mainstream economic thought and exploring it might help me further the project of building – literally building – a better future. Maybe I could help replace an economics of apparent fallacies with one that actually made sense.

And finally, getting down to proximate causes, there was the Crash of 2008, the Great Recession or Great Downturn, the Government Socialist Last Resort Bailout Rescue of Capitalism or whatever it will be known as to history one day. Could that have had something to do with a planet whose resources are severely stressed, whose climate and life systems are under assault? Could we be seeing the beginning of a time when there are so many of us that it becomes evident that, beyond a certain point, more of us means less for each?

True, when it came to the Financial Crisis, there was greed and complicity hiding behind those complex derivatives, paid-for credit ratings and lobbyist-supported congressional deregulators cranking out legislation making it illegal to regulate what was considered the dangerous banking practices that got us into the Great Depression once upon a time in the 1920s. But was something larger yet hiding behind top speculators, brokers, economic theorists, academics and wildly over-paid CEOs, traders and brokers? Could something in the "resource base" called over-stressed nature mean that we are never going back to what we considered the prosperity of the good old days of endless economic growth for an endlessly growing world population? What all that has to do with cities seemed to me to have everything to do with the quality of life for not just us the people but all other living things on Earth as well. Thus my motivation in writing this book is to seek solutions in the way we build both literally, physically, and in terms of building a new economics. Perhaps, in looking at economics as if it had something to do with what humans actually make with their minds and hands of the matter/energy, space/time world we are part of, we could then put economic theory on a much healthier track.

Cities: net positive contributors to a healthy planet

For most of my life I've loved the idea of building beautiful cities, towns and villages stuffed with cultural vitality, surrounded by thriving agriculture and running, hopping, crawling, flying, swimming wildness. I made sculpture in my late teens and my twenties and saw cities as something like three-dimensional sculptures we could live in, works of art, stunning views of and from skylines, clad in wild birds, native trees, gardens and orchards all surmounted by and permeated through with citizens loving to be there. I imagined architecture as wild as the woods and mountains, deserts and ocean shores, as liberating as the mobility of all the animals busy about their lives, as the plants growing in colorful profusion, working away at the literal ground of living being. I could picture myself at home in a neighborhood visited by hummingbirds as a regular thing, walking around the corner to my storefront sculpture studio – I had one in Venice, California for several years – taking an elevator to a terrace level ten stories up to a rooftop café with inspiring prospect overlooking town and country from doorstep to distant horizon. I imagined a ten-minute bicycle trip across town to a friend's apartment or out into the countryside to visit a waterfall. The town could run on one-tenth the energy of today's cities – I'll show how later in this book – while building soils and restoring biodiversity, and not to miss, taking carbon out of the atmosphere and putting it back in the ground.

For all that time I've believed cities, towns and villages could be net contributors to nature's bounty and health as well as to society's.[3] That was designable and buildable. Organic wastes can easily be transformed into rich soil; forests, grasslands and vast peat regions can be protected and holistically managed to add water to soils rather than add to floods, to sequester carbon from the air in enormous quantity while at the same time building fertility. Agriculture, shifting from chemical and high-energy mechanization to much more organic techniques, can do the same. Mangroves, wetlands and corals can be protected to grow and store vast quantities of carbon from both air in soils and water in underwater sediments. The intention to restore natural systems can do just that, from a scale as small as planting native plants in a window box to attract local birds and insects up to the scale of recovering and setting aside land to be rescued from the asphalt desert – as we shrink sprawl back to physically smaller footprint ecocities by shifting hundreds of millions of dollars per new freeway interchange to hiring people to help build cities for people instead of cars in traffic jams.

[3] I'd been saying net "benefit" city for years. Then Sustainability Director for the British Columbia Institute of Technology, Jennie Moore, suggested the best descriptor would be net "contributor" city. I think that's an improvement because a lack of negative features and outcomes can be a relative "benefit," but "contributor" implies the positive gift rather than only the benefit of reducing damage.

The ecologically informed city was, I suspected, the literal, physical concrete and steel foundation for a healthy economics. It would be big enough, provide shelter and organization of the detail in facilities and functions – cultural, social and economic – that would be the starting point for what we add to nature's economics of sunshine, climate and chlorophyll busily working away at the basis of production and all life. So for me, city-building was alluring and more than a little promising.

Economics itself, on the other hand, failed to stir rich imagery in my mind. The subject seemed abstract and dry, the "dismal science" so labeled even by some of its own "scientists." Many of the economists were a self-righteous bunch convinced they and their particular school of economics was the final true measure of all matters important, with other schools of economics deeply flawed and the general public strictly irrelevant other than as numbers of producers, traders and consumers to be studied and manipulated in theories around the self-interest principle. With the exception of those with a sense of humor like John Kenneth Galbraith, those on the right track like Herman Daly and those with style, grace, conscience and originality like Adam Smith, economists seemed like your prematurely dissipated fraternity jerks a little drunk and bellowing well into the wee hours of Saturday morning. It's as if the economists saw the people as machines on automatic pilot, programmed by the economists themselves (ideally of their particular school). They were condescendingly snide in their evaluations of each other, too. Their worship of numbers and constant scanning of charts and formulas in books and nit-picky papers, as compared to engaging in travel, art, music, astronomy, adventure of any kind, looked grim and boring. Their Nobel Prizes for game theory looked like playing around while the Rome of the environment and raging wars burned all around. And, as it turns out I soon discovered, said prizes were not endowed by Nobel's fortune but by the bank of Sweden, the Sveriges Riksbank – how they got permission from the Nobel Foundation to use Alfred Nobel's name when he never imagined a prize in economics I have no idea.

Meanwhile economists' amazingly complex formulas – try this on for size $Pr [T_A<1,T_B<1] = \phi_2 (\phi_{-1}(F_A(1)),\phi_{-1}(F_B(1),Y) (4)$, which you will find here in chapter 15 – based largely on assumed but not certain variables, resulting in unpredictable variance from the supposedly logical outcome – could be nullified handily by reality and quite frequently was. Their claims of discovering economic laws and attaining certainty looked far short of achieving predictability. Each economist was gloating on the obvious failures of the other schools of economics while writing up their own failures as successes. Think free marketeer Milton Friedman's visit to Augusto Pinochet one and a half years after Pinochet overthrew Chile's democratically elected government murdering its President, Salvador Allende, and several thousand others. Friedman adamantly attacked Allende's economics of attempted service to the workers and poor while advising Pinochet to tax the rich and powerful less, reduce regulation and services even further[4] and shrink the government budget another 25% – the military and police excepted. The result: continuation of Pinochet's reign of terror in Chile. Friedman claimed his was a great success.

If my readings about and by mainstream economists were representative – and I admit such investigations have been a recent exploration and hardly a life long career (which may be an advantage) – their numbers turned up rather randomly successful and unsuccessful and often disastrous results. In the real economy, whatever that might be, the matrix of multiple influences on equally multiple results with complex and long chains of cause and effect and patterns of networks of cross influence seemed to make predictability in their field quite chancy. Rolling dice, I thought, would be almost as helpful as consulting economists.

Though they erroneously saw themselves as scientists, as suggested by one of their most famous, John Kenneth Galbraith and by fairly famous World Bank nonconformist economist Herman Daly, most economists' thinking was actually far closer in style and purpose to religion than science, a true faith-based, self-referential and self-reinforcing belief system seeking superiority over other people and their belief systems. They had gotten themselves, each school of economics, into positive feedback loop systems of rationalization and what I will describe later as exaggerated gamesmanship. Dealing with numbers constantly, I surmised and so have a number of other commentators like Daly, economists falsely identified with physicists and mathematicians.

Trying to get at the essence of their mindset and mode of operation I noticed that much of their discipline revolved around "if-then" games. In games that everyone agrees to play there are rules that are made for the game. Everyone playing the game agrees that if this or that is the base condition and if the rules are agreed upon then certain plays based on the conditions and rules produce particular results. Economists play out all sorts of complex formulas based on "if-then" assumptions of agreed upon conditions and agreed upon patterns of changes determined by rules. Fair enough, and you can definitely win or lose games based on the structure of the "ifs" and their unwinding according to the rules of the "thens," if people in the game agree to the original "ifs" and to the rules. But what if the original "ifs" are not certain? And in the real world the real "ifs" seldom are. That's the most basic fallacy I can find in their thinking. (Well, maybe it's tied with the assumption of infinite growth and people as self-interest machines.) Then of course, what happens to the game if someone cheats or drops out or reaches under the table and pulls out a gun or sends in the Marines to grab the oil?

If the economists dealing with agreements people make as to monetary or comparative value of things assess the relationship of the agreed upon "ifs" properly and play by the rules, and if they win, then they get their money from other people agreeing to play the game. In many cases they've actually signed contracts backing

[4] Naomi Klein, *The Shock Doctrine*, Picador, Henry Holt and Company, New York, p.98

the agreements and agree that a court will determine what their contract means (what the rules really are) and who wins if there is a disagreement. In the game, the money that is won is translatable through other agreements as to value, then the winner can take that neutral unit of exchange and purchase some actual "stuff" or services. That makes them feel the rules of the game itself are a reality closely kindred to God-given when in fact only the exchange and what it yields as the physical thing or service is real in any fundamental sense. And, it is delivered only because of the overall agreement that everything has relative value and participants in the larger economics game agree to that.

Or, the real thing or service is not delivered because someone has the power by force to change or violate the rules or outcomes before delivery of what was earlier agreed upon. On the dollar bill in the US we have something that purports to guarantee the larger agreement, the inscription that "This note is legal tender for all debts, public and private" which means the government sanctifies and will enforce that you take the damn thing and fork over the goods – don't even think about refusing it or disputing it's market value if you have something on the open market to sell. No favoritism based on personal likes or dislikes or the like. There's a big game of macroeconomics played on the national and international scale in which our personal and business smaller games are played out. But winning the if-then game we play, inside the big macroeconomics game, is coincidental with, not proof that the assumed "ifs" at the beginning of the game were really valid with the rules meaning something more existentially true than agreements made up by and signed on to by players. In addition, success in "winning" also doesn't prove that the rules actually make sense. It only proves certain people honor their agreements – especially if they think a referee – a government court generally – will step in to interpret and enforce their agreement.

Another problem is the following: Somehow the economists missed that physics is based on not just measurements and math but the uniformity of basic components and principles and various "laws" of what seems to be something like a physical reality: atoms, units of mass and energy, proportional distances and speeds and uniform conditions where tests take place, gravity described in formulas everywhere in the known universe the same, energy dissipating outward from its source as the inverse square of the distance and so on, everywhere the same and dependable if not absolutely, absolutely, absolutely with no possible exceptions. Says one definition of science, it is simply "a means to get reliable information about our world." 99.9999% with no known exceptions is so good one can count on it as some kind of "Truth." If it always seems to work and you haven't found an exception yet, good enough. Play tennis in confidence that the swing of your arm, its angle, the direction and velocity of the ball and the dependable pull of gravity follow nature's rules. Or another definition: science is "truth without certainty." If it gets so close as to work for everybody and fail for nobody it is true for all practical purposes. Finally, science is "the only news. Everything else is he-said, she-said." I read this somewhere, but forgot where, attributed to Whole Earth Catalog creator Stewart Brand. If properly credited, congratulations Stewart. If enough economists say it, they only *say* (their kind of) economics is science – and convince themselves it is and see how many people they can drag along. Missing grounding in nature's basic principles then results in economics massive problems in getting even remotely close to the all-evidence-for, no-evidence-against test of a "reliable" "Truth." It is as if the economist says 51% (estimated!) counts as Truth, not 99.9999%. "Plus, we approve the data."

That's not good enough. Like the religious saying prayers with beads, the more they repeat it the more it becomes true, but in their case, economists call that science, not religion. Since what comes of it often fails spectacularly, as in the 2008 Economic Crisis, one can see the approach is not only not good enough but delusional to its always-and-only-growth-is-healthy, all-exchange-is-selfish, never-learn-from-experience core.

Conversely, in thinking through problems while understanding science, it's educational to notice that so much evidence and tireless experiment and testing supports the proposition that climate is changing radically and people have caused the change. Then one wonders at the conception of science the climate deniers have. They take seriously the claim that science is bunk from the mouths of wholly owned employees of oil companies trying to maximize profits. Beyond the slimmest possibility of doubt, and starting with experiments in the late 1800s, scientists have known a mix of gasses higher in CO2 absorbs more heat, and they know now to what degree according to concentration. They know there is almost 50% more CO2 in the atmosphere now than at the beginning of the Industrial Revolution, 401.3 parts per million[5] as I write compared with 280 parts per million then. Ultimate reasons for CO2 absorbing energy may not be absolutely clear, but it definitely happens this way, just as somehow gravity works to keep the Earth in orbit and tennis balls dropping in a dependable arc. Get used to it!

To deny something proven so clearly is what I call positive denial, denying something for which there is evidence all around. Negative denial is affirming something you want to believe for which there is no evidence, such as getting to a heaven by any particular description among many, a definitely faith-based proposition, to support a much-desired belief or community pressure. In a sort of opposite approach, the positive deniers, the climate deniers, deny the copious presence of definite evidence, "proof positive," to support a much-desired belief: that their powerful government will guarantee high profits to the energy corporations, cheep gasoline to the driver and fuel energy enough that the military will always adequately defend the deniers themselves from external attack. That people can look at the glaciers of the world in rapid retreat and see nothing represents a stunning level of climate change denial. That's nothing. There is no evidence supporting infinite growth in finite environments yet millions of people deny that non-existence saying there's something there, say the King's new clothes.

---

[5] http://co2now.org/current-co2/co2-now/ - Scripts Institute of Oeanography

Then there's the problem broached above. In economics, the basic unit is the individual human. They are not the same in attitude, even more so emotional stability in all things economic. In statistical analysis generally the larger the sample base the more accurate the predictability – until some novel social factor arises, a panic materializes, a religion promulgating suicidal terrorism becomes popular, everyone is shocked by a news item or that the plan for a victory in war didn't pan out that way and a vast number of real people are just plain dead: non-participants in the expected but – surprise! – now non-existent economic system. With people, predictability doesn't necessarily unfold from supposedly reasonable statistical analysis, and since we individuals are at the base of economics, unlike atoms and gravity in science... Under such "real world" conditions in which market and life play out together, economists thinking of themselves as prophets of precision similar to physicists (physicists claiming this only within their stated limits), becomes more than a touch out of touch.

Meantime the immense power of the economics machine humanity has constructed needs to be acknowledged and understood, precisely now, as its sheer magnitude of infrastructure and patterns of functioning are putting life on the planet in the worst crisis since about 50% of all species on Earth including the dinosaurs disappeared 65 million years ago. That was the Fifth Great Extinction Event, the Cretaceous-Tertiary Extinction. The present episode of rapidly growing extinctions is often called the Sixth Extinction Event by paleontologists. It doesn't have an acknowledged name yet but I'd nominate the Infinite Growth Economics Extinction, the Growth Economics Extinction for short, so basic is the fallacy behind infinite grown in a finite environment that the economists, in complicity with practically everyone else, have convinced themselves and others that growth is the basis of health.

But now, what's the largest most conspicuous element in that growth if you stop and think about it? Cities. Go to China and see this writ stunningly large.

Along with elimination of species by overexploitation, habitat destruction and through poisoning by pollution we have in addition climate change to accelerate the pace of the disaster. As this pattern seems to be the case, in some almost ultimate sense we need economists, real economists, who can deal with nature's economy at the same time as our own human economy, economists who understand that it's not just a numbers game (though there's nothing wrong with good math) but has everything to do with what we build and make, how that's laid out on the land, and how we use that created item that is the city, town and village.

There are self-labeled ecological economists but they say precious little about the built environment, how it is designed and its gigantic role in environmental matters – and as mentioned earlier, they should be using the principles and related ways of thinking of ecology to shape economics rather than vice versa. They should be economics ecologists instead of ecological economists.

So who is best suited to guide us when city, state, and national governments are all facing serious financial challenges – or think they are – and need some kind of major change? Isn't that a very primary economics problem? Budgets are almost everywhere in the red by millions of dollars in cities, by billions in states and by tens of billions in national governments. Only astronomy offers larger numbers to boggle the mind than the debt calculations of many governments as we move deeper into the second decade of the third millennium. Bankers' and investors' fates were recently gyrating wildly depending on who gets bailed out for mysterious reasons, if any reasons beyond insider friends, connections through the government/business revolving door, secret quid-quo-pro and the whims of lady luck. The same for large companies while small ones slide into bankruptcy and homeowners give up on mortgage payments and run to any relatives they can find for a bed, couch or meal and a chance to regroup and start over from a lower level.

Solutions here? John Maynard Keynes' deficit spending, but not in general but for investment in something that could solve these problems by building right in the first place then providing good return on investment? Build right and massive new flows of income from best investment can materialize – and did when the US applied Keynes' theory to the Great Depression and the Second World War. But of course it was simpler then when we either invested in fighting and winning or didn't and would have lost. Winning didn't exactly prove deficit spending successful; there was also the spoils of war to the winner and the fact that the United States was the only industrially advanced country whose landscape and infrastructure was not ravaged. But the strategy already was succeeding in various ways in the late 1930s in the US before the War clarified definitely that an investment was necessary for not just reviving from the depression but life or death survival. More on all that later.

3. Creek enters a small town downtown

Natural waterways in cities and towns inform citizens, especially children, how nature works. Thus are flowing waters more educational than designed fountains. Must leave enough depth for the water volume of floods, also educational.

Power, history, resources, capital on our side – if we know what to build

Yet never before has science, engineering, demand for democracy, social justice and ecological health been stronger, education more generally available or communications more broadly accessible and rapid. Never before have people been better prepared, at least in terms of available resources, relevant knowledge and technology, tools for change and the command of flows of mass/energy and money for the task of building a beautiful future. There are immense stores of capital that are being horded, not used, not pressed into service to solve our problems. There are immense flows of capital into war and preparation for war or threats of war to secure good business deals. In other words, something is going gravely wrong that, with a better idea how to spend our capital and activate our responsible, creative work, could be a future of very bright promise. Why don't economists talk about that?

A question arises in the face of all this. If we think in the context of our economy – and that's a context wherein we all live – if we hold the course and continue our consensus economic approaches of grow, bust, bailout and come back to grow even more again on a bumpy but ever higher consumption curve one rising bubble after another believing only an overall growing economy can be a healthy economy, can it really work?

Is there an end to speculative bubbles? Probably not. But how big the adjustments and how destructive are they going to be? They will almost assuredly go on forever in some form as an adjunct of human psychology. Policies to raise and lower interest rates to discourage or encourage borrowing and investing, manipulating the money supply, regulating the market to reduce risk – these policies that are fairly standard by now in the craft of everyday macroeconomics can, if we choose to use them, keep the size of the bubbles modest and their destructiveness in bursting from being too extreme. Such work by economists can undoubtedly do us a lot of good and should remain the core of whatever there is of service in economics.

Is there an end to growth? Yes, in terms of physical increase, but the infinite growth premise of economics is a whole different story than good management of monetized exchange and investment. The accelerating extinction of species, collapse of ecosystems, even the planet's climate system, is shouting loud and clear that there is an end to mass/energy growth in a limited environment, and a very unpleasant end for sure. Yet that is not to say there is a limit to ongoing human creativity and the creativity of life evolving in this universe. To change a set of habit patterns and economic assumptions that go back to the earliest exchanges wherein humans got a little more than mere subsistence and survival that could be saved and preserved or amplified, a little more that is of real benefit to the individual and those near and dear, sometimes called profit – *that* is asking for something dramatic, something to change everything in the assumptions of mainstream early 21st century economics. That is something we might call more generalized generosity.

We can sympathize with the infinite resources notion flying over the Pacific Ocean – it never ends and we are traveling at 550 miles per hour. *Damn* it takes a long time! Environmentalists like me tend to consider absurd the thoughts of the captains of the old whaling ships, that they would hunt their prey to absolute extinction; how stupid could one get? Don't they care about job security? Yet the ocean is immense. Lost on its vast surface, moving at a speed that takes weeks to cross its heaving waters, caught in storms at the edge of your personal oblivion, harvesting large quantities of fish and whale that rise from the infinite depths, given the energy of the sun, the fecundity of the seaweed, plankton, coral and krill, remembering one good year followed by a bad, then a good, then a bad, then a good… Of course it would never give out. There are swirling eddies of prosperity and dearth, fecundity and death out there that seem infinitely cycling on this big planet. In a way, we could well reasonably sympathize some with the no-end-in-sight whalers if we put ourselves in their soggy, salty boots.

But the real crime of economists is in having available to them, if not available to Captain Ahab, clear big numbers data about what's measureable as world decline in resources as their experience and *still* believing in, as economists swear to, infinite growth being healthy. Not to give up the faith so easily, the economist has another twist at the end of the chain of reasoning that even if the resource starts getting scarce, it becomes more valuable, ever more money to be made on ever smaller quantities until finally you've made an enormous amount of money on a very small amount of the last of whatever it is, take your profits and find something else to exploit all over again… maybe. That then bumps up against denial of demonstrated fact from the astronomers and astronauts: the Earth, if big, is still nonetheless just *this* big: finite.

An end to infinite growth on our large but limited planet, bound by cold space on one side and the hot layers of the lithosphere on the other, held down by the force of gravity and controlled by stores and flows of minerals and energy both wild and raw and transformed and made useful to evolution and ecology by plants utilizing their autotrophic (self-made) chlorophyll, demands nothing less than beginning to think like this in these pages – and then building something. It requires an examination of what we mean by prosperity for ourselves, we people, and for everyone else, meaning our fellow life forms on this planet we call Earth. It requires we think in terms of whole systems and not random reaction to immediate problems, seeing cities as whole entities like living creatures in their bioregions and somehow seeing something we could call the planet's economy as a whole systems pattern of mass/energy flows, stores, and new flows with these stores and flows following ecological rules guided by something we could think of as normal, healthy evolution. It requires commitment, hard work and a sense of duty as well as rights for each person's happier fulfillment.

My preliminary thoughts on economics

Contemplating the above notions two years before I started writing this book I found myself becoming more and more interested in economics. Not only did I think I needed to better understand the dynamics of money in my efforts toward building better cities but the sheer presumption of economists and those reporting their wisdom in the business pages began to interest, even fascinate me because of what's sometimes called cognitive dissonance. One day the Dow Jones was in free fall. Not long after the market was rocketing forward. Then the unemployment figures spelled doom. But suddenly a new boom in some crucial industry was the exciting thing to invest in for a real killing. Then Chinese subsidized products were driving America businesses bankrupt, and the oil companies not long after the BP Gulf of Mexico Oil Spill were making record profits. People invested in the stock market or desperate to hear good news about prospects for their businesses who take this wild-swinging reporting seriously must be experiencing extreme emotional whiplash. The "dismal" science began to interest me. The adjective dropped away and science got the quotation marks.

You had to admire the economists' cold-stare self-confidence when everyone in the world of ecology knows infinite growth in a limited environment is prelude to collapse or even collective suicide. Yet paradoxically the complexities of both economics and ecology, with their cause and effect chains and cross influences between countless actors in the total environment, are actually quite similar in pattern. So how then could economists that out of touch with basics about being alive on this planet (ecology) get such admiration and have so much influence in matters that actually matter a lot? And, to say they got credit simply because specialized in money and associated with the rich – and who doesn't want to get close to money and wealth – and were therefore respected in their delusions, might be masking deeper beliefs from other sources, all contributing to planet wide dysfunction. It looked like an interesting puzzle to try to solve and one with important implications.

I was meantime disturbed, because it seemed to me scientists, conscientious activists and even the few people who call themselves "degrowth economists" were failing to deal with the largest thing human beings build, the city, or more correctly, the built environment of city, town and village. Look out over any sprawling metropolitan area – how could they miss anything that big? Where'd their sense of proportion go? Things are *that* wrong with economic thinking. This enormous physical community infrastructure is home to probably around 90% of us, not just the 50% you hear about living in "cities" starting around 2009. Only the rare individual is a hermit in a mountain cave, a herding agriculturalist home on the range or a farmer, wife or child lost in a vast field of corn. The city, taken to mean our designed and physically constructed collective habitat down to the size of the village, is home to almost all of us and largely in its design and layout determines what technologies and life styles fit, what strategies can and can't work for restoration and preservation of agricultural land and natural habitat, what can work for the kind of social and cultural interactions we have.

Why then do the climate scientists, activists and politicians, diplomats and journalists not in denial about climate change mention practically nothing of city design, layout and function in and reporting about the United Nations conferences on climate change? Citizens of European cities, which are much more pedestrian and transit oriented than American cities use roughly one third the energy per person compared with Americans in their cities laid out for cars. Since energy use is so closely correlated with CO2 production and climate change you would think climate scientists and activists would be interested in such a potentially enormous reduction in the production of their prime greenhouse gas. 66% savings off the top is what's called a significant number, real money the economists would say.

Other puzzles interested me. Why is it, for example, when attempting to balance government budgets so few ever discuss going where the money actually is? The military, the rich and the automobile and oil industries wouldn't like it, of course, and editors want to keep their big advertisers and influential friends happy about the silence on the subject, among other things. Politicians get most of their campaign contributions from those three sources directly and indirectly, along with their information, heavily skewed by the swarming army of lobbyists they have to thread their way through to get to their offices. I've been there in the Congress office buildings weaving my way between and stuffed in elevators with lobbyists. I asked them who they represented and they weren't shy telling me. The legislator's story is that they have to get solid data – it's a technical, practical thing – from someplace and the lobbyists heap it up to stuff the agendas of any hearings where their employers and investors can make or lose money. Meantime out on the streets, most otherwise sensible people want to leave open the possibility they too can get rich some day: pinnacle of the ever so democratic American Dream. Dream on! We can all become President, a movie star! Well, identify with them…

More humbly, the great majority doesn't want its boat rocked. So they all quietly conform. After all, most of them work for the wealthy or at least for people who are decidedly wealthier than they are, and about a quarter of the US population works directly or indirectly for the military industrial complex or the automobile, fuel, sprawl development complex – people you don't want to get angry and fire you or tell your neighbors you are a threat.

I call those three – the very wealthy, the military and the car world the three sacred cows of economics in the United States. They are taboo. You leave them alone, you don't touch them, you never talk seriously about milking their wealth and you let them go about their grazing for money – vast amounts of it – without interference. They represent so much money I call them the three sacred *golden* cows. More about them later as they represent reserves of the wherewithal to build a genuinely healthy future and one to preserve the natural world while launching humanity into new realms of peaceful creative accomplishment.

The operative tools here are two: graduated income tax and the knowledge of what to build with the money liberated.

But we don't have enough money to do the job! Nonsense. Or as anthropologist Margaret Mead liked to say, "Fiddlesticks." We just don't yet have the vision and will to apply it well. When applied well, if those with the wealth of the three sacred golden cows worked and invested for the common good, they'd be heroes and we could all be proud of them, which is exactly what, in other fields of activity, already happens with the few among them called philanthropists.

Real economists

Another curiosity: those seriously brilliant people with powerful insights about economics "economists" think are *not* economists.

For example, Hazel Henderson, pointing out economists' frequent use of pie charts to explain their budgets. She likes to take the woman's prerogative of the until-recently-gender-dictated housekeeping and food-preparing role to compare economics to a layer cake. Human economy is built upon nature's economy, the first layer of the cake. On top of nature's economy is the second layer, the layer of the economy of giving and informal exchange, the "love economy" she calls it: family, friends and neighbors exchanging things, volunteering to help one another. Then the next cake layer up is the monetized dynamics of the untaxed and barely regulated black market, the third layer. Finally, there's the official and thoroughly monetized closely watched, above boards and taxed economy, built upon the other layers. It's controlled by government and custom and with coercive powers to force compliance to economic agreements through laws. Hazel considers herself an economist but one highly critical of her profession's mainstream and has often and famously said, "Economics is a form of brain damage." I wouldn't go quite that far, but in the hands of some mainstream economists, such as those who delivered to us the 2008 Financial Crisis, I would at least consider them infected with something dangerous.

Jane Jacobs with her logical reasoning and historic analysis of the economies of cities as the physical engines of productivity and prosperity is another such real economist in my mind. I'll have much more to say about her perspectives anon.

A friend of mine, recently deceased, was Kenneth Schneider. He delivered his perspectives in *The Runaway Economy – the Rhetoric is Growth, the Issue is Freedom* and what it has to do with what we literally build as cities, towns and villages, in his family-published book by that title, 2004, edited by his daughter, Leslie. In *Autokind vs. Mankind*, 1971, thirty-three years earlier, he dared to bring up the subject of the enormously destructive effects of cars on society, environment and economy, both urban and natural, and right when cars were taking the world by storm. With that he managed to get himself blacklisted and thus saw his career as a city planner and writer on city planning and design demolished. He was then forced to make a living at something else, namely printing and distributing colorful post cards of the US Southwest for his "day job" – at least he loved that part of the world and relished the imagery on his oversized post cards while writing subsequent powerful and little known, mostly unpublished books as his real work.

E. F. Schumacher of "Small is Beautiful," influential in environmental circles from the early 1970s, insisted on moderation in scale and economics and links of same to healthy society and ecology.

I include as a writer with powerful economic insights Chalmers Johnson who studied the budget-swamping economic position of the military industrial complex, one of my three sacred golden cows of the US economy and many other economies. There are over 730 US military bases around the world in addition to those at home, plus those "afloat," that is, Navy fleets. He reports on the drift toward the empire that America has become, a pattern in history that often plays out in catastrophic collapse and always in some kind of atrophy and disappearance.

Then there is Naomi Klein in her book "The Shock Doctrine – the Rise of Disaster Capitalism" with its study and critique of Milton Friedman's Chicago School and the catastrophes of his attempts at "pure" capitalism, if the welfare state for the military and police and protection for the already rich and powerful counts as capitalism, which raises the issue of decent capitalism vs. indecent capitalism.

Jared Diamond is another of my economists with his dissection of the ways in which civilizations have collapsed in the past with their many parallels with today's situation including exhausting critical resources, ecological and soil destruction, beneficial relationship with trading partners or wars with enemies and climate change. Building wrongly – even absurdly – as he details meticulously, has brought down many civilizations. As an economist to connect nature's and humanity's he's a real leader unappreciated as such by mainstream economists.

Sociologist Marcel Mauss deepened the analysis of early economics with his studies of gift societies in the Western Pacific and Northwest native cultures of North America. Patterns of economic exchanges there turn out to be well nigh universal as means of distribution of anything saved for a reasonable amount of time – "surplus." This arrangement seems to be an early economic development and notions that people started trading in the sense of barter, Mauss says, is a projection of our own habits looking backward, not evident until historically late in the game of economics. But don't think a gift is just a gift! It's an obligation to give and receive in an endless cycle and an expression of on going relationship for both giver and receiver, each reversing roles next time they give and receive. Exchange in these societies was not something done and finished with the completion of the exchange or redistribution but repeated in a continuing cycle of communities interacting to mutual understanding and benefit.

More recently there is Lester Brown who begins to explore the design and layout of cities involved in economic efficiencies but doesn't take that exploration very far. He doesn't, as far as I have read his work, address the city as an organizing principle and operative meta-technology – a technology organizing technologies –

for economic transition. But he gets close. What he does do – and in doing so takes an internationally leading role – is follow physical resources and technologies people use while tracking their availability according to fluctuating prices and trade, and relating all that to larger issues. He does this in his "Plan B" books citing much of the best most up-to-date information on resources, food, soils, energy, climate, condition of the ocean, transport and practically every other physical variable at play with the intent of helping us make decisions for maintaining a healthy civilization in the face of many threats. Close to the mission of this book, to literally rescue a world in distress, he provides one of the best approaches to planning a strategy for surviving and maybe even thriving. An economist? Can't do much better by my standards.

"But all these are not economists," trained capitalist and socialist economists will exclaim! Why not? They study value and exchange, and often in very systematic and detailed ways. Wade through the endless particulars of Diamond's "Collapse" if you want to see rich detail and exhaustive (some would say exhausting) treatment based on powerful insights and principles, many from the overlay of economics over ecology. For example, archeology shows central Pacific islanders harvesting shellfish that get smaller and smaller over a few centuries as the larger shellfish are harvested preferentially changing the genetic profile of the shellfish, until the people population shrinks to the point of disappearing completely. If that isn't an example of an economics, this time one close to nature's, leading to a serious conclusion I don't know what is. I for one make mental pictures of the details, think it gets me to the principles (inductive reasoning) and enjoy the plodding progress of Diamond's many points adding up to principles, and with many illuminating surprises along the way.

My economists have all dealt with wealth production, accumulation, exchange, hoarding for a rainy day or celebration and distribution as gift/obligations based on recognition of principles in evidence in nature's economy as well as human's. The classical economists have their principles too, but from an abstract, disconnected celestial sphere called free market price setting game theory, infinite healthy growth notions and we-are-selfish-only orthodoxy. You get to decide who is more relevant.

In this book we will be watching the physical form – city layout, architecture, public spaces, networks like streets, water and sewer systems and connected technologies – emerging from religious beliefs as democracy rose from ancestor veneration locked in patriarchal traditions. These traditions were replete with shrines, rigid bowing to small scale authority and locked-down family values that, in the ancient community tending toward cityhood, typically left nineteen out of twenty family members and retainers completely powerless in economics and decision making, i.e. politics. This period in the evolution of economics, not only in the West but evident in many places around the world, is portrayed by Fustel de Coulanges in his book *The Ancient City* which we will examine as we try to follow the threads that unite evolving economics with evolving physical community arrangements. His book is an engaging study of villages rising out of camps and cities out of villages in early Greece and Rome, setting many of the patterns that shaped...

...what sociologist Gideon Sjoberg greatly enriches in his perspectives of economics in that centuries long transition stage between "primitive" society and "modern," as *The Preindustrial City*. That is also the name of his book that I will be referring to. Neither de Coulanges nor Sjoberg address economics with a strong emphasis, but the subject is implied and partially described in the traditions they study. Moreover their work gives us insights into the physical base of societies coevolving with their economies and sets the stage for national mercantilism – government supported positive balance of trade enforced by military power and patterns within that larger pattern. All that leads next into the nexus of early capitalism and evolution theory while cities are beginning to get quite large and complex by all measures: Malthus, Darwin, Wallace and Margulis. Lynn Margulis you might not have heard of; I'll be proud to present her to those who don't yet know her as one of our major evolutionary theorists with strong implications for influencing human economics built on nature's economics.

Then look at the transition to neo-classical capitalism. Then something on the reaction: the labor movement and Marxist theory in the time of monopolies and child near slave labor, and the more moderate anti-trust legislation response (moderate compared to violent revolution) in the late 1800s and early 1900s. Then the Franklin Delano Roosevelt/John Maynard Keynesian way of revolution-avoiding reform of capitalism in the face of world depression and war seeking something more democratic and dynamic yet balanced other than right or left wing fascism or communism.

We will look at the case of China, invaded violently for commercial exploitation in the 1800s with western powers setting up "concession cities" on its mainland and the island of Hong Kong, then later under Communist government welcoming in foreign capitalist investment and business in their former concession cities become Special Economic Zones (SEZs) starting in 1978 promoting a new round of production and trade – but under very different terms. A surprise here: China's connection by way of those SEZs with Lynn Margulis' evolution theory of endosymbiosis. Her contribution adds the cooperative balance to Darwin and Wallace's illumination of the role of competition in evolution.

And not to leave out, we will watch ecological economics rise – largely around "green" and moral jobs – in recent times from those concerns while almost entirely missing the city, largest creation of our species. Throughout, the city and the role of literally building a healthy economics becomes much of my contribution now in trying to understand a better economics for the future.

My thumbnail historic sketch will necessarily be... sketchy, it's so broad, but I hope to hit upon a number of best ideas conspicuously lost to most economics thinking. I'll note certain people have hit the nail on the head – or missed rather spectacularly. I will confront Ayn Rand, Friedman, Reagan, Greenspan, the Gramms, Clinton and the other architects of the financial crisis of 2008 and their continuing influence, not in much detail but featuring them for their more consequential stumbles or outright crimes of greed, greed for money, political power or both. And I'll herein contemplate economic trends and larger patterns generally neglected. We'll be looking for those potential solutions and fresh perspectives that will be new to most readers, some of them quite insightful, I believe. I will be citing my work with the non-profit corporation Ecocity Builders I founded in 1991 and highlighting my most recent work in China and Bhutan, that latter being the Himalayan kingdom of Gross National Happiness – GNH – and world leadership challenging the infinite growth mania of maximum production and consumption GDP, a country with 1 / 2000th the population of China. There should then be quite a range of perspectives synthesized as we wind up.

Along with my views that will be frequently offered throughout this book on economics, its history and perhaps its improved future largely via what we build, maybe I should offer a definition of my own: An economist is someone who has something insightful, well organized and important to add to our understanding of healthy, happy production and use of products and services by, for and of nature and society.

4. Understory, canopy and emergents

The action in rain forests is mostly in the canopy, with a different shadier, calm air environment below and taller trees emerging to tower over the whole forest. One way of organizing a town, too.

BEGINNINGS – SECTION 1

CHAPTER 1

Warm up – First Steps in my Economics Education

When I became an economist

I was impelled deeper into reflection on economics for two reasons: first the worries more and more of us are sharing, which have to do with resources degeneration and the drift toward societal and ecological collapse, which is *not* the main emphasis of this book, and second, what *is* the main emphasis, aspirations for building a better future that have seemed to me ever so clear and easily within reach if…

As I was thinking more and more about all this, I began to see economics in terms of nature's economics with solar energy alighting on the planet's soil, and agriculture tapping into that solar flux with chlorophyll delivering transformed solar energy to the realm of us people via rearranged chemicals from minerals, water and gasses transformed to "food and fiber" via trees, bushes, vines, grass, seaweed and various animals. Also from many living natural sources, medicines and dyes. From non-living nature the list goes on: stone and metal for building and tools for example, water for drinking, salt for preserving food. Then the ecological services: pollination, spreading seeds, fertilizing soils and the non-living services of rain, rivers, oceans, breezes, climate…

Economists like the rest of us know all that but act like they don't, or rather *officially* think and act like they don't. They operate at a higher level of abstraction. They deal with resources, labor, management, capital, exchange and reinvestment with all of it monetized. Have they lost the basis of all their theorizing? Are they really operating at a higher level?

But if Human Economics is based on nature's economics and the economists either don't know that or if they do but neglect the fact for their profit or membership qualifications in a particular school of economics which in turn credentials their credibility, then maybe, I concluded, I'm not such a bad economist myself. Just to think about the subject with an open mind sets the likes of me off from mainstream economists I'd been learning about. I began to think, "I may even be a better economist than many of them are."

My evaluation of my own level of economic insight verged on the smug when I saw a YouTube on the Internet in which Alan Greenspan confessed he hadn't seen it coming.[6] Seen what? The subprime mortgage and runaway derivatives crisis, the Financial Crisis of 2008 that threatened a super-sized crash. George W. Bush who also helped it happen saw it better than Greenspan: "If money isn't loosened up, this sucker could go down."[7] (He knew that much about legit economics craftsmanship.) If the President waited far too long providing the bail out to the wrong people and the celebrated Chairman of the Federal Reserve was blindsided, but not me, I knew I must be a fairly good economist, in fact better, in the things that matter massively, than Greenspan was. I knew exactly what was happening in the macro economy in regard to the real estate market because I was simply willing to look at the conspicuous: the ever so obvious bubble expanding. Call it beginners mind, or just open eyes, or the honesty of not happening to be bought off or dependent on someone of dubious theory bestowing me credentials or paying my salary, benefits and bonuses.

The crux of the matter is in the seeing itself. Watching Mr. Greenspan I had one of those "ah-hah" moments as a naïve realizing, like the child in "The King's New Clothes," that the King was naked and most others were, or at least had been, in the denial of deep conformity, sell out or fear. Maybe it was embarrassment, as it has now been famously recorded that members of Congress simply didn't want to look foolish when they didn't understand Greenspan's gobbledygook and simply took him at his word that he understood subprime mortgages and the derivatives

---

[6] There are many You Tubes available on the internet recording his confession; this one's pretty good and to the point: http://www.youtube.com/watch?v=1bX_vhojH8c&feature=related

[7] New York Times, "Talks Implode During a Day of Chaos; fate of Bailout Plan Remains Unresolced," David Herszenhorn, Carl Hulse and Sheryl Gay Stolberg, Sept. 25, 2008

market and they were all perfectly safe, as well as offering almost unbelievable potential for personal profits. Why they'd be the healthiest things going for the economy. And if not that, the healthiest things going for congressional and presidential campaign treasuries of both Republicans and Democrats filled by donations from speculators, Wall Street brokers and those associated with the big banks.

But could Mr. Greenspan have been lying, that is, did he see this major crash coming but hoped it wouldn't happen on his watch, taking his cue to retire a little more than a year before the plummet? All the reasonable people were saying it was a disaster about to happen; Warren Buffet, no slouch when it comes to economic theory and serious investment, called the derivatives "economic weapons of mass destruction." Or by claiming surprise, did Mr. Greenspan try to protect his profession and the earlier totality of his role in the inflating then bursting of the bubble by pretending he and most self-interest-above-all-else, deregulation market, infinite-growth economists were just blindsided by some rare miscalculation or random, fluky and unlikely to be repeated act of God or Fate rather than a theoretical blunder? Worse yet, had he and they committed moral transgressions granting free reign to greed or even committed illegal crimes leading to what happened?

In the documentaries and YouTubes that cover his mea culpa so well, in Henry Waxman's Congressional hearings among other interviews, he certainly looks like he was honestly stunned by what he didn't understand. He said there was a profound flaw in his "world view." Be that as it may, either way it's good reason to turn to common sense economists like me, and those of the sort I've mentioned above and others I'll be writing about shortly.

I didn't think I was quite ready to think of myself as an economist quite then, however. I needed some more visceral, even tactile experiences to convince me. *That* time was when I was driving with my friend Paul Richards through an enormous housing development being built just east of the San Francisco Bay Area town of Castro Valley, California around 2006. Paul was interested in the layout of the subdivision because the developer was leaving strips of land for walking and bicycling paths along "creeks" – well, almost. The low-lying strips were seasonal drains at best, with flowing water during and seeping water between rains in the wettest of the wet season, not exactly creeks. They'd be creeks if we had a climate like Portland's or Singapore's.

What I noticed was the big houses with wide driveways, hundreds of houses. "How much do these places cost?" I asked Paul. In the $500,000 to $600,000 range he said. That was a little stunning to my ears.

"How on Earth could they afford them?" I had co-owned a house and sold in the already somewhat inflated Berkeley, California market 15 years earlier for $150,000 and to make part of my living I had built and remodeled many houses over the proceeding 30 years. So I thought I knew a little about making mortgage payments relative to income and some basics about real estate and the real costs of constructing buildings.

"Well, a couple with two incomes buying one of these houses figures the market is going up and everyone is making a lot of money on the market. Get a mortgage with nothing down, borrow to make payments for a while if you have to and sell it a year later for an extra $100,000 or so. People have been doing that for a few years now. The real estate agents are encouraging them to turn over the houses – 'flip' them, they say. That way the agents can make their fees flow in faster and bigger, too." Which was the gist of what Paul said.

"That can't go on forever!" said I. I was then and there, even reflexively, intuitively, a better economist than Mr. Greenspan himself. I predicted a coming collapse, he didn't. Being an ecologist in addition to a budding economist, I could also grasp that you can't have infinite growth on a finite planet. Bubbles breaking like they did in 2008 and 1929 prove you can't even have growth that's too unreasonably fast even before you hit the wall of ecological or resource limits. Ecologists have learned that in countless observations of nature. Economists have failed to learn that despite countless observations of bubbles that invariably burst, some with mild, some with disastrous results. To ecologists however it is survey course 101: ecological imperatives and overshoot.

Proportionality

Proportionality, my friends, proportionality. People unwilling to look the six big issues in the eye, the factors that are so large you'd think them conspicuous, like the millions of wildly over priced houses promoted by extremely low interest rates (in the realm of macroeconomics), or the rush of millions of under funded people to dreams of unearned personal profit (in the realm of microeconomics), or for example those who want a big house and have to "drive 'till you qualify," that is, head out of town and keep going until the price of the house more or less matches what you can afford, or think you can… these people can't possibly be good economists. They weren't paying attention to geological depletion of oil deposits and the certainty (long term anyway) of increased prices of gasoline, which has a great deal to do with economics since our machines run on fuels or electricity and electricity itself mostly on fuels.

You have to look at the truth to be good at anything good. To ignore the expanding bubble based on sheer speculation, as opposed to actually making and selling something for good solid delivery of goods and services or investing in same, is ignoring something crucial, especially when even the economists themselves talk about bubbles with respect if not awe for their destructive power and inevitability – *last* time around. Then full steam ahead in forgetfulness again, another word for which is oblivion.

The same for turning your back on corruption, which Mr. Greenspan said he thought would sort itself out with minimal or no regulation from those who think financial gain is the most basic human impulse with trickledown benefit for all justifying unlimited profit for themselves and their small class of elite. Boy! Where'd he get that idea? If one can get away with it, corruption is always the easiest, fastest route to maximum return on minimum investment. It's a slightly more subtle or convoluted form of simple stealing, with a gun or a fountain pen, as Bob Dylan said. Said Greenspan, the greedy would be honorably self-regulating, and he said it with apparent absolute conviction – and apparent shock later on when it turned out that it didn't turn out that way.

The more I studied the more I realized there were countless interesting and often entertaining detours down the path of my investigations, and to my surprise my little exploration was turning out to be more of a pleasure every day. It would have been inconceivable just a year or two earlier to think I couldn't even put the damn books down. John Kenneth Galbraith was one of my favorites – he was frequently outright funny. Even Adam Smith from way back in the late 1700s had the wry wit to make me smile. Short quips in a long history were high points I'll not forget. From the good burghers of New Amsterdam using Indian shell money for lack of coin for exchange and not wanting to talk about it later to the convoluted tale of introducing the paper money of China – with the warning printed on each bill for all to read: "Counterfeiters will be decapitated… the informant will be rewarded with 300 strings of cash."[8] Later the Chinese authorities completely abandoned paper money. Then they brought it back. What were they thinking? It was getting more intriguing every day. I could picture myself watching society as fairly durable commodities like dried grains measured in bags became a medium of exchange then gradually were replaced by uniform bits of much longer lasting metal becoming coins. In China, ever early and active in economic innovations, coins started out as imitation tools like spades and knives so connected were they going back thousands of years to the labor theory of value, upstaging Marx by about 2,400 years (Zhou dynasty, 5th Century BC). Note also the connection in the early years of economics the close relationship, the "grounding" of "spade money" in what we build… with our tools that become literally money, then non-functional "tools" transmuting into real (representations of the real value but with no other utility) money.

Investors in Elizabethan England backed Sir Francis Drake's ventures and other pirates' for a share in their slave trade and profits from loot from attacking Spanish ships, with a 50% share to the Queen with her blessings. (Talk about high risk investing in possible windfall profits – it can get worse than investing in derivatives.) One year, Drake brought back more than half the income Elizabeth's treasury received from all sources combined.[9] Why trade when, with better ships, charts,

[8] Ralph T. Foster, Fiat Paper Money, the *History and Evolution of our Currency*, Published by Mr. Foster, Berkeley, 2009; original quote from Jacques Gernet, Daily Life on the Eve of the Mongol Invasion, 1250 – 276, MacMillan, New York, 1962, p.80, 81

[9] Wikipedia on Drake's life: http://en.wikipedia.org/wiki/Francis_Drake

compasses and clocks (for finding east/west position), weapons and resolve, all you had to do was enslave, kill and steal, tricky though those might be in such high stakes "exchanges" (of cannon balls and long flailing razor blades called swords). Then I remembered being shocked by the pretty young Los Angeles dental receptionist I met during the American war on Vietnam days who, as we walked along the beach, her silky hair tenderly brushed by the breeze over her smooth sun-kissed skin, said she got up to 30% annually on her investments in defense contracting companies. She said, quite coolly, "Where else could you get a better return on investment?" Napalm for the poor half a planet away and riches for her. It was a little slice or reality memory coming back to me on economics as I read on...

Also, I noticed economists seemed to be ignoring what seems to be the *real* economy. Oddly the term "real economy" turns up off and on even among mainstream infinite growth economists. It seems everyone including such economists themselves intuitively understand that to use the word "real" means you are talking about the economy of production of goods and services and their utilization by whomever buys them, trading around in a way that the market says is pretty just and balanced, honest, healthy and fair. Everyone accepts that bankers should store and loan money for good projects and be paid a reasonable profit for the service. No problem with that kind of finance in the real economics.

But the manipulation of sheer hoards of money and the control of numbers that represent money, reduced to microscopic magnetized granules on spinning disks constituting computerized records of various sorts these days, results in the finance/investing/gambling sector of the economy, which produces no product at all but profits to speculators – if they win – represents an amazing 40% of the ("paper") wealth "earned" in recent years in the United States. That's real wealth if you cash in the paper at the right time. Something so physically useless – gambling finance contrasting with the city so physically useful – being a source of an astounding share of the market, struck me as strange indeed. Legitimate and properly proportioned compensation for financial services, no problem. But when that slides into risky gambling on a massive scale and potential economic collapse with millions losing their jobs and life savings... I decided I had to learn more about that too.

5. Desert town at night with stars

Just a massing model, linked on ground level and about four stories up. Water from desalinization – a little expensive in this location near the coast but money is saved on not having car infrastructure so it's available for eco-architecture. If the population of such projects is high, then you salt the waters of the ocean too much locally – several things always have to be considered in as parts of whole systems.

The right title

Coming up with a title for a book can be trying. You hope it will mean something revealing about the book and be catchy. In my case, for this book, I also hoped people would take the enterprise of the writing and reading herein as something important, demanding action. Thinking about the title actually brought up some thoughts I think are worth sharing with you, dear readers.

To get to a basic construct of economics, an early thought was *Shrink for Prosperity*, a kind of slogan title expressing the reverse of the "grow forever" economist's slogan. The logic there, as flawed as the infinite growth notion, is that the fewer of us, the more for each, like in dividing a pie for four people instead of eight you get twice as much for each of the four. But you just need a lot of people to have a vital, diverse economy, to make the pie, so in raw mathematics as a construct it only makes sense as a balance to the opposite extreme. (Also – whatever happened to the other four people?)

Slogans do seem a little crude. But, "It's the economy, stupid," was the slogan that helped Bill Clinton win the confidence of the American people and get him elected President against George H. W. Bush who was beset with an economic recession while running for reelection. Go figure. It's a little embarrassing that simple-minded slogans can really work, along with occasional smart ones, too. That one not only sounds a little stupid, it actually has the word "stupid" in it. But there is something about capturing an idea or an image relating clearly to its context, in few words, with a cadence of sound, and with a meaning that infects the brain like an earworm – "It's a small world after all…" That one is famously, painfully irritating and persistent.

Nonetheless I was thinking *Shrink for Prosperity – Last Chance for a Happy Future.* The first three words commanding action (or trying to) was something like a slogan, maybe hopefully somewhat catchy. The last line, the subtitle, sounded a little sappy as well as bleak, but if we need new definers of prosperity that have less to do with mass/energy consumption and hoarding, hoarding of the stuff itself and/or its monetary representation, it is actually important, in fact, maybe as far as it's real meaning goes, as important as a subtitle can get. Happiness counts. It's even in what passes for the best slogan for the United States of America: Thomas Jefferson's "Life, Liberty and the Pursuit of Happiness." "E pluribus unum," meaning "from many, one" on the national seal and sometimes called the country's motto, means practically nothing, indicates only smaller states coming together but nothing about what the United States should be, do or stand for.

On the other hand the life values suggested by the first word in Jefferson's line, "life," standing clean, separate and emphasized on the beginning side of a coma that separates it from the other words there, could even be interpreted as a commitment to providing a healthy existence for not only all people but the animals and the plants we share the planet with as well. Life itself has rights we should feel responsible to honor. To support, protect and further life strongly implies striving for peace and justice and the avoidance of war. (Sometimes it's hard to live up to slogans, especially national.) Liberty can imply a bit of the "I can do anything I want" impulsive ego behavior with its usually self-centered short-term objectives, but it also supports the notions of free thinking and freedom of many kinds of choices and life ways, which, given our amazing highly evolved brains, suggests we should each of us possess at least that: some serious degree of liberty.

Happiness is something of an ultimate among living things and anyone who has lived with dogs or horses (and cats, a friend reminds me: they purr) knows it is experienced by other life forms going about their own relationships with us and/or with others of their kind. The pursuit part of Jefferson's slogan sounds a little frantic and doesn't imply you actually get to happiness. Maybe you are just chasing it all the time. It also carries the baggage of the hunt: you pursue, kill, take and satisfy yourself into happiness or at least feed yourself so life can continue with happiness a future possibility. In any case happiness is about as universal as anything gets among people and other higher organisms on this mortal plane and the "Happy Hunting Grounds" of some Native American peoples, Valhalla of the Norse, or the Heaven of Christianity and Islam, or other after death paradises other belief systems suggest the goal of life and may be, if life be maybe eternal... would still be some kind of happiness. The "pursuit" notion is the weak link in our era, though presciently apt for the America that unfolded, especially in its 20th and early 21st century, successful celebrity obsessed, capitalist empire-like phase.

Happiness as something of an economics idea started in Bhutan in 1972 when King Jigme Sigye Wangchuck (pronounced more like Wong-chook, which sounds more mellow) was asked by a reporter how the country's GNP, Gross National Product, was doing. On the spot he decided it was more laudable and healthy to have happy citizens than to have them produce and consume as much as possible. I think he had a great idea and it is turning out to have influence way beyond the small size of the country might suggest it would have. It goes directly to that universal, highly desired goal and doesn't depend on picking up a lot of money as life's big goal or to make happiness possible. Yet it defines a great deal about what a descent economic goal might be. It doesn't count life's experience in terms of hoarding or what one can cash in for power and glory. It's the glory itself, like sex with love, dancing on a beach drenched in moonlight one summer night.

So here's my proposed world motto: "Life, Liberty and the Experience of Happiness for All." But it doesn't really work for this book's title. Still it's nice to offer it up as something to strive for, a good idea in its own right, the "All" including the plants and animals, even the climate system, even natural evolution.

Meantime, we need a world rescue strategy at this point in history embraced by the economic powers that build what we live in and therefore prescribe so much of what we can and can't do including damage or regenerate a healthy biological, even climatological world. Some friends have said, "Well, 'World Rescue' is the sense of the book and what we build is much of the means for success, but it sounds grandiose, a turn off don't you think?" Could be. But when Al Gore wrote a book with similar presumption to improve things, as he did in "Earth in the Balance" or when Lester Brown tried a rescue with his "Plan B" books, people said – well, let's see." I'm a relative unknown so I look relatively more presumptuous, unrealistic, a little out of place. But that is what the book *is* about, after all, and I believe it is a direct approach we need. So I think I'm stuck with it and need to play straight and honest. I think it will help.

6. Mural – People love their plants

One of my favorite images from a walk in the Los Angeles, California Hills.

CHAPTER 2

Prioritizing Proportions Properly

The more difficult things can rescue the world

With a few volunteers in the fall of 1989 I was busy organizing the First International Ecocity Conference in a small office in the Berkeley Ecology Center, even smaller because I shared the two tables, one each, with Gar Smith, Editor of the Earth Island Journal, so small, when Gar was facing deadline, like the fanatic workhorse he was – still is – late at night he'd roll out a sleeping bag and crash under the longer of the tables, wake up in the wee hours and start over.

The book *50 Simple Things You Can Do to Save the Earth* was sweeping the environmental community. The 20th Anniversary Earth Day was coming up in five months. One afternoon Gar walked in, book in hand, scanned the *50 Simple Things* table of contents and said, "And what about the three or four Big Ones that would actually work? Like no more than two kids, don't drive a car and don't eat meat."

For some historic perspective, as I'd recalled with Gar at the time, everyone had discussed the 50 things featured in the 50 simple things book 20 years earlier back around Earth Day 1970. Going into 1990, it seemed everything had been sanitized, dumbed down, made easier and more "politically correct." Progress had been very up and down since the first Earth Day, up in environmental progress with Richard Nixon and Jimmy Carter, down *a lot* when Ronald Reagan was President.

Maybe "the simple things" were the best we could muster after solar energy – something very substantial – was trashed in Reagan's 1980s, population activism was classified as racist, elitist, misanthropic and anti-Catholic. Community gardens, vegetarianism and farmers markets were doing OK but not great. Cars and sprawl were making a big comeback after the energy crises of the 1970s slowed growth briefly in paving the Earth, then picking up speed again conquering another few million acres of natural and agricultural landscapes in the meantime moving into the 1990s.

Fast forward to 2006 and with Al Gore's *An Inconvenient Truth* we were still with the 50 simple things: more thorough recycling, better insulation, inflate your tires to higher pressure to reduce road friction to save gasoline – and some money too – more energy conserving light bulbs (taking the place of the "area lighting" of 1970 in which 60 watts would light your comfortable chair for reading rather than 600 watts to light the whole room), and so on.

Why such a lame and dated list I asked myself? The word tokenism kept coming to mind. Nothing wrong with the 50 little ones but where were the big ones and the call to emphasize them? Especially, one decade later, after Gore made such a point of the truly dire climate change dangers in both his movie and book titled "An Inconvenient Truth"? Where was the strategy, the invested time and hard work, the personal energy, the blood, sweat and tears to win this dire battle for the planet he warned us would be coming as sure as night follows day if we didn't rise to its defense?

There was a quick answer. Former Maryland Governor Parris Glendening told me in 2007 about a breakfast he had with the former Vice President. When Parris asked why he did not suggest something really big, like de-emphasizing cars rapidly and advocating shifting city design to fit transit, bicycles and pedestrian accessibility, a beginning on the ecocity solution, Gore replied that the American people were not ready for it.

It's been more than 45 years since that first Earth Day as I write – when will we ever be ready? When do the accumulating years equal never?

There are deeper question. Are we too lazy? Or too dishonest? Are we too fearful? We have such technical knowledge, so many tools, so much material and energy wealth, competence in so many areas to make the mind of just a few decades back boggle. Fearful of what? To paraphrase Frank Delano Roosevelt, we have nothing to fear but what solutions are stifled by fear itself. Is it the fear of actually doing something intelligent? Assuming the vast majority of scientists are actually right, what could be worse than our Earthly environment spiraling toward collapse of the climate system, rise of the oceans and extinction of thousands of species throughout the whole biosphere? In such a situation, why the quiet surrounding the Big Difficult Things Gar Smith off-handedly mentioned as the reflexively obvious yet brilliant retort to the 50 Simple Things?

Climate change is not all, either. There is "Peak Oil" and what I call the "Rust Factor." The first guarantees, at some as yet unknown point, running short of fossil fuels. The second suggests we might lose much of our non-renewable resources through poor recycling and simple attrition. Any way you look at it, human decision based on future hopes for healthy living has to be faced and the random approach that does whatever becomes possible and makes money, which has been the playbook of business in the profit-first market place for generations now, has to change. My point: not only is survival at stake, but on the positive side, thriving. It's a whole systems design problem we can solve if we have the resolve.

Meantime many environmentalists are not taking the forthright lead but should. Consider the BP explosion on the Deepwater Horizon drilling rig in Gulf of Mexico in waters 5,000 feet deep. The collapse of the rig on the 22nd of April, 2010, then the snapping of the pipe to the drilling rig set off the ocean bottom oil geyser that erupted for the next 87 days. I heard no one in the media note that it happened to be the 40th anniversary of Earth Day. The Earth Day organizers and environmentalists in general quietly failed to point out, probably failed to even notice, exactly when BP's pipeline broke and the crude oil gusher poured forth two days after the explosion that killed eleven workers and started the four month and twenty-seven day oil spill disaster. That was a symbolically very powerful date and nobody acknowledged it. Too embarrassing? Welcome to 40 years of... what? Failure to note the coincidental dates, to me, indicates we of environmentalist conscience have proved far from successful. The demand for the oil has not been abated and the structure of the city is the most demanding of all factors in the clamor for more. Environmentalists should feature that fact in headlines but, most of them driving cars and living in scattered housing, simply fail to notice or don't want to notice the connection of urban design and city layout to the problems on which they focus their concern.

And, not only is the cheap and easy oil going to run short in the not too distant future there are other problems arising. The rare earth metals for example. They are a finite resource too and need assiduous recycling and conservation if we are to have many of the fancier technologies we fancy. Or maybe many of these technologies are not worth their environmental and social costs? As the name implies, the rare earth metals are limited on the planet. In current language, these resources are not looking so good for "scalability." These metals include ones most people have never even heard of like indium for television screens, hafnium for computer chips, tantalum for cell phones, terbium for compact fluorescent lights and gallium for solar cells. The best, richest, most economically recoverable deposits of most metals, even the most common like iron, aluminum, copper, nickel and zinc are gone. Even though there is a great deal of these in the ground, the ever poorer quality ores now require ever more energy and more expensive technology to obtain to supply an ever growing population. Some day, if we don't change our trends and ways, these will become economically unavailable from the skin of the Earth at any scale useful to society, reduced to rare trinkets traded by eccentric collectors for investment or the sheer fun or ego trip of possession.

Even iron – and the planet is largely made of iron – has no more high quality and inexpensive ores left to mine while slowly but steadily much that is already mined and in circulation rusts away. Iron and steel are eminently recyclable but small bits and pieces are lost by billions of people and hundreds of whole ships in the millions of tons collectively are intentionally scuttled. At the bottom of the sea they are unsalvageable at any economically feasible price. In fact many are sunk because, due to truly distorted economics, it is far less expensive to turn their metal to salty rust for scuba diving tourists and shelters for fingerling fish (not wholly bad ideas though coral works better) than scrap it for future human uses on dry land or wet water. Worse, military ships are scuttled with their thousands of tons of metals to the bottom of deep in the paranoid fear that an old ship might reveal its secrets to "ship breaking" scrap workers, another casualty of our economically profitable habit (for a relatively small number of people) of war.

Here's another perspective on the Rust Factor situation, from a college textbook point of view. *Human Geography – Landscape of Human Activities* by Fellmann, Getis and Getis suggests the following.

> The extractive industries depend on the exploitation of minerals unevenly distributed in amounts and concentrations determined by past geologic events, not by contemporary market demand. In physically workable and economically usable deposits, minerals constitute only a tiny fraction of the earth's crust – far less than 1%. That industrialization has proceeded so rapidly and so cheaply is the direct result of an earlier ready availability of rich and accessible deposits of the requisite materials. Economies grew fat by skimming the cream. It has been suggested that should some catastrophe occur to return human cultural levels to a pre-agricultural state, it would be extremely unlikely that humankind ever again could move along the road of industrialization with the resources available for its use.[10]

Sounds bad, and would be bad, but consider that we have the richest iron ores that ever existed in the skeletons of our buildings, in all those cars, copper tubing, aluminum siding and countless other things. But, we'd need sharp and extremely hard saws and files which are very sophisticated to make and acetylene and electric arc welding would be out of the question in the above hypothetical situation. How to get at the metal in those enormous I beams after a catastrophic collapse, failing states spreading around the world? Think things closer to today's fanatical Somalia and northeastern Nigeria, Syria's victims of violence, hungry north and central Africans, the flood of immigrants pouring into Europe growing every day more xenophobic in 2015 as the desperate risk their lives and go hungry trying to

[10] *Human Geography – Landscape of Human Activities*, Tenth Edition, Fellmann, Getis and Getis, Mc Graw-Hill, 2008, p.282

get somewhere just plain safe and somewhat secure. Think far worse than what actually happened in the Great Depression, which was bad enough – and bad enough in Europe to prepare the soil for the Second World War. If time ticks slowly in a Dark Age, which Jane Jacobs thinks is coming, and she's pretty smart, it picks up pace for rust and losses to erosion, floods and sedimentation, earthquakes and the like when societies unravel. Alan Weisman's *The World Without Us* informs most entertainingly on those conditions of atrophy over different periods of time.

But of course mineral resources are just the beginning. Then there is the ever-growing list of extinct species, once gone no longer around to help us, much less just captivate us with their beauty, fearsomeness or bizarre wonder. There's the collapse of fisheries, shrinking forests, exhaustion of fossil water aquifers, spreading deserts, retreating glaciers, encroaching seas and other conditions already well into various economic and political scenarios of degeneration toward collapse. With these many crises building up here on our finite planet and with larger crises coming over the horizon like the hot green shadow of an advancing hurricane, where's the commitment to make really serious change?

The disconnect is rather stunning. We go about our everyday lives, some days with bad weather, others perfectly pleasant, and most things function "normally" to outward appearance. The paper's delivered, the coffee's hot, the traffic clots and moves, clots and moves, shoppers continue to descend upon the sales. It's hard to believe it's an actual emergency. The warnings seem… so abstract, the threats so distant.

7. Creek enters a small public space

This was an idea for routing Strawberry creek into the area now called Center Street in Berkeley, California. A bioregional sculpture in the lower center, a little bit to the right with large versions of local natural animals at scale such that each one is about the same size in the sculpture, though not in actuality.

Los Angeles Carcentaurs wreck the atmosphere, lead to changing climate

What do you think are the two most important lessons from the 20th century? We will get back to that.

You will remember I happened to be living in Los Angeles when it was becoming the leader of cities into the automobile age, in the late 1950s and 1960s. So much so it was attracting world attention. So much so, without people realizing it – and *still* not realizing it – it may one day be recognized as the place and time at the fulcrum of humanity's material history gone bad, evolution on the whole planet yanked off course. A friend introduced me to a reporter from Germany writing an article about Los Angelenos as "Carcentaurs": half human, half car with human heads, arms and torsos joined at the waist to automobile bodies with wheels. Millions of us. I thought about that and realized, compared to the rest of the world, our "attachment" to the car, an almost literal attachment butt to seat, really was pretty extreme. I liked the term also since "Carcentaur." Reminded me of carcinogen.

The smog was extreme in those days too. Driving west across the California desert from Arizona toward Barstow and Los Angeles, under the crystal blue skies of the desert and downwind from Los Angeles, you would look up to the mountain range that surrounds Los Angeles on the north and east and see a dark grey-brown miasma with indistinct hazy surface sitting in an enormous geological bowl just waiting for you. With a westerly breeze the mass rises up and spills into the desert like an almost black volcanic vapor miles thick, reminiscent of the evil whatever it was in the 1958 Hollywood horror/science fiction movie called "The Blob," featuring, for a touch of trivia, actor Steve McQueen's first leading role. Drive over the pass and down into it and your eyes and throat burn as hot tears roll down your cheeks. You gasp for air with aching lungs. I was there. I know. I went there for college, the cultural excitement of the place, the art scene, the beach. You just put up with the smog and hoped you weren't going to be one of the officially recorded 1,200 or so "excess deaths" every year[11] in the basin caused by the smog, though none who died would think of themselves as excess. Before they died, that is.

What did we all do there and then? We applied scientific thinking and came up with an excellent target, which was to clean up the air – and we did it. How? By fixing the car.

We clarified the goal: clean air – who could disagree with a "target," a "measure" or "metric" like clean air? Our materials scientists and chemists cranked the relevant theories, revved up, downshifted their thinking and popped into gear. We brought in the engineers, built the prototypes, ran the tests, got the public to "buy in," ran what's generally considered a sterling example of an all-stakeholders

[11] California South Coast Air Quality Management District http://www.aqmd.gov/smog/historical/smog_and_health.htm

successful public process and put smog devices on our cars. We solved about 90% of the local air pollution problem, government, business and citizenry all working in coordinated harmony. This is the literal truth. The sheer increase in the number of cars have sullied the air somewhat since but the fact remains that most of the air pollution was fixed by affixing the smog device with a few bolts to the exhaust pipe. We fixed the car, not the city. We delivered a "techno fix" for a component of the whole system rather than reshaping the whole system.

People failed to note or decided to ignore that the car was just a part, if the most active part, of a whole system which was the car, scattered urban form – often referred to as sprawl – paving in the form of streets, freeways, interchanges, parking lots and parking structures, private and commercial garages, gas stations, drive-in theaters, new and used car lots, junk yards, and, very cheap energy availability: gasoline by the billions of gallons draining vast regions beneath our feet. In fact in Los Angeles, which was earlier a vast field of holes punched in the ground and oil derricks piercing the sky like an erector set forest, most of the oil below was already gone by the 1960s.

But back to our question about the two most important lessons from the 20th century. Some of you might have guessed, as many who attend my lectures have and as I have maintained, that we should have learned from two world wars, Hitler's Holocaust, the atomic bomb and Gandhi's very successful non-violent dismemberment of the largest empire in history, that we need to put an end to wars – and peaceably can. We haven't, of course, and the United States has somehow been at war with someone with almost no break since World War Two: the cold wars and wars and coups against asymmetrically much smaller and weaker adversaries and proxy wars but not all-out wars between big powers.

Twentieth Century lesson number two? We should have learned to stop cars as well as wars. More correctly we should have learned how to build our human habitats, from metropolitan areas and cities to towns and villages with few or no cars. If that seems inconsequential in comparison with stopping the wars that have been something of an eternal curse on the species, think again. Consider that cities, the largest creations of us humans, are already the chief cause of extinctions on the planet by way of climate change and by way of destruction of habitat by displacing natural environments with sprawl and by displacing agriculture, pushing farmland out into natural habitat, paving and building over farmland and nature alike. Finally, closing the circle, remember that much of modern war is to get at the oil that keeps the car-based cities running.

It wasn't as if we had had no warnings. Lewis Mumford had been ranting against Auto Sprawl Syndrome (my term) for two or three decades by the time LA got its smog devices. My own personal wake up was listening to Paolo Soleri, of whom you will hear more as we go through this book. He came to speak in Los Angeles in the mid 1960s. He pointed out that the apparently small houses and modest downtowns of widely scattered Los Angeles county actually constituted a gigantic infrastructure of scattered pipes, wires, asphalt, concrete, redundant walls, roofs and floors, driveways and garages that used up far more construction materials, energy, land, money, time, blood on the highways – everything – than the compact city of many activities close together. Much smaller, leaner, more frugal and healthy was the city of taller buildings designed around pedestrians, apartments without driveways and garages but with public transportation and bicycle culture, something like the cities of Europe Soleri knew growing up in Northern Italy. The taller, smaller footprint city was what we need, he said. He proposed old pedestrian city insights in new modern designs and largely constructed of building materials not available in pre-automobile times, that is, stronger concrete, steel, aluminum and glass, though dressed out in wood, gardens and water features. Vast amounts of land would be saved, no need to pave paradise and farm – they'd be available right outside your door. Just walk or bicycle out a short distance...

But who would pay attention to such thinking while we had fun setting the pattern for cities around the world, there in Los Angeles, city of the future? The ego trip of leadership itself was fun, too. Hollywood, which after all is part of LA, spread the word. We fixed the car, made it look good and who wouldn't want clean air, a great car, zipping from skiing in the mountains to dropping in on the beach in the same day to surf with gorgeous California girls frolicking on the sand, all clean, fresh, young and speedy. Cars were great and I enjoyed them immensely myself.

And a whole world of cities designed for cars followed. So did invasion of agricultural land and natural countryside by the millions of acres. And so did transformation of the atmosphere from about 320 parts per million CO_2 in the middle of that smog problem-solving time, to 401 ppm and growing steadily as I write. Then there is the associated heating of a whole planet by about 1 degree F. since I was living in Los Angeles. Pre-industrial world CO_2 was approximately 280 ppm and temperature about 1.8 F. degrees cooler average world wide than in mid 2010s.

Bottom line: we solved our local air pollution problem, proved cars could be improved and be your friends, convinced the rest of the world to go forth and drive – and we all did just that. We transformed the atmosphere of a whole planet. In terms of destructive effects on evolution of life on the planet, as well as climate impacts, this is well beyond any war, even world war to date, and as we all know, extinctions of species caused by climate change (as well as those from all other causes) are forever. From thinking and acting locally in a way globally contagious we created a disaster of incalculable proportions. Science, playing its part in the episode, provided a half-thought out technological solution, delivered what we wanted to believe, not what would help most in the long term and missed the whole systems perspective entirely – even after being warned. Needing a systems fix, we applied a techno fix and got a world disaster.

The nasty little lesson we still haven't learned as we go about celebrating the supposed positive potential of electric, hybrid, smoothly aerodynamic, quieter and other supposedly improved cars is this: the better the car the worse the city. The better the car the more damage to the planet. This should be one of the two most important "don't do this" lessons of the 20th century. Yet I've never even heard it suggested other than in my own talks. If the true disaster of the automobile/sprawl city were broadly understood and acknowledged, the solution to many problems, among them climate change, would become much clearer. (We don't want "...this sucker ~~could~~ [to] go down."

The top two of the "to do" list would be figure out how to coexist in peaceful creativity and how to build ecocities.

Furthermore, taking the perspective that proportionality actually means something, we need to notice that the automobile is 30 times heavier than the human being, 10 times as fast and takes up around 50 times the volume – standing still and much more when moving at typical (non-stuck-in-traffic jam) speed. What could we be thinking that we design cities where people are supposed to live around and mix with something of such radically different scale and demand for land, energy, speed, money and bloody human, pet and wildlife sacrifices on streets and highways? I've been asked after my talks if it is even possible to have cities without cars and my answer has always been something like, "Cities existed for something like 8,000 years without cars. (That's if we start as many scholars suggest, around the time of Çatlhoyuk, in Turkey, largest town for the next 1,500 years.) Cars have dominated large numbers of cities for only about 100 years, one eightieth of the time of cities, so obviously we can have cities without cars – and do: Venice, Italy; Gulongyu, China; Lamu, Kenya; Zermatt, Switzerland; the Medina of Fez, Morocco, Avalon, Catalina Island in car-crazy California. And there are a few others. So as they say, if it exists (and has in this case for 8,000 years) it is possible.

In any case it is not just that the cities are the largest creations of our species, which rolls off the tongue and out of the mind far too easily. But remember that the car-based cities in the U.S. use about three times the energy and land per person as the more pedestrian oriented cities of the same population and prosperity level in Europe. The form of the city counts powerfully. Plus the implications for lost agricultural and natural landscape next to the city, loss of biodiversity and damage to transit, bicycle and pedestrian infrastructure – we have to include those harms as well.

They insist on and everyone capitulates to championing carbon credits, cap and trade and other market transactions, tagging a good thing on something profitable, reversing the objectives we should have on the subject, which would be to do the good deed as the first objective, not make money (first priority) doing the good deed (a byproduct). These exchanges of monetized contractually agreed upon value are not prioritized for thinking through what it is we are actually building but are literally a second thought. They don't consider the resource base for what we are building, or start with positing beneficial environmental impacts of what we are building much less confronting building a physically different civilization than the one causing the problem. They are prioritized for profit first. In other words, this tradable carbon credits approach conflates doing the planet a good turn with making maximum return on investment, two objectives that in practice have been far from harmonious and when harmonious, just coincidentally so.

Maybe it's time to play it straight. Simply taxing carbon would go straight to the source and get to the foundation of the best sources for solutions. Then to invest in the best solutions, among them, building ecocities that build soils, restore native species, save energy and land massively and generally make for a healthy, loveable environment for us humans to live in and enjoy. Maybe to best get there we'd need a world rescue strategy based on the "few difficult things that would actually work."

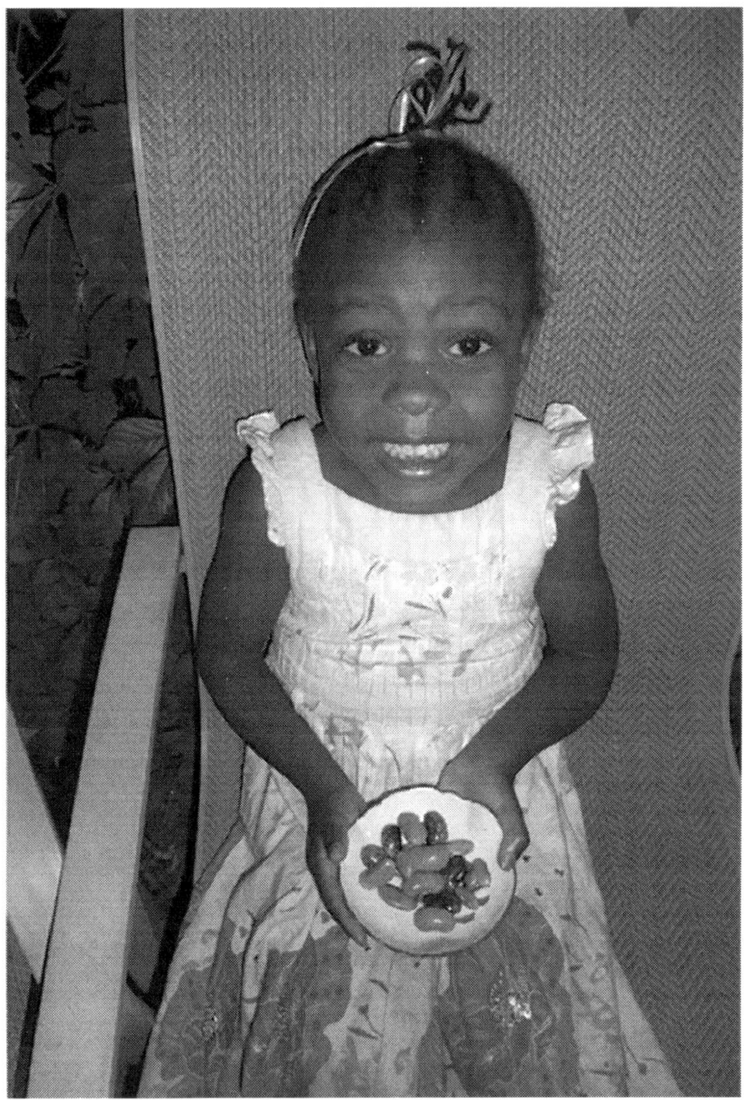

8. Esther Engle-Warnik and her beans from a rooftop garden in Montreal, Canada

Esther is an adopted child from Haiti after the earthquake, at home in a different world.

CHAPTER 3

Preliminaries

The city as the engine of prosperity – and its cosmology

We will start our economics tour through the ages soon and in the same way we started the whole book, with mother's milk. But now, a few basic thoughts as prelude and warm up.

Jane Jacobs gets right down on the ground. She was a remarkable thinker and what some people call an activist. She also changed the course of city planning in New York City and then city planning in much of the world, protecting places that worked beautifully for lively sociability and culture and for the person on foot, that is, the pedestrian. She keenly observed and loved the life in the streets and loved the privacy of her little apartment where she could just pull the blinds and disappear. She could get away from something else she loved that way, too, which was organizing, so she could do yet more she loved, namely exploring ideas and especially her own ideas in her writing. She helped empower the everyday people in the neighborhood, wherever that was, popularized and in a sense coined the term "mixed uses" suggesting a rich balance of happy socializing and commerce in "fine grain" urban places and in defending her beloved Greenwich Village in New York City. She helped educate the world and America in particular to the pleasures and practicalities of density of development of the diverse kind.

Her arch enemy in the days before she left New York for Toronto (so her two sons would not have to risk their lives trying to kill the locals in Vietnam) was the same as Paolo Soleri's and Lewis Mumford's: the automobile. More personally, she was organizing against Robert Moses, master builder of highways and public works, many virtually impossible to get to without a car, and destroyer of low cost and ethnic neighborhoods. And she won. She and her allies prevented the construction of several massive highway projects on Manhattan and all the damaging development they would have unleashed. Years after re-reading her classic *The Death and Life of Great American Cities*, catching up on her later works I was struck by her ideas about *The Economy of Cities* in her book by that name and in *Cities and the Wealth of Nations*. I'd come to think of her as an urban design theorist and neighborhood activist and a very perceptive and articulate one. Now, for me, her ideas on economics rang true and loud. It was a pleasant surprise. Then years later, she wrote *Systems of Survival* and I said to myself, "now there's an economist who makes sense." No infinite growth academic "classical" or "neoclassical" capitalist or even socialist economist would ever think to call her an economist, just as they roundly ignore Herman Daly, another hero in my estimation in their field. But she convinced me. In her economics, the city ranks as the true engine of economic productivity, the place where all the parts, the people, the ideas come together in synergies impossible to imagine (or actualize) out in nature (where by compensation inspiration dwells) or in the suburbs (where television and computer games fight boredom and promote inaction).

What I've come to think is the second most cogent and consequential of her thoughts, after identifying the true economic centrality and power of the city at the foundation of *real* economics, is the idea that cities grow and prosper by importing and copying the best from other cities, usually older, larger and more developed cities – call them mentor cities – through trade, then make those things themselves, with local variation. She called this process "import replacement." In this she wasn't the source – others were already using the term. But she gave proper emphasis to the idea and put it in the context of city-making. To illustrate the notion she convincingly uses Constantinople mentoring Venice. Next, the import-replacing city begins exporting its goods to a second generation of less-developed import replacing cities and so on. In her example, Venice goes on to mentor other cities of Western Europe.

Further, she said this process was more important than the economic manipulations of nation states in terms of economic productivity and prosperity. Nation states could tap into this natural city development process and tax and command the city to some degree while the main deal in building prosperous economies was the import-replacing city itself.

The city could accomplish feats of productivity and even invent completely new products and services (which alas Jane doesn't write about much – I'd love to have heard her thoughts on this) because all the parts were assembled close together in a form that facilitated complementary actions easily and speedily, and it might be added, with minimal energy expended and material utilized for any particular effect. The city was the place with physical structures hosting all its varied activities arranged close together, where the materials, the tools, the shelter of the buildings of a wide variety, the connectors called streets and rails, pipes and wires, the specialized open spaces for markets, plazas and parks and the people themselves in many specializations, all came physically together, everything interacting with and complementing everything else. That the efficient, "lean" as Soleri would say, interactions could happen at all if the city did not exist, or if the parts were scattered far out and about the landscape, would be highly unlikely. Such scattered "cities" in fact did not exist until the advent of the automobile and extraordinarily plentiful, powerful and cheap fuel became available, at which point you could say, humanity began burning its candle at both ends, or perhaps at the far-flung edges of the splayed out metropolis all at once.

I've talked about the solution to this principle for years – decades actually – as "access by proximity." Design the parts to have access to one another simply by being arranged close together. My montra worth hammering in: the shortest route from point A to point B is not a straight line but designing them close together. Then we get access by proximity. In simplest terms, live close to where you work, shop, meet friends and so on. Design and build communities so that this is possible and beautiful. In planning circles this is known as "mixed uses" just mentioned or "balanced development." Living organisms, too, do not scatter their organs out over large areas but gather them together in appropriate positions adjacent other organs and structures and this requires a basically three-dimensional form and a sensible "design." They can't function in a two-dimensional form, shaped like a tortilla say, or in bad design, as with eyes on the backside of knees.

Besides 3-D form and position of parts, is there a time component in nature to give us some ideas for the shape and function of healthy built communities?

What happened before cities in the human record, in ecology, in evolution? There is a time sequence here that Paolo Soleri pointed out starting in the early 1960s. He called the phenomenon miniaturization/complexification and noted that it has proceeded throughout evolutionary time. Actually, French Jesuit philosopher and archeologist/paleontologist Teilhard de Chardin preceded Soleri in emphasizing the pattern and strong intimations of the idea were evident among the earliest ecology theorists such as Austrian geographer Edward Suess who first published the term "biosphere" in 1875 and Russian biologist Vladimir I. Vernadsky exploring ecological and evolutionary thinking in the 1920s.[12]

What Soleri added was that cities would constitute a stage in the healthy further evolution of life and consciousness in the universe. The ecologically healthy city would not only embody, as an expression of miniaturization/complexification,

[12] A. V. Lapo, *Traces of Bygone Biospheres*, Mir Publishers, Moscow, 1982 revised from the 1979 Russian edition, p. 18

a crucial stage in evolution, but be an indispensible stage *of* evolution *for* future evolution.

The total sequence goes something like this: gas clouds from the initial creating explosion, usually called the Big Bang, condensed into stars – much smaller in volume and more compact formations than the clouds of mainly hydrogen and a small percentage of helium from which they were formed. The stars, as they gathered more and more hydrogen and helium through their gravitational attraction then cooked up heavier elements in their high pressure and high temperature interiors. Next, many of them exploded, flinging the heavier elements and simple and complex molecules, dust, water and varying sized chunks and mixes of minerals that didn't exist before out into surrounding space, creating new clouds of swirling material radiant with energy. The first generation stars "manufactured" all that. Thus the explosion of the earlier stars created a second-generation type of gas and dust clouds in space probably also replete with various sized globules of all sorts of elements and chemical compounds.

These in turn accreted by mutual gravitational forces again, but this time into a new generation of starts along with planets, moons, asteroids and comets… as the billions of years went by.

Then on planets life emerged in another miniaturization/complexification phenomenon of immense change creating a vastly more complex universe emerging from a simpler, earlier one. You might say life "emerged;" you might say "was created" or you might even say "is always emerging and creating."

Finally in the pattern, consciousness emerged in life itself in another leap of magnitudes in the complexification and miniaturization pattern. (What happens in this pattern after consciousness? It's a little early to know…)

Soleri's notion was that emergence of later and higher degrees of miniaturization and complexification generally indicates higher states of evolution, a process that seems to be almost a defining characteristic of health in and even of the universe. Following his lead I combine the words (for a more miniaturized and complexified language) – "miniaturization/complexification" – into "miniplexion." The hint from nature and evolution for our built environment of cities, towns and villages would then be generally that those healthiest would most likely reiterate what we see operative in evolution.

Soleri then concluded that the best form for the city would be, for that reason among others, the very compact, generally three-dimensional, small footprint city, the city analogous to the general form of other complex living organisms. Thus he concluded the advancing way to go would be a modern version of the single structure pueblos of the southwest Native Americans, the monasteries of Tibet and the compact, dense and small towns Paolo knew when he was growing up in the mountains of Northern Italy where he experienced something of a beginning in thinking through more up-dated city designs.

His notion was to create towns in a single structure, taking the three-dimensional model to its organic model extreme. He called that kind of structure and the basic idea for it "arcology," a contraction of architecture and ecology. The Italian mountain towns of his childhood and youth, if not in single structures, were close enough to physically unified to essentially function that way. They weren't a bad approximation of the notion he had in mind for built communities of all sizes: compact, pedestrian, providing for "access by proximity," running on very little energy, taking up very little land and therefore producing minimal pollution, perhaps so little that all "waste" could be recycled to new human or nature-enriching uses, such as enriching soil and supporting biodiversity. Hence his term "lean" expressed it all quite well.

In this form, the city would be the chief collective, social physical instrument of consciousness evolving to a higher state functioning something like the human brain/mind. De Chardin spoke of the noosphere, or sphere of knowledge in the biosphere; Soleri saw cities as special physical nodes hosting knowledge advancing in the evolving universe, physical brains for the big collective consciousness of the whole biosphere.

Another thing we will notice digging deeper into this book, is that some things that arise come from "self-organization" of entities forming into new arrangements. Those new things – chemical compounds, and us and everything else – then could be said to have new "emergent" properties. Us complex things called humans have a tendency to believe, since we manipulate simple things into the various more complex things we make, assembling components into things we invent, build and manufacture, that we understand principles of order and are doing the ordering ourselves. So we tend to think that this is the way the universe works. But what seems to have been consistent from the early universe to now is that the things – including us – assembled themselves in successive layers of emergence following the miniplexion pattern all the way down to – or up to – us. So a vast number of us believe that which emerged – higher consciousness – had to exist at the beginning and "create" the whole thing all at once, thus God, the monotheistic Creator. Of course you could say – and some do – that God created emergence too, Creation continuing through time, the universe constantly creating new and fundamentally different layers of itself.

But those considerations are more abstract and seem far away from the day to day of designing, building and living in cities. Not so, Soleri would argue. They are with us in the sense that we are completely emerged in them and to ignore the pattern of miniplexion and the way it functions in the building of our cities he would say, and to ignore that the emergence within the pattern in everyday things taking place, would almost certainly be at our peril. I'd add that climate change, the paving of farmland and natural habitat and the associated extinction of ever more species show that said peril has already arrived and is progressing smashingly. Whether the prescriptions of the "cosmic context" of cities and our present condition of environmental damage is a coincidence or a cause and effect relationship, both exist. In his earlier years Soleri didn't predict all the harms that have arrived while society was failing to pay attention, but he did predict some of them and others, such as climate change, fit the pattern nicely.

This might sound a little too far out and too early in a book about cities and economics, but the emergence phenomenon and its major pattern – miniplexion – in its infinite discreet filigrees, such as the emergence exemplified in the way acids and bases make salts, the way Darwin's finches had very different beaks to fit their different worlds on each island of the Galapagos Islands, the way galaxies string out through space, dark matter tending them to gather together in those strings and dark energy pushing those strings apart and accelerating the scattering away from each other, the way languages form from people making sounds to try to mean something in their evolving world, the way markets with a modicum of regulation set reasonable and useful prices… All these may be expressions of the second of those two most fundamental of the two types of creation in the universe. One is The Creation of religion, and another of the same type, The Big Bang of physics, The Start, you might call it if you want a term to embrace both the religious and the scientific. The second form of Creation is the Big Emergence in which or through which the all and everything seems to constantly, creatively, create new things, forms, types of energy and various patterns, or as Buckminster Fuller called them, "pattern integrities, everywhere in the universe the same." The emergence processes of evolution itself, described in broad outline as "miniplexion," a form of creativity that permeates the whole universe, is a characteristic of the universe as surely as stars condensed from hydrogen pulled together by gravity and as surely as life needs a particular temperature range and certain patterns of proximity and association to reproduce and evolve.

Physicists struggle with representing such a notion in a mathematical formula trying to embrace the most basic pattern that includes all matter, energy, dimensions of space and time. But the quest to reduce Everything to such a formula has always stumped them and probably always will. They love and therefore – I'd speculate anyway – overestimate their physics and math.

But it seems easy enough in English and probably translates universally. You could call it the Common Language General Field Theory, to wit, that the self-organizing emergence phenomenon is common to the very small (quantum mechanics), the medium size where we humans dwell and where chemistry looms large and mass gravity and energy dispersion (to the square of the distance, Newtonian physics) dominate, and the very large where dark matter and dark energy dance their immense choreography in the relativistic universe involving those clusters and strings of galaxies scattered over billions of light years distance[13].

[13] Nancy Ellen Abrams and Joel R. Primac, *The New Universe and the Human Future*, Yale University Press, New Haven and London, 2011, fig. 30, p.49. This book describes the latest theory on dark energy – scattering the galaxies – and dark matter – holding the galaxies together and stretching them out in enormous strings in an expanding universe.

The self-organizing emergence phenomenon operates on all these levels, as Nobel Prize winning physicist Robert B. Laughlin emphasizes as his main theme in *A Different Universe – reinventing physics from the bottom down.*[14]

But stop! Enough of this for the time being and sorry for the tangent, though it seems to be lurking there at the base of so much I deal with in this book. Somewhat more easily grasped, the city is, in less cosmic terms, in its compactness and arrangement, the primary engine of production, consumption and recycling, and in many senses, prosperity. Now we are back to more agreed upon normal economics.

Observations going into my study of economics

In early 2010, scanning the field of upcoming events I thought looked promising for learning more about economics, I discovered a conference was coming up on "de-growth." (I prefer degrowth, so I'll use that.) Certainly cities needed to "degrow" to a smaller more compact infrastructure. Maybe degrowth economics would be the theory to fit ecocities like hand in glove. It looked like a place to learn what others were thinking, a great place to test out some of my thinking. I presented my case as a potential speaker assessing a city-based strategy of degrowth and the conference's organizers added me to their list of presenters. The conference was called the Second International Conference on De-growth for Ecological Sustainability and Social Equity. It was held in Barcelona, Spain in March of 2010. Pertinent to my own themes, my host informed me that of the central area of this beautiful city only 6% of the land was for motorized traffic. That compares with about 60% in Los Angeles.

At the end of the first three-hour plenary secession with all assembled in the elegant grand hall of the University of Barcelona – I wasn't a featured speaker yet – I stood up from the floor and pointed out that I'd missed the words "city" and "urban" in all the opening presentations. I mentioned it was puzzling to say the least that the largest physical thing we humans build, and something at the base of economics was missing from the conversation. If there were ever something that needed to "degrow" in land area, physical materials and energy consumption and shrink its destructive impacts it would be the city. We should feature, I suggested, city design and layout and associated policy and lifestyles at the very center of any discussion of a new and healthy economics. The audience looked like they were thinking hard where to put that comment, or just looked a little blank like they hadn't heard it. No one in the audience or on the panel of original speakers made a peep. One young man milling in the foyer during the coffee break told me he appreciated the point, and being fresh to the notion without yet much to say, moved quickly on.

[14] Robert B. Laughlin, *A Different Universe – reinventing physics from the bottom down*, Basic Books, New York, 2005

9. Three families share a country house that's almost an ecocity fractal – explained later.

People live here with children, multi-family "home education" in the country, residential space, potato and wine cellar, shared (co-housing) kitchen and dining area plus private food preparation areas, big garden with orchard, tree house/play house with slide to pond, telecommuting and home crafts for cash "crop" of products, pretty nice.

The main speakers focused on Gross Domestic Product and promoted using quality of life indicators. One mind-bending notion: just ignore GDP and it will fade away through growing irrelevance and increasing evidence to the contrary. I ignored television and for me it withered away 45 years ago delivering hundreds maybe thousands of hours of potentially creative peacefulness and freedom from relentless ads. So I was alert to the idea that such ideas might spread. But of course, television has hardly withered in mainstream society. But maybe ignoring GDP while Bhutan popularizes their Gross National Happiness initiative, which has many very substantial and positive results and while other leading thinkers like Herman Daly, Robert Costanza, Hazel Henderson and others champion replacing or augmenting GDP with a Human Development Index, the Calvert-Henderson Quality of Life Indicators or other related measures actually puts GDP in its somewhat useful but hardly domineering place.

One idea that struck me as important at the degrowth conference was the "Jevons Paradox." William Stanley Jevons was a British mathematician and economist of the mid 19th century. In 1865 he pointed out that increasing efficiency would seem to benefit the economy in terms of better resource use and impacts on society and environment. Think again. He used coal as an example. Historically, making the burning of coal ten times as energy efficient in improved machinery in the early days did not improve conditions by nine times over - because conditions were anything but static. It turned out that use went up 100 times during the next few decades as efficiency progressed ten times over. Thus we saw roughly a ten-fold increase in pollution and other problems from burning coal – not to mention a growing rate of depletion of the resource. Regarding mineral depletion and availability of rapidly disappearing resources, Ugo Bardi says, in his book *Extracted – how the Quest for Mineral Wealth Is Plundering the Planet*, "...the system may allocate more resources to keep production ongoing, also in the form of technological improvements. This behavior leads to a higher amount of resources being extracted, but in so doing it exacerbates the depletion problem and causes the system to crash after reaching the productive peak. This is a counter intuitive behavior typical of dynamic systems: actions that at first glance appear to solve a problem [increasing the efficiency of production] turn out to worsen it [generating a more rapid collapse when the postponed disaster comes.]"[15]

As we asked earlier in reference to the City of Carcentaurs down in Southern California, does this apply also to smog devices solving local air pollution problems and bringing on climate change? The record is that it does and it has. The Jevons Paradox is deadly serious.

In more general terms, most of those growth worriers and degrowth warriors present at the conference wanted to dump capitalism. But they didn't put up a really

[15] Ugo Bardi, *Extracted – How the Quest for Mineral Wealth Is Plundering the Planet*, Chelsea Green, White River Junction, Vermont, 2014, p. 160

strong alternative. So I suggested something more like reform than revolution. Why throw out the baby with the bath water? Why not take the best from what is commonly thought of as capitalism (accumulation of wealth under individual or corporate control for profit for multiple purposes including reinvestment in positive, productive enterprises) and the best of what is thought of as socialism (responsible sharing and provision of and public investment in facilities and services for the common good) and admit both have a great deal to offer? This more cooperative approach, known as "win-win" rather than the polarizing either/or, seemed to me to solve a lot of problems in both theory and practice. The notion was novel enough at the degrowth conference as to spark some lively conversation in the breakout group where I suggested it. It surprised me that it wasn't a more emphasized theme throughout the conference.

A closing point from thoughts at the degrowth conference sums up a lot in my mind: Where the abuse of environment and where the gap between poverty and wealth is extreme, seriously graduated income tax with no loopholes is an exceptionally good idea – *if* society has good ideas about how to spend the money and what to build with it. Researchers in more and less economically equal societies give a lot of attention to heightened envy in making societies with high degrees of inequality rate low in health, education, satisfaction and other indicators. But I believe we can ignore much of that unpleasant and largely ego distorted emotion and can very beneficially give much increased attention to what is actually built in the efforts to spend tax moneys in best possible ways, including in building ecocities. In any case graduated income tax was a very large and largely neglected issue there. We'll think this through more later as a moderate, non-game-like approach: cooperate, compromise, solve.

The cultural artifact list

Shortly now I will try touring us through the history of economics as I see it in my recent and continuing "follow your nose" study. But before then a last bit of background thinking and that has to do with our cultural artifact list.

My first real job, a summer job when I was 16 years old, was digging up Indian ruins along the New Mexico-Colorado border for the New Mexico Museum of Anthropology in Santa Fe, New Mexico. I was the artist adjunct to the dig that was unearthing pit houses scattered across the San Juan River Valley about to be flooded by a new dam. The rock and earth dam to be surfaced with concrete was the politically correctly named Navajo Dam now backing up the lake which has flooded the homes of the present day Indians' ancestors, the lake also named Navajo, just to make sure.

These pit houses were dug into the ground for around 100 years around the year 800. The pits were spanned over with logs, then branches, then twigs and then dirt. The roofs caved in hundreds of years ago and the pits filled with sand and silt.

Over the centuries they were grown over with bushes and grasses. In the early 1960s they were flooded with the waters of Navajo Lake. When occupied, these dwellings benefited from what is often called geo-exchange these days, tapping the stable temperature of the earth a few feet down to help warm in winter and cool in summer. The earthen walls and thick roof, also of earth, are what makes the Southwestern American adobe buildings so comfortable. Exceptionally and pleasantly quiet too. As I recall, the pit houses ran from about ten feet to twenty feet in diameter. The present Native American's ancestors lived in those relatively warm in winter, cool in summer underground abodes. You often need a disaster as an excuse for money for archeological digs. This dig was typical; the bottom of the valley where soft alluvial soil was good for building pit houses is now flooded under 300 feet of water.

At night on the job I helped glue shards of old pots together sitting around our small "fly camp" dining room table in a rented adobe house in the middle of nowhere. I don't think we ever put a whole pot together. Mostly I drew pictures of matates and manos, the Indian's big mortars and pestles for grinding corn, and an occasional sandal, strap, pouch, etc. We called the list of their products their "artifact list." Including the pit houses themselves and sub components like mud wall plaster, I doubt if the list would fill two pages double column 12 pt. Times New Roman. There were articles of clothing, skins, some hunting weapons, cutting and digging implements, baskets and pots. Those things and not too much else. Pots were the high tech of the times requiring fires in some kind of structure leaning toward kilns operating at high temperatures. Knowledge of clay properties and proper good timing needed too.

Think about today's artifact list. It would probably fill a hundred books as thick as a telephone book – or, since we don't use those so much any more, *Photoshop for Dummies*. Millions of items, fine print three or four columns, some things we think of as crucial, many useful, convenient or educational, many with entertainment or distraction value only, some for pure display of status, many with toxic by products in the making or use and many, like weapons systems, and all their sub components and sub-sub components and tools down to machines for making the threads on a specialized screw specifically designed to support destruction.

Such a gigantic artifact list has many implications. One implication is you need an immense work force and many different work places and tendrils out into the supply chain and beyond that, means to get at the resource base – roads, trucks, digging machines and so on – to create each item on the list. Where the workers toil (or hang around the water cooler engaged in the realities or fantasies of building an effective corporate culture) and where they live have to be relatively close together – or close enough to drive – and naturally the people thus employed double as customers who need shops and schools nearby. In other words, the size of our cities is in similar proportion to the size of our artifact list. In fact the size of our population itself multiplied by what might be called the artifact list number might well turn out to be a good basic indicator of our impacts on the entire planet. A very long artifact list, then, implies an immense work force, big cities and high population. Which comes first? They grow up together.

We will return to this observation later around consideration of exercising better choices in what it is we put on that cultural artifact list, and that will deliver us to consideration of boycott and purchase lists as well, and all that could be guided – and improve greatly – by building ecocities.

10. X-ray village with keyhole plaza and view to the mouth of a small river.

In trying to express different features of ecocities, ecotowns and ecovillages, I've invented a few devices to help visualizing ecocities. Here, by making the higher, farther parts of buildings transparent we can see the layout of the streets and the fronts of the buildings facing us.

HISTORY – SECTION 2

CHAPTER 4

4.5 Billion Years of Nature's Economics

Original gift

We now start our nature/human economics history, not with the Big Bang about 13.8 billion years ago, but here on Earth. Miniplexion patterns from cosmic ancient times gives us some broad guidance. Now we move closer to the here and now zooming up to about 4.5 billion years ago to the formation of our own solar system and our home planet. What's going on from then on is what I'll call our total economy, nature's plus human's here on Earth.

Readers of the popular press as well as scientific papers know these days, some planets, including ours, revolve in orbits in the temperature range at proper distance away from their star where water can exist in its liquid form between freezing and its gaseous state. This zone is sometimes called the "Goldilocks Zone," not too hot and not too cold. Fortunately, water also dissolves many substances and takes part in endless chemical reactions. It serves as a medium in which, through mixing, all sorts of elements and molecules can come into close proximity to one another and react producing a wide range of materials friendly (and sometimes hostile) to the formation of life.

At present 99.97% of the energy arriving in our biosphere comes from the sun. That's an enormous quantity of energy if diffusely distributed as sunshine, diffuse and weak compared to, say, the searing heat of a river of lava or a gallon of kerosene erupting in flame in a Boeing 747 engine high at the edge of the stratosphere. But imagine the vast area of the whole world's lands and waters on which this free flood of energy is alighting. This light and heat, in both visible and invisible spectra, warms and powers various chemical reactions in the atmosphere, hydrosphere and lithosphere of the Earth[16].

The big lessons for nature's part in real economics here are the following: Though large, the planet's complement of minerals is finite and its energy input is close to steady in quantity arriving from the sun. On the capitalist's bullish side, the solar energy is for all practical purposes available essentially forever. And it is only deceptively weak: world wide it runs the whole biosphere in all its fecundity and rich variety, providing immense build up and storage of energy concentrating biomass in forests, grasslands, fossil fuel deposits and so on. (Except for a small fraction of total biomass in very deep seas and in micro cavities in the crust of the Earth.) Sunshine is diffuse enough that it takes mechanisms to collect and utilize all that available solar energy, natural mechanisms called plants with various services provided by animals, and human created mechanisms to burn energy in and build... our artifact list, including our cities. Thus nature's matter and energy enters human economy. The energy it takes to create all our products, structures and tools is called "embodied" energy.

First, and understood by more and more people every day, fossil fuels, maybe better called fossil hydrocarbon chemicals, were created on Earth in serious quantities during only three time periods with zero chance they will ever be replaced as we use them. The formation process was too slow and a long time ago. Coal came from forests between 360 million and 290 million years ago. Then along came microorganisms that evolved to eat and degrade the forests into gasses that literally went up into thin air. So that isn't about to happen usefully again any time soon. Oil was laid down in shallow waters for a few tens of millions of years, around 150 million to 90 million years ago, in shallow water sediments rich in dead algae and plankton precipitates. That is also not about to happen in a timely manner in human resource utilization terms ever again.

Then there's the "Rust Factor" earlier mentioned. Rust happens. Corrosion and loss through dispersion to below economically viable quantities for recycling etches away at the base of Human Economics. That means in the long run without extremely efficient recycling our basic mineral resources will dwindle away in rust,

[16] Wikipedia says 99.97% of energy arriving at the surface of the Earth from above (about 340 W m-2) is solar energy and a much smaller amount, 0.025, arrives from below, left over from the heat of formation of the planet as its immense mass cools, and from fission of uranium in the matter of the Earth itself. Very small amounts of energy relatively speaking come from tidal action of sun and moon and even smaller from light and radiation energy from distant stars and the thermal radiation of space and the friction with the air of meteorites.

corrosion and simple mechanical attrition buried in soils, sediments and landfills. In terms of what is lost in the mass component of the mass/energy we have to work with, not just ships that bubble down to Davey Jones' locker, lost to the deep blue sea in the tens and hundreds of thousands of tons of good metal each, but bottle caps and bits of wire, paperclips, bent nails, greasy aluminum foil, worn out, filed down and broken tools, small things melted in fires, things lost in floods, earthquakes, accidents or thrown "away" in disinterest. All these are multiplied by the billions of people we have on Earth today. As the virgin resources become increasingly scarce, more, not the same old amount of energy, is needed for new mining, recycling and manufacture.

Either the population has to contract to maintain something fairly close to in balance or people's average consumption of matter and energy, or both. I've mentioned making that negative into a positive – shrinking for prosperity – but from the capitalists' point of view, that's one of the bearish factors, the Rust Factor.

On the bullish side again, the Earth actually can absorb a certain amount of pollution and the energy income from the sun is awesomely large and patiently enduring. The industrialist polluters for a time acted on the slogan, "the solution to pollution is dilution," raising smokestacks taller so the locals would complain less – and last longer as underpaid workers at the nearby factory. Environmentalists, the labor movement and social justice activists would throw all that back at the industrials with a sarcastic twang when obviously the more distant forests were dying due to acid rain and chemical dust and pollution-related diseases spread over vast landscapes.

The oceans are big but not big enough to avoid the phosphate fertilizer and nitrification waters at the mouths of rivers draining agricultural areas like the Mississippi Valley into the Gulf of Mexico Dead Zone, and not big enough even as the Pacific to avoid the Pacific Gyre Garbage Patch, and not big enough to escape acidification of the one World Ocean from absorbing CO2 from the one World Atmosphere. Scientists thought the Ocean was so big there was no way it could acidify as quickly as it is happening, but surprise! The ocean doesn't seem to mix as much as anticipated; and acidification for the upper layers, where most of life is, has gone up a whole coral-damaging, seashell etching .1 on the acid base pH scale. The fastest natural acidification scientists have studied took place took over a 5,000 year period approximately 56 million years ago in what is known as the Paleocene-Eocene Thermal Maximum totaling .4 on the acid base pH scale. The rate of acidification now is about 1,200 times as fast, which makes sense since the entire reservoir of preserved carbon "fuels" is going toward gone up into the atmosphere largely to diffuse into the ocean in about 300 to 400 years when it took many tens of millions of years to accumulate. Not good!

Then there is the total number of people and especially at high consumption levels using and discarding non-degradable products and byproducts that can and do overload natural capacity to buffer pollution. That's the Rust Factor I just mentioned.

Adding these negatives together, well before they were as negative as today, the original authors of Club of Rome book, *The Limits to Growth*, came up with a chart tracing industrial output, food, pollution, population and resources. They produced a chart of bell curves for all factors but resources. That resources line on the chart follows a trajectory gliding gently then dropping more rapidly downward. All trends tend toward stabilizing in a much lower range heading out of the graph on the right side. (See the charts next two pages.[17])

Yet some pollution can be absorbed, and in some possible if-today-only-dreamed-of future we can imagine levels of pollution that are neutralized and an ecological footprint well below overshoot, a rich and magnificent biosphere coming back. Such pollution absorbing capacity and "geo-ecological services" could be delivered by slow-moving but massive ecological and geological forces and the beauty of sunshine and chlorophyll restoring forests, grasslands and oceans – while nature absorbs a modest amount of what looks and acts like pollution today.

Another thing in understanding nature's economics is noticing and appreciating what chlorophyll in plants does by capturing sunlight and changing it into useful chemicals – sugars and starches, oils, fats and cellulose – that store energy and serve billions of other uses. This energy can be released later in plant growth and, next, after animals eat the plants or other animals, in animal growth and in the power of working muscles. Follow that chain of chemical reactions from chlorophyll through yet more geological conditions of heat and pressure in strata of soil, sand, gravel, etc. producing hydrocarbon chemicals called fossil fuels. This stored energy then operates human-made machines of a wide variety for production, use and exchange of wide ranging other things and objectives. Our very thinking, too, is powered by this string of chemical reactions from sun to plants, through chlorophyll, to us, through our stomachs to our veins, muscles, organs, nerves and brains.

All this about resources, sunlight and the action of chlorophyll, as well as the lessons of the principle of limits, is rudimentary in our mass/energy physical reality. Yet it is somehow irrelevant to classic capitalist economists banking on any old kind of fuel, all assumed to be replaceable for ever more growth. What the knowledge about the chlorophyll link implies in protecting the biosphere – life in all its ecological interactions – is crucially important. It describes the resource base and transmission system delivered from sunshine by the chlorophyll to plant stored energy in "primary producer" life forms like algae, seaweeds and land-based plants to "first level consumers" like butterflies, deer and cows and "second level consumers" like dragonflies, wolves and people. Fail to appreciate the relationship of the plants and animals to fertilizing the soil for healthy functioning of photosynthesis and you fail to understand such things as why biofuels have a strictly limited utility for human use under current conditions.

The bottom line here regarding what we literally build, in our early 21st century context, is that our enormous world population and structural dependence on

[17] Ugo Bardi, Ibid., p. 169

driving cars, linked to our building of the scattered city, eliminates biofuels for any practical purpose from a role in a healthy economics, both natural and human. This situation will probably last, optimistically speaking, one to three generations while we try to mend our ways, (if we actually try). As Lester Brown points out, one full tank of ethanol in the average SUV requires the same amount of land as needed to feed a person for a year. [18] Ironically, biofuels such as simply wood, ethanol from a limited acreage of corn and sugarcane and oils from oil palms, will in the long run, if human demands for energy are radically reduced, be a sustainable source of easily portable and convenient fuel energy for many uses – Richard Branson flies Boeing 747s on the stuff – into the deep future if we can get ecocity infrastructure and the others of the Big Six figured out.

Also among the basics regarding nature's part in the total economics of both natural and human-constructed economics is the fact of uneven distribution of mineral and soil resources in varying degrees of purity and ease or difficulty of extraction and purification. In all cases it takes matter in the form of tools and machine energy, in whatever form, to extract and render the resource materials such as ores and chemical feed stocks into a useful form. By this point in history, as *Human Geography – Landscape of Human Activities* noted in similar disturbing words, what's easy is gone, and what isn't gone, isn't easy any more.

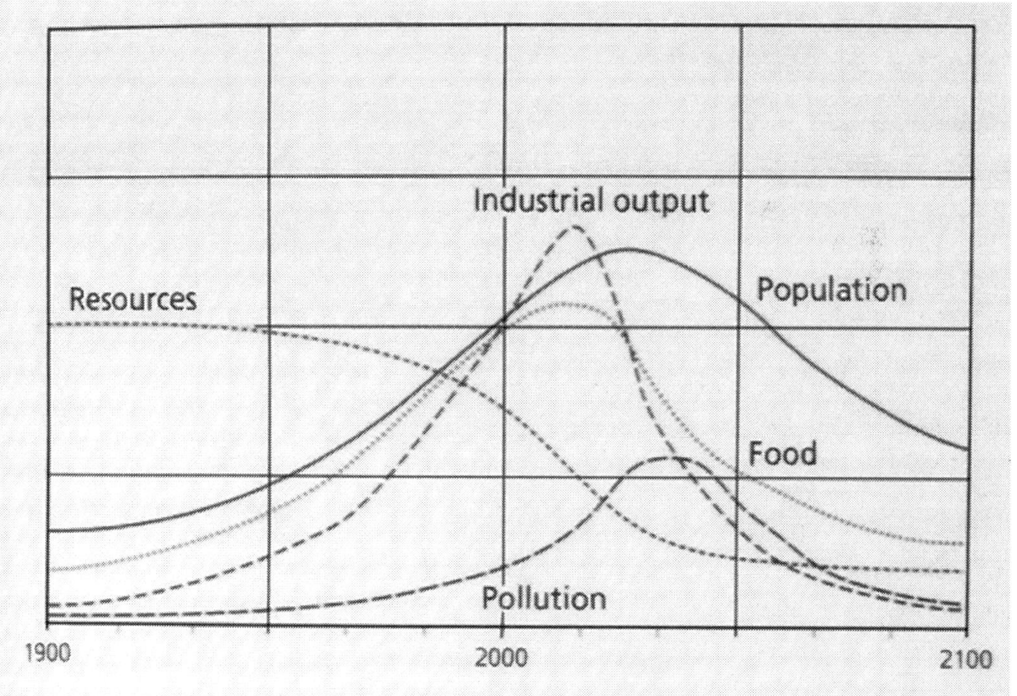

Caption next page.

[18] Lester Brown, *Plan B 4.0*, Norton, New York, 2009, p. 49

11. Chart in the book *Extracted* from the 1972 Club of Rome study and book, *Limits to Growth.*

Critics said these predictions were wrong, as we obviously were not seeing collapse yet, that is before around 2020. But the projections were based on large generalizations assumed even at the time, 1972, not to come due until sometime in the 21st century. But at a glance we can see the prognosis is bleak and some of the lines in 2015 as I write are obviously not that far off.

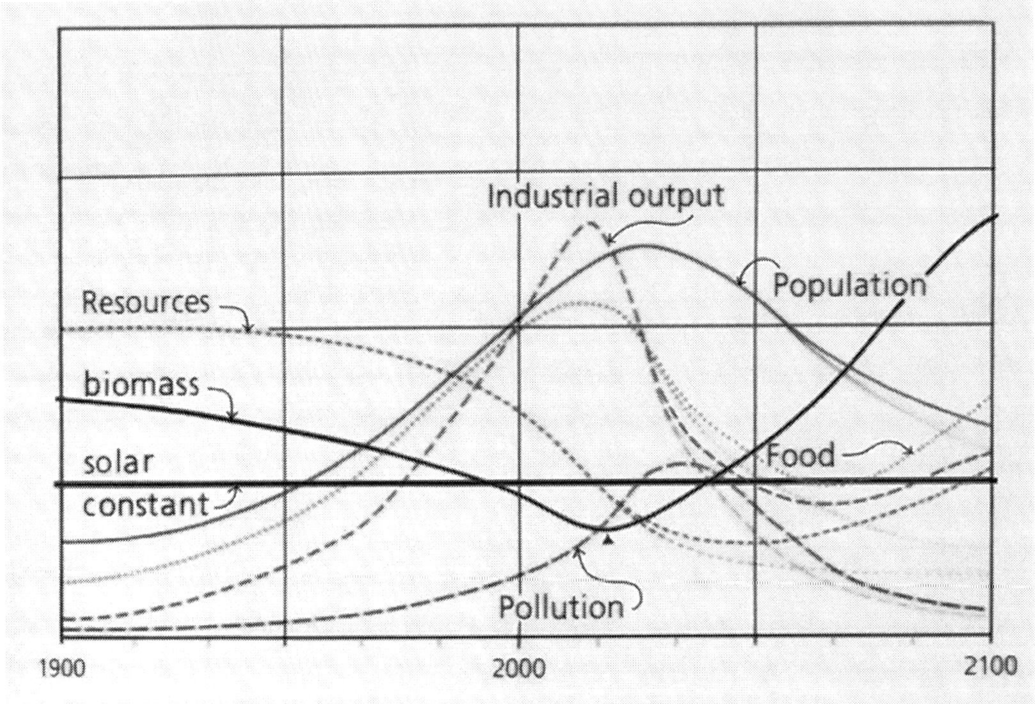

12. Limits revised. Adding solar energy and recovering a high biomass planet.

This is my chart (left) adding the massive arrival of solar energy as base of the total economy, natural and human economics together. Here I call it the "solar constant." Thanks to plants and chlorophyll it's massive in energy and biodiversity supporting terms. The high biodiversity line is labeled "biomass." The biomass upswing point is designated by the small triangle about the year 2020 if we catch on. We can achieve that in ways to be discussed later in this book. Look for the term "Natural Carbon Sequestration." All the negatives improve; I show the Club of Rome rough projections in fading lines for comparison. As biomass goes up and people more intelligently use biological resources, things can improve greatly: partially because the projection is for declining then later stabilization of human populations and mass/energy consumption. Pollution will decline not only because of less mass/energy throughput and fewer damaging products and byproducts but because we become smarter and more conscientious. Plus I've assumed growing ecocity infrastructure. Plus very thorough recycling. The "improvement" is relative, though – to a much more biologically rich and far less material- and energy-wasteful arrangement of infrastructure, lifestyle and set of values. Possible? Only with major attitudinal changes on the part of humanity. My prognosis: hope for positive surprises to help us get there.

Meantime the fossil "fuels" can be burned or, used as chemical material feed stocks, made into paints, sealants, adhesives, lubricants, medicines, fertilizers, pesticides, building materials, pipes and wire insulation, asphalt, paraffin, detergents, furniture, synthetic rubber, strong fiber, flexible fabric, plastics products of countless descriptions, some food additives, preservatives, flavoring and even artificial limbs and body replacement parts. It gets so personal that even my own innards are held in place by an artificial plastic kind of apron inserted in a hernia operation after I literally coughed my guts out – gross but true – in a Beijing smog attack.

But if these fossil chemicals are burned, "You can't have your cake and eat it too." In fact, though the popular chief concerns with the resource are pollution, climate change, ocean acidification and eventual depletion to unavailability that results from burning, they are so versatile it might one day be realized that its amazing range of other uses will be missed more than the energy release for which it was destroyed. After all, fossil fuel energy could be replaced harmlessly and without much effort and intelligence by wind, sun, falling water, heat of the Earth and judicious use of biofuels when food needs are more equitably met.

In the realm of the economics of the biological, if and when extinctions occur, that particular linkage between nature's economy and ours is interrupted and, say, if the Japanese and other friends of sushi continue insisting on eating blue fin tuna down to the very last slice of *maguro*, another piece of our resource base disappears forever, along with whatever wonder or beauty we might have seen in our lost planetmate. The Japanese restaurants will never make another cent on blue fin. Every creature's millions of years of continuity gets down to microscopic string of DNA connecting one generation of organism with another, through inside soft protective living layers sheltering the reproductive process from a pretty harsh outside world.

The scale difference between the stuff of the genetic material and the size of, say our own bodies, the parent-offspring link from one to the next adult organism, is just amazing, the organism being millions of times larger, the DNA link barely existing at all in physical scale. Yet species endure with slow changes through hundreds of thousands or even millions of years making human constructions and whole civilizations look fragile and ephemeral in comparison. Even hard stone mountains well up and wash away in those time spans while squishy microscopic strings of DNA march on in their patterns of continuity and slow mutation for literally thousands of millennia protected only by the bodies and behavior of the ever changing guard plants and animals in which they exist and thrive quasi-eternally.

For all species there's also the external-to-the-organism ecological support system, the environment, to keep millions or even hundreds of millions of years of slowly changing genetic continuity going. Gradually, very slowly changing sets of chrono-species evolve, one species morphing into something different through time, along with the other species also evolving, but connected in an ancestral line that goes back to life's beginning on the planet. Every generation goes back to those compact strings of information in their DNA. Wondrous, as one might say. But if the number of individuals becomes rare, extinction can occur and that species' entire history of millions of years is lost forever.

Shameful to cause an extinction just for a flavor rush or for not being willing to think about city design's massive impact on the biosphere, thousands of species at a time. Again, and in keeping a focus on economics, you can never again make money on an extinct species. (Unless you were a naturalist selling the last ones to a museum after The End, which has happened a few times. Then ethics caught up to the tragedy and *they don't do that anymore.* Or so I hear.)

These flows and limits of nature's capital become ultimate factors in understanding nature's economics, from massive flows of solar energy laying down whole forests to micro energies arranging DNA. I'd guess these ultimate factors include:

1.) whole systems limits: finite size of the Earth and various resources.

2.a.) dependable and steady long term but limited flow of energy from the sun that needs tools and an investment of energy to capture and utilize, or

2.b.) by way of the biological tool called chlorophyll, the transformation and storage of energy in plant and then animal protoplasm and in the fossil fuels and,

3.) the absolute irreversibility of loss through extinctions.

These macro dynamics become the bedrock foundation of the *real,* the total economics around here on planet Earth, the double economics that conjoin as nature's and human's together, or we sink back to nature's economics only, and a greatly impoverished nature at that. The economists consulting practically every government on Earth can ignore or try to deny the reality of something as fundamental as Peak Oil and what I'm calling the Rust Factor all they want, or they can claim that if those resource limits do exist we'll just find a replacement. But if they continue much longer in such influence on human conduct, from policy and physical design of our infrastructure to life style choices advertised into existence, their economics will collide with the *real* economics on the planet and guess which will survive? As they say, "nature bats last," though it will not be like nature wins since it will be so much impoverished. But it might also be more like "nature shoots back."

Enter people

Much of this book is an effort to see if we can understand the dynamics of nature's and people's economics as one whole system. At this point we are shifting from mass/energy space/time parameters of nature's economics to those systems people create by shifting flows of material and energy to the uses of individual people, societies and the collective works of Homo sapiens. Certain financial services are harmonious with nature's economics, such as loans to build a healthy, nicely profitable businesses that are also healthy for the community and the environment. These exist as genuine services: "green" and "fair trade" businesses. But, they are not sufficiently placed in a larger economic theory of the sort I'm trying to develop here, and very specifically, they are presently almost completely uninformed by the significance of geographic placement in the potentially healthy city, town and village structure as conceived as nascent ecocities in their bioregional and often ecotropolis contexts. "Green" investment and business is growing and getting educated step by step but isn't yet "place conscious" in the sense of their relationship to urban layout and planning.

Did I just say "ecotropolis"? That's the ecologically healthy metropolis. While we are busy defining new words in the necessary vocabulary we all need, in order to understand the kind of cities we need, it might also be useful to call the city dependent on cars that makes a couple billion of us dependent on cars "automotropolis." I admit that sounds a little ludicrous, humorous, chiding and condescending. But maybe that's good.

Meantime the economics of speculation that produces no physical product or practical service, that amounts to gambling on the part of wealthier people and those who just can't resist taking higher risks for hoped for higher profit, at the more extreme reaches of what Aristotle saw as dangerous and damaging and called *chrematistics*. Today we can see how such "finance" morphed into the crises of 1929 and 2008. But for now, let's start closer to the beginning.

Since I think the simplest, most generic term for the combination of natures' and society's economy would simply be the "total economy," that's what I'll use below. To simplify and provide a reference point for terminology, here's my brief outline for "the whole picture":

The Total Economy – Total Economics

Nature's Economy – Natural Economics
The mass energy world, including biology on planet Earth and undoubtedly on other planets if life exists there too

Human Economy – Human Economics
The mass energy world we humans create, along with means of production, created products and services and expedited means of exchange; completely based in and on, spatially and temporally, Nature's Economy, which is why I indent Human Economy to the right of Nature's Economy

Gift Economy – Gift Economics
A social extension of primordial parent to child giving between relatives, friends, acquaintances, even strangers

Capital Economy – Capital Economics
socialist economics – socialism
mixed economics – just... mixed economics?
capitalist economy – capitalism

In my reading the seldom-mentioned term "decent capitalism" caught my eye, as did the supposedly socialistic economies of northern Europe and China. Northern Europe's economics have been a democratically approved and "voted-in" mix of what's usually thought of as socialism and capitalism while in China there is a centrally planned version of socialism supported somewhat by the people if not "voted-in" but with capitalist Special Economic Zones (SEZs) and capitalist businesses flourishing throughout the country. I don't have a good term for the capitalism/socialism mix yet. Decent socialism... would that be the same thing as decent capitalism, a workable win-win midpoint? Just plain decent capital economics since socialism and capitalism are both capital based.

Milk, again

Now we get back to mother's milk, back where I started this book. In the early mammals, milk makes its appearance as a biological gift from one generation to the next long before people even evolved much less started making things and storing things, giving and sharing things and trading..., seeking profit, investing in, pooling resources for and building complex enterprises and so on. The gift of life itself goes back about 3,500 million to 3,800 million years. For your structurally basic mammals zoom ahead to about 125 million years ago. Breasts and milk, most paleontologists believe, seem to have evolved from modified sweat glands and a specially enriched sweat becoming milk. We might think this development encouraging to gift giving, sharing affection, cooperation. People pretty much differentiated themselves – ourselves – out from other mammal species around 2 million years ago or only about $1/60^{th}$ the time of milk on the planet.

Reciprocal services, a most basic form of trade, go back way before even mammals' proximate forbearers and the appearance of milk. I'd guess cleaner shrimp were busy extracting and eating bits of flesh from the teeth and keeping gum infection at bay for predator fish, while the big scaly marine vertebrates waited patiently. That practice, one type of what's called symbiosis, I'd estimate from reading charts of geological eons, eras, periods and epochs went back around 300 million years and that's about 175 million years before the gift of any kind of mother's milk. (Admittedly the above is a wild guess – but shrimp go back at least 520 million years, sporting perhaps the first cardiovascular system, by the way. Think about that ordering your next shrimp cocktail. If by 300 million BC they were trading dental services for bits of food, they were early innovators in nature's economics who knew a good long-term investment when they saw one.

One of the oldest of exchanges, maybe the oldest of profound consequences, was theorized by Lynn Margulis in the 1960s while updating and adding considerable support for an idea from 1905 by Russian botanist Konstantin Mereshkowski, further developed in the 1920s by biologist Ivan Wallin, and now called endosymbiosis – symbiosis (living together) one organism inside (endo) another. In this case inside a single cell. In a sense we complex organisms with our bacteria resident in our mouths and digestive tract have that kind of endosymbiosis going on inside us. But she had something a little different in mind. The notion, now generally accepted by biologists, is that some early single celled organisms were "invaded" by particular bacteria with different capabilities, or conversely were "engulfed" by a "host," like an amoeba might do these days. Both host and prospective food and/or misinformed invader – the engulfed one – however, ended up getting along, probably with a great deal of mutual irritation, like two people of a cantankerous but creative couple, sharing, specializing and expanding capabilities together. The smaller ones inside the larger became organelles within the larger single celled organism, such organelles as chloroplasts for photosynthesis, or mitochondria for exchanges of energy to produce motion and even the nucleus itself, suggested by the fact that the early "prokaryotic" cells had no nucleus.

The new relationship turned out to be a mutually beneficial chemical and physiological economy between smaller cells becoming organelles within the larger cell starting about 2 billion years ago.[19] Prokaryotic (simple) cells thus changed – and rather quickly in evolutionary time – to eukaryotic (complex) cells with many more

---

[19] www.scaruffi.com/science/endosymb.html

This most interesting article is mysteriously without a cited author, apparently from something called "Thymos: Studies on Consciousness, Cognition and Life." Scientific American and other sources say it is difficult to date appearance of the eukaryotic cells but seems to have been between 1.7 billion BP to 2.2 billion BP or a "little" farther back.

powers. This was a massive breakthrough in cellular, and hence, all of evolution, and also is thought to have greatly accelerated the pace of evolution.

Could the total economy be something like that, nature's economics hosting the human economics for an enrichment of the whole environment and a massive advance of normal, healthy evolution, that is, an economics analogy or even *case of* largest-scale – anywhere in the universe scale – endosymbiosis? Could such comparisons be valuable and carry through from biological sciences to solid economic theory? Could this thinking place economics in its true context as part of evolution in the miniplexion pattern? The larger context, nature's economics in this case, informs on how all components of any economics might use or abuse knowledge about the total picture of the total economics. For example, people might like to embrace and amplify the burning up of the planet for short-term luxuries and design, as indeed they have in many places, exactly that.

But back to our main line of thinking... In our human world, as said in this book's introduction, the mother for her milk receives back something wonderful beyond words, that, to be not so poetic about it, might start with reflexive physical pleasure. She and her man got into this situation through the mutual pleasures of sex built into, some geneticists and neurologists say "hard wired," for the survival and thriving of, again, life itself. Sex had to be a big pleasure for both parties or why even think of it? A little pleasure like massage +? That doesn't sound like quite enough to guarantee continuation of species through evolutionary time. But I digress.

Other basic exchanges: father brings home an animal or a skin pouch full of berries to eat; mother and eight year old child, with lots of scraping, pounding and washing make a blanket of the furry hide that keeps the three warm at night. They all share the harvest and results of the personal initiative that started with an invention somewhere, by accident or intent, that delivers a piece of skin clothing, hunting weapon, utensil to use, cooked meal, thorn and fiber to stitch and thread and so on. Mutual sharing looks like gift giving and receiving, earliest trade, if in close and simple family and small band exchanges.

Invention and creative ideas? People are good at that and once discovered or invented not often soon forgotten. Take fire. Obviously there was a fair amount of it around and big fires since no one was there to effectively fight them when lightening struck or a river of lava flowed into a field or forest. A spark of spontaneous combustion occasionally lit up the oily hot and getting hotter chaparral on sunny slopes on dry summer days in Mediterranean climate zones like around the Mediterranean Sea, much of west facing coastal California and Australia. In a few rare places there were even exposed coal seams that, like oily brush on a hot day, spontaneously ignited and burned steadily. There were even oil seeps in the Middle East, which many believe were the sources of the Zoroastrian religion's interest in fire and the burning bush of Old Testament tales. Someone, and probably many, overcame the fear animals have for fire and the shock and awe of seeing it slash down out of the sky with deafening thunder, convulsively disgorged from a volcano with truly apocalyptic accompanying events or maybe even mysteriously "spontaneously" appear in an innocent looking summer scene on a hot day. Our imaginative and curious ancestor picked up the cooler end of a flaming brand to impress his or her friends and introduced fire for fun, for a little proof of solid competence and ego, utility and defense, all pretty much at the same time: impress your friends, cook your food, scare away predators.

Fire goes way back and one idea is that cooking accelerated human evolution and traded a big digestive tract and small brain for a small digestive tract and a big brain – let the cooking do most of the digesting before you put the food in your mouth. Invent pots and you have external stomachs to get digestion started with all sorts of advantages following on. Michael Pollan reports on this in *Cooked – A Natural History of Transformation* calling it the "cooking hypothesis." "The hypothesis," he says, "is an attempt to account for the dramatic change in primate physiology that occurred in Africa between 1.9 and 1.8 million years ago with the emergence of *homo erectus*, our evolutionary predecessor." He points out, "The chewing and digestion of raw food of any kind requires a big gut and strong jaws and teeth – all tools that our ancestors lost right around the time they acquired their bigger brains."[20] *Much* bigger brains; chimpanzees' brains, by comparison, are smaller than one-third the size of the human brain. Of course they don't use fire or cook.

In terms of gift giving the advent of use of fire and cooking elaborated human activities and increased cooperation and specialization considerably, suggesting that someone with one skill would, naturally, share with someone else specializing in something else, presenting gifts back and forth. Pollan points out that cooking saves enormous amounts of time chopping grinding, chewing and digesting, time available for further specialization, more time for developing language through conversation and time for pondering life's mysteries gazing into the fire. Also, making more time available for making things: birth of industry, more babies.

Sharing in some senses was the socialistic idea – from whom according to their ability (modified according to willingness, which is often a contradiction to this day) and to those according to their need (which is obvious enough with children and with someone cooking while someone else goes out hunting to bring back something to cook.)

Early exchange

Looking at the exchange functions that lead into market place dynamics and conventional capitalist theory, where might have exchanges of resources, products and services gotten started? If we go back far enough in sharing and exchanging

[20] Michael Pollan, *Cooked – A Natural History of Transformation*, The Pinguin Press, New York, 2013, p. 56 & 57

we'd probably be in an era before language was much more refined than among chimpanzees who engage in preening, ridding each other of irritating lice. One chimp provides the benefit of relieving itchy skin and to the other, we might presume, in the process receives the pleasure of popping a tasty morsel into his or her mouth, as filmed and reported in scholarly papers. One act, one unit of exchange, two beneficiaries. Another explanation for the preening/snacking might simply be the pleasure of sociability, comfort of company, banishment for the time being of loneliness plus safety in numbers. Maybe the service was quite negligible and the lice flavor not so good after all. Economic exchange is *not* singular in motivation and content, not simple, despite careful studies supposedly testing just one thing at a time conducted by many economists running the studies they base their theories on.

13. Small shop on the edge of Bhaktapur, Nepal with running dog, people shopping, conversing

Just one of my favorite photos taken from a hurtling mini-bus, with a real sense of both country and village, commerce and life.

Even very early on it seems likely that credit emerged in a kind of innate sense of balance, justice. Asymmetrical benefit in the exchange might have raised its sense of injustice with the inkling that it wasn't such a good deal for one of the parties or was an off balance deal now waiting for later rebalancing. Wait too long and it would be an obligation shirked. If the preening itself was experienced as having more value than the flavorless mites that you couldn't just drop on the ground because they'd immediately climb back on, then after a while the preened would owe the preener, whether words were there to focus on and emphasize the fact or not.

Come people and at a certain point there would be words. "You owe me one, Buddy." Thus was born credit communicated in sound frequencies leaving a set of vocal chords and vibrating a pair of eardrums somewhere else. The first hint of "are you going to be good to your word?" appears, and an implicit agreement eventually becomes explicit and reinforced by the spoken word.

For example, what if Howard needs to borrow an arrow – doesn't have time to make one before this afternoon's hunt – will return it a few days later. Bill agrees to provide him with one. Howard has the arrow for a few days but loses it way down in a precipitous canyon. Probably it's shattered anyway, the canyon strewn with rocks, both point and shaft. Howard is set to return a replacement of same size and quality, but when he arrives at Bill's, Bill says, "Linda came over yesterday looking for an arrow for her husband. I said, 'Hey Linda you make excellent pots and I need a nice medium sized one, but I don't have an arrow now. However, Howard borrowed one and is supposed to return it or one like it today or tomorrow. Why don't you give me one of those nice pots you make and you can collect your arrow from Bill?'" So Linda agrees and brings over this pot a few minutes later, and now she gets to collect the arrow.

Voila! Money! Verbal money. And Linda holds it, the instrument of credit, in her memory. It has the three essential characteristics of money: serving as 1.) a medium of exchange, that is, representing something of value but not being the thing of value itself, as 2.) a store of value over time agreed upon by those in the system, the agreement itself being the store of value, in what we will call the market, which is the activities together in this set of transactions also in general character agreed upon more broadly by the society the three are part of, and as 3.) a means of counting proportionality, accounting using numbers or agreement regarding scale or quantity, even quality, one good arrow being worth one medium sized pot in this case, one not so good arrow worth only a small saucer. Thus a string of words expressing an agreement used to facilitate exchange of real things and services held in the memory becomes the first kind of money. This kind of spoken money works if people have good recall and are good to their word, that is, share that particular common value, or in most rudimentary terms, have a sense of balance and react negatively to imbalance, or you might say, asymmetry in the exchange, have an innate sense of injustice if someone gets cheated – or justice if people "get even" with a debtor. It also helps if your culture's artifact list is short and the time intervals in the exchange are not too long since trying to remember lots of things flowing around in agreements held only in memory becomes a challenge as memory fades over time.

Later, with written language, an IOU gets recorded and the clay tablet, papyrus, parchment or paper record serves to augment forgetful or slippery (intentionally forgetful) memory. Rerunning our example with an IOU the story follows the same minimalist plot but the transaction gets recorded. Bill doesn't want to look distrustful so he says, "OK, but I want you to write that down. It's not that I'm uptight or don't trust you Howard but you know how busy we are getting these days now that we have written language and all those forms to fill out, tax records to keep track of, so many new types of products coming around, so many things each of us own, one of us just might forget." The same story unwinds but now, Voila! Money! Money of a new fangled sort on clay tablets, parchment, scrolls, paper maybe. If verbal money was where capital economics was conceived, here is where it burst into the world, born and delivered.

Another step in the history of money comes when a lot of people have shells with a drilled hole on strings, like necklaces. Maybe they *were* necklaces, beads on a string. Each shell bead has the work value of the finding, gathering, filing and drilling, plus the physical existence value of the material itself, perhaps of attractive color and sparkle. The shell beads become a fairly standard unit. If the shells are of approximately the same quality and size, and let's say color too, they are of the same value. People adorn their bodies with them, give them for special occasions. They are not of high value, but if you have a lot of them...

Of course shell money actually was used in the American Indian community. A surprise to me though, before I started digging around for information about economics about two years ago, was that the New Netherlanders in New Amsterdam had no money for exchange when they arrived among the American Indians on Manhattan Island and neither did the British also recently arrived in New England in the Boston area. The coins of the Netherlands and England that the colonists brought with them were so few they were close to useless for exchange. So they traded with the Indians between New Amsterdam and Boston using Indian shell money when supply and demand didn't match for direct trade in beaver pelts, dried fish, lumber, corn, tools and so on. The shell beads could be conveniently loaded on strings fairly efficiently and lubricated exchange through a fairly wide range of geography and value.

Something to notice is that materials like obsidian stone for arrowheads, straight sticks from trees for arrow shafts, fine mud for pots, animals for food, if you knew where to find them, kept appearing from nature. Some materials came from the ground itself, some from the sun's energy working on the plants, minerals, air, water, and all requiring work by people in hunting, growing, shaping to various uses but always available and in human hands constantly being created as some were wearing out or being lost. This was real economics and being "in balance," that is not significantly depleting nature, in fact enriching the kinds of healthy activity going on the planet, the total economy operating well. Specialization and exchanging things through one means or another, sharing within families, barter one to one in the exchange on the spot, without time lag or third party or "neutral medium of exchange" involvement, and keeping track of who owned the land, that is, who had rights of tradition or custom and occupation, with or without paper proof, or who purchased those rights... in some way of agreement all these transactions played a large role while money was getting started. Money, meaning the physical representation of value, not the spoken word money I started out with here to emphasize agreement, was a good way of not worrying so much about who owed whom what. It helped in moving a few extra things around more conveniently.

There were other ways of seeing it, though. The view of the Indians in what is today the United States northeast for example regarded the shells and strings of shells as something they called *wampum*. It functioned something like money but money *plus*, which was more than a medium of exchange in that this money, this store of value, carried a more ancient view that the strings of shells represented gifts exchanged to confirm agreements and be a reminder of said agreements with expectations of some form of return into the future. It represented not simple debts resolved or items accounted for moving from person to person.[21] Value was in the complex understanding of social ecology, not just reduced to number. Wampum was not just a store of material value but also balancing of mutual benefit gifts. Strings of shell beads of two colors representing different values by color, one purple bead equaled five white for example, among the Indians around Long Island Sound, and thus among the early Dutch and English in the area. These shells of white or purple, from near where La Guardia Airport is today and shorelines east, were arranged on their strings to create different patterns to one way or another indicate agreements and obligations, to indicate resolution of earlier conflicts and new or recommitted friendship and trust.

The exchange of the belts of beads then were like a language, but being simpler and not so specific, word for word, required that the arrangement of beads be rehashed several times among participants to the exchange and before witnesses and essentially memorized together so that the meaning would be remembered when the bead belt was viewed as a reminder again at a later date. The position of the changing pattern of beads served as a mnemonic device as well as record of value in its sub parts, the shell beads themselves. The whole thing had value beyond the agreed commodity value of its components, *way* beyond, like the number 100 on the Franklin US bill on paper worth much more than the 1 on the dollar bill or the paper itself. In fact, some belts of beads, these wampum belts, were documents recording rights to the use of land for dwelling and farming, for trees for cutting, animals for hunting, waters for fishing and so on. They amounted to real estate records, up graded by inflation to hundreds of thousands of today's dollars or many millions. Contrary to those who say Indians were foreign to the concept of land ownership these semi-written records functioned in many ways like deeds. They certainly had concepts of use of the land and who should have rights to those uses often specifying where one could build a village and hunt freely and cultivate the land or even establish a military fort. These wampum belts essentially documented transfer of rights to use of the land and often enunciated various specific uses, often attached to a pledge of friendship and mutual support should a conflict break out with a third party. In a very essential way the Indians dealt in land and sealed deals with their *money plus* that amounted to highly qualified deeds, with rights to this and that involved: hunting, fishing, cutting trees, etc., even development rights for architecture in building villages.

But being seen as gifts between friends, essentially treaties plus more personal commitments of representatives of various groups of people, these particular belts

[21] My main source on shell money: *Shell Game – A True Account of Beads and Money in North America,* Jerry Martien, Mercury House, San Francisco, 1996

implied on-going relationships and obligations. For the deal to stick, though, you had to be able to read the wampum belts and come to future agreement as to what they meant. Thus the Indians were in an interesting world half way between keeping one's word and honor using verbal money and written contracts and paper money. They had a semi-literate system half way between verbal money and paper money, between some sort of ancestral customary claim to use and physical record of that use with a demand for just continuity or transfer or sharing of such a claim.

What was to be remembered and when strung into patterns of beads on wampum belts was often quite consequential in terms of society and politics, too, declaring who was friend and who not, whether the French, English, colonial American or other tribe would be the enemy or friend and so on. Much discussion preceded exchange of wampum at times of treaty, and later, interpretation was made largely on the basis of what everyone remembered – or agreed about in reading the lines of those mnemonic devices, the bead belts.

The white European colonists had a much more precise language for recording in writing, but as history proved out, they would disregard written agreements simply as a matter of outgunning the Indians and sending them packing on pain of death. Many that didn't go packing were in fact killed, along with their children and old folks. The subtleties, the being together, in theory as to friendship or at least being allies, the commitment to trying to reinterpret the meanings as recorded in the pattern of beads of the earlier exchange and concomitant obligations – no problem in the view of the white man at the time: possession was nine tenths of the law when you were a superior being with true religion, more advance material technology with guns and outnumbered the natives many times over, whether the agreement be recorded in beads or the letters of an alphabet.

With the Indians there was mutual gift giving. Balance was restored by obligation exercised as reciprocal further gift giving in the opposite direction, seeing each other off and on, learning something about one another, resolving new problems maybe, and – the dark side of long debates among parties to a set of exchanges – gossiping about some group outside of that set of meetings and discussions around the wampum belt, beginning to see them, for continued absence and growing ignorance, and often border issues, as something of a gathering threat and possible future enemy. For there is only so much time to deal in such detailed debate and reiteration and interpretation with so many people.

In any case it turns out to be surprising how close to universal the early attitude about "trade" as mutual gift giving with detailed discussion, almost ecologically complex in nature, actually was. It popped up all over the world.

Mauss: gifting societies – "A barter society never existed"

French sociologist Marcel Mauss, nephew of Emile Durkheim who has been generally considered the founder of modern sociology, suspected something was amiss with the constructs of his contemporary marketplace economists during his investigations in the 1910s and 1920s. By 1925 he had written his influential essay *The Gift: The Form and Reason for Exchange in Archaic Societies.*[22] He favored socialism and cooperative ventures organized by independent groups, was not strong on strong state socialism at all, was horrified by Bolshevik terrorism and "means justify the ends" thinking which he though also characterized much that was wrong with marketplace capitalism. He wanted to learn what contemporary "primitive" people had to say about economics and exchange. So he dove into his studies of the Samoa Island cultures and the Kwakiutl of the North American Pacific Northwest coast looking for barter economics or something different than what was disenchanting him at the time. He rapidly discovered that barter was not what the people in the western Pacific and Pacific Northwest engaged in at all. In fact he began to wonder if any society had ever used barter as the main means of exchange. He soon began to wonder if a barter society ever even existed.

I've wondered about that myself having lived in "alternative" rural communities – back to the landers we were – where barter was something of an economics ideal more anchored, in theory, in the soil, more community oriented: you harvest or make something and simply trade it with something someone else in the neighborhood harvested or made. The thinking was, "What might they have that I want and what might I have that they want?" Maybe the idea was to seek more simple, manageable life ways separate from the American War on Vietnam and other nasty, complex and meaningless – or negatively meaningful – things that were going on at the time (which isn't to imply that such things are not still going on or that a lot of nice things were not going on at the same time then).

But somehow we never got around to doing much bartering. It went about this far: "My truck's broken right now; how about if I borrow yours for a wood run," (meaning scavenging the National Forest for fire wood), "and trade you about a quarter of the firewood we gather?" Or, "I'll babysit Sally Saturday night if you babysit little Thomas next Friday night." More generally when it came to any special possession or product of some skill and labor, person number one never seemed to have what person number two wanted when person two had something person one wanted at about the same time and of about the same value. Even waiting a while for reciprocity hardly ever worked out. If the ideal of barter wasn't a fantasy of capitalists in the monetized economy trying to imagine where their system got started, what else was it? Because it seemed close to negligible in my experience and in the much more studied, closer to the source, scholarly experience of Marcel Mauss.

Insofar as barter does exist, it is more like a little icing on the cake of near self-sufficiency rather than something basic or substantial in economic flows: many even in the United States as late as the very early 20th century raised most or much of their food, sewed a lot of their clothes, built their humble country houses with one

[22] Marcel Mauss, *The Gift: The Form and Reason for Exchange in Archaic Societies*, Norton and Company, New York, 1990, originally published 1925

quarter the square footage per person as today's suburban average and repaired their farm tools and machines themselves one family at a time. I know my grandmother's parent's family did. Those things they couldn't provide for themselves with their own hands they bought with money, not traded, though they didn't need a lot of money to do that in the larger scheme of things because they didn't need money for most of the many things they did for themselves. Even within the families they didn't really trade in a systematic way, they just gave things back and forth, made and handed toys and clothes down from older kids to younger, sewing some new clothes to add to the stream of hand me downs, buying the cloth from a store in town, and so on. This kind of economy that is largely but not wholly self-sufficient and at the same time is partially monetized is why many of the poverty figures used around the world create distorted impressions of how badly off some groups closer to personal, family or village self-sufficiency actually are. These studies sponsored in the much more monetized economy of the wealthy world make the better-off people feel they are, in comparison, yet more accomplished and advanced than the others when maybe they either are not or their excellence is exaggerate. For the developing countries such figures justify receiving foreign aid and can therefore be actually quite helpful.

How can anyone actually live on \$100 a year or \$8.00 purchasing power a month or 27 cents a day? Well, they don't. They live on \$100 plus \$10,000 worth of what they produce and pass around the partially self-sufficient "love economy" as Hazel Henderson calls it which has in its proper environment no monetary evaluation measures and doesn't involve tit-for-tat trade of goods. It's based on giving, receiving, giving back, receiving, giving, round and round.

Back to Marcel Mauss. I'll quote David Graeber, Professor of Anthropology at Yale University, from the freewords.org website, from his essay about Mauss called "Give it Away." "First of all," says Graeber,

> ...almost everything that 'economic science' had to say on the subject of economic history turned out to be entirely untrue. The universal assumption of free market enthusiasts, then as now, was that what essentially drives human beings is a desire to maximize their pleasures, comforts and material possessions (their "utility"), and that all significant human interactions can thus be analyzed in market terms. In the beginning, goes this version there was barter... The problems was, as Mauss was quick to note, there is no reason to believe a society based on barter has ever existed. Instead, what anthropologists were discovering were societies where economic life was based on utterly different principles, and most objects moved back and forth as gifts – and almost everything we would call economic behavior was based on a pretense of pure generosity and a refusal to calculate exactly who had given what to whom.

Well, this rang true to my own experience, "back to the land" in a mountain village in New Mexico. Graeber adds,

> In gift economies, Mauss argued, exchanges do not have the impersonal qualities of the capitalist marketplace: in fact, even when objects of great value change hands, what really matters is the relationships between the people; exchange is about creating friendships or working out rivalries, or obligations, and only incidentally about moving around valuable goods.

Mauss' description, based also on observation of Northwest Coast North American peoples, seems close to the Northeast US Indians I've mentioned with their shell money and added mnemonic tools, the wampum belts. One can see the relationships of obligations of Samoa Islanders reflected in the tradition of debating the meaning of exchanges until understanding was established, agreements cemented and, frequently, friendships launched or strengthened or relationships broken off. But maybe the use of beads for money and tying that in with the beginnings of a system of accounting and statement of agreed upon valuation – the use of wampum belts for both purposes and as the beginning of some sort of proto early writing and number system – speaks to the kind of transition we might see from advanced hunter/gather and early agriculturalist economics to the village becoming ancient city, to the stage which some call the preindustrial city economics and those a transition into our current industrial city market capitalism. But a glance at gift exchange systems before we transition to the earliest cities.

Polanyi: gifting economics hits the lengthening artifact list

Like Marcel Mauss, economist Karl Polanyi also took the gift exchange society seriously. His best known work *The Great Transformation – The Political and Economic Origins of Our Time,*[23] published in1944, examines the economics of ancient cultures before cities and he also cites studies of his "primitive" contemporaries, the ancients still among us – at least still among us then in the early 1940s. In particular he contrasts very explicitly the patterns of the gift and obligation exchanges of reciprocity with capitalist patterns of economics and thinking. He identifies three characteristics of these early economies: symmetry, centricity and householding. As a very general pattern, it seems they may well together be a step in an evolutionary sequence of something that started as simplest gift giving moving toward higher levels of complexity.

---

[23] Karl Polanyi, *The Great Transformation – The Political and Economic Origins of Our Time*, Beacon Press, Boston, 1944

14. Plaza, Santiago, Chile

Looks and expressions link, everyone doing something, everything so lively in public spaces around the world.

In describing symmetry he focuses on the gift exchange in which individuals among small numbers of people give things to one another. Sharing – mutual gift giving – would seem especially natural among us humans in earlier times when care during childhood, requiring obvious gift giving to the young, would constitute such a large fraction of life, given very short life expectancies compared to today's. One can imagine the hunter brings home, the homebound provides the home. This reciprocity, this symmetry in giving back and forth, Polanyi points out, is reflected in systems of duality that pervade, in the division into moieties, which are divisions of peoples larger than small bands into two closely allied but separate groups. Typically even in small tribes men and women marry outside their moiety and into the other, with the positive effect of forging alliances with neighboring people and reducing genetic inbreeding problems.

Gifts come largely from the fact that seldom would early people have something someone else wanted right at the time they wanted or needed it, though with a short artifact list the coincidence would be more likely than for us up in the New Mexico mountains. Typically one would give something on one occasion and receive something on another occasion at some time later. Each separate exchange would be one way. Trade and barter, on the other hand, implies simultaneity, assigning roughly equivalent value and not having to remember obligation since the whole deal was executed in the exchange and agreement of value on the spot.

Contrarily, the gifting method of distribution had to be back and forth, like tennis, but with proper time lag and active use of memory, but general and somewhat vague and not precise. To have wanted or expected immediate return would have made it no longer seem like a gift. Besides, if immediately returned, then appropriate deliberation and time for expressions of various sorts – ceremony and ritual – would have been curtailed. Especially if you don't see one another that often, why cut a good thing short? Party a while, get tipsy, sing and dance; your future wife or husband will likely come from that other moiety, tribe or band after all… It's a social occasion for social meaning as much or more so than for exchanging stuff. It must have been a more culturally complicated thing than at first appears, and something that lost a lot in translation, to have gone from gifting to immediate trading. How boring!

Another circumstance to consider at this point is that among early people, all of nature was there for the taking, even if the taking was difficult and often dangerous. The predator animals had a hard time too, lots of work to create the opportunity to eat. The "just taking" wasn't "just" for early people but it was picking up what was available and fashioning it to human purposes, largely for food and self-preservation. You didn't pay the deer for some venison – you chased it, shot it, cut it up, cooked it, added spices, had another party. Viewed this way all of nature was a "commons." The commons might have been the "green" the citizen could use to graze sheep in common as a residual town green still resides in the middle of Amherst, Massachusetts, called the Amherst Town Common, and various other towns in English tradition. But for early people, all of nature was the commons. Nature/the commons was for everyone to do the best with that they could, taking but due to small numbers, seldom taking enough to disturb the natural balance. (Actually we know this isn't strictly true since our ancestors are by almost all scientific consensus now known to have destroyed most of the megafauna on the planet, but that is a slow motion story for another telling.) People took and then fashioned (built) what they could for their own use, and for "higher" reasons of expression and appreciation in craft and art.

Related to the commons is also the idea of "customary usage." People didn't need to write down what they agreed upon as to their prerogatives of taking, calling them "rights" at a later date. Customs were good enough, provided order and allowed latitude for free ranging and random harvesting. Customs changed with time, of course, but the notion in a group of some sense of proper, socially accepted ways of relating to nature, the resource base and the distribution of the wherewithal for survival and thriving was there and remains in the meaning of customary usage. Custom and money both are most fundamentally based on social agreement as to the value of things we might possess or control.

But back to Polanyi. The most primitive of trading partners, he points out, meet to give to one another in pairs of symmetry, taking mental note of who in the future owes *approximately* more of what to whom: the obligation next time, if not one of numeric or monetized precision called tit for tat or quid pro quo. Polanyi says that this ceremonial gift giving, structured by strictures of protocol and witnessed by many people on both sides of the gift giving, amounts to a best approximation of an accounting system for people without written language or numeric system for keeping more detailed accounts. In essence this pattern reflects an innate sense of fairness in distribution, the roots of a sense of justice contagious to other affairs in which we people find ourselves entangled. He points out a typical case on the Trobriand Islands of the western Pacific just northeast of New Guinea to illustrate such exchanges he believes were near universal at a particular stage in human social and economic development, "...each coastal village on the Trobriand Islands appears to have a counterpart in an inland village, so that the important exchange of breadfruits and fish, though disguised as a reciprocal distribution of gifts, and actually disjoint in time, can be organized smoothly."[24]

He points out a pattern, that the receiver of the gift – say the coastal village-representing fisherman when breadfruit is placed at his feet – feigns disinterest as if saying he doesn't really need the breadfruit. He rises above it all eschewing any signs of greed or material self-interest either for himself or on behalf of his fellow fishing villagers. It's important to all concerned to be the individual "giving" or represent the generous social group. After a time, acting as if his interest is growing and his skill at discerning a good breadfruit when he sees one is clearly known, he finally picks up the gift and accepts it – on behalf of the others, to whom he will later generously distribute much of it, taking a little more than average for himself as proper for the trusted negotiator/gift receiver and giver of the group. Then after various expressions of satisfaction the ritual is reversed as the fisherman generously offers a goodly part of his group's catch to the inland breadfruit tree climbers on behalf of his colleagues, but in theory based on past gifts not present.

At about that level up in the sequence in scale and complexity of exchange there comes the "Big Man" of many societies, the more skillful representative and often a better hunter or fisher, the magnetic personality that interprets custom best, who may be trusted in things hunting, fishing, healing or spiritual. This is the level Polanyi calls "centricity," by which he means that redistribution through gift giving becomes more organized due to larger quantity of stores and more complex variety of traded items, centered in containers, often involving larger numbers of people and often in sheltering buildings and under the watchful eyes of acknowledged leaders.

At this point in the evolution of economic systems, means of preservation and storage are improved. Items such as salted and spiced foods, drink preserved in alcohol, and even media of exchange such as shell money representing agreed upon value are now kept in granaries, storehouse, ceramic pots and bottles and proto-treasuries. The common folk are expected to give, though the contribution is getting to be more like expected to pay a tax in kind and in some cases in money (shells,

[24] Karl Polanyi, ibid., p.51

grains or other agreed upon medium of exchange) to the spiritually and socially wiser or politically stronger "Big Man" who then redistributes while taking responsibility to save and guard some of the stores for times of scarcity, dislocation through war, typhoon, fish scarcity or other emergency. These societies, operating without what we'd understand as a market, certainly not a self-regulating market of supply and demand and automatic price setting, range from small village scale groupings all the way up to the systems of the Pharaohs of Egypt and Kings of Mesopotamia, getting more monetized as scale increases, with the Big Man getting disproportionately ever bigger, more powerful politically and wiser in the ways of religion. The big man who exchanges for the benefit of the collective, small or large, is at the center of activity and the controller of centralized stores, thus Polanyi's focus on "centricity."

As we've noticed, as cultural products become more numerous, the functional usefulness of money with its three main characteristics – neutral medium of exchange, holder of value over time and value assignment by quantity and quality – would be growing along with the length of the artifact list. What we are seeing here, if I read it right, is the transition between gift giving exchange with memory and obligation crucially important and monetized exchange as the only practical alternative as the artifact list lengthens.

In transition from giving and receiving to selling and buying, we are seeing the emergence of monetized trading, concentrations of wealth become the norm, under the control of the Big Men and their families and friends, along with ease of extending loans, two conditions leading directly to banking – where your money can be safe in safes, where loans are available at reasonable rates – or maybe not so reasonable. Thus emerges the specialty work and professions of finance.

Sometime around the time monetized economics was taking over from gifting economics, different times in different places, and the period of a mixed economy of the two was shifting from a mainly gift oriented condition to a mainly money oriented condition, householding kicked in. This notion is well developed in the studies of the ancient city by Fustle de Coulanges coming up shortly but I'll mention here that the key notion that a family, generally extended, with enough members well organized, with all contributing – "giving" by tradition, that is to say in the customary usage – to the whole unit creates a system in which the basics of sustenance are covered. Generally this comes about in the stage of agriculture shifting from herding to cultivating crops on the land, Polanyi says. But it's interesting to also think of householding as starting in the first division off from the commons, which is the cave, wind break, lean-to or shelter of sticks and animal skins, claimed and defended (as regarding caves) or built to shelter a small number of people. This private space is divided off from the commons of nature all around and becomes the house, then the yard, then the yard with a wall and later a city with a wall and finally a country with a defense department, a ring of radar stations and well armed military aircraft. The house-based farm can be humble or it can be the manor house plus many support buildings housing many family members and appended craftspeople, servants, even slaves. The redistribution agency of the "Big Man" here reincarnate is the patriarch.

"The third principle," says Polanyi, "which was destined to play a big role in history and which we will call the principle of householding consists in production for one's own use." He goes so far as to say, "The individualistic savage collecting food and hunting on his own or for his family has never existed. Indeed, the practice of catering for the needs of one's household becomes a feature of economic life only on a more advanced level of agriculture; however, even then it has nothing in common either with the motive of gain or with the institution of markets. Its pattern is the closed group."

What we will see of Polanyi's thinking as we tour economic evolution later in these pages comes down to the notion that economics has been, is and properly should be, imbedded in and controlled by society rather than running on its own mathematical imperatives – self-regulating – and controlling society. But what he also seems to be saying but not emphasizing, is what I want to emphasize: that the built environment of the house itself, the community of physical structures, is indispensible and defining in human social and economic relations.

Laissez-faire is a fantasy: only law can make private property

Down here at the dawn of *really* modern economics, another principle that we need to discuss is the idea that individualistic Laissez-faire style economics can exist at all. Like barter being economic's first step, it's nothing more than something certain capitalists would like to believe, so they do: "I think therefore it's so." What does it actually mean to say we should be able to make what we want, sell on an unregulated market that finds its own balances, pay no taxes or practically none and everything would work out just fine? The best government is the least government? Or as Ronald Reagan said in his Inaugural Address of 1981 as head of the US Government, "Government is not the solution to our problem, government *is* the problem."

Why not "the best government is simply the best government?" That is, government with rules (regulation) to produce what society decides is healthiest for society itself?

When agreements of value get started – Bill's arrow borrowed by Howard equals Linda's pot – is it really an unencumbered valuation and trade agreement simply between two freedom-loving people? It might seem like it, but strangely, other people chime in, the "group" Polanyi was talking about two minute's reading back, if you read at the same speed I do. Bill's son says, "Hey Dad, you got gypped. No way that pot's worth a good arrow. Takes a really long time and lots of skill to make the points. You have to find the straight stick, dry and harden it, attach the feathers..." But his daughter chimes in, "Says you. Linda has to dig up the right kind of clay and it's miles from here and build a big oven and gather and burn all that wood she has to gather up to fire the clay. And that's not even including how good she is as making the pot itself which is pretty beautiful." "Relax kids, you're just playing gender prejudice roles. I'm above that being one of our tribe's wise elders and I can tell you what things are worth..." Etc. Through that sort of thing we develop a cultural consensus called custom. This amounts to early, generally somewhat looser "law" – though cross the customs and you might die an embarrassing death, or maybe just not be invited to the next fire circle... for the rest of your life.

When it comes to the value of money (remembered agreements, shells, coins, paper money, checks, electrons configured for an international bank transfer) the agreement is a consensus among vast numbers of people and institutions as to what things are worth, even if changing in value, usually fairly slowly over time.

Further, when it comes to contracts, who enforces? We are used to everyday transactions, so much so we usually fail to notice the weight of society behind the agreement when deemed a solid, obligatory, even legal agreement. Adam Smith said enforcing private contracts is one of the basic needs for and obligations of government, right there at the birth of modern capitalist thinking, along with provision of highways and other public infrastructure private business would find difficult to provide profitably and the system of justice itself with courts, a role business couldn't play due to frequent conflicts of interest. Then there has to be a government monopoly of rights to economic and violent coercion called taxes and law enforcement. Thomas Hobbes called the institution with such enforcement powers the "Leviathan," meaning a great big authority or government that keeps order and peace among those under its watchful eye for the benefit of all by overwhelming force when called upon by conflicts within the local or regional polity. In any case, we don't in everyday life think that much about enforcement as we go about our normal economic exchanges; it's there so we don't *have* to think about it that much. There's a broad and assumed consensus that backs law or society degenerates toward fascism or monarchy – dictated law called upon to force compliance with violent coercion – or toward chaos, gangsterism and war lords.

Say in simpler society someone refuses to honor a contractual agreement. When Howard says, "Well your arrow was very poorly made so when it hit regular dirt it snapped into five pieces and even the head broke in two. So I just left it there – pure junk. You should feel guilty about making arrows like that – and I don't owe you anything after all. In fact you should owe me a lost day's hunting, a week of eating, some antlers for making tools and a skin for a much needed blanket." Who settles that? People take or don't take one or the other's word and Howard gets away with it or Bill and his larger male relatives convinces Howard to pay back in some manner. Some societies would say, "Yeah we know all about Howard and that's the sort of thing he does. This is one too many and we are now going to shun him. Out of the village, jerk." Ultimately, though, "they pass laws about this sort of thing." What does that mean? Coercion to enforce private contracts. Write them down, have witnesses, sign and store at least two copies and jump into those more complex arrangements – and they are submitted to the community's judgment if conflict arises. If instead you kill the object of your disagreement, along comes the Leviathan to lop off *your* head. Short of that, reasonable law with consensus and voluntary compliance for the harmony of all makes for a much happier society. It all starts with customary law held more or less consistent through verbal reiteration and such arrangements evolve into the sorts of written laws we have today: enforceable by courts, jailers and in China, death for people like Bernard Madoff.

To be more refined about the legal/economic theory here, Cass Sunstein, lays out the "basis" of Laissez-faire – and how it has no basis – in his book *The Second Bill of Rights* about Franklin Roosevelt's unwritten (something like "customary") transformation of the US Constitution – or at least its interpretation. Roosevelt didn't think Laissez-faire, small to microscopic, non-interfering government made any sense. That was Herbert Hoover's problem that helped lead to the Great Depression.

"Roosevelt's attack on the idea of laissez-faire had a long legacy. Jeremy Bentham, the father of utilitarianism, was a great believer in private property. But he also said that 'there is no natural property, because property is entirely the creature of law... It is the law alone that can enclose a field and give myself to its cultivation, in the distant hope of harvest.'" For good measure Bentham adds, in Sunstein's book, "'"Before the laws there was no property; take away the laws, all property ceases.'"[25] To this way of thinking customary traditions could be considered an early version of law and have the weight and consequences of law, written and officially codified or not. But enforcement – or threat of it – in complex societies is the follow up, shall we say, that guarantees smooth economic exchanges. Similarly, if not so finally, there is enforcement in advance expressed by the old saw, "They put locks on doors to keep the honest folks honest." That is, the law protects private property, joining with the locks to declare this belongs only to the owner. Looked at like this, Laissez-faire – the freedom to own and exchange without the hindrance of regulation – is far from even being possible according to most people's evaluation of human nature, admitting self-interest and therefore deciding to write laws. Without saying self-interest is the only or the most important thing, it is universally recognized for getting out of hand from time to time, such as in 1929 and 2008.

[25] Cass R. Sunstein, *The Second Bill of Rights – FDR's Unfinished Revolution and Why We need it More than Ever*, Basic Books, Perseus Books Group, New York, 2004, p. 20

15. Ecocity San Francisco's Union Square

CHAPTER 5

Early cities: ancient and preindustrial

Beliefs, walls, shelter, family property and patriarch power

The general picture probably looked something like this: Scattered societies of families and small bands moved from gathering and making a small range of things that accumulated and wore out to putting down roots with physical structures that stayed in one place. Natural shelter like caves and burned out or rotted out big trees like the baobabs of Africa, served as a start. Hey! Even insects, birds, lizards knew to hang out under big leaves or wide branches during downpours, millions of years before we even existed. But then for us came rude huts and later more sophisticated architecture. Some things had to be consumed quickly, like many foods. With a sheltering place some things lasted a little longer like grain, dried meat and salted fish, given container and the built container of the containers – architecture. All sorts of things could then be stored for later use protected from animals, insects, rain, freezing and excessive heating. Architecture-protected stores could be built up for later use or exchange with others. Then came the collective walls of towns and cities and finally territorial walls like the many walls of China and the Maginot Line after World War I constructed by the French to try to stop the Germans in case of another war. All this protected many thing including the build up of what economists call surplus.

There, in constructing the shelter for long term accumulation we see the primal linkage between the building and surplus, of the literal building of an economic system where the very potential for exchange was stored at the ready, a built physical system to get ahead of attrition, a means to stretch out prosperity for ourselves and posterity – and a basis for speculation – through time. Architecture was the bedrock, then, of the "stocks" and reserves for "flows." Providing a physical place called a bank, with vaults, the building also served as the focus of gold in safety deposit boxes, abstract economic value and physical records under the eye of the banker and the banker under the eye of the government. And, how about the physical place called the mint? And all of this inside the city where the pieces all come together behind a defensive wall or city limit *and* the walls of law.

But well before sheltering structures were erected, believed Lewis Mumford, the city of the dead preceded the city of the living by giving an anchor to the memory of people gone that did not move about the land but were buried in it at a particular place, the grave. There, said Mumford, "…the dead were the first to have a permanent dwelling."[26] People would linger, remembering their departed family members and loved ones at these locations. There also, he suggested, was the likely origin of agriculture where discarded seeds from gathered foods would, when visited later, be seen to produce new food plants. There too the place for venerating and amplifying heroic ancestors, their bones under foot, into gods and ultimately God. Thus and there architecture, agriculture and community physical design, were most likely to have sparked and expanded into the first glowing idea of a permanent community place, the physical beginnings of Polanyi's householding, maybe where we started trying to find our place in the household of the gods, an important step in religion and questing for understanding of the cosmos, the powers that move, the thoughts and emotions of contemplation, meditation, prayer and poetry.

But there were others around the grave and the fire, those not yet born and a sense through the mere contemplation of time, of what and who was to come, obligations to the future as well as to honoring the past. The dead would want some of that accumulation of that love expressed, maybe a few material tokens of respect, some sacrifices. The not yet born would need our dedication to keeping the sacred traditions.

Then there were also others from other bands and tribes beyond the circle of trees, in the next valleys, beyond the mountains, rivers, lakes and seas, out there in the distance. The foreigners might come and take some for their own greed, or perhaps need. Thus there were four forces working against increase in the artifact list and each item on the list: use that wears down until useless or simply gets lost, the ravages of storms and pests and predators, the dead needing sacrifices, and the attacks and pillaging by strangers.

[26] Lewis Mumford, *The City in History*, Harcourt, Brace & World, INC., New York, 1961, p. 7

Fustel de Coulanges in *The Ancient City, a Classic Study of the Religions and Civil Institutions of Ancient Greece and Rome*[27] chronicles the Indo-European ancestors' belief systems, very similar in Greece, Rome and Hindu India. The period he covers starts generally where we have just left Polanyi's studies and carries through to the building of the cities we learn about in school and the revolutions in Greece and Rome that led to experiments in democracy, but still not to capitalistic market economies. The sequence in western tradition goes from the gift society through the householding origin of the ancient city – still strongly gift oriented – to the preindustrial city in its medieval form then morphing through mercantilism, nationalism and even Christian theology into modern capitalism, neoclassical capitalism to global capitalism and the movements against its excesses. I'll also talk about the Chinese new economic hybrid, but quite a bit later in these pages.

De Coulanges picks up approximately where the gift society is complexifying and beginning a reorganization leading into the ancient city. Somewhere in this period coinage becomes quite popular as we slide from Gift Economics with limited artifact list in small villages to monetized trade involving a much longer list produced and sheltered in early larger villages, sometimes considered small cities. In my outline on pages 79 and 80, this is approximately where we see the transition in Human Economics from the Gift Economy into the Capital Economy by way of 1.) a neutral means of exchange (money) 2.) something holding value over time (money) 3.) all accounted for in quantity and quality by value rated by scale of value, based on numbers and proportionality (money again, with numbers printed on it). We are not talking capitalist but rather capital.

(An explanatory aside here: "Capital" is often used for human talent and social arrangements expressed as "human capital" and "social capital." I'm talking here about the literal coin, paper or arrangement of electrons stored in computers to back up agreements and systems of production, storage and exchange of value that characterize a newer more complex economy emerging from gift economics in both history and evolution. "Human" and "social capital" may be useful terms in known contexts, but here I'm using "capital" as being simply money in its various forms.)

De Coulanges' perspective is one of looking at what earliest texts, most of them written in Greece and Rome's age of glory, said about the period trending into the oldest cities in the Indo-European Western Tradition. In those times long gone, without a written language and not properly studied, he says, at least at the time he was writing in the 1960s, he demonstrated that the social context set the economic pattern and was all important, but the extended society of the dead and not yet living – past, present and future – was an equal or even more controlling factor. In fact, "the religion of the ancients" set an even broader context for the social context of

[27] Fustel de Coulanges in his book, *The Ancient City – a classic study of the religious and civil institutions of ancient Greece and Rome,* Doubleday Anchor Books, Garden City, New York, 1956, originally published in 1964

the economic pattern. Lest economy following religion seems foreign to real money-making thinking today, recall as I've mentioned earlier no less important economists than John Kenneth Galbraith and Herman Kahn remind us that the beliefs and ideologies of neo-classic/market economists today are far closer to religious than scientific.

De Coulanges' "ancients," the pre-city people in those cultures, who had transformed their life ways from hunting, herding and gathering to land-anchored agricultural and house-building, edifice-centered traditions, saw their ancestors as something like gods ("ancestor worship") anchored to the grave, with past generations honored with an eternal fire at the hearth. Something like God, too, God the creator, the ancient departeds did in fact create much that lived on in the present, from buildings, tools and stores, to language and customs of social expression and order and control... and the very bodies of the descendants carrying the "same blood." And who didn't want to believe he or she was descended from some sort of god or God?

Each household had somewhat different beliefs and rituals from the neighbors and different gods – of course: since they had different ancestors, each with different personalities, accomplishments and legends about them. These rituals, tales and supplications directed to ancestors-becoming-gods were the secret, utmost private property of the families. But the central belief that the spirits of the dead were somewhere in close proximity to the grave and these spirits of the departed could be satisfied and made happy with sacrifices of food and ceremonies of respect – that was everywhere expressed in these cultures. If you kept the rituals and brought up your children to maintain the sacrifices and beliefs you'd be reasonably secure in expecting a happy if hazily defined and locally confined afterlife too, as your children and grandchildren would go about making offerings to your spirit in the traditional family rituals anchored physically in tomb, hearth, shrine, repast, home, yard and property wall. Instead of playing harps, walking golden streets and hanging out with angels, you'd be kicked back watching your great, great grandchildren grow up playing in the same old yard, courting, dancing and singing within the familiar walls, having their families and children forever. You'd be remembered, the venerated ancestor still enjoying the meals of the world you once lived and loved in, accepting sacrifices burned on the alter entering the world of the afterlife through the medium of crackling fire and curling smoke through familiar air.

De Coulanges points out how important it is to try to put ourselves in the mind set of the people of a time if we hope to understand what was really happening – and what that still may mean. Today, with monotheistic religions and their various realms of afterlife, religions espousing reincarnation among the living and atheism that doesn't believe in life after death at all, the notion that the spirits of the dead are somehow still present near their bodily remains, even if just ashes, still haunts us. Why else sayings like "whistling past the grave yard," the strange sense of time and presence of others unseen but "felt" in cemeteries, the near universal edge of fear, sadness and longing there, innate from childhood on up? It turns out that the continuity through time and types of commitment to property that evolve on that base are quite important in economic thinking – or should be. We all want to leave a little to our children, be remembered, contribute something to the future and continue living in the memories of the people we loved but had to leave. And there you have it: eternal money, or aspiring in that direction anyway (streets of gold?) with its main functions intact, whether the legacy is small or large: valuation agreed upon, at least basically and we hope, being a medium of exchange, mostly of emotions, between the dying and others, in this case into the future and *that* value stored deep into the future in memories aided by small reminders like shrines, hearth fires and these days family photos.

The period of pre-village and small village cultures, studied by Mauss and other anthropologists and sociologists interested in economics, leads into the earliest of the preindustrial cities. We'll proceed now from the pre-village and village cultures with the gift economies we've touch upon to the ancient city. Here we see in the gifting phase of human economics shifting into capital economics beginning to be very solidly anchored simultaneously in religion and in the form of the family habitation where the notion of powerfully vested property becomes established. Economics in this pattern could be seen as something of a natural development of rising degrees of material accumulation and complexity in societies and human adjustments to their world view – ancestors, gods, descendants and all. Not just more products but more types of products – longer artifact list – were building up.

Anchored to the land and the family grave and delineated by a surrounding wall or consecrated open space, was a house constructed in the middle or back of the property: a large field or in the early villages, a smaller yard or lot. This arrangement, quoting numerous classical Greek, Roman and Indian written texts that were in turn reporting on the traditions and customs of an earlier pre-literate time, says de Coulanges, is where the Western tradition of private property, especially land ownership, became established and solidly secured deep into the future we occupy today. The property, however, did not belong to the living family member but to all family members past, present and into the future. The living residents were seen as stewards and guardians more so than fee simple owners in today's sense. They were not allowed by religion and tradition to will property to any person by choice – only lineage rules and only oldest son stewards were recognized and sanctioned by religious tradition to have control of the property while alive. Love and affection come and go but family lines can and must go on forever for who would take care of the ancestors if the living did not?

The family wasn't who gathered round the ritual repast but also the ghosts of the departed hovering in the shadows and the children of the future awaiting entry into this life. It would be a blasphemy to the religion and fatally destructive to the family to sell the land to another family, put out the fire of the hearth and move on, that important was their anchor to the physical ancestors/heroes/gods that gave the present generation land and the built infrastructure. Only war or the most desperate plagues, floods, earthquakes, fires or famines could excuse a move. The tradition was so fiercely territorial that even generations later when cities had arisen in the tradition and two houses were located side by side, says de Coulanges, "Isolation of property is so obligatory that two domains cannot be contiguous, but a band of soil must be left between them, which must be neutral ground, and must remain inviolable."[28] In most Roman towns a distance of approximately 2 1/2 feet between properties was required no matter how dense the habitation.

This rule of inheritance of property – ancestor-given in the Indo-European village tradition and ultimately God-given at birth to princes and kings later in the preindustrial city – transmuted into the social acceptance of rights of inheritance of kings that we may now be seeing in their last vestiges in the early years of the 21st century (unless societal collapse wrenches us back to a far simpler state). This landed right of inheritance was essentially anti-democratic, insofar as democracy is based on the sanctity of the individual, and promulgated by the idea that the gods going back though family bloodlines and, in later history, to God Himself calling his people the chosen people, dispensed that grand gift to theirs or His bloodline. If gods or God determined what family you were born into, it follows that that is where you belong.

Thus in the order of the universe was bestowed privileges, property and obligations, and in societies all the way up to the industrial cities of capitalistic times, a certain powerful strain of fatalism was solidly established. *That* democracy began fighting against, ever since its first revolutions in Greece or wherever in less noticeable places it raised its independent, "why not me too?" head. A more recent version of this is the notion that the wealthy are better than most of us or, if God has the powers attributed to him, he would not have given them the advantage of fortuitous birth.

The ancient city – from family compound to the preindustrial city

The early city, sometimes called the feudal city, was complex for its day compared to surrounding villages but very simple in technologies and small in population compared with today's much larger and more complex cities. Further, only a small fraction of the total population lived there. It arose, says de Coulanges, when families having similar traditions and something to share, specialties to exchange, came together in small clusters of families called phratries. The families and the phratries would share essentially the same pattern of most important components at two different scales. For example, in the new higher level of organization a new layer

[28] Fustel de Coulanges, *The Ancient City*, Op cit., p. 111

of gods to be worshiped in common were adopted and a shrine celebrating the phratry gods as well as those of the family. As long as the old worship and laws still prevailed in the family compound and advantage was gained collectively, the higher-level associations were entered into. Thus a cluster of families in one valley might unite at this higher organizational level for enhanced security and to better thrive and build surplus relative to the vicissitudes of nature and the competition of family clusters in the next valley over.

Later, phratries joined in a yet larger unions called in Greece the curies then in tribes, about 100 of them in the territory of the Greek peoples of the area called Attica, clustered into the twelve confederations that formed city sates. For comparison it was something like houses with fences, then precincts, then neighborhood districts, then whole cities in our times, but with a strong religious/political tradition (power over mind and body) at the core. A fifth and final layer was added when twelve city states were united in Athens and all the layers of organization below were left without interference to follow their own rules and worship within their own subdivisions.

We could call these different expressions of the general pattern "fractals" of each other, the smaller ones "nested" – a popular term recently – within the larger. A fractal is a fraction of the whole that has all the essential physical and functional components of the larger scale present and well organized. Actually, the larger pattern is also considered a fractal of the smaller too, as in the Mondelbrot series of patterns repeating infinitely into the small in one direction and large in the other direction, celebrated by theoreticians and fans of chaos theory. But I use the term mainly in relation to the smaller versions of the larger pattern, rather like a neighborhood in a city being functionally complete, almost like a village within a city.

In any case we will see this concept is important in understanding ecocity design later on in these pages. Implied also is that there seems to be corresponding psychological fractals at different levels as well, which some anthropologists and psychologists have called "cultural pattern models." We see it here in similar worship and habits from the household to the city-state.

De Coulanges points out something especially important in these transitions of scale retaining basic pattern: how power magnified and produced an elite that controlled and shaped the ancient city, modeling many aspects of the later preindustrial city as well. Within certain families their numbers multiplied with ever more children and servants and slaves, all those unrelated by blood, also known as "clients." Many families simply became much larger. Whatever they did for sustenance and trade and whatever they accumulated in products and architecture and whatever natural leadership was possessed by their patriarch, could elevate that family and person to leadership at a higher level of organization as most influential group and chief of a phratry or, one level higher in organization and scale, curie, and so on to the highest, the city-state. Thus certain families evolved into a gentry or *gens* that transmuted into a near permanent hereditary elite with powerful dominance over their particular lower fractal divisions. As suggested, this dominance was in no small measure due to the protecting walls of architecture and accumulating surplus as well as accumulating belief and tradition to which the people submitted.

Parallel to this worldly ascent in prosperity of certain family lines into leadership at higher levels of organization, the gods of their families, having delivered prosperity and good fortune to theirs, might also gain general attention and worship at the other organizational levels. Since everyone wanted to share in the good fortune delivered from such successful gods, their worship augmented the already revered place of household gods. Thus Athena, the goddess worshiped by the tribe in the Cecropidae line, originating in a time lost in antiquity in a particular family, due to prosperity in production and trade and victory in conflicts of that line, was adopted by the city named after her: Athens.

Going back to the family level, servants were initiated into the worship of the family gods and became faithful retainers with their own privileges, if locked into less honored and permanently subordinate roles. Their children, in turn, were born into these roles. As the system evolved, many such underlings transformed into the retainers of the courts of higher orders of organization and in the domains of the most powerful families of the later dawning preindustrial or medieval city. As this system developed in the ancient city, its rigidness was reinforced and became the essential social/political/economic and especially religious framework for the typical preindustrial city.

If we tend to think the Roman and Greek householders tending to village and city life had a notion of freedom of action and thought anything like archetypical cowboys and enterprising settlers in the old wide-open American West or IT entrepreneurs in Silicon Valley, think again. According to de Coulanges, for the Roman,

> … his house was for him what a temple is for us. He finds there his worship and his gods. His fire is a god, his walls, doors, his thresholds are gods; the boundary marks that surround his field are also gods. The tomb is an altar and his ancestors are divine beings.[29]
>
> He steps out of his house always with the right foot first. He has his hair cut only during the full moon. He carries amulets on his person. He covers the walls of his house with magic inscriptions against fire. He knows formulas for avoiding sickness, and others for curing it; but he must repeat them twenty-seven times, and spit in certain fashion at each repetition.[30]
>
> He leaves his house and can hardly take a step without meeting some sacred object – either a chapel or a place formerly struck by lightning, or a tomb; sometimes he must step back and pronounce a prayer; sometimes he must turn his eyes or cover his face to avoid the sight of some ill-boding object… He offers sacrifices to thank the gods… to appease their wrath.

[29] Fustel de Coulanges, *The Ancient City*, Op cit., p. 211

[30] Fustel de Coulanges, *The Ancient City*, Op cit., p. 212

"Liberty of thought in regard to the state religion," de Coulanges tells us about the Greeks, "was absolutely unknown among the ancients. Men had to conform to all the rules of worship, figure in all the processions, and take part in the sacred repasts." Or else, in Athens for example, be fined. "Ostracism and banishment from the city were the punishment for 'incivism' – that is to say, for the want of affection toward the state." Of the Athenian of this period says de Coulanges, "His principle religion ... is the worship of ancestors and heroes. He worships the dead and fears them. One of his laws ... forbids him to pronounce a single word that can call down their anger... If a priest introduces the slightest innovation into the worship, he is punished with death... The ancients, therefore, knew neither liberty in private life, in education, nor religious liberty."[31]

How did the famous democracies of Greece and Rome materialize then? Says de Coulanges again, there "was a class of men who found themselves outside this city organization, and who suffered from it. These men had an interest in destroying it, and made war against it constantly." The "clients" in Greece and commoner Plebs in Rome vastly out numbered the patriarchs of the families. The family members *themselves* outnumbered the patriarchs many times over. De Coulanges said, "The inner constitution of the family was the first principle of inequality" and often greatly resented within the family. Outside the family the inequality was magnified even more at higher levels of organization. Within the family not even the eldest son was a citizen of most Greek and Roman ancient cities and could not participate in debate and decision-making – he had to wait until his father died. Then there were the younger brothers never to be in charge or have rights or citizenship, all the blood related sisters and the wives, and within the household, the clients including servants and slaves. Outside the household walls, whole families of outcasts who dumped their earlier families, foreigners and some of the ever untrustworthy traders who dealt with the outside world, and, to remember again, sisters, daughters, wives, mothers, that whole half of the species called women.

There were reforms, revolutions, assassinations as step by step the old religion and authority lines were etched away, householding beginning to give way to civic engagement, black sheep leaving the family, if not ostracized first, to try new means of working and surviving, joining the traders, tradesmen, the sailors, the warriors, the builders, the artists, the philosophers, the academics, forging into new territory as the city grew and needed people to help it grow.

De Coulanges says in addition to a sense of injustice needing righting, the other major influence leading toward democratizing was, "...ideas resulting from the natural development of the human mind." What we should notice in addition is that the accumulation of total cultural artifacts and growth in their variety, and es-

[31] Fustel de Coulanges, *The Ancient City*, Op cit., p. 222

pecially as they focused and accumulated in the city, showed up ever more conspicuously in the ancient system that tried to maintain security through, shall we say, the sacred status quo. That old sense of economic imbalance, that lack of the symmetry Polanyi thought was so important in the gift society, was getting too extreme to be maintained.

The customary usage of the commons outside in the grazing land or hunting land of wild nature, and the more private farming land and the customary usage of the grounds, buildings and accoutrements of the household, began to grate philosophically against one another. Like electricity building up in a thundercloud, a rebalancing, or close to it, had to happen. If it were the "natural development of the human mind" or as simple as the human mind of the child rebelling at age two when a sibling gets something and *I don't*, it probably actually is natural to not just humans but all animals trying to stay alive and thrive, to get their fair share, plus a little advantage. My point here, though, is that the material circumstances have consequences economically and politically – and my theme in other parts of this book is that the material circumstances called the arrangement of the city itself has consequences for the life of people and all other fellow travelers on our planet Earth.

I might add another point of interest. The artifact list and the city itself appear to have grown in close relationship and they both conspired to overthrow the totalitarianism of the rigid religion and the power of the top patriarchs. As the artifact list grew, so the infrastructure and city that sheltered, supported and helped physically organize by proximity and good accessibility to resources, tools, talents, producers and customers. That meant that there were ever more new jobs in making and distributing the new products and rendering new services for all those disaffected, powerless, righteously indignant and ambitious younger relatives, clients and women. They had a small share in the prosperity of the city and therefore enhanced opportunity to plan their revolution, one little eroding chip at a time, and eventually by uniting, overthrowing old and writing new laws – or by adding pressure until the old order was destroyed through collapsing consensus.

Regarding the origins and growth of cities, De Coulanges notes that villages in our times tend to grow by simple accretion, one building near by another, expanding incrementally. After a certain number, add a general store with Post Office, then more villagers, producers, traders and customers, together growing onward. Toward the center, some buildings get torn down, replaced by larger ones, a dirt street getting paved and widened, the village becoming a town, then a city.

Not so with the preindustrial cities appearing in the Indo-European tradition. A cluster of buildings in a village could not grow in the religious system of the ancient city in this tradition by sale and purchase and new larger construction, by any rearrangement in fact that would disturb the graves of the ancestors; it could not be allowed.

Therefore a whole new city had to be built. And it was traditionally founded in a single day. The founder, the chief religious figure of acknowledged leadership, in ideal circumstance would use a special copper bladed plow personally steering it behind a white bull and a white ox, to cut a furrow through the soil delineating the walls and outer perimeter of the city. The founder would be accompanied by other chiefs and spiritual leaders chanting and singing, the founder lifting the plow and carrying it over the spaces that would be the gates to the city, all this replicating a higher fractal of the household fractal with its wall on the property edge surrounding its grounds and buildings and shrine to the family gods and hearth and graves. The furrow in the earth would be the base of the new wall around the city and none but enemies would ever thenceforth attempt to cross over. The founder would also dig a small hole called the *mundus* in Roman lands and the heads of the tribes planning to construct and live in the new city would place small clods of earth from their homes into the *mundus* connecting their land, ancestors and gods to the grounding of the new city. Fire from the hearth of the founder's home curie or city would also be transported to this place to create the flaming new shrine to the gods, heroes and ancestors. A more contemporary version of such founding took place for the town of Auroville, India in 1968, in the eastern Hindu tradition wing of Indo-European heritage. Auroville was – and is – aspiring to be a city for all humanity in its earthly and spiritual evolving. At the founding ceremonies small containers of earth were gathered from people who had brought samples from their 124 homelands, and placed these offerings in an urn at the center of the aspiring city's outdoor amphitheater, maintaining with slight change, the ancient tradition. About 30 feet away, a fire was lit, and this new city too was thus founded, though the walls they built were the forests they planted on the formerly denuded grazing land. (Stripped also for the wood for building Pondicherry, India and as an explicit effort, I was told when visiting, to keep tigers away.)

In our narrative here, informed by de Coulanges, the essentials are seen in the linkage of the religious beliefs, the edifices and the central focus around a constructed place of powerful social and economic control and order.

This means of creating a new city by starting whole and fresh served the Greeks well in establishing colonies. It implied powerful patriarchs with control over substantial material resources backed by firm social agreement held together by religious belief and cemented to a hopefully powerful parent city somewhere across the sea. But also, closer to home, the whole process was a means to assiduously avoid disturbing what the families owned in towns established earlier, keeping their land, buildings and religious lineage intact, avoiding demolition and forgetfulness and to de Coulanges' view, the source of today's capitalist idea of sacrosanct, not necessarily grounded in real estate, property rights. One might add, it could represent the deep roots of the preservationist movement in addition, though the two sometimes conflict, especially with the later capitalist mobility of money at the base of ownership and the loosening of the order that strong customs of usage provided, everyone doing what everyone expected of one another. More restrictive than today's stiffest zoning codes, one couldn't raise money, hire professionals, produce plans, convince the authorities and fight the neighbors, buy a family compound, raze it and raise a new building. There was the prohibition against sale or transfer by gift of family real estate and there were the ancestors and gods who would be very unhappy and angry and visit disastrous bad luck on anyone committing such a spiritual crime. Then there was the inherited rights to that exact spot of land and set of walls, buildings, hearth, fire, shrines and tombs that were to be the birth rights of those to be born deep into the future. For this reason, in addition to strategies for set-up-and-build-fast colonial conquest, a new city all at once was desired.

The subsequent history of Greece and Rome that followed and their demise is not the subject of this book, but a last point should be made about this particular transition. At a certain point Rome and Greece were losing their traditions and collapsing of internal disintegration. "Barbarians" were invading and the alienated black sheep sons and clients, traders and the growing crafts and commercial producers were often working with writing, producing their own records, and using coinage that was missing or rare in the early stages de Coulanges reported on. Then rather suddenly arrives Christianity to throw a curve, to move the entire civilizational pattern toward capitalism and individual initiative. How so?

This religion said all people, down to the poorest and most afflicted, had equal access to the glories of companionship with not just the gods but God the Creator of all the universe, and in addition, the realm called Heaven where total bliss reigned after death. This was a dangerous attack on the venerated, worshiped ancestors-become-gods, removing the holy from the grave, shrine and hearth and placing the holy and loved in the cosmos everywhere – in all people – outside of as well as inside the household and in the heart of each individual. Also, the prerogatives of inherited ownership/stewardship of the household founded in the family gods and providing a structure of unchanging, inherited privilege could perhaps co-exist with this new set of beliefs, but only if different rules applied to God's world and the elites' world. That door was open by the often quoted pronouncement, King James version, Mark 12:17, the Holy Bible, "And Jesus answering said unto them, Render to Caesar the things that are Caesar's, and to God the things that are God's. And they marveled at him." (Various translations have slightly different wording.) Indeed they should be amazed by such a statement since it seemed such an open door to all sorts of contradictions. And thus it came to be! It would be centuries and we still haven't sorted out who is supposed to get what.

At the heart of it all was the doctrine of the sanctity of the individual before God, with all equal in His eyes. This was quickly distorted by religious orders, historically by the Catholic Church in alliance with the various elites in the realms into which Christianity spread. But the cat was out of the bag. The commercial interests, the traders, the producers, the black sheep, even the women and slaves, all now had religious justifications to bring strong criticism against privilege and to go their way with a higher rationale for and actual degree of personal initiative that would have been taboo, cause for banishment or even fratricide in the ancient city.

Now we end the discussion of this stage of city evolution and next look at preindustrial cities all the way up to the beginnings of the modern industrial city, the city of classical and neoclassical capitalism now both – physical city and economic patterns and theories – needing in the early 21st century some rather drastic changes.

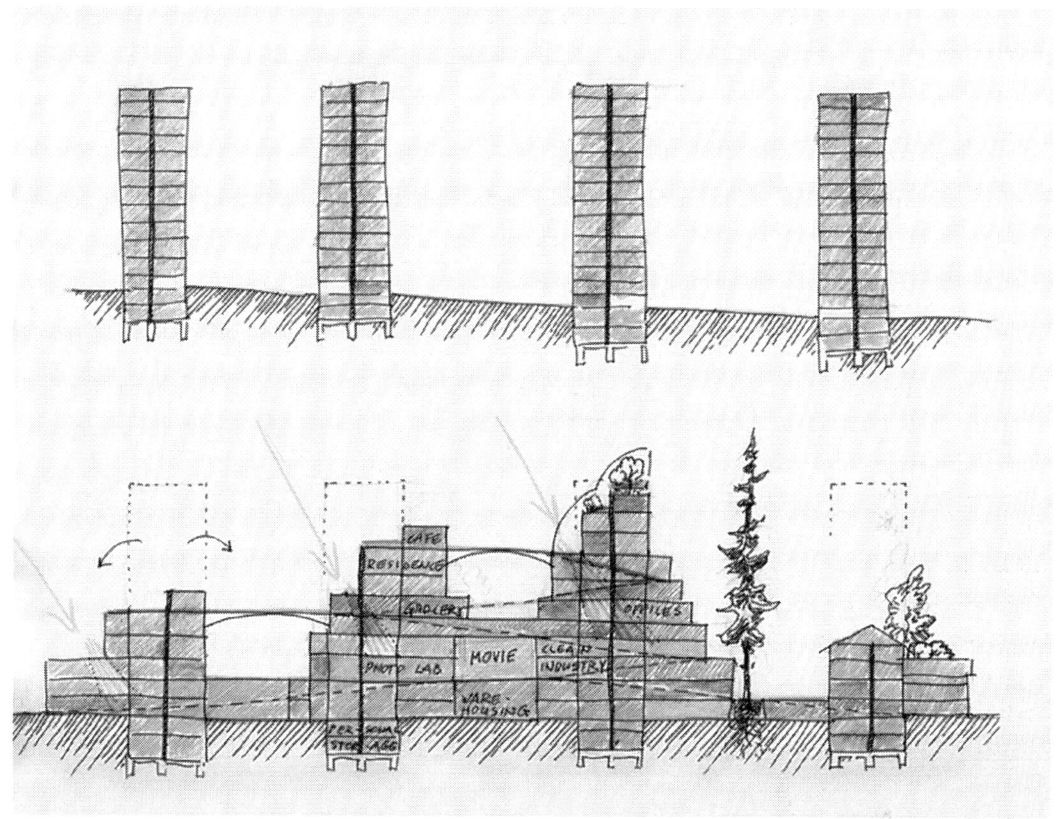

16. Modernist towers and slabs vs. ecocity complex mixed use

The towers and slabs of modernist architecture, top drawing, with open space around – called "towers in a park" by many – is a simplistic, energy consuming design. Same population but with work, commerce, warehousing, socializing, etc. This represents single use, above vs. whole community design, below.

The preindustrial city

Gideon Sjoberg in his sociological study called *The Preindustrial City, Past and Present*, starts off carefully justifying his approach that seeks and studies overall patterns throughout city history. He admits to much criticism from other sociologists maintaining that his approach is too general, that the range of different patterns in different parts of the world, they say, make it exceedingly difficult to tease out accurate patterns of commonality much less, since sociology claims to be a science, to be accurate enough to predict much. Then again, does mainstream sociology that does *not* seek patterns of some consistency have a better change at helping predict and thus help create a healthier future – and maybe a better sociology? He says of sociology, "…as a 'science of society' it must establish propositions that have cross-cultural validity." "Many propositions, once widely accepted as true, are coming to be recognized as excessively culture bound." He illustrates: "Among some writers it has been fashionable to attribute the emergence of the conjugal family that is the norm in present-day urban America to the urbanization process per se. Such a narrow view could not have developed in a climate that stresses cross-cultural research… The conjugal unit… is a consequence of industrial urbanization; it most decidedly is not the ideal pattern of the preindustrial city."[32]

Important distinction, but in addition I'll mention the ecological perspective that affirms the value of noticing similar patterns almost everywhere living systems are present. This supports Sjoberg's assertion from another angle and seems particularly valid from my point of view having grown up involved in the arts and noticing the swarm of ideas and influences at play in that world when the artist seeks to synthesize influences and perceptions in any particular work or try something new. Maybe some patterns are fantasy but if you don't use imagination and explore, how will you actually find the patterns that swirl together into meaningful wholes, which can produce complete works of art, maybe even find basic truths? The right fantasies backed by discipline and clear insights often turn into realities in the hands of inventors, artists, scientists, engineers, architects. But you have to seek, discover or invent your way forward navigating such patterns. Looking at the complexities of economics, weighing land, labor and money, credit, interest and reserves, considering bullish confidence, bearish panic, sure thing and risk, profit and loss, trends and new technologies out of left field, protective tariffs and "free" markets and subsidies, investment in plant, "job creation," mergers, takeovers, taxes graduated and regressive, efficiencies of scale and the Jevons Paradox of the inefficiency of efficiency given various variables, insurance, loan guarantees, blue chips and toxic derivatives, dynamics of bubbles swelling and popping and on and on and on… What could be more like the interconnected complexities of natural ecosystems than the economic system, of whatever variety you are talking about?

And then the various varieties all link together in harmony or clashes, endosymbiosis cooperation or Darwinian competition, often to the death.

To get a sense of proportion and begin appropriate prioritization, to find the important patterns within and in relation to the natural and social environment, the patterns that could bring health at a time when in the early 21st century many "fundamentals" look bleak and powerful forces are gathering momentum in destructive directions such as toward climate change and so on… If basic patterns of ecology do lend insights to the patterns of economics and vice versa there could hardly be a

---

[32] Gideon Sjoberg, *The Preindustrial City, Past and Present*, the Free Press, New York, 1960

more important endeavor than exploring these patterns. So you can see I come down strongly on Sjoberg's side.

But to continue with the nature of the founding of cities, looking now at an inner pattern of relationships and moving forward from some of de Coulanges' observations, moving from ancient to preindustrial cities, sliding out of Gift Economics ever deeper into Capital Economics, Sjoberg assumed a physical structure and social structure came to be and existed all at the same time, of a piece. They appear to be what I see as a "dimensional pair:" each, without the other, nothing. Energy and matter is a dimensional pair. You can't imagine and there couldn't exist one without the other. Time and space is another. Male and female in the universe of us mammals. The universal and unique are united in a pattern the Oriental ancients beautifully represented with their "yin-yang" symbol. If it is a powerful reality that the physical substance and form and the social transactions of cities – cultural, political and economic, not to speak also the mental, psychological and spiritual – are linked in this absolute way of dimensional pairs, perhaps the ecologically healthy society and its economics will need the physical ecocity or will never come to be. According to this notion, vice versa as well. They "evolve" and "emerge" as a unity or not at all, like the laws of chemistry and the chemicals themselves.

The period we are talking about now is from the time villages started becoming more complex and larger more populous constructs as at Çatalhoyuk, Turkey close to 8,000 years ago, with a simple structure beginning to complexify and with 4,000 to 10,000 inhabitants and amazing, thoroughly unique art. More commonly this period is thought to extend from the Sumerian civilization of Mesopotamia of about 4,500 years ago, until the 18th century, gaining momentum until about then, overlapping after that with the beginnings and growth of the industrial city and capitalism over the next approximately two hundred years. A few basically preindustrial cities in transformation exist right now such as Kathmandu, Nepal and a number in the world of Islam for example, with both preindustrial social systems and physical structures, mostly giving way to democratic and capitalist social/political/economic structure and pedestrian physical structure giving way to machines in factories and transport and heavy use of energy. Motorcycles get their narrow tires in the crack of the door, pry it open some and cars follow, bulls in the china shop of those last surviving preindustrial cities.

In addition, there are much larger populations in cities in recent times, the higher density pedestrian centers cut off from the open spaces of nature and agriculture by low-density development ringing and isolating city people from nature and agriculture. Sjoberg says the preindustrial cities, with slightly different time tables in different parts of the Old World and with a later start in the Americas, were to be found as far ranging as in Europe, North Africa, Middle East, Central Asia, India, China, Korea and Japan, and then a few centuries later, in Mesoamerica and the central Andes.

The antecedents of cities, "folk societies" Sjoberg called them, had few tools, small agricultural surplus and little specialization. "This paucity of specialization," says Sjoberg, "obviously inhibits the development of a class system. Even in more complex folk society, one that supports a few full-time specialists, not enough persons are liberated from the day-by-day struggle for subsistence to permit the development and utilization of such a complex tool as writing."[33]

Due to the limits of the technological tools at the time, the fact that almost all energy expended for production was from human and animal muscle power and due to the relative poverty of the farmer/hunter, the peasant and small craftsperson base, the small city and the society that emerged could only support a proportionally very small elite. But the elite was key. "The upper class sets the pace for the total society. It alone can maintain an extended family system, acquire formal education, and fulfill all the ideal religious norms. In general, the upper class shuns economic activity, one organized in the city along guild lines."[34]

As with the ancient city, power had to be rigid, understood as part of the order of the universe as seen by religious belief and enforced by physical prowess, read police and military: Robin Hood's nemesis the Sheriff of Nottingham. How else could such a small group maintain order and material accumulation of buildings, roads, metal working tools, taxable market places, cisterns, food stores, furniture, utensils, clothing, weapons, adornments, arts products, early libraries and other property and castle itself usually at the core of a city that kept slowly growing in scale and diversifying in function?

The elite controlled the land by blood, that is, hereditary privilege, as in the earlier ancient city, and also with blood as the double edged sword of privilege and duty, of police and military functions, with the elite risking their lives defending the realm from those outside and keeping those within submissive to their order. They had dominion over this world and were closely allied with the religious elite with power over entry into the next. With their force of arms to simply take from the peasants, the small minority of hereditary elite exacted tribute, but not so much as to destroy the base of their economic system. Once in China's economic history the Emperor raised taxes on market transactions from 3% to 10% to replenish his treasury and suddenly nobody was trading and everyone was waiting. But they didn't have to wait long. The whole economy shut down overnight. The tax was back to 3% in only a few more days. Moreover in systems that were more generally called "feudal" the serfs of the realm were pledged to their lords for in kind tribute – a pig, a goat, at few bags of grain – some coins where in circulation too. The serfs were pledged to be foot soldiers in war while the lords were pledged to the leadership and proctors of the serfs, church, guilds – everyone in their realm – from outside aggression and recruited for their own aggression. They also were responsible for distribution of stores in times of famine and other emergencies and responsible to some

[33] Ibid. p 9

[34] Ibid. p 11

semblance of justice in civil disputes and private transgressions, not that unlike the "Big Men's" responsibilities in the gift economies before them.

The religious elite was literate and protected by the property and power elite – only under such patronage could the time be found to learn to read and scribe. They not only spoke the telltale dialect of the power elite that separated them from the great unwashed and commanded access to the written religion, history and politics but in Catholic realms used a completely different language, Latin. Most churchgoers just sat there under social and political pressure wondering what the hell was going on in services (or more likely just blanking out like children usually do in today's services). But they did generally follow customs and outright orders that *were* translated. They had better!

The radical egalitarian strains of early Christianity were, after adoption by the elite, set in terms of profound paradox, rather than logical contradiction, mystified and obscured. The pattern of householding and authoritarian power was amplified despite the weakening or death of the ancient religions of multiple gods and small dictators in every house. Powerful princes with their subjects came to replace the patriarchy of much smaller aggregations of family members and clients that prevailed in ancient city times. It's tempting to suggest that the parallel between social and cosmic/religious realms was actually fairly tight when the relatively weak and multiple patriarchs were replaced by the more regal, distant, powerful and singular prince or king and the small gods of the grave, shrine and hearth gave way to the God of all creation. The largest paradox in this being, obviously, that such an immense and ever present deity should also claim intimate personal concern for and contact with the least and weakest, even most sinful of all people. In fact, cared so much He would experience death and excruciating pain as a human would to absolve their sins.

A general sense of innate proper function (something like early thinking on rights and clearly in the lineage of customary usage) leading into the era of earliest cities, was for people to be able to live somewhere and range about on the commons for agricultural and productive activities of living on the land with the understanding – not written down – of tradition securing tenure, that is, being able to stay somewhere and make a living over time. Concepts of property and responsibilities between those with less or more "stuff" and less or more influence took the form of private property recorded in writing, especially of real estate, developed over time.

But my own guess as to what was shaping up for the transition to the modern world, albeit gradually over centuries, more fundamental than private property was a means to something more essential, which was the build up itself of material things of increasing variety, whether seen as private property or society's property. Accumulation of the king's property such as the infrastructure of the city, walls, castle, granary for redistribution in emergencies, administered by the governing elite, armories for the defense was in a sense both the king's and those living in his realm; there was always some ambiguity between private property and public on that level, and this in some degree was a contributing element to the occasional common cause and mutual support between royalty and the more common folk against the non-royal family aristocracy – read competitors and potential assassins – and later, the wealthy merchants and bankers moving into positions essentially aristocratic. In addition, whereas the simpler societies tended to give things away as a means of redistribution while replacing them as they wore out, and in the potlatching societies outright destroying much of the "surplus," by the time of the medieval city and powerful princes and kings, deferred maintenance of pubic works and wars might also set back material progress.

Nonetheless, the artifact list, overall, continued to expand. Mechanisms for preservation and increase of societies' products prevailed in the long run. New inventions kept coming over the horizon picking up pace century by century leading to levels of complexity requiring new types of social and economic ordering. Thus non-monetized gift exchanges gave way to lightly monetized feudal systems and later yet, feudal/preindustrial city systems gave way to much more thoroughly monetized capitalist/socialist systems (both in the capital system) as the industrial city replaced the preindustrial city. The cities themselves and their ordered complexity continued evolving and growing right up into the launch of the industrial city, and then, both kinds of city, preindustrial and industrial, overlapped for many decades. Now as I write, the preindustrial cities are almost gone, though we can see their influence everywhere.

Producers and traders gain ground

But what was the engine of productivity in the preindustrial city? There was the peasantry producing products of the soil: food and fiber as we are prone to say today, including wood from forests and from fields, meat and milk and skins, leather, wool, cotton… even silk in China from the silk moth larva eating mulberry leaves. The power source: solar energy by way of chlorophyll and photosynthesis in plants and the metabolism of plants and animals. The material source: productive soil, and far less emphasized, "ecological services," which as compared to today's usual "pollination and distributions of seeds" by the bees and the birds, included the wild animals to hunt and wood from the forest to be cut for fires and building. Of course some mining and metallurgy was going on too, bridging over into another world, the world of the craftsmen and their guilds. And in addition to the producers, the craftsmen and craftswomen, there were the traders who transported the specialized crafts from one city market place to another or directly to the courts of elite customers, bringing things useful and in demand – some tools, utensils, textiles, salt and spices and domesticated animals. They also arrived with other more exotic faire from longer distances, such as precious metals, gems and objects of art and adornment.

The guild members and traders were essentially business people, but business people of two different sorts, one engaged in production for needs without the overlay of today's business people who manufacture demand via advertizing, lost leaders, styles, fleeting discounts and the like as well as products and services of utility and pleasure. In the preindustrial city products of the guilds included some items of luxury for the elite. Among the traders, though, something else was going on – and none of it was actually making something. This shifting of goods for a profit in coins, bullion or a build up somewhere of products of value stored in a building, was kindred to another activity called finance today, and when seen as extreme – or to exist at all in some religions including Christianity through the Middle Ages and Islam today – usury.

So business people in the pre-industrial city were held rigidly to a particular place in society largely separate from those below, meaning the peasants and outcasts, and firmly separated from those above, the elite. Some, if far inferior, were in service to the elite directly in court or in service to the government bureaucracy, from Europe to China and later in Korea and Japan. Some, a large proportion of the citizenry, and almost completely ignored in most sociological studies of the preindustrial city, says Gideon Sjoberg, were in the manual labor group living squalidly in the city or immediately adjacent. The builders of the city itself and castle – masons, carpenters, gardeners – sweated through the dust, moving about, almost invisible to the historian and with status approximately as low as the peasantry in the countryside. A cut higher, craftspeople were on the streets, often living above their metal work, shoe making or sewn goods shops or near by the market where food and crafts alike were sold or otherwise exchanged. They could be making tools for the farmers and themselves, weapons for hunting and for the aristocracy-lead army. There were clothes, crockery, carts, wagons, furniture, household utensils of various levels of sophistication depending on when in the city's evolution and who – elite or commoner – was to have them. It was not a long list compared to today's cultural artifact list, but products in variety close to impossible without the city's physical structure providing proximity to market, stores of resources for manufacture and variety of specialization. Most of all this, no matter where in the world the preindustrial city was being built and functioning, was rigidly organized in guilds or their equivalent, with firm standards, generally very slow change in technology and technique and lifetime commitment for their members, usually passed on from father to son resigned to "their station in life". Do not rock the boat!

But here also is where it starts getting interesting in terms of economics in that the elite "shunned trading." This is a condition elaborated by Jane Jacobs in her book *Systems of Survival, A Dialogue on the Moral Foundations of Commerce and Politics*[35] that we will be exploring soon. This sounds counter intuitive today, with business people, traders, financiers and speculators among the wealthiest and most influential

[35] Jane Jacobs, *Systems of Survival, A Dialogue on the Moral Foundations of Commerce and Politics*, 1992, Vintage Books, a division of Random House, New York, NY

among us, the nouveau riche of a short time ago by now almost ye olde aristocracy. But in times of landed wealth and control in rigid hierarchies of power in the early stage of slowly complexifying cities, shunned they were. The elite shunned money lending at interest as immoral usury. They didn't need loans, after all, with privileged inheritance and tribute, stone walls and benedictions of the clergy for the hereafter and armed guards in the hear and now, and backed by the law – mainly of their own writing. For the Christian elites in Europe it was largely the Jews who filled the gap in the economy providing those services. For Moslem elites in and around what is present day Iran, Pakistan and for the Hindus of the northwest of India, it was mostly the Parsis, believers in the Zoroastrian religion, filling the gap. The degree to which the elite shunned the commoners in business and trade was news to me as I dug into the story. Said Sjoberg,

> A few merchants, though ideally excluded from membership in the elite, manage to achieve high status. Most are unequivocally in the lower class or outcast groups, however. As a consequence of their wide interpersonal contacts with the lower orders of society, their necessary recourse to manipulation (as occurs in money lending) as a means of getting ahead, and other factors, they threaten the authority structure of the elite. Nevertheless they must be permitted to thrive; the city depends upon commerce for its very existence."[36]

The elite, moreover, shunned work of the hands in general and when it came to trade, they looked with particular suspicion upon those who might bring new ideas into the city from abroad. Any unfamiliar idea could threaten the established order. Here we see the pattern of elevation of a few in profitable businesses, as they gained wealth, as part of an on-going if slow change in the evolution of the city. Toward the end of the preindustrial era, approaching the time when the industrial city was taking over, a considerable number of wealthy business people of a wide variety were buying hereditary titles in Europe and China by marrying into the traditional elite families that were doing less well financially. Some becoming successful in business were paying scribes to investigate or even forge documents to prove that back in their lineage there was some elite bloodline ancestor to help justify this elevation in status and rank. In pre-preindustrial city times, that would amount to faking your supposed descent and rights from the gods of your family, tribe and city.

Something very crucial, amounting to rearrangement of agreements, prerogatives and control was happening, shifting from inherited landed privilege, wealth and power – feudalism essentially – to do it yourself production, commercial wealth, finance and reinvestment – basic capitalism – as the preindustrial city was becoming more complex and morphing into the industrial city.

---

[36] Gideon Sjoberg, *The Preindustrial City – Past and Present*, New York, 1960, p.121

Note at this juncture that the capitalists of the lower orders must have assumed much more democratic values and politics than the elite, but the most successful among them in amassing wealth switched sides, so to speak, to join the elite if they could and shift holdings from smaller things and money to real estate and title with claim to broader, even mythic and God-granted privilege. The notion emerged, "God must favor us or we wouldn't have been born with fortune on our side."

Mscl. preindustrial city

Now, a few more observations will round out a workable picture of the preindustrial city at this juncture as we try to connect some important particulars in economics history and ideas.

Take religion. In preindustrial cities everywhere the religious establishment and writings provided rationale for the privileges of the elite and the religious hierarchy all the way up to king and God. Sometimes government and church coincide in godlike kings, or deities on Earth. As the sovereign is hereditary through family blood in the preindustrial city, so the Dalai Lama is – or was – hereditary through reincarnation in the city called Lhasa. The religious texts and traditions in this way declare the world changes little or not at all, the order is fixed in heaven as on Earth and there is almost nothing you can do about that. You accept your station in life as born. The slogan of the preindustrial city should be "Get used to it." The commoners, and especially those who lived in the countryside far from the cities, may have their folk superstitions, their fairies and trolls kindred to ancestors and gods, and beliefs brewing under a show of acceptance of the religion that dominates the realm, but in the city, sheer closeness to and participation in the churches, mosques, synagogues and temples makes for people closer to true believers in the mainstream religions.

The outcasts as well as the religious scribes played an interesting part in continuity through time and the holding of literacy in their nooks and crannies of the city. Some were from outside cultures, races and religions expelled by prejudice elsewhere or were personally adventurous people seeking and seeing more of the world and thus they held particularly tightly to records of what was unique in their cultures – while learning a great deal about others and gaining the survival skills and sharp wit required. The best example of this is probably the Jews maintaining their religion and religious traditions and – very noteworthy, their literacy – the written word providing continuity through time while otherwise minds and mouths may change the story or minds just plain forget. Worth noting, as such outcasts were often business people and in many places the only real early bankers, they were, beyond the scribes of the religions in the sovereign's court, keepers of and innovators in business records and low profile patrons of the arts and sciences as well as preservationists of religious scriptures. In the history of writing the famous cuneiform script of Mesopotamia, the first scratches or imprints on clay tablets, were recordings of transactions in quantities of grain, bricks and other items of production. The Jews were present there and undoubtedly paying attention as a survival necessity, and no doubt actually conducting some of the business. That business writing with enriched vocabulary later moved into boasting claims of power among the monarchs and finally into refined communications unto law, math and astronomy, poetry, philosophy and prophesy, from the practical to the sublime.

The scribes of the church, mosque, synagogue or temple, besides those in the outcast commercial class just mentioned, commanded almost all that there was of written records and the knowledge of reading and writing in the early preindustrial city. Even the sovereign was usually illiterate. Just a few of the elite in various courts and departments of government, were privileged to have the time and leisure, that is, to not be in materially directly productive pursuits or engaged in its management. In addition, as mentioned earlier, religious texts were also in a language foreign to the common people in syntax, pronunciation, vocabulary or simply a completely different language. Thus secrecy about the lines of authority and power from heaven and city to earth-bound peasant village and countryside maintained ignorance. Machiavelli wrote that the prince must keep the commoners off balance by arbitrary acts of raw power, meaning violence, along with courts of justice to right wrongs, keeping by confusion and mystification more power to himself. Christian sanctity of all people and radical democratic egalitarianism on the spiritual plane notwithstanding, the prince had to keep stability in decidedly undemocratic ways: to God's what's his and Caesar's what's his, a great "paradox" of practical accommodation.

A word about Heaven and Hell in the preindustrial city, whether of the Christian variety or as seen in the tankas of the Himalaya Mountains with the gods dancing on severed heads, flames and clouds swirling around the icy peaks in the background. War of extermination, slave taking, rape, punishment by torture, maiming and grotesque execution by beheading, dismembering, burning and stoning were seen as God modeled, God sanctioned, even required, and, as far as the violator of tradition and rules – or just plain arbitrary rule on high levels – was concerned, well deserved. Even in compassionate Tibetan Buddhist Lhasa one could be flogged mercilessly if kept alive until the end of the flogging. If the punished died later because of the wounds it was not considered connected to the punishment that our contemporaries would say caused the death. God, karma or fate had stepped in at that point with the advent of Hell. Order was thus preserved not just with a death threat at the arms of the sovereign and his agents but death and excruciating pain forever in the next life as well. On the other hand, be good in this poor Earthly life and expect the sort of pleasures, real or imagined as seen in the ostentation of the elite; you too could get there after death, streets of gold.

The situation for women must be mentioned. The preindustrial city and its hinterlands was a man's world, and more so the higher one rose or was born into in the social, economic, political structure. Women of the elite class, other than ordering servants about, were outside the economic structure entirely. They were not allowed to debase themselves at menial tasks and denied the education and participation in administration of the realm – except in the case that an individual woman might not have an eligible male heir to such responsibility in the family. Then queens or wives or daughters of the elite could reign supreme until a similarly qualified by inheritance male turned up. At the lower end of the scale, among outcasts and peasants, life was so close to the edge all hands were needed and often men and women worked together in the fields, though specialized more at their humble homes. Guild workshops were controlled almost exclusively by men though often their wives would take over when a husband died, then delivering the inheritance to sons, not daughters. In many guilds, women did much or most of the work, especially in textiles, brewing, bread making or similar trades that had origin in or adjacent the house in earlier times.

At the upper end of the scale, Sjoberg writes of women as carriers of status that reinforce the notion of unchanging social stratification. In the preindustrial city, "women, utilizing elaborate dress, make up, coiffures, and/or display of jewelry, reflect, indeed advertise to other women of the elite, the family's socio-economic position, their own exemption from physical labor, and their ability to spend long hours in self-adornment."[37] Their treasures on their bodies, he points out, provides an additional rationale to keep them secluded to interactions only in elite circles as elsewhere they'd be "targets for thieves and all sorts of aggression."

The extremes to which these feudal arrangements separating women of high birth from men and most of the rest of society is most conspicuously exhibited in the traditional Islamic cultures where even the architecture and clothing is designed to keep prying eyes from the family's women's faces and bodies from adolescence until death. The buildings have special quarters for the women – harems – and doors are arranged so that any visiting men cannot catch a glimpse of them. But one of the most intriguing, beautiful even, descriptions of this segregation I've seen was in a quote Sjoberg uses from Osgood.[38] By day the high elite women of Seoul, Korea were secluded in their fine homes, but...

> "At night... ladies walk through the streets under the most extraordinary circumstances, as the thoroughfares of the whole city were turned over to them alone, except for blind men and officials. This situation came about after dark when the fire beacons converging on the capital brought the evening message that the kingdom was secured and peaceful. Word being conveyed to the palace, the royal band played appropriate music, the great bell

[37] Sjoberg, *The Preindustrial City*, Free Press Paperback, 1960, New York, p. 166

[38] Oh great! He says only "op cit." and page numbers and there's no other reference to Osgood, whoever that is, or title of Osgood's book in his chapter notes!

> was rung, and the guards closed the gates of the city... Until one in the morning, women were free to walk abroad, and any man found on the streets apart from those mentioned above as specially exempt was subject, if caught by the patrols, to imprisonment and severe flogging. The women carried paper lanterns as they strolled, but in even so little light they protected their faces with their silk jackets."

A last observation before moving on to more recent times: the elite's prejudice against the experimental sciences yet support for math and theoretical science. The latter tended to promulgate the ideas of permanence and hierarchical structure. Astronomy and math, associated with the heavens and gods, then God, unchanging through time, were associated with and patronized by the religious and political/economic elite, and the geometry that built monuments, castles and cities made of stone that rose firmly from the land of the elite were the sciences utilized for social, political and economic control of the people and for the practical physical projects of building the city.

Meantime there was the prohibition against the elite using their hands, which would erode the differences between themselves and the commoner and threaten their power structure. This caused the elite of the preindustrial city to shun the experimental sciences that dissected living matter, planted things (like peasants do) in the dirt for study or insisted on running experiments and trying out new inventions. Any and all of these activities could lead to developments threatening the status quo and thus there was little patronage for such work. On the other hand, as trade grew a pace over the centuries and technologies did crawl forward and spread from one city to another around the world in a steady advance, new ideas and products, slipping through the sieve of elite opposition, wars of destruction and pestilences of disease and hunger, did accumulate and add to the city's wealth. Given the elite's dependence on acquiring and using a goodly portion of the wealth to bolster their power and maintain control, the practical sciences and technologies were given a begrudging nod but at the same time a restraining hand. In this regard, the practical, experimental and technological sciences were at once a source of power and a source of danger to be managed with great care. Like business and trade in general, which explored the Earth and distant societies, about the exploring and inventive sciences, be most careful.

Next we'll take a brief detour from our scan through history from the point of view of cities and economics co-developing and address a kind of time jumping idea connecting very contemporary conditions back to the times of the pre-industrial city. I'm convinced the influence is still great and from her usual outsiders' viewpoint, Jane Jacobs gives us some long-term historic perspective. Then we'll rejoin our outline history at approximately the point where the preindustrial city meets the industrial city, where feudalism leads through mercantilism into the capitalism of

Adam Smith, Thomas Malthus, Karl Marx influenced by Charles Darwin and others. Take it away Jane, woman of extraordinary insight.

17. Lights at night

A view through the dome of one of the three atriums of the City 7 project in Changwon, South Korea just before closing time. The view is down from my hotel room. The project itself is getting close to an ecocity fractal, a highly mixed use set of facilities – housing, offices, hotel, conference center, movie theater, clothing stores, food stores, restaurants, cafes, bars, day care nursery school, workout gyms… – all linked with bridges and rooftop gardens and sculpture gardens.

CHAPTER 6

The Takers and the Traders

Systems of Survival – Jane Jacobs

In *Systems of Survival – A Dialogue on the Moral Foundations of Commerce and Politics*, Jane Jacobs sets up a conversation in the New York City apartment of a retired publisher who has gathered four of his past authors to help him think through some of his disturbing observations about honesty and dishonesty, honorable everyday work and corruption working away at the base of the economy. The retired publisher host had recently done some consulting in Germany, got his fee, went to a bank and turned it over to complete strangers for wiring back to the US. Pointing at numbers and, everyone looking like they understood and with no language in common, off went the money, or some agreement about it, through freezing, radiation bathed outer space, to an orbiting satellite and back down to his bank account. Back in New York at his apartment he told the assembled how remarkable it all was when you stopped to think about it, and how it hinged on a network of agreements and arrangements that at any point, one might think, could be flawed, maybe "diverted" by excessive self-interest. People were keeping to the game book and if a certain larger than very small percentage did not, such transactions would be impossible. The agreements were held together by honesty, fair play, a moral sense and without them, no transaction of anything like the sort could happen. Morals at the base of economics?!

On the other hand, how about the corruption so prevalent from fudging here and there to grand larceny in business suits and wildly asymmetrical deals in which someone is tricked and grossly exploited and another enriched, and with no sense of guilt whatsoever in the deceiver and with admiration for his "success" – because he made lots of money? What, thought Jane Jacobs' fictitious and curious host, could be the cause of such attitudes and behavior? Conversely, how and why do economic arrangements work well when they do work? What are the deeper currents here, the ones when known might help us along our better way?

It seemed like an important puzzle, couched in the work life of the great majority of us, delicately balanced and in need of conscientious understanding and maintenance. Jacobs' retired publisher seemed to cringe with the possibilities for catastrophe if the honor system, even if backed by significant regulation, should fray out. (If only his character (Jane's) had been written after the Crash of 2008 instead of in 1991; I'd love to see his (her) perspective on that.) The publisher host then says to his guests, "So I've come to the conclusion that we must try to think in a systematic fashion about morality in practical working life."[39] He asks for attendance at future dinners and lunches with the guests. He urges them, one at a time, to prepare some informal notes on relevant thoughts. "The only ground rule," he continues, "is that we cleave to the behavior people use, or are supposed to use, in their work." He exempts delving into personal behaviors, to keep the investigation on track of the economic ideas I know Jane is about to delve into having read her earlier books, and he sends them off to mull over the thought for a month. Then they reunite.

One of the guest authors at the publishers initial dinner decides to field the first report – very informal; can be simply note cards – and comes back with notes plus a list of two "syndromes." She'd collected precepts people hold that fit two distinct classes of people. The two sets are remarkably different. Some of the guests at the second meeting are shocked at how different.

As they explore what they mean they come to agree that "moral syndrome A" is a set of values embraced by people in business, trade and finance. Remember the traders and lenders just four or five pages back, including the outcast foreigners protecting their heritage, religion, literacy and sheer survival. Jane's shorthand for those who cleave to this moral code: the traders.

"Moral syndrome B" is a set of precepts for those taking the responsibility for the land, taking the tithes from the peasants and defending it all to their death or to the death of those who challenge their order or threaten to take their personal or family property or that of others in the realm for which they have some or a great deal of responsibility to defend. This set of precepts is for the second group: the takers. Remember the animals and the earliest human bands taking by customary usage what just happened to be there, provided by nature; remember that "taking" was often difficult and dangerous to accomplish and closer to honorable work than conventional notions of theft or lazy harvesting of fruits and nuts; remember the earliest

---

39 Jane Jacobs, *Systems of Survival*, ibid., p.20

householders anchored by ancestor precedent to that spot with assumed eternal justification for harvesting the near-by commons because it was always there for them. Of course they had even higher justification for all that which falls inside their constructed house and yard walls, most of which they would have created themselves collectively as a family, class or generation to generation on-going administration.

I think Jacobs has hit on something here that helps explain our modern roots in the history of cities and the way their societies evolved, something clearly resonant with Mauss, Polanyi, de Coulanges, Sjoberg and other curious, probing folks. The traders look very much like many of today's liberals and the takers much like many of today's conservatives (diluted and confused somewhat by some recent changes I'll discuss later). Put yourself in the shoes of people in the category you consider yourself *not* to be in while thinking about the list of percepts of *that* moral syndrome, and keeping its history in mind, which is, not coincidently, largely the history of the pre-industrial city and going back even farther the earlier gift and taking societies. Then a number of things tend to get clarified.

The traders are the business people and agree to certain rules of opportunity, competition, inventiveness and reinvestment in their projects. They tend to tolerate and even like a wide range of people – the better to trade with them – and knowing them, tend to gain some sympathy for them as well as develop networks of trust. Sometimes they even fall in love with an "outsider" which would be more contrary to the values of the takers, but complicate things even among the early traders. In general the traders have the courage to travel, skill to learn foreign languages and face the unexpected with creativity and resilience. The takers see them as a tad cowardly, eschewing violent defense and war as they do, which tends to get in the way of trade. That the traders would hire defenders from the fighting elite to guard their caravans, which is what some knights were hired to do, only increases the disdain for the traders in the eyes of the takers. The traders tend strongly to literacy because their accounting requires knowledge of numbers and writing that explains what the numbers and agreements mean and sometimes what behavior and patterns in whole cultures mean. Much less anchored to one spot than the takers, their riches have to be far more portable, thus the use of notes of credit then paper money gives them a literally light-weight, highly liquid way of transporting value and exchanging value, about as opposite as possible from holdings in land and architecture. Also, writing gives them a much more powerful grip on their history and customary, personal and asserted rights than they would have without it. Having no land and buildings, often no security of tenure anywhere to point to, they could still pull out a sheaf of paper, parchment scroll or stack of clay tablets and point to proof of their traditions and rights they could at least then claim exist. With any luck a high authority of the land would consider correct interpretation of such agreements as controlled by law or allowable by custom – and enjoy enforcing such law largely because involvement in it gives intelligence of the exchanges such that taxing can become regulated and more dependable.

The takers are the enforcers of traditions, transactions and those who watch over the conduct of the whole society, the regulators in the largest sense. As we saw in the Crash of 2008 they, in the form of government, were those to bail out many of those who created gigantic economic disasters, along with some of the victims. In this we can see them playing the gift society's role of the patriarch, Big Man, king or modern day philanthropist redistributing wealth at strategic times, if generally in ways that try to maintain the same economic structure and patterns of privilege called class. The takers risk their lives as police and military people and expect appropriate resulting privileges. They are the guardians. (Less emphasized in Jacobs' book, they are also the conquerors of other people's territory, who kill and loot and bring back spoils and glory with a certain percale down to the entire realm, something quite significant in economic strength and prosperity of the general populace in the taker's realm.)

The takers lie and keep secrets for the general defense, for history is full of other people's deception and surprise attack. That is, *their* takers, those people from outside *our* territory, have often overpowered *our* takers, and with serious to dire consequences for many, most or even *all of us*. The takers are also, in other words, the defenders. They follow orders while learning the ropes until they are competent and then, when they have earned rank or proved themselves capable of exercising their family or class connections strategically they give orders and expect obedience. They negotiate the law with the high cards in their hand, judge and enforce the law for the general good and to within tolerable limits for their own benefit, and punish, even take revenge – for if punishment is not carried through, the order of society will soon enough be shaken. They dispense a tough love, tough duty social justice. Knowing the well-armed takers in the other territory think like they do and, at home in their own opulent digs, knowing the envy their land, possessions and privileges stoke in their own people and especially in the aristocracy and members of their own family who may be friend or foe or wildly envious, these guardians tend to be suspicious and untrusting, hire poison tasters and depend on force – which Jane labels "prowess" – as well as secrecy, stealth, outright lies of deception and threat. Their honor is in carrying through with these duties. It's a tough job but someone has to do it. Put nakedly they assume for themselves as God-given and permanently in the order of things, a monopoly on violence. Violation of their laws and violence among their subjects and other elements of the population in their realm is dealt with by harsh judgment and even greater violence: two eyes for an eye and two teeth for a tooth, ye olde code of deterrent taken seriously and sometime arbitrarily, preemptively.

The takers expect their privilege because they stand ready to defend the whole realm and because of "who they are" by blood. They tend to think of themselves as the good and the better people, the clean and the righteous. The peasants and urban poor they see as almost another and inferior species because of their own higher noble code and life-on-the-line responsibilities, their sometimes ceremonial duties including periodic acts of generosity and patronage, the always necessary *noblesse oblige* – obligations of the noble class. Unlike the traders, who need good relations with foreigners in their line of work, they are, because they believe they have to be, suspicious of outsiders. Their code is ancient going back to the earliest householders and they expect it will flow down their family bloodlines deep into the future. They see the traders as upstarts that only go back to the democratic rebellions in politics and religion of the ancient Greeks and early Christians who, though spiritually insightful, got it all wrong in the physical world, real newcomers in the eternal order of the universe.

Since this construct rings true to the history of economics and society in preceding pages here, or so it seems to me, I'll record Jane's two columns of precepts here.

Moral Precepts Syndrome A Traders	Moral Precepts Syndrome B Takers
Shun force	Shun trading
Come to voluntary agreements	Exert prowess
Be honest	Be obedient and disciplined
Collaborate easily with strangers and allies	Adhere to tradition
Compete	Respect hierarchy
Respect contracts	Be loyal
Use initiative and enterprise	Take vengeance
Be open to inventiveness and novelty	Deceive for the sake of the task
Be efficient	Make rich use of leisure
Promote comfort and convenience	Be ostentatious
Dissent for the sake of the task	Dispense largess
Invest for productive purposes	Be exclusive
Be industrious	Show fortitude
Be thrifty	Be fatalistic
Be optimistic	Treasure honor[40]

Jane has one of her dialogue participants, there in the Manhattan apartment, shocked that such values as moderation, common sense, mercy, foresight, judgment and wisdom are left off the two lists. That's what both camps have in common, is the retort, and of all the values held in common courage is the master value, "be courageous" the master precept. I'll return to that later in this book because it is the

[40] Jane Jacobs, op. cit., p.23

worst stumbling block I can think of preventing society from doing what it should do to survive and thrive. The lack of courage – physical, intellectual and moral – is precisely why our society of those two syndromes and a smattering of unique and crossover people is headed toward, as Jane says in her last book, by the title, *Dark Age Coming*. C. S. Lewis, Jane reminds us, called courage "the master virtue because it makes practice of all the others possible."[41]

Taking and giving in pre-village times

Now let's do a brief flashback to before the preindustrial city, even before the agricultural village, to hunter gatherer times, to times even earlier than the settings for most of the work of Marcel Mauss. One of the characters in *Systems of Survival* says, "I think we have two distinct syndromes because we have two distinct ways of making a living, no more no less. We are unique in having the two. All the other animals have only one."[42] What she meant was the animals take what they need from an environment generally in approximate balance between producers and consumers. Carrying capacity, powered by solar energy moving through the alchemy of chlorophyll together with the resources of soil, water and air, serves as the "invisible guiding hand." The point in Systems of Survival: only people trade in the direct sense.

So here we have an interesting rule of economics: something new and unique is created by people. We not only *take* to maintain individuals and the species, but in trading we simultaneously create and explore a whole new economic territory. Yet lest we humans risk disaster, we can't let our creativity and the heady excitement of exploration go to our heads and forget our economics rest on the foundation of nature's economics.

Trade requires build up, accumulation – a surplus – and thinking in some way about the future, and not just eating more by impulse and/or genetic programming like a bear putting on fat for hibernation. But think now of making things, crafting things, things that can last through many seasons. Bringing in a crop is making something too, baking bread also. A major theme in this book is that today's economists don't think that much about the largest case of just that – making – and miss proper evaluation of the role of the build environment – cities, towns and villages – in civilization, ecology and economy. So getting back to where making gets started might hold some interesting insights.

---

[41] Jane Jacobs, ibid., p.25

[42] Jane Jacobs, *Systems of Survival*, ibid., p.51

William Calvin takes us back to those times in his book *A Brain for all Seasons.*[43] To get the sequence right, people – or rather what paleontologists refer to as hominids, that is whatever was descending from our common ancestors with apes that was not yet quite human nor still that common ancestor and definitely different from the apes – started making use of sharp-edged rocks, either found that way or intentionally broken, as implements for scraping or cutting. That was as far back as 2.6 million years ago.

Calvin tells the story of a bonobo named Kanzi, bonobos being a close but smaller relative to chimpanzees, very similar in looks though with the bonobo having redder lips and generally longer, straighter hair parted stylishly down the middle. This one lived with archeologists Glenn and Barbara Isaac in Atlanta, Georgia. Kanzi was having trouble copying Glenn's way of smashing a small rock on a larger rock, "future tool" on "anvil." Eventually Kanzi flung his future tool at the ground in frustration, having little luck to that point, and the ground being a concrete slab, the rock broke and there he had it. A sharp edged tool. Kanzi recognized it for what it was and used the sharp edge to cut through twine that bound a box with his food inside. Kanzi didn't have the idea for making the tool himself, he was copying. But then his Bonobo ancestors might have realized a broken rock lying about in Africa three million years ago, instead of in a house in Georgia just a few years back, had a sharp edge – like teeth – and might be handy for cutting or scraping something, maybe digging for roots or grubs? Maybe said ancestor, direct descendant from our common ancestor with Kanzi, would throw a smaller rock at a larger one to break it thus bringing tool making into the world. Actually, a fair number of animals, Darwin's finches on the Galapagos Islands or a similarly enterprising bird somewhere else that used cactus thorns to dig insects out of rotting wood or from under bark, might have beat the Bonobos by millions of years. Some insects too. The rock breaking business might have been original to people, though seagulls provide a great hint when they drop shellfish from 30 feet onto the rocks below to shock them open; people might have been students of tool using birds or of seagulls as Kanzi was of Glenn Isaac in this story.

Actually, the nest making abilities of birds – their form of architecture and when in colonies like cliff swallows', city design and building, though said to be instinctive and genetically hardwired – undoubtedly had small personal variations. Then there are the famous fabulous termite towers more than 15 feet tall, presumably preceding birds by a couple hundred million years. Could these be life's beginning cities? Could the slight variations be the beginning of creativity and learning? So thoroughly embedded in the natural world, could these householding acts by other animals represent the seeds for ecocities that I believe should be the locus, protectors, organizers and generators of the next generation in the lineage of life making things?

---

[43] William H. Calvin, *A Brain for all Seasons*, University of Chicago Press, Chicago, 2002

The hand ax: the first, the basic industrial revolution

In any case, before 1.7 million years ago intentional making of tools was well underway; hominids were crafting worked rocks of several designs for scrapers and cutters. By 1.7 million years ago, they were proficient at producing something archeologists decided to call a hand ax. It was about the size of your hand and became extraordinarily common in much of Africa spreading north into Europe and east into Asia, apparently being manufactured until about 100,000 years ago. The hand ax is often found in association with the edges of past shallow ponds and the margins of lakes where animals went to drink. Many hundreds are found at some such sites. These were chipped into a somewhat teardrop shape. They were fairly heavy and somewhat flattened with a thickness to width ratio of something like 1 to 3 and getting thinner to about 1 to 5. When viewed looking at the flat side rather than on edge, one end of the teardrop-shaped disk was much more pointed than the other, like the classic shape of the pointed upper end of a falling drop of water. The mystery about this artifact is that it was not an ax in what hundreds of thousands of years later became a conventional tool designed to be bound to a shaft or handle. And it wasn't a chopper or scraper with a sharp edge or pointed end on one side and a smooth rounded back to fit in the palm of the hand on the other. Its edges were sharp all around. Big puzzle for the archeologist, one of the biggest considering how long it seemed central to our antecedents' lives among the food animals, almost 400 times longer than all of urban civilization if dated from the Sumerian Civilization to now. Use it to chop or scrape and expect a lot of pain and not much force at the business edge or pointy end. The other mystery is why once it came into being it just kind of froze there in time being used and recreated millions of times with no significant design changes over the next approximately 1.7 million + years, which is a long time.

William Calvin theorizes, after hefting a large number of such implements, that they were hunting weapons. Some archeologists half jokingly call them killer Frisbees. Without significant pain the hand ax could be accelerated to sufficient speed to cover considerable distance when thrown but be sharp enough to hurt, even sometimes draw blood. For millions of years grazing animals, the base of the ancient human economy in many well-explored places, gathered in tight herds to drink at the edges of ponds and lakes. They formed up in such ranks in large numbers to better defend their rears, literally, which constituted a disincentive to leopard, lion and hyena attacks. What Calvin noticed was that predators, like lions that make about one kill per six chases, can't get too close before the heard bolts, presenting fast retreating rear ends and powerful legs with hooves for the predator to try to get past, a very tricky, risky, dangerous kill. So crowding around the water hole seems to work for the would-be prey. The predator's strategy is to attack from an oblique angle toward neck and shoulders area of the victim, a weaker, usually older animal left behind or an unguarded young one.

16. Pedestrian world

Not to encourage every one to work this hard (but maybe why not?), but much is possible with foot power in the pedestrian city. These women in Bangalore, India illustrate solidarity in work – notice they are all on the same foot, in step, making the work a community effort in "solidarity" with one another.

But a long hard throw of a hand ax by a human or hominid could span the distance the grazing animals would expect harmlessly separating them from this rather small two legged almost hairless skinny animal. The shape, says Calvin, sets the hand ax to fluttering around a ragged axis averaging generally point down. It doesn't matter how it's thrown – over, under or side arm. The pointy end is a little heavier relative to the other end's air resistance. Often if the object lands in mud or sod point down it will be disposed upright, exposing the other more rounded but also sharp edge to the animals legs like a knife, edge up. The sequence is that the fluttering falling "ax," or many of them coming in at once, hits one or more animals wounding them slightly. The animals have a reflex to collapse to the far side of the blow or stumble to their knees. Dependably this causes pandemonium and some animal or several are wounded trying to escape and then easily attacked by the ax throwers, perhaps with sharp wooden spears that would not likely be preserved hundreds, much less hundreds of thousands of years, much less 1.7 million years. Like the American plains Indians' technique of herding panicked bison over cliffs, this technique did not require bows and arrows, long range spear throwing or atlatls. Thus an effective tool that provided food and material for many other tools made from the bodies of the game animals settled into use for over one and a half million years. People – or hominids – were on their way to slow innovation and long, long traditions. Making things was now firmly established at the base of human economy. Was this as fundamental as it gets, backing up Marx' labor theory of value? This sounds odd enough to be some kind of joke but I think it probably means a lot.

Succeed well enough in the hunt for a little surplus to start accumulating and we have the ancient taking syndrome getting established as a surplus begins to make trading practical, or Mauss would say, the kind of trade called exchanging gifts. Probably one of the most important of early gifts was the hand ax itself, made by the father, given to the son, along with the secrets of how it was made – education beginning its debut in making things – a gift. It would seem the making of the gift would figure in very fundamentally in this primal exchange adding value, as we like to say these days, to whatever is exchanged; unlike sharing berries collected, say, such a made gift would have the special imprint of the maker's knowledge, skill, maybe in some detailing, even personality.

As in the situation where the preindustrial city was slowly gaining technologies and education of those making the products of those technologies, while gradually picking up tempo, so too the same pattern prevailed earlier but moved glacially more slowly as the cultural artifact list picked up the use of skins, hides, sticks for shelter, the beginnings of architecture, and the acquisition of fire. Fire could be found and used briefly after a lightning strike, forest or grass fire. It could be nurtured from burning twigs left over from fires of natural causes long before tools generating friction or flint sparking into flammable material were used to actually start fires. The estimated dates for first utilization range wildly between 125,000 years ago to as far back as 2 million years in the hands of *Homo erectus*, the earlier the dates the more flimsy the evidence.[44]

Education of a more rudimentary sort but more advanced than the other animals teaching their offspring was no doubt evolving then too, probably the first sounds of serious language formation as well, perhaps differentiating tools and products at the same time as naming plants, animals and the individual people themselves.

The taking syndrome morphing into potential gifting/trading with the beginnings of accumulation and production, in other words, seemed to be rising from animal reality from the absolute irreducible case of taking and giving down all the way to the microbe level as basic as it gets: eating and giving life to the next generation. I think Marcel Mauss would see this making sense and probably Jane Jacobs

[44] Wikipedia, http://en.wikipedia.org/wiki/Control_of_fire_by_early_humans

too. But says Jane, in her earlier books, *The Economy of Cities* and *Cities and the Wealth of Nations*, which preceded her final book, *Dark Age Coming*, there is this very major point: whole societies can lose their knowledge base and even the memory that it ever existed. She cites, for example, lost skills and memories of crafts and even how to use old tools in Appalachia after several generations of increasing poverty and associated disuse of the tools: the build up can reverse. The culture and the economics are linked in this decline, slow or rapid, and in its more severe form it's called collapse.

For our thinking about economics, though, it may be important to note that the build up itself creates higher levels of abstraction and more and more items and services separated ever more from basic sustenance. Luxuries become considered necessities and all manner of meaningful distinction dissolves while distinction itself, that is, differentiation of our created things and their variety, multiplies. What to give if nothing really connects with basics any more? What does the rich kid really appreciate at Christmas? Then again with so much variety, monetizing everything actually serves a purpose kindred to anonymity in preserving privacy and personal development in cosmopolitan cities. Whether the detail – all that *stuff*, all those products useful, useless, profound, nonsensical and outright destructive swirling around an economy – is healthy and meaningful probably has a lot to do with how well how much of it fits with the basic needs of the times. More on that in a later discussion on simplicity vs. complexity.

But for now we can see accumulation of "enough" to create a gift society tending into "so much," a more commercial form of economics that actually makes sense for a complex creative society, then tending into "too much," to the point we are now burning out our sources of sustenance. The process seems to be happening over very long stretches of time, society observing, learning, inventing, teaching, neglecting, destroying, forgetting, rediscovering and inventing all over again, and all of this producing a society and economy on its way to the industrial city. This is not to say there was an ideal good old times on the "enough" to "too much" continuum – all sorts of environmental and societal overexploitation and wars set back the whole artifact expansion pattern when various degrees of collapse visited past societies we know about – it is only to describe the economic pattern relative to resources and biocapacity and human capacity for privation abuse and suffering.

But we are reflecting on Jane's precepts for the takers. The elite, especially the highest, don't just give and expect some reciprocity, they must also, like the Big Men in the western Pacific and the chiefs in potlatching societies, dispense largess. The largess never comes without expectation of some sort of return, definitely expected and major return if earlier gifts in the cycle are major. Largesse in Jane's construct on the part of the takers, the landed, the territorial elite, and in the complex hunting and gathering potlatching cultures of North America's Pacific Northwest, as noted by Mauss, was not just a generous gift. It just plain demanded reciprocity. Something had to come back from the beneficiary of the gift.

Digging a little deeper into the gift giving notion, Yale University anthropologist David Graeber discusses how gift giving may have been distorted into the American work ethic gone strictly materialistic, by way of Christianity.[45] Graeber reports sociologists Alain Caillé and Gérald Berthoud were discussing a conference they were attending on the subject of gifts.

> They came to the shocked realization that it did not seem to have occurred to a single scholar in attendance that a significant motive for giving gifts might be, say, generosity, or genuine concern for another person's welfare. In fact, the scholars at the conference invariably assumed that "gifts" do not really exist: Scratch deep enough behind any human action, and you'll always discover some selfish, calculating strategy. Even more oddly, they assumed that this selfish strategy was always, necessarily, the real truth of the matter; that it was more real somehow than any other motive in which it might be entangled. It was as if to be scientific, to be "objective" meant to be completely cynical. Why?
>
> Caillé ultimately came to blame Christianity. Ancient Rome still preserved something of the older ideal of aristocratic open-handedness: Roman magnates built public gardens and monuments, and vied to sponsor the most magnificent games.

In *Systems of Survival* and as a trait of the elite in the *Preindustrial City Past and Present*, here comes the largesse that expects something unstated but real in return for the gift, maybe something as non-physical as loyalty, or as physical as taxes and required military service – or as twisted as in the following example, continuing on in Graber's article:

> But Roman generosity was also quite obviously meant to wound: One favorite habit was scattering gold and jewels before the masses to watch them tussle in the mud to scoop them up. Early Christians, for obvious reasons, developed their notion of charity in direct reaction to such obnoxious practices. True charity was not based on any desire to establish superiority, or favor, or indeed any egoistic motive whatsoever. To the degree that the giver could be said to have gotten anything out of the deal, it wasn't a real gift.
>
> But this in turn led to endless problems, since it was very difficult to conceive of a gift that did not benefit the giver in any way. Even an entirely selfless act would win one points with God. There began the habit of searching every act for the degree to which it could be said to mask some hidden selfishness, and then assuming that this selfishness is what's really important.

[45] David Graber, "Give it Away," on the website: www.freewords.org/graeber.html. This is actually a side note in Graber's article which is mainly on Marcel Mauss and his gift societies observations.

> One sees the same move reproduced so consistently in modern social theory. Economists and Christian theologians agree that if one takes pleasure in an act of generosity, it is somehow less generous. They just disagree on the moral implications. To counteract this very perverse logic, Mauss emphasized the "pleasure" and "joy" of giving: In traditional societies, there was not assumed to be any contradiction between what we would call self-interest (a phrase that, he noted, could not even be translated into most human languages) and concern for others; the whole point of the traditional gift is that it furthers both at the same time.

Mauss himself says of transactions in early societies he has observed that, "In particular, such exchanges are acts of politeness: banquets, rituals, military services, women, children, dances, festivals and fairs in which economic transaction is only one element, and in which the passing on of wealth is only one feature of a much more general and enduring contract."[46]

So don't worry about generosity, he suggests. Enjoy it! Remember it. Be open to surprises. Give back what seems appropriate and timed into the future in a way that seems right. Here where things get so convoluted and introverted there's a lot to say for just relaxing and moving on with intuition and social reality checks helping guide the way. It's called variously, in addition to acceptance, expressions of friendship, brotherhood and sisterhood, solidarity, bonding…

But there are other dimensions to this reciprocity, maybe call it symbiosis. It might be that the back and forth of the evolving relationship might not balance in material terms, but that's not all that's going on. We are after all used to people being paid for services, even advice based on some class of knowledge. But what if someone has something of exceptional beauty and not much mass/energy, like advice, but also no monetizeable value or material utility to give, maybe just an enduring story, maybe taking someone on a walk to draw attention to an inspiring view remembered for life, without charging for the tour. Or maybe someone saves a life? To gracefully accept such a gift is simply to appreciate a large benefit and not feel indebted forever because something of equal value simply can't be delivered. For example, setting up a very dangerous situation for your friend so you can save his life too, is not such a good idea. Not all things can be made equal – we can gracefully accept that. But where inequality is extreme we can see, and will look at later, the problems that ensue. Nothing that a little generosity via graduated income tax can't fix at least a bit.

[46] Marcel Mauss, The Gift, first English edition, Cohen & West, 1954, quote from the Routledge edition, Milton Park, UK 2010, p. 7

Monstrous hybrids and rancid cooperation

But what happens if the traders assume to take taker roles, asks one of the diners at Jane Jacobs Systems of Survival salons? And what if the takers assume to take trader roles? Jane has her character on the spot call these "monstrous hybrids." Such as that would never happen in the preindustrial city because the gulf between the commoners and elite was so immense, the trader being much more closely allied with the commoner than the elite. Just one glance at someone's clothes and you'd say of the pretentious commoner, even a rich one (until the industrial city was getting started), "What are you doing wearing those extravagant clothes? Waste your family's meager savings for your vanity? Trying to make a target of yourself, your family, your business associates with your unseemly pretentions?" As for the elite, they would never stoop to wrecking their status among their class, embarrass their family blood line and risk losing their privileges by going into business handling everyday transactions with lesser beings. Their loss and their families' in prestige and community standing would be enormous. Such black sheep would get cut loose, ostracized, lose their inheritance.

In our times, as rich business leaders, inventors, successful artists and athletes, very top professionals like "starchitects" and famous lawyers, even executive directors of the large NGOs and labor leaders flirt with the styles of and become as elite as the landed aristocracy, some buying large acreage of land themselves, and as literacy of everyone dissolves many of society's barriers, people lose some of Jane's "syndromes" pattern and hybridization becomes more commonplace. But, theorizes Jane, considering the relationship between the two separate but dynamically balanced syndromes, commoners and elite, traders and takers, hybrids are not just inappropriate to the maintenance of society, they can cause great dislocation and damage. Take business deciding to go into governance: the Mafia is a good example, ersatz insurance business pretending to be like the government's police force running a protection racket, levying an "informal" or off the books tax. The "people's" experience is one of constant ignorance, pervasive fear and occasional violence. We can see why do it yourself guardians playing the Levithan, making money "off the books," who usurp agreed upon division between takers and traders, are a serious problem, from strictly self serving criminals to bands of volunteer vigilantes and lynch mobs.

As for government going into business inappropriately, there is the case of government selling itself, or rather it's holdings and responsibilities, from selling national parks attempted in a grand manner by Ronald Reagan when President of the United States. Selling public holdings makes it easier to balance budgets, increasing the revenues... this year. A few big sales can avoid raising taxes, which tax payers tend to support, until their parks are closed. Outsourcing an outfit like Blackwater**,** a for-profit security "contractor," for military duties in Iraq was supposed to save money, but they aren't supposed to be in on military intelligence so we can expect their job to be half baked, even if costing us less or the same as or even more than just having a military. Blackwater famously abused its armed prerogatives killing numerous non-combatant bystanders generating enough embarrassment to be banned from Iraq and to change its name to Xe, pronounced Zee, supposedly somehow related to the noble gas Xenon, an attempted, largely successful, anti-mnemonic device. Who now knows who Xe is? Where'd Blackwater go?!

To this point I may seem to be wandering over a wide range of topics and some might seem tangential to our investigations into an economics built on what we build. But I don't think so. So far I've been preparing the soil. I'm hoping themes of real meaning are appearing and beginning to weave together. In the next chapter I'll hope to draw them together more clearly, make something of a coherent pattern of them and bring us more up to date. Then we can look at the really big violations of Jane Jacobs' syndromes in the Financial Crisis to 2008, ongoing, and maybe see more clearly that patterns embedded deep in history are playing out. Most importantly I hope that such background will bring us to a point where we can then make real sense of what to do next.

19. Tableland

Imagine an infrastructure like this provided in concrete and steel to support a community taking up 1/10th the land of car based suburbia and running on 1/10th the energy, and using 1/10th as much concrete and steel as freeways, interchanges and parking structures for the same number of people. Just inset buildings, landscapes, elevators and bridges... A little fanciful and symbolic, but representing the three-dimensional in a way I enjoy.

CHAPTER 7

Launching Capitalism

Real money, verbal and early

Meantime, a little on the history of money itself. Actual real adult money goes back to the early childhood of societies and probably really did start with the sort of verbal money I hypothesized earlier in these pages. Some people like solid coins in hand and see paper money as too flimsy, etherealized. Some insisted on pegging economic value of the medium of exchange on the value of gold and backed by gold, supported the gold standard which said bring in your paper money and the bank or national government has to give you gold. I don't know if any such people exist any more since no one is obligated to provide gold for paper money these days, and the world of economics continues to go around. Verbal money must make such people, if they exist, sweat and shake if they can't get to understanding money is just an agreement, miss that it is the agreement itself that makes the money in whatever form it takes. Maybe seemingly paradoxical, but real, the agreement, the idea, is very much as real as existentially *there* in the exchange as the printed paper or minted metal, as the material/energy products or services produced, stored, delivered and used. In a book talking about building as the basis of human economics it may seem contradictory to say "it's all in the mind, you know."

Actually, I think it is another case of a dimensional pair, the agreement between people represented in this case as a valuation given to exchanges *and* the thing itself, the thing acquired – animal bodies, sharp stones, gold, cities... – made, built and put into action. My point in this book is largely that it is enormously important to make (to build) the right *thing* which requires more of the best *thought* about what gets built. You might think of this as the thing/thought dimensional pair of value. (A service qualifies as a "thing" here too.)

But to sound more prosaic and historical about it all, less philosophical, it seems more than a little likely that things given in a society based on redistribution mainly through gift giving and reciprocal obligations became part of a flowing set of socially valued relationships. But some things that could last a long time, like hard shells and beads, and better yet, bits of metal small enough to be carried around but large enough to be easily manipulated, could be exchanged over and over naturally falling into use as an exchange medium. Things that disappear with use or quickly decompose, such as food, don't make a useful medium of exchange. Items the wrong size don't work either. In Ralph T. fosters book, *Fiat Paper Money – the history and evolution of our currency*, he mentions and features a photograph of the copper money of Sweden issued in 1644 that was a slab of copper 12 inches wide, 30 long and so heavy it was next to impossible to use. Silver coins were worth 100 times as much in metal value than copper, so the copper money of similar value weighted 100 times as much as the silver. Government economists had not yet figured out they could just declare small copper coins to be worth in exchange value as much as coffee table sized slabs of copper, though in addition the citizens would have to trust and use the system. Finally 17 years later they tried out Europe's first paper money, copying China's first issue 637 years earlier.[47]

Measured amounts of longer lasting food served as money long before Sweden's copper slabs – dry grain in jars, baskets or bags for example – were also used as money, greasing the speed and ease of exchange. Since everyone can use grain, just as everyone can use money, and it lasts a reasonable time, like money (if kept dry and cool), it has utility as a medium of exchange over many months. Gold? As long as you can avoid losing it, spending it or seeing it disappear into a thief's pocket.

Ralph Foster relates in his book,

> Long before the advent of coinage, ancient civilizations refined gold and silver in the form of jewelry, art and ingots. These metals were measured and valued by weight. Sumerian clay tablets reveal that as far back as 2400 BC official standards existed for the weighing of silver for use as money... One of the earliest passages in the Old Testament reports that Abraham "weighed

[47] Ralph T. Foster, *Fiat Paper Money – the history and evolution of our currency*, self-published, Berkeley, California, 1991, p. 59. This book is a treasure trove of information from many relatively obscure and worthwhile sources. As far as I know available only from the author, located in Berkeley, at: tfdf@pacbell.net.

to Ephron… four hundred shekels of silver, current money" to buy a burial plot for his wife, Sarah.[48]

(The shekel was initially a measure of weight, maybe grains or ingots, probably not coins since metal objects in that form were found corresponding to later dates.)

Cowry shells were used as money in China as early as the Shang Dynasty around 1400 BC, contemporary with later Egyptian times. As with the American Indians making shell beads used as money by themselves and the Dutch and English colonists mentioned earlier, these shells in China had the hardness to last through time, and would usually have holes drilled through them to function as beads.

Somewhat later – we're still in China – around 1200 BC farm tools, especially spades were used as money and could be traded in various number representing value for the purpose of purchasing things. Considering the proportion of farmers in the society, these could be used by the vast majority, like grain but lasting longer, for function as well as exchange. You can imagine they weren't all that convenient. But in any case, here comes Marx labor theory of value again. Perhaps he would have noted approvingly if he'd studied Chinese history in the origins of money. Maybe he did…

But quickly the "circulating tools" (the spades, the "money") were switched out to be made thinner, weaker as people thought why have all those tools not used for digging hanging around? But they were allowed to retain the approximate same value and got yet smaller. People were beginning to realize the agreement as to value could be established beyond functional physical utility. Interestingly the tool money, when it became more symbolic and less utilitarian for farm and building, got inscriptions stamped on it to represent cities. That's the earliest link of cities to money, at least as declaring geographic location and eventually official government sanction for economic value, that I've turned up so far.

The tool coins and metal cowry coins lasted until about 350 BC, by which time coins that look roughly like today's coins began replacing both. These were usually of bronze, but with square holes in the centers of round disks making them easily assembled on strings, like beads on a string. Now there were strings of "cash," a Chinese word for one or more coins.

Why square holes I always wondered, with the string-pinching corners of the squares more likely to wear through and break strings than if the holes were round? These coins were cast, not struck with dies, and had rough round edges where a little molten metal leaked out of their molds. A square rod was thrust down the middle of a large number of coins after casting and files were used to plane off the excess metal from the edges of the coins, to thus smooth the edges. A round hole in the middle

[48] Ralph T. Foster, Ibid., p. xiii.

would have permitted the coin to turn, rather than resist turning when being filed, thereby make filing more difficult. Therefore, square holes.[49]

The first items that began to be about the size and more or less the shape of modern coins appeared earlier than that, though, in what is now western Turkey about 640 BC in the kingdom of Lydia. These looked something like very fat coins or flattened egg shaped globules of metal with an image, typically of a lion and sun on one side, and a crushed-in area on the backside where the metal blank was placed on some sort of anvil when it was literally struck with a die turning it into a coin.

Herodotus says the Lydians were first to strike coins of gold and sliver, in those separate metals. Soon after, the naturally occurring gold/silver alloy called electrum became the standard – apparently. Aristotle begged to differ saying the first coins were electrum and he credited Demodike for minting the first coins in Lydia. Though she was from Kyme, part of ancient Greece, she married King Midas of legend who is likely King Mita historically, King of Mushki, Mushki being near Lydia. Thus the legend of Midas turning things to gold apparently starts with Mita, his wife shaping gold or electrum into coins, another case of males getting all the attention.

Not long after the flatish eggs or fatish coins a newer version appeared that looked almost exactly like today's coins followed Greek colonization around the Mediterranean and spread to meet in trade with coins that may or may not have been invented independently about the same time in the Indus region.

A key step on the process would be the role of government, establishing the money's value by fiat. Fiat, says Ralph Foster, is from the Latin *fieri* for "let it be done." Thus government mints or prints and simply proclaims the value of money. Law and punishment under law for defiance of the proclamation makes its value relatively dependable. It also reinforces the essence of capital in emphasizing that it is created by agreement, in this case an agreement forced from above. Base metal in the small quantity of coinage would have little value as a commodity and paper much less. But if there is agreement in the market place and enforcement by some power able to "exert prowess" in Jane Jacobs terms or play the role of the Leviathan in Hobbes' construct, produce lots and let the exchanging begin! Besides, if you're a government you can get a lot of stuff when you first issue it. Or give it to your friends who are then obligated to support you one way or another.

In the history of paper money, individual initiative and in that ever so early civilization of China, things get rolling like this and Foster gives us some dates. The Chinese invented paper in 105 AD, ink around 400 AD and block printing necessary

[49] Calgary Coin and Antique Gallery, Chinese Cast Coins website, http://www.calgarycoin.com/reference/china/china1.htm#round%20hole, is a good source on early coinage in China. Looks conscientious.

for consistent images on the paper around 600 AD. Also around 400 "religious money" made its appearance.[50]

For many generations in China as well as in the tradition of the ancient cities of Greece, Rome and the Indus Valley, people made sacrifices to their more heroic and longer remembered ancestors, kindred to or actually become gods in the eyes of the householders. These sacrifices were often portions of the repast the living family was sharing round the table, sometimes burned, becoming rising smoke and steam. There was something ethereal, eternal, almost ghost like about the drifting, sometimes delicious-smelling incense smoke curling into the air and out through the trees, mountains, clouds melting between the stars. The vapors seemed to be a medium, a bridge over which to carry the meaning of sacrifices from this world to the ancestors and gods, speaking in a similar language as the quiet fluttering and flicking of prayer flags. Maybe food sacrifices wouldn't make the journey but the smoke seemed to make it through.

Approximately in the early in the 7th century AD, the practice of burning paper to represent the value of possessions or money appeared. I called up Ralph to ask him how sacrificing this "religious money" worked. To be explicit I asked Foster, "You mean the people making the 'sacrifice' wrote down what something they owned was worth, burned the note as a sacrifice to the gods, but continued to own whatever was represented on the note?" He said with a voice that sounded like a smile, "Being a practical lot, to really destroy anything of value made no sense. Just destroy what is imagined to represent the value you have. Here lies the very root of our whole financial structure today. Absolutely nothing!"[51] (Well, if that's the definition of an agreement not being connected to something physical anyway…)

But it seems even then some people found the arrangement a little fishy. Foster referred me to a story in his book that was written and perpetuated to allay doubts that went like this, quoting Ana Seidel:

> At first people feared they were cheating the spirits out of more useful offerings by replacing them with mere paper… A man named Shan-Lung… was frightened when crossing paths with three ghosts. He apologized saying, "In my ignorance I did not recognize you gentlemen. When I return home, please let me prepare some things. But I don't know where to send them." The three ghosts then said, "Burn them beneath that tree on the river bank." Later [Shang-Lung] cut up some paper to make "money" and "silk" which he burned beside the river after also setting out some food and wine. Suddenly he saw the three men (ghosts) who had come to thank him. "Thanks

50 Ralph Foster cites Anna Seidel for his information on these dates and on the history of "religious money." The book for reference is Seidel's Buying One's Way into Heaven: *The Celestial Treasury in Chinese Religions*, Yale University Press, New Haven, Connecticut, 1978 p. 424-425 1978

[51] Ralph T. Foster in e-mail communication with the author

to your keeping your word," they said, "we have received these valuable gifts. We truly appreciate it."[52]

About 150 years later, around 750 AD, a new kind of money was coming into circulation. This money didn't aspire to satisfy the demands of the other world but rather work smoothly in this one. It was emerging out of the more personal, more like contractual notes between individuals, negotiated in the money shops. It was called "flying money" because it was used over great distances. If "money shops" on moist coastline would honor paper representing real value in the distant dry cities on the silk road far to the west, and vice versa, then merchants and other travelers need not carry heavy bags of strings of cash. By the 900s AD flying money, essentially receipts proving there was a place where the paper could be cashed in for cash in iron, bronze, copper or, if available, silver, was easily negotiated all over China and its distant central Asian outposts. That system was initiated privately by the financial services institutions of the time – then the government took over, profiting its treasury but also geographically expanding a means of greatly facilitating trade.

Where paper money appeared for the common folk, not just the long-distance traders, was in the western province of Szechwan. There, fairly remote from the rest of China, copper cash for exchange was worth considerably more than iron, but there was a copper shortage. Instead of ounces of copper for exchange, many tens of pounds of iron cash had to be used. Says Foster, "A housewife had to carry to market one and one-half pounds of iron to buy one pound of salt. A merchant cashing out one ounce in silver bullion received ninety pounds of iron cash... In 1011 AD sixteen merchant houses, accustomed to honoring each others' receipts, joined together to create a uniform paper note. ... People began to deposit their iron money in money shops and exchanged deposit receipts to transact business." These receipts became real money, now universally exchangeable in that part of China.

Twenty-two years later officials of the imperial government, recognizing something too successful to be resisted, plus they'd like to extend it to the whole realm, took over and issued their own paper money, declared a government monopoly and required all people to accept it "...for all debts, public and private" as said on the United States paper dollar – and the rest is history.

[52] Anna Seidel, Ibid., p. 216

20. Elevated over floods: New Orleans

The idea of building on elevated fill – just piles of dirt – goes back 4,500 years to the Sumerian Civilization. Simply build higher than the floods, nobody hurt, no damage done, no insurance payments or claims. This solution that can work for about one billion people in flood prone areas today fits perfectly with compact pedestrian ecocity design. Notice steps down to natural wetlands. Such an environment also protects from hurricane-generated waves and if the mounds are high enough, elevation prevents tsunami destruction.

Transitions: Feudalism to nationalism to mercantilism to early capitalism

Now, speaking of history, we look at some democratic strains and economic patterns that lead from the preindustrial city and elements of feudalism that followed the Fall of Rome and into next phases in the development of cities and economics. Other city cultures are going through other changes in China, India, the Americas, some similar some different but I will deal much more with the Western story, the European story due to several centuries of dominance.

The drift I'm talking about continues in fits and starts, mostly in slow motion, so slow people hardly noticed anything was changing or could change – except when punctuated by violent battles of shifting feudal and religious competitions throughout Medieval times. Then the drift moves into the Renaissance and nationalist mercantile times and eventually into modern times – and "post-modern" times of globalism and new eco-bioregionalism, Internet and climate change. I would hope also, into the beginning of the age when humanity realizes what we literally build has a great deal to do with economics, society and nature.

Remember the ancient authoritarianism based largely on the customary authority of revered ancestors and gods, the authoritarianism of the landed patriarchs owning real estate but only on behalf of the collective, the extended family, up to substantial defensible architecture with adjacent landscapes and surrounding walls, turning into castles whose aristocracy was responsible for the defense of adjacent towns and hinterlands. The patriarchs with customary and family heritage claims to that real estate who were the most wealthy, powerful or influential rose, as did the tribal leaders in Greece, to leadership over much larger domains than their contemporaries. They became the lords of the Middle Ages, the most powerful yet, kings.

But to be a king one needed the loyalty of others of the aristocracy who benefited by the concentrated power in the strongest among them, often for coordination of mutual defense and in the more regular course of daily affairs for favors that might be granted, as in the gift societies studied by Marcel Mauss, if in the earlier social evolutionary steps on a much smaller scale than kings could deliver in their obligation generating largess.

Formalizing advice and consent from the aristocracy was the advent of councils and related institutions in Europe. The succession of councils, later called parliaments, started in Iceland in 930 AD and in England after 1066 when William of Normandy instituted his Great Council, or *Curia Regis*, King's Council, of tenants-in-chief (nobles renting land from the king and having considerable control over resources and commoners residing there). Also included in his Council were ecclesiastics. From the two groups he sought advice before proclaiming laws. These councils of William's were made up of barons, earls, archbishops, bishops and abbots. The King unpopular among the barons, John of England, 149 years later, was forced to sign the Great Charter, or Magna Carta in 1215. When he failed to honor the agreement – after all he *was* forced into it – rebellion followed. He was remarkably unpopular for insulting the nobility in various ways and instituting an array of "innovative but unpopular financial measures," in the words of one scholar. He levied traditional "scutage," payments from lords in lieu of military service – when there was no war in progress – increased charges levied against widows who wished to remain single, sold charters for building new towns, including Liverpool, sold charters for operating market places, sold sheriff appointments, instituted an income tax where none had existed before, proclaimed new import and export taxes and even land taxes, after which if the barons failed to pay, he would confiscate their land. He hoarded the silver he collected and melted it down for new coinage for financing his castles and occasional wars, but reintroduced it in smaller quantity than collected and thus made commerce more difficult for scarcity of money. And he charged taxes called tallage preferentially levied against Jews but also against those Christians who had borrowed from them. Little wonder he was unpopular.

Shortly after signing the Magna Carta William abandoned his part of the bargain bringing on a rebellion of many of the barons, but he died of dysentery a year later. His son, nine year old Henry III was crowned, with expectations of far better management of affairs of state ("can't get much worse…"). Henry's Lord Protector of the Realm for the next few years being a respected noble, and Henry III's long reign, the first of more than 50 years in England, amounted to the cementing of the tradition of the English Parliament. At first there was only a House of Lords, but in 1264 a House of Commons was also created, if for only men of means, if not titles, including some farmers who owned their land and some of the more prosperous and influential townspeople. Thus in that degree, democracy from the top down, if not very far down, was activated.

Overlapping historically, between 1222 and approximately1370, an innovation in bottom up democracy paired with proto-capitalistic commerce, was launched in Southwestern France. These communities, called bastides from the French for "to build," created a kind of new economic system within the feudal system, which is interesting from the point of view of our thesis that one needs to know what to build to solve economic problems. In this case, build centering the community on production and commerce rather than religion. This must have been something of a breath of fresh air for this was right in the middle of a period of almost ceaseless, horrendous religious wars. The physical innovation was that the market was in the center, the church to one side. They even named this kind of city after that notion linking building with their foray into what was beginning to look a little like capitalism.

The first bastide was founded by Count Raymond VII of Toulouse. The wars were at that time and place pitting a religious sect call the Cathars, also Albigensians (centered early on in the town of Albi) against the Catholics and vice versa. So may people were killed in Raymond's lands he dedicated himself to quitting old towns and founding new ones. To settle them as quickly as possible he offered what we would call for the time an extraordinarily liberal charter.

In the following 150 years about 600 such towns were built in the region, many founded by other lords following Count Raymond's lead. The new citizens of the Count's bastides were required to quickly build a house and work place so that the town would appear all at once. The lord would extract a tax of up to half the cost of building but then the new citizen would be a free man. There would be further taxes of a manageable amount levied on exchanges in the market place between producers and between them and traders from outside, but not levies on production. The taxes were reasonable enough that many citizens thrived as craftspeople and merchants. The citizens would elect their own council for local governance and would have freedom to chose which religion to embrace, pay relatively small taxes to Raymond in return for which he would build fortress walls around the said towns and undertake their defense. He would also build a market place scaled to the projected population of the particular towns. [53] Though feudal arrangements varied in detail considerably from place to place, here the new townspeople were given a plot of land in a regular right angle grid work platting of city blocks and streets, a layout designed for simplicity, a minimum of difficult decision making and influenced by Roman military city planning; this was in the far reaches of the Empire when it collapsed approximately seven centuries earlier. These new towns had a plaza and were centered on the marketplace rather than the church, as said, upgrading economic life and downgrading the emphasis on religion.

The role for the elite with the lord at the apex was very much in the command-and-duty pattern of Jane Jacobs' takers. The economic arrangement in the market was designed to be open to inspection by all and rigorously consistent, honest and fair in weights and measures, valuation and taxation. Now everyone in this charter-guaranteed new deal had a higher stake in the town's success and many of the towns did well over the ages since. Thus another step further was taken in policy, rights and city building leading toward the age of the industrial city, along with greater democracy and basic capital economics as compared to latter day capitalistic economics and it's tendencies toward monopoly, gambling in the finance sector, quasi-religious belief in Growth and various reactions to regulating economics into good citizenship. Remember, other than quick attacks, things changed very slowly, and the attacks, which still came, came much less frequently. Was the focus on the new kind of building, along with its economic management innovations a distraction from the obsession of religion and violence and a much-improved model of existence? Maybe.

Consolidation of smaller political units into nation states was the next political, social, cultural step, usually complete with an ever more standardized and generally used unifying language, literally speaking: old French, Spanish, English... Political units had consolidated and disintegrated many times before in China and of course in Greek and Roman times and a similar pattern prevailed everywhere in the world, including in the New World, as Gideon Sjoberg recounts in *The Preindustrial City Past and Present.* Now, in Europe, centered on larger past tribal groupings and around common heritage, customary usage and common language and in close alliance with the prevailing religious order, nation states began to form, trade quickened a pace, armies and navies expanded and the next phase on the macro economic level was nationalistic mercantilism.

In the mercantilist economic system, as it was coming into existence, advisors to kings, ministers and some bankers who played the role of early economists, were theorizing that a positive balance of trade must be maintained for the security and superiority of "our" particular country. A few centuries later, Winston Churchill

[53] James Bentley, *Fort Towns of France – The Bastides of the Dordogne and Aquitanine*, Tauris Parke Books, London, 1993 – main reference for information on the Bastides

called the goal "mastery" which, beyond security and superiority, includes the notion of control, considerable exploitation and at home, patriotic personal association with national glory and a higher mission which was… to unabashedly dominate and exploit. In the early mercantile days freelance robbers, "highwaymen" and pirates plagued trade, caravans on the Silk Road, shipping on the Mediterranean, Indian Ocean and elsewhere. Traders had recourse to employ military style, elite trained defenders including those called knights and later military units from the sovereign to defend "our national interests" meaning our businessmen bringing profits and products back to our country in another of the uncomfortable but necessary but more greatly empowered relationships between the takers and the traders. Warfare became almost constant between various states in Europe at any given time as kingdoms sought to gain ever better advantage over and wealth from other countries as well as the subjugated colonies

The overall pattern according to Steven Pinker in *The Better Angels of our Nature* was this: "Europe had five thousand independent political units (mainly baronies and principalities) in the 15th century, five hundred at the time of the Thirty Years war in the early 17th, two hundred at the time of Napoleon in the early 19th and fewer than thirty in 1953"[54] – that much were powers consolidating and Leviathans growing in power each, securing peace within borders, but continuing almost constant warfare between the ever larger states.

As the scale of political unit increased through the Renaissance, mid 1300s, and into the age when science and technology was getting firmly grounded, say the mid 18th century, world exploration and aggressive pillaging of the "undeveloped" "primitive" parts of the world took off in the tradition of Greece, Rome, and by then, Islam, and not to forget Chinese empires and those of central Asia. The Aztecs in Mexico and Inca in Peru weren't doing too badly either. It became the times of discovery and exploitation so glorified in western school textbooks, the time of establishing colonies, stealing precious metals, extracting resources and proudly striving for empire, the British Empire leading into and through the Victorian age, being the largest and proudest empire of all. Unlike the aggressions and trade, forced and cooperative, of the single great empires before, the European nation states were contemporary with one another and not united and fought bitterly against one another. Virtually all European countries of any size, then the United States, Japan and other countries joined in the scramble for maximum extraction of wealth from trade and colonies, outright pillaging of resources and even extraction of the people themselves in the form of slaves for the homeland, as in the United States, and before it in Islam,

[54] Steven Pinker, *The Better Angels of our Nature*, Op Cit., p. 74 The book title comes from a quote from Lincoln's Inaugural Address of March 4th 1861 expressing a desire to avoid war between the North and South of the United States. He said, "We are not enemies, but friends. We must not be enemies. Though passion may have strained it must not break our bonds of affection. The mystic chords of memory, stretching from every battlefield and patriot grave to every living heart and hearthstone all over this broad land, will yet swell the chorus of the Union, when again touched, as surely they will be, by the better angels of our nature."

or in the colonies over the seas as the Spanish and Portuguese did in South America and the British everywhere.

The general idea was to best the national competition in trade, seeking more sales to foreigners than purchases, such that gold, sliver and resources of a wide variety would be always flowing toward the homeland faster than away, ever building up a positive balance of trade. As to production, with the growing wealth of the realm the system would produce more at home than buy from abroad, something of a nation scale version of Jane Jacobs' much emphasized "import replacing" economic strategy for thriving cities. Also, success in mercantilism meant a general prosperity stored physically in manor houses and buildings of commerce and business, mines and factories, roads, canals and urban infrastructure. All countries had land, but what you put on it and could wring out of it in metals, energy, wood and crop production was all contribution to the wealth of the realm. All manner of physical things were an addition to prosperity, from silverware and furniture to carriages and horses, from quarters and food sufficient to keep the peasants and workers alive and working to splendid digs for the ostentatious classes and, again, what there was of city infrastructure at the time – all were valuable embodiments of wealth.

Mercantilism backed by government, something like the business/government "partnerships" of today, grew large and crossed over eventually among the most powerful into imperialism. The essentially mercantilist positive balance of trade goal, still backed by military violence and threat, glossed over by late 20th century globalism, is still with us in the policies of the United States, in the ambitions of others. It was obscured by Capitalist vs. Communism ideologies and propaganda in the Cold War for a time and lurks beneath the surface in the rise of consolidated power, whether acknowledged or hidden, in the national ambitions and block alliances that are still with us, major players being, in addition to the US, China, the European Union and other looser amalgamations that might be forming in South America, Africa and elsewhere, going deeper into the 21st century.

But back to earlier mercantilism… In one particular kind of economic activity extreme profitability was guaranteed – if you had bloody courage, if you lived, and if you had few scruples about killing. Even the Royal treasuries sanctioned and invested in the practice: piracy, such as that of Sir Francis Drake for Queen Elizabeth I. It was a gory business but for those willing to fight, kill and risk violent death, it could be extraordinarily lucrative. Private investors as well as royalty paid for this kind of import-only business for greatly asymmetrical mercantile positive balance of trade from their pirates stealing the treasure of ships, as England did from Spain's bullion fleets. This hoard, we recall, was earlier extracted by violence – and by accident through introduced diseases – from the people of the Americas. And why not to advance the country's fortunes? The assumption was that other countries would do the same if they could: the Hobbesian trap it's called: better strike them first if you think they might strike you – or plunder someone weaker before someone else strong like you does. It was a violent consensus shared by almost everyone. War was the iron fist inside the silken glove of trade, as some mercantile-becoming-imperialist strategists would comment. Everyone noticed the math that to steal was one benefit to the thief and one point down for the opponent, while killing the opponent just plain cleared the field. That's even better than trade!

Meantime, in this overall development and economic context, science was advancing rapidly in the 18th century after Galileo Galilei, with Isaac Newton, Carl Linnaeus, Comte de Buffon, Earasmus Darwin, Jean-Batiste Lamark, Johan Wolfgang von Goethe and others contributing. Technology too. The Renaissance period, leading into the age of reason and rapid advances in science, around 1300 to 1600, had invoked Greek and Roman literature, science and technology, legitimizing learning about the physical world and making the elite of the preindustrial city perpetually nervous while the printing press of Johannes Gutenberg, put to work about 1440, rapidly expanded literacy many times over. Moveable type itself was invented in China by Bi Sheng around 1050. But his ceramic characters chipped easily, his wooden ones didn't create a sharp image and wore quickly and the number of characters was enormous and very difficult to work with. The Chinese dropped the movable type idea and stuck with wood block printing.

By 1377, however, the oldest known book printed in moveable type, the "Jikji," a Buddhist religious text from the 11th century (hand written in early stages), was printed in Korea – and it wasn't the first, just the earliest to be preserved. The French have a copy, maybe the only one, and won't give it back to the Koreans. Its influence, said of all people among other scholars, Al Gore, spread across the Silk Road through central Asia to Europe and almost certainly influenced Gutenberg and his contemporaries. It took more than sixty years to get from Korea to whatever influence it might have had on Gutenberg.[55] This was the big computer/internet leap of the day, and probably much more basic as it took literacy from scant to relatively common, whereas our electronic marvels may be taking us from sufficiency in things that matter to infoglut in things meaningful and meaningless that are scrambled almost indecipherably.

Movable type facilitated commerce and democracy both at once: people rather suddenly wanted in on more of what they were learning about. Countless other advances in invention, exploration and resources and materials were converging in Europe. The artifact list had taken off and all sorts of new possibilities were sliding into production and availability in tools, products and services. The pressures on the Earth's resources and ecology were now beginning to multiply again as they did during the rise of other civilizations, especially Rome's and China's earlier extractive practices.

But for now, or rather next, let's get more grounded. Let's get physical.

---

[55] This from six or seven sources from the Internet.

21. Early ecocity pioneer, architect Paul Downton's rooftop garden

Rooftop gardens as social areas are coming on strong in the 2010s after decades of promotion by ecocity activists. Paul was one of the early ones, shown here with the native plants and community picnic table at the Christie Walk project of 30 units, apartment style up to five stories tall. Downtown Adelaide three blocks away is in the background.

Wood – the foundation source of material and energy for civilizations

If we follow the materials and energy flows that underlie nature's economics, "follow the money" as the investigative journalists would say, but in a more basic physical sense, then "our economics built on nature's," becomes a pretty dramatic story – at least I think it does. As the sun pours energy into leaves of plants and they enrich the soil – massively! – thus are the stores of energy built up. The forests represent storage that takes, if cleared, in the temperate zones, one hundred to four or five hundred years to re-accumulate a deep mat of living power all over again: the climax tree cover and all associated with it down often deep into the soil, roots, fungus, insects, worms in enormous total weight and energy – read carbon fixing activity. The forest is, relative to the tribes of people, stunningly immense, apparently endless, the biomass of all animals, in fact, only about 1/1,000 that of the plants.

But as to the endless forests, John Perlin's book[56] *A Forest Journey* recounts their stripping by every civilization that ever existed except where there weren't any forests, and in such places civilization only as far outposts of a distant center. With some efforts by conservationists seeing the full value of the resource and understanding the dynamics of sun and soil, replanting and significant restoration was pursued, and in some cases successfully.

Early on wood was used directly, burned for heat and illumination, going back as far as whatever the controversy eventually comes up with for first use of fire. And of course wood was used as one of our first tools, along with simple rocks, for throwing, prodding, stabbing and whacking. Wood-wise, then there was the stick, then lever and club, then probably the non-wood "hand ax," then spear, then atlatl (two sticks), then bow and arrow (two sticks plus cord)... The first of these go back almost as far as our prehensile hands with opposable thumb, which of course evolved grasping the wooden branches of the trees of the "woods," in which our primate ancestors lived their arboreal lives. In all likelihood the first simple tool was born when one of our proto-human ancestors reached for a dead branch, accidentally broke it off and fell some distance to the ground holding said future tool, aka broken branch, still in hand, noticed some interesting things about striking things with it or perhaps throwing it in anger or maybe frustration from his or her embarrassing, probably painful fall.

Wood and rock again, piled up and maybe with the addition of a little mud and leaves or grass, and arranged to break the wind and provide the simplest of shelter, were also our first building materials of architecture. In thinking of the importance of wood, a side note: it was an unexpected, not altogether unpleasant eventuality for me in my own career in ecocity work, that support for my endeavors in the field was very weak and so I worked in wood like hundreds of millions before me to make my living, to, in my case, keep studying and trying out ecocity experiments in activism and hands-on projects, drawing and writing. I paid my way by working in wood. As many of us with a passion for something else jokingly call it, carpentry was my "day job," wood the material of my deliverance.

By the advent of agriculture, humans had barely taken a chip out of this vast biological storehouse of phytomass – the living and decomposed material of forest trees and other plants, detritus on the forest floor, in carbon-rich peat and in quasi-infinite fragments of organic matter in the dirt itself. But all that was about to change. Once agriculture kicked into serious production in the Mesopotamian Valley and Fertile Crescent, agricultural fields and deserts began peeling back the forests, and

[56] John Perlin, *A Forest Journey – The Role of Wood in the Development of Civilization*, Harvard University Press, published by W. W. Norton & Company, New York, 1989

ever more rapidly, one civilization after another. Viewed time lapse from far above, it would have looked as if a strange vapor spread outward from the centers of civilization dissolving the dark green areas on an ancient Google Earth image and leaving a thin film of low lying yellow green crops or, in many areas, nothing at all but tan, yellow and rust colored sand, dust and barren stone. The civilizations of Mesopotamia, China, Greece, Rome, even the Americas and Australia where the early arrivals used fire to clear and modify the landscape and whose numbers increased rapidly as they pushed the forest back and back.

Agriculture wasn't even necessarily the first assault, though it became the big one for a while and remains gigantic today. Metal production, starting at approximately the same time, largely to make implements that advanced agriculture gave us hoes and plows and don't forget the shovels in China that became our first coins. Also there were real axes, chisels and saws, knives and pots, arrowheads and swords, and on and on. Forests were stripped for wood for heat and light and for melting ore to extract metal, then for heating again to cast or forge metal into implements of various sorts. Between 4,700 and 4,600 years ago copper and gold were mined near the Nile upstream from Egypt in the area called Nubia, now Northern Sudan.[57] The Greeks mined silver at Laurium, providing one of the chief sources of wealth for the Athenian state. Lucretius, a Roman philosopher, thought that wood and mining brought civilization itself. Says Perlin,

> Great fires [Lucretius wrote] "devoured the high forests... and thoroughly heated the earth," smelting metal from rocks embedded in it. When people saw these metals lying on top of the ground, "the thought then came to them," Lucretius continued, "that these pieces could be made liquid by heating and cast into the form and shape of anything, and then by hammering, could be drawn into the form of blades sharp and thin as one pleased, so they might equip themselves with tools..." Tools, in turn, Lucretius remarked, made forestry and carpentry possible, enabling humans "to cut forests, hew timber, smooth, and even fashion it with auger, chisel and gouge." In this fashion, according to Lucretius, civilization emerged.[58]

The Romans reduced the forests of Cypress to straggly remnants mining for copper, the forests of northern Spain for silver, England's for gold, silver, tin, lead and iron. The trees were cut for fuel for heating the ores to melt out the metal. Early mining started with pits in the ground or against slopes or walls where veins of the ores met the surface in a technique called open casting, which was simply building a very hot fire, stoked with wood against the ore surface, melting out metal if possible or getting the surface so hot that when flooded with water, thermal shock would

[57] Wikipedia, http://en.wikipedia.org/wiki/Mining

[58] John Perling, Ibid., p.29

fracture the rock in smaller pieces out of the vein of ore. So loosened, next the material would be dug out and collected, crushed and heated again in a separate fire later to create bars and ingots and then heated yet again to be cast or beaten into shape as various implements and sometimes coins.

In larger operations a process called hushing was employed in which ditches and aqueducts were dug and constructed to bring water to storage dams where it was released suddenly and with enough force to not just shock the stony ore into smaller pieces but flush away the soil covering the ore and help force bits and pieces free, for further breaking, heating and melting. We are accustomed today to think it is next to impossible to find metals, as we wander about various landscapes "in nature." But very early in history, before we humans scoured the surface of the planet a thousand times over and mined anywhere there were hints of metals or other valuable minerals on the surface, perhaps where forest burned, it was likely to come across some shiny, strangely malleable yet very strong stuff that today we call the various metals, just as Lucretias surmised. Maybe, being resistant to erosion, strange dribbley lines survived on the surface and could be found fairly commonly oozing from stone, red orange for copper, reflective mirror called silver, luminous yellow called gold, flat black/gray now lead. These must have struck our ancestors curious.

Techniques developed quickly and people burrowed into hills and pits and eventually pierced the earth's surface entirely with tunnels following the veins of ore ever deeper, in this case requiring more wood for posts and beams to keep the artificial caves from collapsing while digging out the ores. More wood was needed later for carts and wheels, and, to smooth out the rolling surface for the ore carts' wheels, the first tracks being thick planks. These too were usually made of wood, though sometimes of stone and later of metal. In the earlier times, including Roman times, in almost all cases slaves were used for labor and the labor force needed food, some cooked over wood, and housed, if miserably, inside wood.

Coal was known to the Greeks and used as early as 400 BC. Wood in Roman times, in some locations was simply burned to clear forests to get seams of coal and ores, then the coal burned to melt metals from other ores (in addition to coal) ores. I won't even get into charcoal, which is wood burned twice, first in limited available air to drive out almost all but a carbon residual, then a second time to very high temperatures with a clean flame that wood can't otherwise produce and which was necessary for metals with a higher melting point or in making pure metals or carefully mixed alloys. This required even more cutting, sawing, chopping and burning.

Different stages of the process with different actors had different manias for things demanding this vast supply, whether for burning or building. The Romans were famously addicted to hot baths. Earliest glass making was from Mesopotamia turning into a real industry in Constantinople then Venice. Perling tells us that in England many centuries later, glass making demanded so much wood for fuel, its production was for a time banned.

Whether for fire, construction, for delivering services like baths, or making products in style at the time, or raw clearing the surface for energy stores and minerals underneath, in all cases the forests were the losers, that vast store of energy almost as dense (energy available per unit of weight), about 70% as energy dense, as coal itself.[59] All these uses of wood were in fast burn in the European Roman Empire. And then, collapse. Taking Britain as an example, south of Scotland and the Wall of Hadrian, after 410 when the Romans left, mining and tree cutting on any significant scale ceased immediately. People did not resume coal mining for another 800 years. Then on the coast of Scotland, where coal seams were long open because of erosion by waves of the North Sea, very small coal operations started out all over again. That was around the year 1200, about the time of the Magna Carta. South, in England and Wales where the Romans had so thoroughly cleared the forests, the woods were now almost completely reestablished. Then started the next phase of deforestation.

But we can learn from that the lesson of the great productivity of solar energy teamed up with chlorophyll and soil. The Earth is bullish, it does abide. It does regenerate its forests if given a chance. The immense spread of forest was the main energy source by far for the Roman Empire and others before. Add building in wood and fashioning implements of great variety directly and through making things of metals and add the food growing of agriculture, directly in plants and indirectly in animals used for meat, milk, wool and so on, and realize also that all of this can be largely restored when forests have a chance to build soils again. The obvious key to sustainability here and the lesson to learn is to not use too much, to understand limits and the ecological concept of carrying capacity. Just maintaining minimal carrying capacity, however, is the pessimist's compromise with nature. More optimistic, seeing our own human potential to understand and create, there's another lesson: recognizing the immense power of plants and sun to repair the damage of human mismanagement of humanity's economy, if we don't screw up *too* totally. Way beyond taking care to keep nature just a little above minimal carrying capacity, if we allow forests, grasslands and phytomass in waters to thrive, there lies the immense power to actually reverse global heating through natural carbon sequestration.

Meantime society is pouring out the poisons. But here is another positive side, that toxics produced, if small in quantity, very slowly do get disbursed, diluted and absorbed in concentrations harmless to nature and deposited in the sea waters and the bottom of the ocean. There, under accumulating layers of silt it is out of sight, out of mind and out of danger of harming biological systems for millions of years. Environmentalists hate hearing this because they are so carte blanche anti-pollution and for the most part they are very right in the opinion. But the fact remains that off the shores of continental plates where subduction occurs, the materials

[59] Wikipedia, http://en.wikipedia.org/Energy_density, wood about 16.2 megajoules per kilogram, coal about 24 megajoules per kilogram. Best book on the technicalities of energy: *Energy in Nature and Society*, Vaclav Smil, MIT Press, Cambridge, 2008

considered polluting on the surface when more concentrated and associated with living animals and plants, are gradually transformed chemically while sliding deep under continental edges, being acted upon by increasing heat and pressure the deeper they go. Tectonic plates are burying, heating, diluting and detoxifying pretty much all the evil stuff. A small fraction of such material, in six or seven million years, changed considerably in chemical form, will boil and blast up in volcanoes. The vast majority of the material will not be returned to the light of day in this manner but is thrust up as new mountains in tens or hundreds of millions of years later in sedimentary or metamorphic rock to be worn away in the tens of millions to billions of years, back to the sea, diluted to insignificance.

The lesson here is that the planet does actually give us a little grace in the usually joke line formula once mentioned already "the solution to pollution is dilution," but only in an extremely small degree relative to the rate humans are currently putting waste and pollution into the soil. But citing the various positives adds to the notion that we do have some cards in our hands if we get ambitious about helping, and if you hear, "It's far too late to reverse climate change or realistically prevent most extinctions," think again.

And here's another thought: There is an organization called One Planet Living which advocates that humans not take more than their share, leaving for nature enough to thrive as well. I'm proposing half planet living to claim only about half of what we think our maximum might be, to give nature the slack it needs should our calculations be a bit off, to play it safe, to dedicate ourselves to better than just fair play for the other life forms and have the magnanimity and grace to actually give something, be generous, to learn at least that much from Gift Economics and the entire gift of nature's economics to us humans.

Industry, Phase 3, comes steaming in

Why industry, phase 3? Remember the "hand ax"? Society settled in on a certain form, having perfected the basic hand ax – Industry Phase 1 – and stayed there for an amazing 1.7 million years, give or take a hundred thousand or so. Then at a certain point an Industry Phase 2 started and hundreds of new tools poured forth from a new "basic tools" mindset: spears, arrows, pottery, baskets, items of clothing, needles, fish hooks, string for fishing line, bows and clothes and fire makers. Then ropes for leading animals around, plows, fences, buildings, Phase 2 being part of and support for Agriculture... Industry Phase 3 would be what we normally think of as the Industrial Revolution to now, machines being very complex tools, generally with multiple usually moving parts, part and parcel of yet another mind set, each machine something like a complex living organism, something like the integrated whole that is the city itself, home of the machine and machine maker and that which enabled their success.

I mention all this because it might stand as a wake up lesson for our own stuck-in-the-growth-economics-notion of ever expanding mass/energy machine based industry, even hyper complex and subtle machines like computers when what we need now is Industrialism Phase 4, the ecological industrial revolution that shrinks for prosperity after strategic proportionalizing and prioritization. That in turn means another mind set required, like the post hand ax mindset that liberated people into countless tools and products that were, in another step, magnified by machines and intense fuels and have now produced our bloated and largely nonsensical and destructive artifact list. The next mind set may be defined by miniaturization, as suggested by de Chardin – miniplexion – as suggested by they hyper miniaturization characteristic of advanced electronics and by the need to "shrink for prosperity," the sustainability mandate, you might say. Those three signposts provide a crucial guidance – all in the same direction – for the next phase of "industrialization." Maybe Bucky Fuller said it best in saying we could "do more with less." ("Less is more" which we hear once in a while is more poetic, less really clear and rational, but what the hell…)

Be all that as it may be, and back to our narrative, looking at technology now, what's commonly called the Industrial Revolution really takes off moving from wood and basic mining to coal with innovations in transport and machinery. The first "rail roads" date back to ancient Greece. Wikipedia's rendition of the period starts with the following:

> The earliest evidence of a wagonway, a predecessor of the railway, found so far was the 6 to 8.5 km long Diolkos wagonway, which transported boats across the Isthmus of Corinth in Greece since around 600 BC. Wheeled vehicles pulled by men and animals ran in grooves in limestone, which provided the track element, preventing the wagons from leaving the intended route. The Diolkos was in use for over 650 years.[60]

Wagonways began appearing more commonly in Germany around 1550, made of wooden planks tied together with wooden "ties," so that wagons, made also of wood, could be pulled smoothly over the ground by horses. These rails made roads passable in the muddy winter season for carts carrying coal, wood and metal ores about the mines and to distribution points, whereas before, carts would sink to their axles in icy mud and the mines had to close down for the soggy seasons. By the late 1700s stone and iron had largely replaced wood rails around Europe with wagons still powered by horses and still used in mining areas for heavy loads of ore, metal or coal. The rails usually had directing grooves like those the Diolkos. This all changed when in 1789 Englishman Thomas Jessup devised the flange on the wheel, one on the inside edge of each wheel, to keep the vehicle literally on track and keep

[60] Wilipedia's history of railways, further citings therein: http://en.wikipedia.org/wiki/History_of_rail_transport

the amount of material comprising the track, now iron, to a minimum for the job. This innovation quickly became the standard and remains so as a glance at any but a levitation train or monorail reveals today.[61]

In 1712 the first steam engine was made by blacksmith Thomas Newcomen in England to pump water out of mines. James Watt, Scottish inventor, is often cited as the father of the steam engine. Though he improved greatly on Newcomen's machine he didn't have first claim to the basic idea. Watt's career, during which he made many incremental improvements, spanned from about 1775 to 1819. In 1802 Richard Trevithick put a steam engine on a wagon, creating the first locomotive. Many incremental steps followed: published visions of how a new system of rails and steam locomotives could link cities – the science fiction of the times – starting with Englishman William James and American Oliver Evans, both around 1810, began creating a climate of interest, even excitement like the imagery of space exploration in the 1950s of illustrator Chesteley Bonestell that helped inspire the commitment to go to – that got to – the moon. (I'm an inheritor of that tradition with my attempts, through writing and drawing, to create interest in a revolutionary, new type of city that aspires to bring space age science fiction down to a practical grounding here on Earth.)

By 1829, a 35-mile rail line connecting Manchester and Liverpool was built for freight. But the public wanted in on the deal and the railway owners began making money hauling passengers as well. Soon railroads were expanding all over England and, shortly after, spreading across the United States and Europe.

Looking at industrialization in general, and in sync with the railroads in the total orchestration of the Industrial Revolution, factories were shifting from animal, water and some wind power to wood and coal powered steam machines – cotton spinning machines and looms for making cloth, for example. The cotton gin had productive precursors to American Eli Whitney's machine, though in most histories he is credited with its invention. Technically, in 1794 he patented the device in the United States but various devices were used in China, India and the Middle East for similar if less efficient effect for the job hundreds of years earlier.

Caribbean cotton gins ("gin" is short for engine) with foot-powered treadle and flywheel for smooth, steady action were already putting out 25 to 40 pounds of cleaned cotton a day with the power of a single person, a vast improvement over simpler tools and hand separation. [62] But Whitney's gin was so simple that small operators could copy and modify it slightly, both manufacturers in competition with

[61] Just as a note here: this section of wood, coal, mining and inventions comes mainly from *A Forest Journey* and many sources from the internet, glued together in so many small pieces it makes little sense trying to credit each factoid.

[62] Real cotton gin inventors... The site I'll mention is a very interesting review of a book by Angela Lakwete, *Inventing the Cotton Gin: Machine and Myth in Antebellum America*, Johns Hopkins University Press, Baltimore and London, 2003: http://www.h-net.org/reviews/showrev.php?id=9530

Whitney and farmers building their own do-it-yourself gins. The effect was enormous as gins replicated across the south, as old farms and new territory were turned into cotton plantations. Around 1800, a person could turn out 120 pounds a day. By the 1850s one large capacity steam powered gin could turn out five or six bales a day, an increase from 1800 to 1850 of 29 times over.[63] Whereas slavery was sliding away in 1800, the gin became a "gin" of another sort: an economic engine that reinvigorated and greatly expanded the slave-based economy of the US South. This in turn became one of the reasons for both the war launched by the United States against Mexico, known in the US as the Mexican-American War of 1846 – 1848, and the US Civil War. In both cases the industrial north feared the spread of the South's economic power and slavery – both linked to cotton now – through the hot weather states from Texas all the way to the Pacific. Nationalist desire for simple territorial expansion was another major cause, and both plantation economy south and industrial economy north wanted as many of the new states in their camp as possible. *Whose* manifest destiny was it to be?

[63] Cotton gin economic history at: http://eh.net/encyclopedia/article/phillips.cottongin

22. Ataturk and young Turk at Istanbul's Grand Bazar (Previous page)

Another of the photographs I like just because of the juxtapositions one gets in special urban places, and for the happenstance composition of the image. Ataturk was the father of modern Turkey and a hero there like Washington, Jefferson and Lincoln are in the United States all rolled into one.

The physical economic component

In my rendition of this period why emphasize sunshine and soil, minerals, air and water chemically squeezed, as it were, through chlorophyll into vast sheets of forest teaming with life and deep beds of fossil fuels that used to be solar energy-powered protoplasm? Why dwell on details of the cutting and burning of forests, and the burning of coal in this super skinny history of the preindustrial city society and mercantilism next heading into industrialist monopoly capitalist/organized labor trust-busting times? The answer is that I'd like to build up a sense of society's economics evolving as a physical and cultural series of changes interrelated and happening roughly simultaneously and these descending from nature's economics, nature's flows of energy, materials, products and recycling. I want readers to almost feel the physicalness of it all. Then maybe the physical and the cultural can be seen as linking increased production and consumption with a growing pressure for democracy from spreading and elaborating knowledge and capital economics from evolving systems of production and exchange. Remember that's capital economics, not capitalist, economics with deep involvement of the neutral medium of exchange that followed gift economics when the cultural artifact list became otherwise unmanageably long.

The expanding "artifact list," a terminology I think one can also actually "get your hands on," a changing quantitative condition requiring a qualitative shift, is a crucial element in this evolution. In this pattern the phase changes, the real leaps forward, are often brought on by the physical spark of a brilliant new insight. (As you might guess, I think the ecocity is another such insight.) Here's a big one in early times: imagine what it was like to see just after a forest fire a glistening stream of hard metal that had run out of the face of a steep rock slope. As Mr. Lucretius said: "...that these pieces could be made liquid by heating and cast into the form and shape of anything, and then by hammering, could be drawn into the form of blades sharp and thin as one pleased, so they might equip themselves with tools..."

This particular, very physical image contrasts almost stunningly with the broad generalizations in this book, mercantilism sliding into industrial capitalism, for example. Jane Jacob's construct of takers and traders, as much as I admire and feature it and feel it is both useful and in many ways profound, doesn't adequately deal with the creative, the new spark of discovery and invention, the emergence of the new in evolution. We need to emphasize that too.

Also, the broad brushstrokes of religion changing along with political structure, ancestors becoming gods and gods becoming God while patriarchs turn into princes then kings, maybe tending into great transnational corporations, is another pattern of general change through time similar to biological evolution. Shifting economic theory is another, away from the practical of everyday life into abstract theory and deep into the mathematical formulas of game theory in neoclassical capitalism that win Faux Nobel Prizes in Economics and help produce disasters like Milton Friedman and the derivatives obsession that contributed mightily to the Financial Crisis of 2008. If the connections don't hold with some relevance, legitimacy, or accurateness of generalization, then the more abstract levels can conceal rather than reveal. And if "the truth shall make us free" or at least give us best options for solving our problems, then keeping the connectors honest between the physical small realities and the larger generalizations and principles is very important. In something as powerful as economics, getting those connectors wrong and devising the wrong formulas on the abstract side could be a mistake as big as losing most of the world most of us have come to love.

Economists John Maynard Keynes and John Kenneth Galbraith saw aggregate demand as particularly important, like the enormous drift of, say, the Gulf Stream in the Atlantic Ocean – aggregate flow you might say – for the whole North

Atlantic. Aggregate demand is pretty much like what it sounds like it is, the consumers, or buyers side of GDP, gross domestic product, all added up. It's the sum total of what consumers demand and express by buying something. Total supply would be the other side, the producers side of GDP, GDP being a measure of all that crosses that exchange divide between producing and consuming, figured in monetary measure of total activity. Keynes believed governments could and should manipulate aggregate demand to produce full employment (among the many other things they should do). Controlling large general patterns by raising or lowering interest rates on loans across whole countries, manipulating protective tariffs for attempting national prosperity and so on – all these are grist for economists trying to make their whole big oceans of macroeconomic flows, healthy. And this discussion leads into Adam Smith, generally held to be the father of modern capitalist economics, appearing in late mercantile times, maybe the first to make a serious, in depth study and analysis of what worked and didn't in effecting these larger flows of wealth between and within nations.

Adam Smith and self-organizing systems

I lead into thinking about Adam Smith, 1723 – 1790, in this way because one of his chief concerns was that something was wrong with the mercantile notion of highest possible importance was, in each country, always to turn a net gain in relation to other countries, the idea that you always had to sell more than buy to have a steady influx of wealth for your country and thus generally to its inhabitants, especially its elite, among which he was one, that is, a property owner with a little leisure and time to think his thoughts and write them down. No everyday farmer or blacksmith had such luxury and supportive literate environment. What I'd like to suggest is that he may well have had, as the key insight, that all this growth oriented thinking, focused largely on the national gold and silver amassing of mercantilism, was not so healthy and needed a whole lot more subtlety, a much more valid connection to physical reality, to get at what really was healthy. Maybe there was a disconnect between this large generalization called a positive balance of trade – *for us* – at the heart of mercantilism and the way economics really should work or actually did work (in the last half of the 1700s). Maybe he thought his contemporaries didn't really get economics but with an effort such as his, could. Perhaps also in looking at the larger patterns, the aggregate flows, Smith might well have felt the same discomfort looking at the balance of trade growth-fanatical economics of his time that some of us today feel looking at the growth-fanatical GDP economics of our time. Maybe Smith's eyes were the X-ray vision to see through the political games and power manipulation, the self centered interest in obfuscating, keeping secrets and even lying about the real dynamics of the economy to keep most of the powerful players in the game powerful or getting more powerful all the time.

I'm particularly suspicious this is the case because then, like now, there was an enormous silence in economic thinking (at least in my readings trying to look into these things over the last two years) regarding the role of the violence of warfare in the game, just plain killing and stealing to maximize the inward flow of wealth to *our side*. Study the cutting of forests and you find that the end point of the investment in divesting the forest of its trees was very largely in making ships for navies and burning wood for melting metal for enormously heavy cannon to take the bloodiest line straight to net positive imports of mercantilist value: simply stolen. Sometimes the royal forests were cut down in large parcels to sell to builders to help raise money for war. That other countries did exactly the same thing justified this extraordinarily bad habit maximizing positive balance of "trade." It was an especially bad habit from the point of view of sailors shanghaied after drinking a little too much at the neighborhood pub to wake up on one of the battleships of their day far out at sea.

Income from this harsh but lucrative edge of the national economy – piracy, pillaging in war, "preemptive strikes," etc. – of England and the other European nations Smith was studying, which were engaged in colonialism and almost constant nationalist wars, was perhaps something of the icing on the cake, and I'd suppose he didn't deal with it much (as far as my reading discovered) because it would have touched a raw nerve in politics and especially in his class that believed it collected wealth from the process and deserved it. I further suspect that the threat of force and its ability to swell national treasuries, either directly or by taxing the profits from those investing in piracy was to defend the more mundane flows of profitable trade, the steady massive flows that constituted the bulk of the "cake" for which the spoils of war was "icing."

So Smith dealt with most of the system by looking at internal exchange and foreign trade, the largest flows around, the less bellicose dynamics of production, exchange and consumption at home and with trading partners. To genuinely sort out whether this is a mistake or not, that perhaps the real deal was the constant warfare, I'll only suggest here might turn up some nasty surprises that might apply as well today as then. Maybe the gun, even more than the gold, was then and is now the true but unacknowledged key to maximum leverage for material wealth and power, for both earlier mercantile kingdoms and later capitalist empires alike. I don't know; I only raise the question.

In any case, looking at some of Adam Smith's ideas proves very interesting for thinking through much that is right or wrong, leading toward health and happiness or dysfunction and misery, in today's economic circumstances.

Probably his most famous observation was that the market place buzzed along setting its own prices and optimizing the effectiveness of everyone's role in the market. That appropriate range of prices would be about as little as a producer or deliverer of services could charge considering his or her costs plus a reasonable profit to live on and save a little, and as much as the buyer would be willing to pay for the item or service desired in the exchange. Go too low or too high and one or the other party would be unwilling or simply unable to make the deal.

Today we might call the market economy a self-organizing complex whole system. And the whole thing could be seen as emergent from its circumstances of resource base and number of players and products. With enough participants – those trading – and enough components shifting about – the exchanges themselves of products and services – the system guides itself. In physics this is called an emergent phenomenon and among the countless examples, Robert Laughlin in *A Different Universe – Reinventing Physics from the Bottom Down*[64] points out that there isn't the slightest indication in an atom of the iron compound called magnetite that can be measured or theorized to predict that when many of the atoms come together a magnet with the power to attract iron would result, but result it does, as trade phenomena like price setting does with enough people participating. It takes two to tango, and in these cases, the power of the magnet and the power of the market, quite a few more, though exactly how many, who knows?

Smith's often quoted line from his book *The Wealth of Nations* published in 1776, the same year another history-changing revolution was being launched, was: "By directing that industry in such a manner as its produce may be of greatest value, he intends only his own gain, and he is in this, as in many other cases, led by an invisible hand to promote an end which was no part of his intention." This was the insight to launch the abandonment of mercantilism and adoption of something being refined (or obfuscated) to this day: capitalism. The "end which was no part of his intention," of course, was the harmonious workings of the market for the smooth running and general benefit of society.

When Smith says "... he intends only his own gain," however, he is himself exaggerating his own larger meaning because he acknowledges elsewhere a great interest in "the other" as well as "the self." In fact, "...he (who) intends only his own gain" actually intends the gain of his wife and children too, and maybe a circle of friends he invites over for roast beef, good grog and heavy bread, plus the gain in satisfying services of whomever he sells his products to. The myth, in other words, to launch *that* revolution, starts off with an exaggeration, a one-sided preference in the first "game theory" of capitalism that's way short of the whole story. Most capitalists ever since have exaggerated on the "self" side and extended the exaggeration to say that only self-interest in the final analysis (whatever "final analysis" is supposed to mean) exists or is necessary for the collective good.

Adam Smith's sentence might mean essentially that centrally planned maximization of growth – controlled by kings and their advisors in the mercantile system of his day and more generally interpreted as regulation by governments today – is not as useful, powerful, meaningful and healthy as the mysterious forces of the market organizing itself, Robert Laughlin's "emergence".

The insight is as deep in my opinion as recognizing that self-organizing systems happen, including language and complex ecological systems themselves – and

[64] Robert Laughlin, *A Different Universe – Reinventing Physics from the Bottom Down*, Basic Books, New York, 2005

within them, living organisms. The insight – "unseen hand" – implies that self-organizing is basic, "happens," is in the nature of the dynamic continuities in evolution through all time. What do self-organizing systems do? They create emergent phenomenon. It says something important of the similar dynamics of language forming itself as people in large numbers use it, a comparison I've mentioned earlier. No individual or committee says, "let's make up a language" and does just that. No organism says, "I think sharp teeth for cutting are better than flat ones for grinding – think I'll grow those." No bioregion says, "I think I'll put the big trees on the top of the ridge where it rains a lot and the trout in the rivers that flow down the up-wind side and the cactuses on the down-wind side." It just "evolves" or "emerges" like that because of some mysterious internal way the changing universe with its changeless laws, including new ones, evolves.

The physical arrangement of cities has been something of a self-organizing system, too. Villages organized themselves by collective tradition over many generations, like language, and got the multiple basic functions together in general physical arrangements that were elaborated into cities at later dates. The professions of urban planners and designers were called into action later in the evolution of the built community only relatively recently to try to discipline cities into shapes and functions that would avoid worst problems and provide better services as people came to understand city dynamics better – or think they did. Though you could complement the planners for the effort, it seems they obviously misunderstood more than they understood, and that is proved true in the colossally destructive rise of the city dominated by automobiles and its real planners: everyone who, without knowing or wanting to know what kind of forces for damage they were causing, bought into that particular layout and associated set of businesses, professions, government functions and lifestyles when they bought or manufactured, fueled, insured and maintained their cars. The most effective participants in shaping the automobile city – owner/managers of car companies and oil companies, developers and real estate agents, the makers of movies and writers of ads glamorizing cars and the drivers themselves – were only vaguely aware of what they were creating as the new city in the way a person fluent in English but having never had a class in English might be unaware of the structures of grammar and the tricks of rhetoric, something like, as they say, a centipede walks without thinking about it and would probably be in trouble if it tried thinking about it. When Paolo Soleri spoke to audiences in Los Angeles, which included me, back in the mid 1960s, when he talked about the changing structure of the city, the role of cars and low-density development as contrasted with the more compact and functionally diverse pedestrian city, the collective shrug of the shoulders left him with practically no support from then through the rest of his long life. In both cases, while creating the system the agent of that creation, those speaking the developing language and those building the developing city, didn't really understand what they were creating. Thus the form of Los Angeles and the cities it reshaped worldwide. The city self-organized itself more than by people.

Ecological systems, too, are self-organizing systems finding the optimum number and pattern of organization of participants – living organisms – for any dynamically balanced (changing but within certain parameters true to ecological principles) ecosystem and bioregion. No animal is planning its future, its long-term relationship to its environment, much less designing its ecosystem. As the price of exchange in economics is the action edge between seller and buyer in the market, one species eating another, whether predator or disease microbe, is the action edge of ecological balances, whether munching them raw, alive or dead, preparing them in tasty meals with sauces, spices and wine or by scavenging or decomposing the other species. In both cases, economic and ecological, physical flows of material and energy are in aggregate mainly self-regulating at the point of exchange, and number or quantity relationships figure in to determine "value" or "price." The "price" of a certain weight of vegetables, for example, is about one tenth that of a living animal in material and energy terms. That is, it takes about ten times the weight of a steer in vegetable matter to produce a steak from the steer itself as compared to eating vegetable protein, minerals, vitamin, sugars, fats, etc. This has definite implications about number of individuals of a species, or more usefully understood perhaps, amount of biomass transfer, required relative to another species in the exchanges called eating.[65] This has everything to do with "biocapacity" and the closely related notion of "carrying capacity" – and "overshoot" when biocapacity is exceeded, carrying capacity violated. Then the number of species being carried collapses, rarely but sometimes to extinction.

Another example of measuring such relationships and getting a sense of proportion about them, from island biogeography, a subset of ecology and evolution studies: it takes about ten times the land area to produce a doubling of number of species that an isolated island or isolated mountain system can host. In economics this is similar to the role of scarcity or abundance of particular resources and population skill bases available for production and services in a geographic area – the extent of which produces variables to trade too, longer arms of trade being more expense in transportation fuel, dangers en route, etc., demanding higher ultimate price, or if not achieved, less trade in the particular item or a ceasing of trade in the item altogether. Later we will see how interesting mathematical general patterns like this became wonderfully impressive, a kind of esthetic in their own world, but became illegitimate for general conclusions in neoclassical capitalist economics when the "medium" (complex math and game theory + belief in previously-established dogma) overtakes real observation – the "message", the "content", and unpredictability of human participation in the enthusiasms and panics of economics. I'm talking 2008.

Not so selfish after all

Back to Adam Smith. Smith was clear that self-interest was dominant over charity in practical market transactions and probably in virtually all transactions between people outside circles of family, friends and groups of special personal interest, post gift societies, that is. I find the following quote a little easer to read in our times than the invisible hand one: "It is not from the benevolence of the butcher, the brewer, or the baker, that we can expect our dinner, but from their regard to their own interest."[66] Yes, but, you could say, if not also in the interest of the customer, no sale and eventually bye-bye to Smith's business or Smith himself if he persists in satisfying only himself in his transactions.

Smith's influence on capitalism tended, though, and as suggested earlier, to an exaggeration, almost certainly to support the self-interest of the wealthy, comfortable and powerful, the class of which he was a secure member. His recognized self-interest is primary, but failed to mentioned by his followers, that it is not *sufficient* for a prosperous economy. His formula did, however, provide a rationale for the wealthy powerful class's desires for ever more and more and more.

In his book *The Theory of Moral Sentiments*, Smith equivocates his famous *Wealth of Nations* saying, "How selfish soever man may be supposed, there are evidently some principles in his nature which interest him in the fortune of others and render their happiness necessary to him though he derives nothing from it except the pleasure of seeing it." Wow, from Adam Smith is that not wonderful? How, or better, *why* did later capitalists miss that one? (More money in the other?)

In a similar vein he said in *The Wealth of Nations*, "Man has almost constant occasion for the help of his brethren, and it is in vain for him to expect it from their benevolence only." But from their benevolence somewhat and more so their self-interest because we are all connected and need a community and the community needs mates to reproduce the species. We can notice that he does not leave out benevolence but only says you can't imagine society operating economically with benevolence only. But who would suppose that?! Here we have an economist, some would say the first, in a wild, extreme exaggeration.

[66] My information on Adam Smith comes from several books, but here I'm using a concise collection of good summaries from the Library of Economics and Liberty at http://www.econlib.org/library/Enc/bios/Smith.html

23. Stars over country ecotown center

No cars, no vast scattering of streetlights, no smog, and the stars come out.

We need to think in terms of sequence: for individual animals trying to keep themselves alive, each has to be number one. That's why on the airplane the safety announcement at the beginning of the flight tells you, "In the event of a loss of cabin pressure, when the oxygen mask drops down from the overhead, put your mask on first before helping others." There's a reasonable sequence here. Step one does not assume not taking step two. In fact in many cases it's the first step for something more important, even maybe saving your child or your whole family in an emergency, getting ready to do the best you can with altruism, absolutely natural to the species, and many other species too for that matter.

So, as with most religious texts, appropriate to the genre which economic "scientists" buy into, Smith's revelations are contradictory yet broadly inclusive leaving it to the believer to select what he or she believes to be true or, and especially in the theory of economists and among them, profitable.

Those who interpreted Smith in the selfish exclusive – and it got worse with "social Darwinism" around 100 years later – were like people imagining driving a car with an accelerator but no breaks. Skip the regulators, full speed ahead – which is a little dangerous and has led to many ever so well documented and later ignored economic crashes, just as car crashes ensue when breaks fail on automobiles or someone in panic hits the accelerator instead of break pedal.

Driving as fast as you can and insisting you don't need breaks – now that's nuts! There were 19th century bank runs and big crashes in1929, 2008 and others, local, regional and world in scale. You'd think economists, who study economics, would learn. True, the function of the automobile is to move about and that doesn't happen without power for locomotion, which is the main point of cars, controlled by the accelerator pedal and in some ways analogous to working for self-interest, that is, the power for the main thrust forward. "Specialty" driving can move backward when adjustments need to be made, as in parallel parking or backing out of a driveway, or say when a company downsizes for a changed strategy or an investor sells some stock for bolstering something else with his or her capital. But there is the other part of the economics formula which is that there are other forces at work in the other direction, namely in the case of altruism, real giving, in addition to occasional restrains on forward movement for various reasons of reasonable control.

In trade you might just think of it as something kind of friendly going on when caring about others and being concerned that what you sell benefits me, the one "making the sale," *and* that the thing or service sold really is a benefit, similar to a gift, to the one making the purchase. Pride in craftsmanship, that the person using the product enjoys and gets real benefit from the item or service purchased and understands its quality, or the rosy warm feeling that in all this exchange one is part of a community is hardly a stranger to exchange and is not strictly self-serving. Altruism can be an outright gift to your baby, your mother, your lover, or even as faux "abstractly" to your society, as attempted by people who work hard for peace, for example, and aren't even among those risking to be in front of the reporters' cameras, who are often accused of ego games. Or an anonymous outright gift to the needy, the young, or some other species as seen in those donating to social justice or environmental organizations? In the more pure altruism, it comes back to benefit the altruistic person in simply delivering a happier, healthier world to live in. As David Graber said, linking giver and receiver in an earlier quote in this book, p 136, "...it was very difficult to conceive of a gift that did not benefit the giver in any way. Even an entirely selfless act would win one points with God."

Aggregate benefit and happiness, call it, in rough rhetorical sympathy with Keynes' and Galbriath's aggregate demand. If that is seen as something basically selfish, the person seeing is as through dark gray glasses, as generous, through rose colored lens. It's simply in the eye of the beholder – or maybe a social filter called collective consensus, maybe social pressure, maybe threat of being fired. There are the more cynical acts of altruism too, the establishment of foundations to clean up a company's image with a small fraction of its earnings increased by resulting public misconception, for example. But overall, the exchange for both self-interest and for benefit to others can, and often does, benefit all.

To wind up these particular thoughts about Adam Smith's contributions we should list a few more items than just his free market construct and reasonable restraints on it: 1.) He opposed mercantilism vigorously, favoring trade without tariffs or only small ones, presaging today's "globalism" and influencing future free-trade economists from David Ricardo to Ronald Reagan, Bill Clinton and beyond, 2.); He explicitly saw that government regulation was necessary from issuing patents to encourage innovation, enforcing contracts when disputes arose and through proper taxes and other regulations – the breaks as well as the accelerators of economics – 3.); He felt that government initiative to build public works like roads and establish a justice system with courts and police was necessary and proper, and 4.); He did factor in war as often a major drain on the economy even if other of his themes were either stronger or more broadly reported and debated. (How much he factored in the other side of the ledger, the value of the spoils, slaves and indirect income, or if he factored in these things at all, I have to admit I don't know yet.) 5.); And lastly I'll mention his rejection of gold and silver in the national treasury as the measure of ultimate wealth in favor of the work it takes to make things and deliver services. The traditional Chinese, incidentally, called this the difference between "stagnant wealth" and "flowing wealth," a summation I think Smith might have approved of.

This gets as basic as the very first sentence – and he must have very consciously taken that as important – in his book the full title of which is, *An Inquiry into the Nature and Causes of the Wealth of Nations*. His first sentence therein is: "The annual labor of every nation is the fund which originally supplies it with all the necessities and conveniences of life which it annually consumes and which consists always either in the immediate produce of that labor or in what is purchased with the produce from other nations." Did you notice the role of "labor"? Marx's labor basis of value? Was iconic Smith ironically father of socialism as well as capitalism? Maybe I'm grasping at threads but I wonder…

Overall, said one of Smith's students about the time *The Wealth of Nations* saw print, Smith was actually less interested in economics than in several other subjects, which the student, John Millar, listed in order of Smith's pleasure:

- natural theology first,
- then ethics,
- then jurisprudence and
- lastly, economics.

I'll mention one last contribution: he saw the main cause of prosperity as the increasing division of labor and I see this as directly related to the increasing length of the artifact list, which demands the specialized labor base and powerfully influences the population of cities. I'll be amending that later to say the artifact list itself can go from reasonable to the absurd, from healthy to destructive, in its particular times and that has a lot to do with prosperity.

Changing thinking while capitalism was emerging

Long time ago, going back to the Renaissance, back to Leonardo da Vinci's times, thinking was opening up in Europe close to one thousand years after the collapse of Rome and after the very long intellectual chill that followed, opening up ever so slowly. Leonardo (1452 – 1519) knew freedom of thinking in his world had to progress cautiously. He wasn't only measured in how much of his really radical thinking he put forward but kept much rigorously secret. He knew the Catholic Church killed people in incredibly painful ways whose thinking they did not approve. He was successful enough to have solid patronage most of his life, that is money and respect enough to have a studio closed off and accepted as a kind of privileged refuge for a national treasure or city state treasure at least: Leonardo himself, the genius artist inventor, not theological rebel.

As for Aristotle, who lived approximately 1,800 years before Leonardo, he was regarded among Leonardo's contemporaries bold enough to engage in philosophical and scientific thinking, as the highest authority. This is probably largely because Aristotle imagined the world as immutable, just like the Church liked it, though with the church's addition of the notion that the world was all created at once, or at least in six days with a day for rest. Aristotle wasn't famous for saying how it all came about, just that it looked much like this and such and was pretty much unchanging in its list of species, characteristics of minerals and energies and laws of relationship between all aspects of reality. Everything had its proper place in the ranked and filed Great Chain of Being, every human and creature a proper station in life with options limited by higher law and order. After him and for adopting his immutable universe, the curious and creative could begin a new wave of investigation of the natural world without (at first anyway) challenging Church authority.

One almost off handed observation of Leonardo's – or maybe he just wanted it to look that way, and it wasn't noticed for centuries – was that fossil fish and shellfish in the rocks in the Italian highlands must have been living creatures very long ago buried in the Ocean floor. He had seen layers of silt deposited by any old delta in any body of water from major river deltas in the ocean to tiny deltas in a puddle where a small trickle might enter and deposit sand and mud in the familiar (to him) fan shape. The layers of sediment from river systems containing the bones of the fish and other creatures must have been buried in the silt and must have been turned to stone and lifted up over very long periods of time, elevating the fossils into the mountains. Volia! Evolution and basic geology all in one observation. The church didn't have to hear the news. And it didn't gain general acceptance for another approximately 250 years.

Next in loosening up ideas about evolution in particular and the natural sciences in general, oddly enough, we'll mention Sir Walter Raleigh (1552 – 1618) famed explorer, naval commander and consummate risk taker, though not everyone was listening to him either. Raleigh was thrown in prison, accused of taking part in a conspiracy to assassinate King James I, who followed Queen Elizabeth I. He wasn't proven to have been involved and was later released so that he could continue his explorations in the waters around South America. But while incarcerated he wrote an ambitiously, some would say grandiosely titled book *The History of the World*. In it he noted he was a ship's captain and sailed the most advanced ships imagined to have ever existed and there was no way Noah could have gotten all those animals into any ship, especially ships inferior to his, which, presumably, much earlier ships had to be. Maybe all of the animals in a couple miles of Noah's neighborhood, maybe aboard a surprisingly enormous boat, but certainly not all those animals in the rest of the world, and he knew a lot about the animals as well as ships because he had seen many in that rest of the world, many more than any churchmen back home. Because the animals looked similar but substantially different at the same time, he said animals must have escaped the flood and migrated all around the world, changing over long periods of time – flexible thinking, evolutionary thinking.

Adam Smith was a contemporary of Erasmus Darwin, Charles Darwin's grandfather. Eight years older than Smith, Erasmus was already producing evolutionary theory in the hard-to-decipher stanzas of his poems in discussion in intellectual circles of the time and place. They thought his writing was normal. By those days, the days of the emergence of capitalism and the place being Western Europe, thinking was getting far more flexible, Linnaeus, born 14 years before Smith, was meticulously classifying plants and animals, carefully emphasizing the immutability of species in conformity with Bible scriptures, which he said he believed in with complete confidence. By the time Smith was writing, Linnaeus was established as the absolute authority on classification of species taken to be in total support of the biblical start-at-once never-changing list of species, aka "special creation." Late in his career one of his students brought him an innocuous flower quite familiar, a *linaria* or toadflax. It had five spurs, not one. He called it a monstrosity, a one-off freak – freaks did happen once in a while – classificationally speaking, so what? Everyone had run into a freak or two. They were something like somehow wounded individuals, healed in weird ways and often still functional, unique, an exception, incapable or reproducing their monstrousness in offspring, not to be taken seriously by theory enshrined in natural law. Then the little toadflax proceeded to reproduce further five-spurred flowers.

Linnaeus was deeply troubled. When evidence also arose that species in some circumstance would crossbreed and produce something new, a hybrid that began flouting it's difference like it might be a new species, he became even more agitated and depressed. Finally, with the courage of the true scientist, "He now made a complete break with his previous confession of faith. 'Life originated at a single initial point from which creation began and gradually spread.' This was pure evolutionary theory, fifty years before Lamarck and a hundred years before Darwin." Herbert Went in his book *In Search of Adam – The story of man's quest for the truth about his earliest ancestors* continues: Linnaeus was expecting a firestorm of criticism for such a 180 degree turn around, but… "He was not mocked, nor applauded. The experts simply ignored his revolutionary statements. They loved and admired the Linnaeus of 1735, the systematizer. They could make neither head nor tail of the skeptic of 1759. That authority of the Classifier of Nature had become so great that no one, not even himself, could challenge it."[67]

But the cat was out of the bag. The intellectual drift was toward opening minds and serious speculation about practically everything. Something was wrong with, or at least misunderstood and poorly directed, about the economics construct of the monarchy-commanded nationalistic mercantile system that capitalism was beginning to emerge from. That flexibility of thinking etching away at the old was based largely on the advances of science, but probably even more so, on what science delivered in terms of the products and services. More convincing than the scientific method were probably the new inventions, engineering and ultimately in the experience of people in the times, that expanding artifact list, increasing aggregate *stuff* you could get your hands on, work, play and live with. The branch of science most profoundly flexible – evolution studies and theory, which confronted what most people thought of as Christian theology and Aristotle's code of permanence – was just lurking in the background as far as economic forces were concerned.

But maybe not. The literature is replete with all sorts of people in Europe from the 1700s on delighting in digging up fossils and collecting beetles, many of them "churchmen" and "amateur naturalists" and wondering why on Earth they thought *that* – digging up fossils and collecting beetles – was so damn interesting. If potentially troublingly "scientific," they at least had the excuse that they were exploring God's Creation, with all due respect, even awe and reverence, "reverence for life" as Christian missionary, doctor, philosopher Albert Schweitzer one hundred or so years later called it and made the theme of his life's work. Maybe thinking about economics just had to be stirring because of something we might think of as a general growing aggregate demand for satisfying human curiosity. We can note children's innate curiosity – reigned in by parents in a dangerous world "for their own good" – repressed by dogmatic patriarchs to maintain home rule of law and order. But what if the world becomes more prosperous and secure? Repression of curiosity becomes harder to rationalize.

[67] Herbert Went, *In Search of Adam* – The story of man's quest for the truth about his earliest ancestors, Houghton Mifflin Company, Boston, 1956, p.72

Meantime also sympathies for people, "We the People," the democratic impulse, the belief we are all valuable – was no doubt stimulated by ever more people being empowered not just by slowly increasing security and prosperity but also literacy. If economist theorists could talk about "aggregate demand," how about "aggregate prosperity?" complemented by the communications revolution of the time: books. That sets the stage for feelings of righteous rights all the way to fair sharing. The poor and dispossessed just logically *had* to have inherent rights (plus Jesus said so).

The Christian tradition itself, by giving high value to the individual and direct contact with the Deity through prayer, even entrance into Heaven, had helped sow the seeds of open-minded democracy and individual rights to an implied share of prosperity. Wouldn't it simply follow that all people should also have rights to share reasonably in the general prosperity?

Jane Jacobs introduces us to broader thinking

In trying to understand this transition from mercantilism to capitalism I find, once again, that Jane Jacobs cuts to the core. I'll follow her train of thought and add a few observations along the way.

In her 1984 book *Cities and the Wealth of Nations – Principles of Economic Life* she starts her story about 50 years before Adam Smith's *The Wealth of Nations*. The French economist Richard Cantillon (1680 – 1734) suspects there are problems with the mercantilist positive balance of trade definition of wealth. He wonders if larger more fundamental forces are at play. He has the following to say, sited by Jacobs:

> If the increase of actual money grows from mines of gold or silver in the State, the owners of these mines, the adventurers, the smelters, refiners, and all the other workers will increase their expenses in proportion to their gains. They will consume in their households more meat, wine or beer than before, will accustom themselves to wear better clothes, finer linen, to have better furnished houses and choicer commodities… [The] demands for meat, wine, wool, etc. being more intense than usual, will not fail to raise their prices. These high prices will determine the farmers to employ more land to produce them in another year; these same farmers will profit from this rise of prices and will increase the expenditure of their families like the others.[68]

[68] Jane Jacobs, *Cities and the Wealth of Nations – Principles of Economic Life*, Vintage Books, a division of Random House, New York, 1983, p. 9-10

"Cantillon's answers to himself," Jane Jacobs summarizes, "propounded what we now call a demand side theory of economic expansion, meaning that demand for goods and services lead the way in an expanding and prospering economy while supply to fill the demand follows in its wake." Henry Ford must have said, "Hey! Good idea!" He suddenly raised the pay of his workers almost 100% in 1914. They'd be happier, more loyal, stay with the company longer, work more enthusiastically and productively and – very demand side – have the money to buy Ford automobiles themselves, recycling their money back to the company. Worked quite well.

But Adam Smith, in the pioneering days of capitalist theory, with about 50 more years to think about things than Cantillon had, was a supply side economist. "That is," Jacobs continues, "he attributed economic expansion to expanding production and trade, with expanding demand as a by-product and consequence." He would, in this case, be in the camp of the industrialists who believe in high profits and low taxes for their companies so that they can invest more in production and make more money, hire more people and thus contribute to growing prosperity while profiting well personally. It was not an idle claim either to say that the process under their control of investing in and producing things in large volume reduced the price of many things making them much more broadly available, even in many cases to the poor.

As typically happens in human intercourse, this polarization between demand and supply side was historically emphasized, one side vs. the other, for higher stakes in the game, whether those stakes be real money and who gets how much, through business leadership, or worker skills development and organizing, or for the economists for the intellectual capital, sense of power from higher academic degrees or fame through published books, television interviews or whatever other games we buy into to best our competition, or simply be the best or find the truth of the matter first or at all. From greedy grubber trying to get rich fast but not so good at it to exalted Faustian bargain, from stepping on and over that jerk one up on the ladder to becoming a multi-billionaire or discovering the laws of economics, winning a so-called Nobel Prize in economic game theory, those in the game at whatever level and in probably in all human endeavors tend to exaggerate and make their side as important as possible and as correct. The other side has to be bested, shown to be wrong and unimportant. Never mind that most of the time all might be partially right and partially wrong. Often, from the point of view of those in the game, it's the more heat and less light the better, the objective being to "win" in the eyes of a largest possible number of fans of the sport or get the most reward for the effort and skill. Often the gamers' positions drift far from what's really going on. And so, economists have taken sides ever since the early days of demand-side vs. supply-side debates and built theories, practices and reputations around one side or the other as *vs.* the other. But in playing that game, by keeping our eyes on the prize of a game we may fail to see the whole scene of which the game is only a part. We're stuck in exaggerated gamesmanship.

Jacobs has this to say about that: "Several centuries of hard ingenious thought about supply and demand chasing each other around, tails in their mouths, have told us almost nothing about the rise and decline of wealth. We must find more realistic and fruitful lines of observation and thought than we have tried to use so far." She credits Cantillon and Smith with looking into the real mechanisms of production at the level where production actually takes place, shifting the balance of thinking away from the balance of trade in things someone else made, which with closer examination might just turn out to be more powerful in generating real wealth and prosperity than most of what is often called monetary policy. Implicitly they, those two early capitalist economists, were getting more fine grain in their analysis, less stuck in elite, authoritarian thinking, broader and at the same time more local and "into" minerals and foods coaxed from soil and carboniferous strata of the planet by burning wood and coal, spreading dung fertilizer on soil and applying real toil and the leverage of early complex machines like mechanical looms, steam engines and water pumps. They were getting more real in looking at where things were actually made, not just traded and stolen from one another in war.

What the first capitalist theorists began to zero in on, and Jane stands ready to advance, is perhaps exactly how prosperity does arise: through the agency of her "import replacing cities," cities being the meta-tools, the technologies of many technologies assembled for smooth functioning. From her point of view when using the word "import" she's not talking about countries' importing gold while exporting products, selling and loaning more than buying and borrowing, the mercantilist's positive balance of trade. Instead she's talking about cities gaining the power of their own productivity by first making things for themselves, and then second, to trade with others. Sequence counts. What they are really importing is the *idea* of the thing that would otherwise be imported so that the thing itself now becomes a local product. How they are really acting is as living complex organisms (this I'm adding).

But getting back to the demand side vs. supply side tangle, we might be seeing a game of exaggerated positions, of a false choice between two things that both work to explain things if in different ways. Her notion that what's really going on in economics is a cycle and not something based on a major single cause, that supply side and demand side are two integral parts of a whole neither more important nor empowering in the cycle than the other. It is all very "ecological" in pattern and style of thinking. If greased by dollars, exchange and investing producing more dollars, exchange and investing, the economic system might be noted to have close parallel with ecological systems that run analogously on calories, eating and reproducing giving rise to further generations of creatures running on calories, eating and reproducing, both systems ecological and economic, in that order, ultimately powered by the sun: solar energy, which I was writing about in 1972 for the Los Angeles Times! (Of course I'd put an exclamation point on it, proud of my early support of solar.)

Bringing up our magnifying glass and looking a little closer at the productivity/utilization cycle, you might call it, and we see more refined theories around specific components in the whole process. Marx for example emphasizes to a high degree the role of labor in the "labor basis of value" idea. *Labor über alles* you might say. But why over emphasize that when the cycle includes real physical resources such as iron, wood, coal and agricultural produce plus in most cases tools and component parts down the supply chain necessary for production, plus the skills of invention and design of products and capital investment and management in their production? For food, the plants and animals are workers too. For crops the rainfall, the rivers, the weather and climate are the workers; for minerals the action of tectonic plates and volcanoes; for the vast quantum of energy the sun. For patterns of consistency through the immensity of time, it's evolution. It's the big, big world of unified economics, natural and human.

More conventionally stated we are talking about ecological services like pollination and soil fertilization, the physical resources themselves delivered as solar, climate and tectonic services. Why give all the accolades to those with the talents and imagination of inventors and entrepreneurs when the credit accrues to everyone else too?

The answer to "why?" is that the contest of gamesmanship becomes more important to most people than the content of the argument, the on-the-ground reality. All games have defined boundaries and rules players accept and what's off the field of action is defined out of bounds and in fact if you pay too much attention to the sidelines you are almost certain to fail to attain the goals of the game. The play intentionally ignores much or all of the extraneous external information of the more inclusive "real" world all around. Meantime if tradition has it that winning gains you money, attention, respect, power, sex it's easy to be seduced. It's one of those things we have to think about and resist, like addiction. People like and get carried away in sports, cards, speed of car, size of house, ego points and other games: exaggerated gamesmanship. Economics provides many opportunities to take that to extremes.

The "why" with Marx, more narrowly focused, was undoubtedly a sense of identity with the workers and some righteous anger at the industrialist capitalists for causing such injustice and pain through their low wages, terrible working conditions, child labor and unwillingness to share decision making (democracy) and prosperity (materialism) more broadly, though many benefited by lower steel prices. There was much justification for "his side" so Marx exaggerated to win a point and maybe improve things. One might think his gamers' exaggerations also warped into one on the most bizarre fantasies or maybe misunderstandings to ever occupy political and economic space with his idea that a dictatorship – his dictatorship of the proletariat – should and could emerge from democratic process among the workers, run things (as opposed to the dictatorship of the owners and managers running things) then dissolve away into a classless society with far more equal decision making power (democracy) and share of prosperity (happy, shared materialism) to absolutely everyone (but maybe "Nature").

Bad choice of words, almost certainly helpful in establishing the Soviet Union, but much more what common language meant by "dictatorship" than he seemed to have had in mind. Even the Communists in vast numbers around the world abandoned ship when they learned from Nikita Khrushchev what a monstrosity Stalin had wrought as an actual functioning government for the Soviet Union. The "dictatorship" working for "the people" contradiction was just too much. The real dictatorship was, well, a pretty typical... dictatorship.

To get extreme, or even adopt the language of the more extreme ("dictatorship of the proletariat" for example, sure to alarm most people with a penchant for democracy and personal liberty), to focus on one aspect of a complex situation or only half of a pair potentially in balance... does that really make sense? Is it an effective, healthy way to proceed? Exacerbating conflict to supposedly clarify a position, win a battle then get on with reasonable reforms when the battle itself would be unreasonable, unnecessary and often deadly destructive isn't such a good idea. Strategists often say people won't even work for something if they don't go to the extreme of fighting for it. More fun? More like sports? A way to show prowess and skill, win admirers and social power? Maybe so, but that is a very serious problem. We'll deal with it later in thinking through what "generosity" means as one of the "Six Big Ones" humanity needs to prioritize properly. Perhaps it's the biggest problem we can imagine. That's the gamers' exaggeration, the battle for its own sake.

Evolution theory in the middle 19th century becomes important in understanding economics. Malthus set the tone with his concern that population was outstripping the sun and soil's capacity to provide and with his worry that famine was then likely to follow as population multiplied. Darwin followed up with his notion that the fittest among a species growing in population survive to reproduce and evolve the whole species. Notice that "fittest" doesn't necessarily mean the most forceful, ultimately violent, which was the robber baron self-justifying interpretation called Social Darwinism – but that which fit its environment best, perhaps taking and delivering mutually supportive services most efficiently. Malthus and Darwin gave some real foundation thinking to the idea that Human Economics connect with what happens in Nature's Economics.

Economists' thinking, however, was exaggerated in the manner just described as the gamers' ploy to prevail, to "win." The notion of survival of the fittest in the sense of nature's battles red in tooth and claw, both for food – predator vs. prey – and within species – for the privilege of mating – did characterize the selective patterns of evolution in some species. But half of the pattern was neglected, the cooperative half of what was going on at the same time. I'll describe that later in looking at Lynn Margulis' endosymbiosis ideas that enrich and balance the total scene, giving us together with "Darwinism" a much fuller and more true-to-the-evidence notion of evolution's mechanisms. That notion may not be as viscerally satisfying as "winning" the argument but healthier.

Economists, meantime, socialists on one side and capitalists on the other, continue to embrace the battle metaphor and tactics, still draw their lines in the intellectual sand, harden their minds for battle – and miss much of what is really going on in the total economy. But meantime Jacobs makes that link very particular and real, the snake with tail in mouth. Are the distinctions, as supply side and demand side really that meaningful, the demonizing of theirs opposite by capitalists and socialists? Quipped John Kenneth Galbraith, "Under Capitalism man exploits man. Under Communism, it's just the opposite."[69]

24. Foot and rail bridges of Detroit, Michigan

Detroit, for its key role in saving democracy in the Second World War – replacing car production with weapons production – in double edged sword style, gave us climate change, in that cities around the world bought its cars and followed Detroit's example. Result? Car city infrastructure is heating up the whole planet. With its present open space it could build new ecocity infrastructure while bringing back natural habitat and reviving its historic rich agricultural production.

[69] Cited by Al Gore, *The Assault on Reason*, New Penguin Press, New York, 2007, p. 95

CHAPTER 8

Modern Times

Declining violence

Reading Steven Pinker's book *The Better Angels of our Nature – Why Violence has Declined* takes a mind for statistics and a cast iron stomach, but it's worth it. How so? From the point of view of basic economics, it should be admitted that much of production has been based on violence at the base of economics, in the transference of energy and materials called food, clothing and architecture – killing animals for food, fiber, skins, tools and cutting down grain and trees even wasting countless acres with fire to create more open space for agriculture and architecture. Then how about slaves, and near slave labor? Competition for resources from productive food producing landscapes and water to digging up metals and fossil fuels…? So much of it has been based on exploitation that is essentially violent in nature, often leading to wars.

But the message that violence is declining in many forms is encouraging and supplements my own observation that we humans have never been in better shape than we are now for tackling our "insurmountable" problems – if we have the ideas, commitment and courage to actually do it, because we have the tools and information for splendid success. (Though not knowing what to build, a problem this book hopes to help us solve, is more than a small impediment.)

We start this chapter with the sort of information Pinker deals with, information to better grasp larger historic patterns leading from the diminution of violence as we move to next focus more carefully on "Modern Times."

Looking back it is almost unbelievable how coldly violent and blasé about violence society has been, and the farther back toward our supposedly "natural state" in a hunter gather stage, the more violent and accepting of violence according to Pinker's copious statistics. The gore is an everyday experience for the hunter or the person on the action end of your hamburger, and happy for it too since it means food and other useful things to be made from the body of the killed, from leather products to money. So it was in ancient times, and still is for many people, about killing and dismembering. Recognizing we are animals too, only Konrad Lorenz's "identity factors" and anti-violent acculturation "factors" prevent what to us these days could be staggering numbers of murders, individually or collectively, by private initiative or government policy.

So believe it or not, times keep getting less violent, at least in the very broad drift over long time spans. "No matter how small the percentage of violent deaths may be, in absolute numbers there will always be enough of them to fill the evening news. So people's impressions of violence will be disconnected from the actual proportions," says Pinker. Not withstanding the Islamic State slitting throats for Your Tubes or escalations in warfare to drone attacks in which the no-risk killers are sanitized screen watchers pushing video game buttons. Pinker adds, "…distorting our sense of danger is our moral psychology. No one has ever recruited activists to a cause by announcing that things are getting better, and bearers of good news are often advised to keep their mouths shut lest they lull people into complacency."[70]

The media makes money stoking this largely false impression of massive modern mayhem, we might add, because we all tend to buy sensational news. My guess is it goes back to the necessary fascination with dangerous situations, the better to avoid stepping on the rattlesnake. Not an altogether bad thing but one with dynamics we might improve on if we want to improve our world.

Pinker starts his story with Otzi the Ice Man discovered in the Tyrolean Alps emerging from a melting glacier in 1991. "Only when archeologists spotted a Neolithic copper ax did people realize that the man was 5,000 years old." He was celebrated as a very clever and well-equipped hunter who, theory had it, must have fallen into a crevasse or frozen in a storm. It wasn't until ten years later when,

> "…radiologists made a startling discovery: Otzi had an arrowhead embedded in his shoulder… he had been murdered. …Otzi had unhealed cuts on his hands and wounds on his head and chest. DNA analysis found traces of blood from two other people on one of his arrowheads, blood from a third

---

[70] Steven Pinker, *The Better Angels of our Nature – Why Violence has Declined*, Penguin Books, New York, 2001, Preface, p. xxii

> on his dagger, and blood from a fourth on his cape. According to one reconstruction, Otzi belonged to a raiding party that clashed with a neighboring tribe. He killed a man with an arrow, retrieved it, killed another man, retrieved the arrow again, and carried a wounded comrade on his back before fending off an attack and being felled by an arrow himself."[71]

The book is full of rich detail – call it graphic – with many more stories like Otzi's, enough to give the reader an almost witness, even involved position in the various conflicts: wars, genocide, cannibalism, racist violence, religious exorcism and sacrifice, lynching, murder, suicide (violence to self), infanticide, family feuds, clan vendettas, dueling, assassinations, drone attacks with "collateral damage," slavery, torture, executions, physical suppression of women, rape, animal cruelty, hunting to extinction, even spanking children and eating shark fin soup, that much – to all out war. Has society's circle of concern against violence spread its protective "civilizing" embrace through changing customs, taboos and laws to embrace protection from nuclear weapons to helping unfortunate children and sharks? Then there was killing a goat or some other innocent bystander rather than a more guilty but privileged human: the practice of scapegoating. How did these things seem so reasonable, normal once upon a time, that a good Medieval entertainment extending into early modern times, with a moral lesson at the end, was to take the kids down to the plaza to enjoy an execution?

Pinker's objective is to make a method of it after securing as much data and contextual detail as possible: good general numbers over a long time span. As I do in these pages he calls for a good sense of proportion as crucially important: "It is not coincidence that proportionality has a moral as well as a mathematical sense. Only preachers and pop singers profess that violence will one day vanish from the face of the earth. A measured degree of violence, [Hobb's Leviathan] even if only held in reserve, will always be necessary in the form of police forces and armies to deter predation or to incapacitate those who cannot be deterred."[72] The essence of his book is to assess the reasonable, the meaningful proportions regarding violence. The essence of *this* book is to get a sense of proportion about our natural/human economy, the mass/energy and biological dynamic of it all, and what the things we make has to do with it. Given the enormity of expenditures on war and hyper expensive ongoing violent conflict distracting from and wasting resources needed for building the right things, Pinker becomes most relevant.

As he scoured the literature Pinker was horrified by the prevalence of violence among early humans, not as absolute numbers compared to today's violence, but number of people who must have been intentionally killed as a percentage of those dying by all cause. Pinker presents a graph for best estimates (saying where the

---

[71] Steven Pinker, Ibid., p. 2

[72] Steve Pinker, ibid, p. 646

estimated come from) for archeological sites, hunter-gatherers and hunter-horticulturalist and other tribal cultures – "non-state" societies and "state" societies.[73] The earliest archeological sites reveal that approximately 15% of the deaths were killings. The hunter-gathers were marginally less violent with about 14%. And the hunter-horticulture and tribal groups scored worse at 24.5% deaths by human intent. Later in historic sequence, in state societies, we see a massive decline, for example contrasting parts of England (Oxford in 1300 for example with London in 1900) shows a decline of more than 99%, from slightly over 100 killed per 100,000 per year to slightly fewer than 1.[74] Why he suggests? "Self-control has been credited with one of the greatest reductions of violence in history, the 30 fold drop in homicide between Medieval and Modern Europe."[75]

Declining violence is part of an overall phenomena Pinker calls the "civilizing process," a term he adopts from Norbert Elias (1897-1990) who Pinker calls "the most important thinker you have never heard of." Why again? Because of the power of the concept in understanding the decline of violence and the shift from brutal social norms to vastly more reasonable, peaceful, compassionate ways of life. Pinker chronicles the decline in the 1,000 years since the collapse of Rome like this:

The Renaissance, 1400s through 1600s;

The Age of Reason, science and the Enlightenment, late 1600s through early 1800s;

The "humanitarian revolution" starting in the later part of the Age of Reason, late 1700s through to today as a broad category, which saw the end of slavery in the West, the end of brutal and public executions, progress in voting rights and so on;

The Long Peace, which starts after the out-of-step First and Second World Wars, about 1945 to about 1990 with no large state vs. state wars and markedly lower violent crime rates around the world. By out of step Pinker meant the general decline was gradual and fairly steady with the major exception of the pair of world wars linked by many related causes that weren't addressed in or after the first of the two.

The Rights Revolution, from late 1950s through today – human rights, civil rights, women's rights, gay rights, children's rights, animal rights, the rights for the planet to have a healthy climate system, and;

The "New Peace" which pinker names and says is, minus the anomalous 9/11 attack and Middle East wars, small in comparison with the World Wars, a period marking, from about 1990 through to the completing of his book in 2010 or

[73] Steve Pinker, ibid, p. 53

[74] Steve Pinker, ibid, p. 60

[75] Steve Pinker, Ibid., p. 592

2011, another drop in violence by almost all measures proportional. (I wonder about the up-turn in the Middle East and Africa since then…)

But in general the civilizing process continues in fits and starts but has maintained an overall vector down in violence throughout. Two notable big hiccups on the down-swinging graph were the fanatically violent European wars of religion in the 1600s and, as just mentioned, the strongly linked two World Wars spanning just 31 years in the first half of the 20th century. Probably, Pinker suggests, the religious wars and the two world wars and mega-death pogroms in the Soviet Union plus the civil wars and violence-induced famines in China were hopefully atypical and trend-bucking in the pattern of reducing violence. The two world wars, he suggests, were technology-magnified in ways that had not been anticipated: mechanized and massive, so much so that many people before 1914 expected that extreme new weaponry would put an end to war itself. Such a hopeful expectation seems less fanciful when we note that the deterrence value of nuclear weapons may well have prevented yet more massive multi-state and big-state all-out wars in the late 1900s. Maybe it was freakish and almost accidental in the case of World War I with poorly thought out mutual defense pacts that spiraled out of control. Maybe it was a mix of punishing World War I reparations, the Great Depression and the bizarre, messianic, mesmerizing, person of Adolf Hitler in regard to the Nazis' war.

On the positive side, why otherwise the continuing jagged graph line ever downward? The civilizing process, Pinker says, plus probably the Mutually Assured Destruction – MAD – stalemate that helped keep the US and USSR from all out military imperialist ambition. The deterrent, to this way of thinking finally got so large, war between large states really did become unthinkable.

Norbert Elias, born 57 years before Steve Pinker, didn't have death statistics by cause to work with but he did see the larger patterns in conspicuous relief as honor, glory and vengeance was being, by fits and starts, replaced by self-control, dignity, rationality or what could be called enlightened mutual-interest, maybe even a slowly growing capacity to see things through other's eyes, even as Jesus suggested, an enemy's: empathy. Elias gave great credit to, of all things – a surprise to me – all sorts of books on etiquette becoming stylish in the 1600s and 1700s. Self-control, cooling out, being reasonable, simply having "manners" was advancing early in the civilizing process, becoming a significant social influence. Pinker adds that the upper classes had a rational for exploitation and war due to the "gross" ways of the poor, gross being a word he entertainingly pursues into all sorts of habits of the lower classes, sneered at by the elites locally with assumptions that other similar characteristics prevailed across borders. But as traces of graceful manners percaled down-classward to the middle class and then to the lower classes as they all tried to look more like the upper classes, the elites just naturally had to ever more so accept their inferiors as human after all. As the lower classes became more restrained, polite and refined subtle changes spread though society.

An example of a particular change in the larger general cultural drift is dueling. Without much promotion, "Dueling petered out in the middle of the 19th century... Historians have noted that the institution was buried not so much by legal bans or moral disapproval as by ridicule." When "...solemn men went to the field of honor only to be laughed at by the younger generation, that was more than any custom, no matter how sanctified by tradition, could endure."[76] Today, said Pinker "... 'take ten paces, turn, and fire' is more likely to call to mind Bugs Bunny and Yosemite Sam than 'men of honor.'"[77]

Leading into the Humanitarian Revolution, and one hundred years earlier than Adam Smith launched capitalist theory into the mainstream of capital economics and the Founding Fathers launched the version of the democratic theory embodied by the United States, Thomas Hobbes had pointed out something that became known as the Hobbesian Trap, sometimes called the security dilemma – that in the pre-state state of humanity you can never know that if you don't shoot the competition first he might shoot *you* first. His cast of character and philosophy was perhaps influenced from the start: he was born under the threat of the Spanish Armada Invasion, which terrified his mother. He recalled that, " My mother gave birth to twins: myself and fear."[78]

Said Hobbes, there are three causes for pressure for extermination of the perceived competition, all based on self-interest, survival and reproduction: gain, safety, and reputation. Reputation helps with relations of influence and gaining mates. Its more inflated version, magnified by wealth, secrete knowledge, number of followers and accomplishment of high stakes deeds, is glory – the more dangerous and violent the more glorious. The sexual prize for top predators in society is often paramount: multiple wives up the large harem scale and Henry Kissinger supposedly having revealed this truth saying, "Power is the ultimate aphrodisiac." This somewhat bleak picture is the basis of Hobbes' most famous proclamation, that "the life of man [is] solitary, poor, nasty, brutish and short." ...unless you are among the well off, which he was, his mother's fears not withstanding.

But he had a solution to the more general condition: a higher authority which he called the "Leviathan," which I've mentioned a few times already. A more powerful force with a monopoly on violence (police and military) and legitimized by law (legislatures and courts), namely a government presiding over a relatively large domain. The Leviathan could limit wasteful violence and thereby protect its subjects and prevent the destruction of resources and items representing prosperity, or one could say, protect the expanding artifact list. The Leviathan would serve its subjects

[76] William Oliver Stevens, Pistols at Ten Paces: the Story of the Code of Honor in America, Houghton Mifflin, Boston, 940, p. 280

[77] Steve Pinker, Op. cit. p. 23

[78] Thomas Hobbes Biography, Notablebiographies.com, 2009

and "keep them all in awe." It would not exist to serve the rulers but to serve everyone based on this idea: "that a man be willing when others are so too… to lay down this right to all things; and be content with so much liberty against other men, as he would allow other men against him."[79] He was aware that such arrangement provided a more dependable tax base and wealth delivery system to the Leviathan's royal coffers than a condition of violence. In general – and this should be big in economic theory – to not have violence constantly hacking at society's collective assembled wealth, the artifact list and quantity of each item on it – provides for maximizing the post-GDP genuine prosperity indicators.

Political philosopher Immanuel Kant believed democratization, trade and participation in international associations leads to a reduction of violence and had a general civilizing effect, and Pinker added, as mentioned, a little straightforward rationality and proportionality: evidence indicates only a small minority gains much in war – while most of us lose, and often in spectacularly unfortunate ways, like our one and only lives. With a little more detail Pinker describes a force for liberation from the Hobbesian Trap: "…in real life people can confer, and they can bind their promises with emotional, social or legal guarantors. And as soon as one side tries to prevail on the other not to injure him, he has no choice but to commit himself not to injure the other side either. As soon as he says, 'It's bad for you to hurt me,' he's committed to 'It's bad for me to hurt you,' since logic can't tell the difference between 'me' and 'you.'"[80] Note that when such systems are around for awhile without abuse, people relax and completely forget about such fears assuming at least *that* society is peaceful, non-threatening: a major accomplishment of the civilizing process.

But worth special notice in a book interested in economics, cities and learning what to build that is healthy, economist Edward Glasser had a relevant item to add. The co-related rise of democracy and cities.

> "Oppressive autocrats can remain in power even when their citizens despise them because of a conundrum that economists call the social dilemma or free-rider problem. In a dictatorship, the autocrat and his henchmen have a strong incentive to stay in power, but no individual citizen has the incentive to depose him, because the rebel would assume all the risk of the dictator's reprisals while the benefits of democracy would flow diffusely to everyone in the country. The crucible of a city, however, can bring together financiers, lawyers, writers, publisher, and well-connected merchants who can collude in pubs and guild halls to challenge the current leadership, dividing the labor and diffusing the risk. Classical Athens, Renaissance Venice, revolutionary Boston and Philadelphia, and the cities of the Low Countries are examples

[79] Steve Pinker, Ibid., p. 160

[80] Steve Pinker, Ibid., p. 647

of cities where new democracies were gestated, and today urbanization and democracy tend to go together."[81]

Winding up thoughts on the civilizing process and the evolution of human rights, Pinker says,

> "Insofar as violence is immoral, the Rights Revolutions show that a moral way of life often requires a decisive rejection of instinct, culture, religion and standard practice. In their place there is an ethic inspired by empathy and reason and stated in the language of rights… This conclusion, of course, is the moral vision of the Enlightenment and the strands of humanism and liberalism..."[82]

Capital, not capitalist, Economics

So let's assume we are inside that envelop of relative non-violence and we can proceed with healthy production, consumption, and not to forget, fresh invention and creativity. It gets down to the ever so physical logic of the productivity utilization cycle. Says Jane Jacobs in her introduction to *Cities and the Wealth of Nations*, her 1984 book mentioned earlier,

> …creating prosperity where it didn't exist and maintaining it where it did… differed under the influence of differing ideologies, but less than one might suppose. For example, when Soviet and American governments competed for allegiance of a poor country by offering economic aid. Rather the two competed to supply much the same dams, roads, fertilizer plants and irrigation systems. The economic programs Poland's government adopted were largely financed by West German and American bankers. The bankers disapproved of Communist state ownership and probably many other Polish arrangements as well; all the same Polish conceptions of how an economy expands and develops, what it needs for the purpose and how it earns the wherewithal to carry and repay development financing were perfectly familiar conceptions to capitalist bankers: conventional, logical.[83]

---

[81] Steve Pinker, Ibid., p. 179

[82] Steven Pinker, Ibid., p. 475

[83] Jane Jacobs, *Cities and the Wealth of Nations*, ibid, p. 4

It seems not only is there a guiding hand fixing prices but it is beginning to look like other aspects of the system that derive from the basis in resources and the nature of exchange are out of the supply side/demand side debate and into something maybe not that well worked out yet. It is not just the market but the market as it has to function while nature in all its physicalness, neither proletariat nor bourgeoisie – or rather probably both – is giver, not exactly dictator, of economic law. The guiding hand emerges again, and it turns out to be Nature herself, which I'd call nature's economics here, not some kind of mathematical formula cooked up among economists. This time She's telling us we need to build right, get it all physically right, if we hope to have a healthy economics. For example, compost that urban organic waste and turn it into the soil if you want that field of chlorophyll to crank out a big grain harvest. In general, figure out organic farming as a mega-recycling program.

John Kenneth Galbraith, leading mid-20th century economist and Franklin Roosevelt's price fixer during the Second World War, examined an important element in this shifting from mainstream economics too, getting around to the physical-all-so-anchored kind of economics that links nature's with human's by looking at the powerhouse that emerges when the production utilization cycle gets *really* complex, companies get *really* big and the artifact list gets *really* long. The quantitative increase seems to be leading to a qualitative shift here, somehow changing the rules. Galbraith acknowledged this transition by shifting the focus to examining the big players that produce the most products and services and move the most capital. His son, James Kenneth Galbraith writes an introduction to his father's 1967 book, *The New Industrial State*, which says it quite eloquently. I think you will see how it leads directly into interesting themes, both the anchoring of economics in the physical design and form of the city by way of insisting on looking directly at the physical production utilization cycle and in some new thoughts about what to make of the capitalism/socialism gamers' exaggeration.

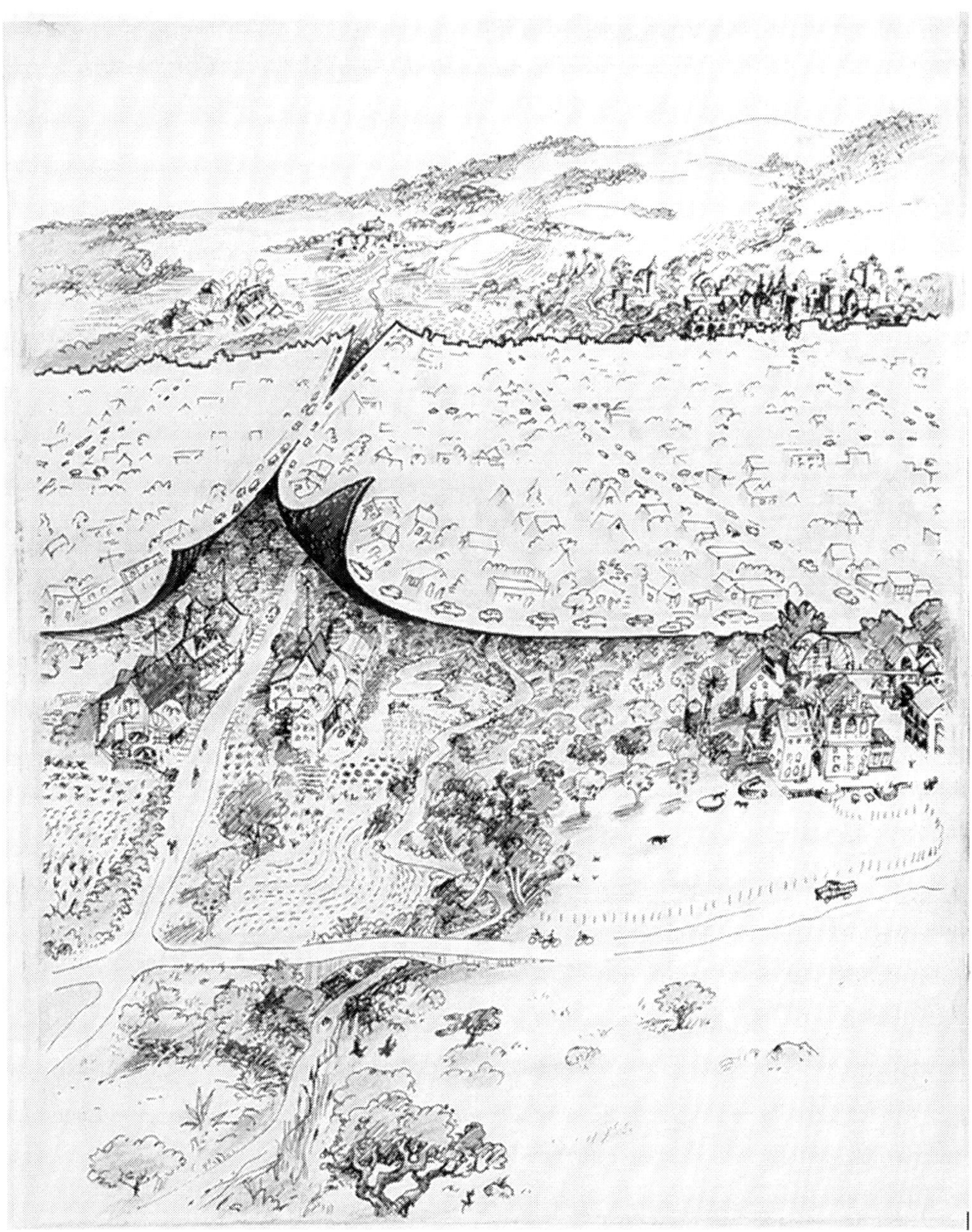

25. Roll back sprawl

Long term transformation of cities has to be toward active centers of high diversity, from small neighborhood centers becoming small villages through district centers becoming ecotowns to downtowns to ecocities and whole metropolitan areas to ecotropolis areas – galaxies of centers of all scales, each like a complex, healthy living organism well fitted to its bioregion.

> The economics of organizations stands in opposition to the economics of markets. In what Galbraith called "the accepted sequence," consumers' preferences come first. Firms place their products before a discerning public, sell what they can, discount the rest, and then repair to study how it might be done better next time. In his own "revised sequence," larger firms start with the design and technology of new production. They see what is possible, they conduct "market research," they decide what they like. They then engage their advertising and consumer-finance staffs to ensure that the result can be sold.
>
> For Galbraith, this was reality; he did not oppose it. Complex technology dictates that markets must be controlled.[84]

James continues: Large corporations reduce uncertainty of the market by "...forging the future for themselves. [They] often even replace the market altogether. This they do by integration: replacing activity previously mediated by open purchase and sale with activity either internal to the corporation, or between a large, stable enterprise and its small, specialized suppliers," who often are "forced" by the dependable and profitable volume of whatever it is they are providing, to sell exclusively to the larger company and function almost like a department in the larger company, taking "orders" in two senses. The large company coordinates all this through extensive planning, not so much accepting and trying to understand Smith's invisible hand as replacing it with their own much more visible hand: planning, planning so that the inner workings of the company by teams and committees can coordinate with one another for smooth, as predictable as possible operation. There are teams for design and production working with teams focused on procurement of tools and materials, teams for market analysis, and advertising departments feeding information back to the research and development wing and back to the designers all influencing the main production stream of the company with decision makers coordinating, budgeting and financing the whole. Smooth functioning internally needs to be matched by dependability of supply at the start side of the production process and sales at the other end. Customers have to be convinced to buy dependably – bring on the advertising department. Advantageous laws have to be planned as best possible – buy friends in legislatures and government executive positions by hiring lobbyists and contributing to political campaigns.

The process Galbraith identified and emphasized in 1967 became, *was*, he said, the new capitalist strategy shifting from endorsing the more genuinely self-regulating market of the sort that brought us to the Crash of 1929 to not a government organized set of regulations, but a corporate new way of driving government regulation from the field to replace it with their own market planning around the idea of

[84] John Kenneth Galbraith, *The New Industrial State,* Princeton University Press, Princeton, New Jersey, 1967, with 1985 Introduction by John Kenneth Galbraith and 2007 Introduction by James Kenneth Galbraith, p. xi

maximizing the profits of investors and the ever richer executives and people in charge of finance. In fact, they pushed a kind of regulation in the negative, euphemistically and meaninglessly calling it "modernization." Their tool of regulation: make regulation of the really profitable (and dangerous) transactions just plain illegal.

The "free market" capitalists thus drove the regulators from the field only to see that their planning didn't effectively replace it but instead "creatively" planned the market's own collapse (we are getting close to up-to-date now) through all those sub prime loans, derivatives and the like so meticulously devised as genius game theory formulas they thought they understood, all part of an overall plan. Rather they sought, in an up-dated strategy identified by Galbraith, a market they hoped to control – and still largely do. 8.4% of US GDP was in finance in 2011, where beyond some limited service in legit loans and investments, there is no physical product or service at all. In the 1950s, for comparison, finance accounted for about 3% of US GDP,[85] probably about right for the real productive and distributive economy. So their plan worked out for the biggest among them (while costing millions of other people the loss of their homes, jobs and retirement security – thanks suckers for buying IRAs when you could have had even better than your present Social Security benefits).

Then the very designers of the derivatives inflating the doomed bubble extracted hundreds of billions of dollars from the Federal Government in socialist style bailouts to save the country's supposedly capitalistic economy, money from the usually vilified ("…the problem *is* the government") collective assets and actions. Far from giving the market a free unseen hand, the deregulators controlled it by nursing its overheated growth until it collapsed. Then they succeeded in controlling government in a stunningly large way: "Thanks for your hundreds of billions, tax payers!" Perhaps that was part of their planning all along knowing the "too big to fail" doctrine would rescue the large and successful, who after all run most things (think Goldman Sachs) while so many almost-as-bigs hope to be among those bailed out too. (To the physically productive capitalists' credit, and in the spirit of gamesmanship *not* exaggerated, the bailouts (negative spin) were mostly in reality loans (neutral spin) that in a number of cases, after some reorganization and unevenly distributed equity gains, were paid back ahead of schedule such as General Motors' bail out loans.)

Another detail: whereas in the old capitalist model from the late 1800s ownership and control were in the same hands, the very large corporation coming out of the Second World War era and since became something controlled by executives and managers with ownership just too broad to be much more than an irritant to boards and executives. Because things became so complex that not only do most of the stockholder not have a clue, their opinions are therefore of little worth. Proportionally grows the power, then, of the board and executive. Often the interests of

[85] Think Progress Website http://thinkprogress.org/economy/2011/12/14/389487/financial-sector-gdp-recession/?mobile=nc

owners, enormous numbers of stockholders in most cases, and the executives in the very large companies, are very different. For example, the executives often have privileged information on the condition of a company and can engineer their exit with a lucrative golden parachute payout just before a company suffers a serious reversal or collapses, often partially *because of* the actions of the dearly departing. The decision makers of such corporations, in controlling much of the information flow, can skew and provide the information claiming that they deserved not 30 times the pay of the average employee as in the days of the 1960s but more like 300 times the pay by the 2010s.[86]

(Separate question: why do company boards of directors reward such destructive execs who abandon ship and other companies later hire them on? Don't really know but it sounds like honor among thieves to me, in which the code in the club is to create conditions "I," each individual in the club, could later exploit.)

Galbraith called the large firm's organization pattern the "technostructure." In coining this term he was identifying the fact that very large complex productive companies, due to their internal functioning, had to be relatively autocratic, that is, not regulated and controlled over much by government or bankers. Galbraith was particularly hard on bankers saying, in his son James' paraphrasing words,

> [They] were powerful but not fit to govern. Far from being a blown-up version of the avuncular small town specialist in local business acumen, the modern banker bestrode the corporate and the political worlds without understanding much of either. In particular, he could not understand much of the technical work at the heart of the major corporation, and therefore he could not exercise practical control over strategy or performance. The Banker's power was mainly of the destructive kind: he could squeeze business; he could wreck business – but there was no magic whereby from the rubble a better business would emerge.[87]

Their power, misunderstood, left bankers feeling like the Chosen Ones to engage in pushing for their options in the business of magnifying paper value and cashing it in for real wealth in the real economy of real possessions and less volatile investments with good timing so that others, not them, would get caught in the crashing. That the bankers, Galbraith thinks, don't really understand the complex business enterprise and the same for government, helps explain, if he's right, the dynamics of the historically recent bubbles they influence.

---

[86] Figures vary fairly widely but the increase in executive pay relative to average employee compensation from, say, the 1960s to 2010s is several times over. One example: In 2007, CEOs in the SP 500 averaged $10.5 million annually, 344 times the pay of typical American workers. Landy, Heather, "Behind the Big Paydays," The Washington Post, November 15, 2008

[87] John Kenneth Galbraith, Ibid., p. xix

Looking back to the late1800s when capitalist economic orthodoxy was getting firmly locked in and the ways of the robber barons in that incarnation of giant corporations, relatively early industrialism, shifting from the age of iron and coal to the age of steel and oil, it seems there may be more parallels than Galbraith seems to acknowledge and fewer real contrasts, he too exaggerating his thesis for its advantage and popular entertainment value – one sells more books that way. Plus, it's more fun to write them that way – one can tell he enjoys his use of words as I sometime do my own.

The decision makers of the early giant companies striving to create monopolies – think late 1800s and early 1900s – lobbied in their own way. Never mind that they were owner powerhouses instead of their one-century-later executive reincarnations with proportionally far smaller stake in their companies. They were building "trusts" with the power of the executive by ownership over the sources of the money flows, factories, hardware, mass of products pouring forth and so on. The force of their institutions and internal and external dynamics in the role they played shouldering through in the larger economy wasn't all that different from today's largest corporations. Many of the robber barons, like many of the robber CEOs, bought government support or stepped back and forth through the revolving door themselves, even then, seeking monopoly on one hand and attempted purchase of government decision making on the other. They set up distribution systems and crushed competitors not subtly at all, and they abused workers at home probably as badly or worse than today's corporations abuse workers in foreign lands. Think child labor for example.

But they did drop the price of steel low enough to build the railroads and skyscrapers, factories, wonderful ocean liners and horrible weapons, and gave – or rather sold – us telephones, long distance travel, movies and convenient home appliances at affordable prices for tens of millions, then hundreds of millions and now even billions of people, not to leave out building, well or badly, our cities. And they were partially humanized by the labor movement, in Pinkers world of mellowing levels of violence, mostly against their will. But most people today would acknowledge the great majority in advanced countries enjoys a far more comfortable and entertaining life than in pre-industrial days. So it is quite a mixed bag with all of us mixed up in it. And, we don't have to buy all those things "bad" corporations produce.

The earlier giant corporation concentrated massive amounts of money as do today's corporations and though they polluted worse locally, they had nothing on climate change. The differences, between economic understanding and strategy then and now, with the period in the middle examined by Galbraith, meaning mid 20th century, seem real to me but what he cites looks more like a matter of degree and style – up to this point: Mostly what is different now is that we are flirting with the collapse at the resources base world wide, we have crossed the quantitative line into a new qualitative world – at risk. We are being forced to examine the direct linkage between Natures Economics and ours.

But even in these times Galbraith's distinctions may help us understand important economic patterns, and, there is a more important idea lurking there in *The New Industrial State*. We can compare his thoughts with Jane Jacobs comparing the productive part of economies, meaning the entities that actually produce something, in the US and the Soviet Union back in 1984: "the two competed to supply much the same dams, roads, fertilizer plants and irrigation systems..." etc. I'd add, that at certain levels of complexity, these entities have many parallels with everyday complex living organisms, just as cities do, and that they, the large business firms, may have less to do with mainstream capitalist vs. socialist theory than with the inner logic of living organisms in their ecological world of sustainable productivity vs. blowout and collapse.

Here's Galbraith's thinking leading in that direction. Remember, *The New Industrial State* was written in the early 1960s and remember also that his technostructure is always trying to liberate itself from external control, in fact control enough of its environment to thrive like a living organism in my analogy.

> In sum, it seems likely that the Soviet resolution of the problem of authority in the industrial enterprise is not unlike that in the West ... Full social authority over the large enterprise is proclaimed. Like that of the stockholder and the board of directors in the United States, this social control is celebrated in all public ritual. The people and Party are paramount. But in practice large and increasing autonomy is accorded to the enterprise. This is further suggested by the trend in decentralization, so-called, in the Soviet and other Eastern European countries. This has accorded greater authority to the firm over prices, individual wage rates, production targets, investment and other employment of earnings. In the West, especially among professional ideologists and volunteer propagandists, this has been widely hailed as a step toward control by the market. It isn't. There is no tendency for the large Soviet firm to become subordinate and subject to uncontrolled markets for its products, production needs or labor supply. ... There is no tendency for the Soviet and the Western systems to converge by the return of the former to the market. Both have out grown that. There is measurable convergence to the same form of planning.[88]

Though I'm sure Galbraith enjoyed putting forward a hair raising, perhaps history-of-economics-changing idea, I'm also sure he took it to also be the conclusions of dispassionate inductive reasoning: everything pointed from his data and information to its synthesis and into a new conclusion perhaps on the way to a new

[88] John Kenneth Galbraith, *The New Industrial State*, Op cit., p. 135-136

economics theory. Compared to much of his thesis that large companies, not markets are the real guiding hand of the real economy, he considered another thought he called "yet more disturbing."

> Might there not be a convergence between the great bureaucratic organizations of capitalism and those of the socialist world? I spent the spring months of 1959 traveling through the Soviet Union, talking with Russian plant managers and economists in the belief that this might be so. I concluded that there was such a convergence. When this conclusion was published – in the Soviet Union eventually as well as in the Western industrial lands – there was another kind of convergence: Critics in both East and West united in condemning what seemed both socialist and capitalist apostasy.[89]

Was there gamers' exaggeration suddenly at risk? If they took Galbraith seriously would all the Cold War posturing begin to look a little ridiculous with a great lessening of the differences between the camps? Would fear of nuclear was go poof? Would scare tactic fail to scare voters into voting for *me?!*

But now more on gamesmanship. Practically everyone loves games and spends an inordinate amount of time focused on them. Think spectator sports, card games, gambling, investing in long-shot high-return things, poring over the stock reports in the business pages, smashing your business competition and waging war. The real heroes are, and the real glory is to, those who are not spectators but players who get the focus and winnings – or losings. The exaggeration attracts attention, builds careers and often makes for successful politicians and warmongers, plus winners in scoring sex mates, which is the best most of us can do but definitely worthwhile. Throughout, vicarious involvement is obviously satisfying to billions of us humans who get swept up in the emotional, sometimes to their own destruction, which in different degrees of exaggeration, befell those buying way overpriced houses and derivatives in the early 2000s, not to speak their friends and family members and millions of others all over the world, buying their dream house to try to flip it, or to get extreme in the pattern, the Germans who signed up for Hitler's SA and SS getting all patriotic over the growing war hysteria. The problem of "exaggerated gamesmanship" is when the game gets unfair or destructive in the real world, when proportions get way out of control.

Back to Galbriath: He goes on to say perhaps even "Keynesian macroeconomic policy should itself be seen as part of a larger planning process, one seeking to minimize for the corporation the manifest uncertainties deriving from large random fluctuations in the aggregate of demand for goods and services."[90] That is, the model for serious economic theory needs to shift to whatever is producing real goods

---

[89] Galbraith, Ibid. p. xli

[90] Galbraith, Ibid. p. xli

and services and the almost organic dynamics of that, the *that* being the technostructure in its full cycle relating to its total environment. It's the human economics harmonized with natural economics, sometimes, I think only half consciously called by conventional economists, the "real economy." Could the prime physical manifestation of the technostructure be the thriving built and well-ordered structure of the city?

But many would say, the Soviet Union collapsed two decades after Galbraith's thoughts on the similarities across the Iron Curtain; doesn't that prove that something very different in the economics was very important, socialism was lacking and capitalism fundamentally the correct system? But what collapsed in the Soviet Union was an oligarchy/dictatorship, closer in many ways to a fascist dictatorship than a system to empower labor, help the poor and make for a materially more equitable society. In that rather crucial way the insensitive, brazenly cruel Soviet system was radically different from the semi-socialist, multi-party voting democracies of, say, contemporary northern European countries where capitalism and socialism has for all intents and purposes converged.

But back in the 1980s the two systems, generally centrally planned Soviet and democratic capitalism, had physical function closely aligned in their technostructures as viewed as mechanisms for the productivity utilization cycle, trying to tap products and happy lifestyles out of the mass/energy flows. But also, trying to contrast, exaggerate and prove themselves in the world contest against an enemy led them into the staggering expenditure on the military during the Cold War. In more simple natural and capital economics terms, the Soviet Union more likely just ran itself into bankruptcy, exhausting itself in the arms race against countries with much greater resources. Gorbachev may have liberated some thinking there that helped opened the door to new possibilities too. We will never know all the ways such influence unwound in the Soviet collapse, but my guess is those were, in order, reasons number one and two.[91]

How lack of regulation crashes markets (as if not obvious)

The market has a powerful tendency, very dramatically demonstrated in the late 1800s and again in the 1920s, and we could add in 2008, to grow and

91 Could America's vast military spending we are seeing today and flow of arms world wide be such a path to collapse when we need the money to build a sustainable future now? The US spends more on arms than the next eight countries together and maybe we really are approaching that downward "point of inflection" on the Club of Rome graph here on page 79.

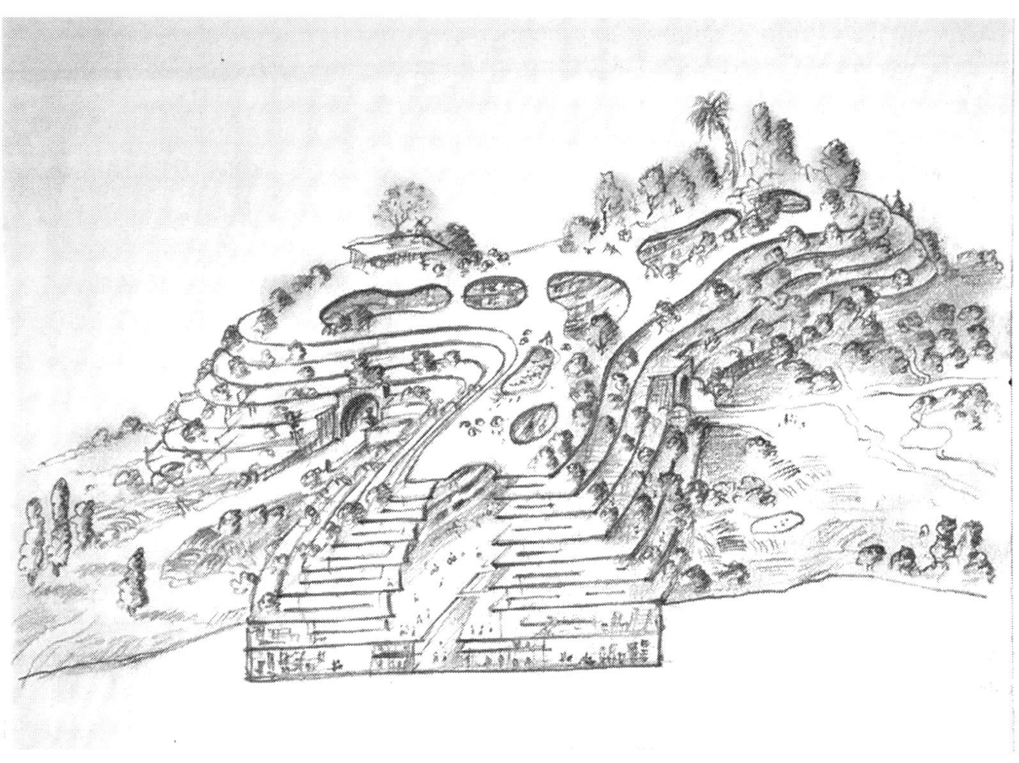

26. Town as hill

Idea from California architect Gene Zellmer re-interpreted by the author.

concentrate wealth and greed until it crashes. This was a very clear history the logical conclusions of which the capitalist chosen few and their mainstream economists chose to ignore. But Keynes and Galbraith didn't. In 1890, due to public disgust with the trusts and their greed, manipulated high prices, rise of a few large companies to monopoly over large chunks of the economy and use of local price wars to destroy competitors or employ deception in buying and secretly running smaller companies that falsely appeared to be competitors, and on and on, including the hiring of thugs to rough up and intimidate anyone in the way…, due to all this and more, in 1890 the Sherman Antitrust Act was voted in with only one opposing vote in the US Senate and a completely unanimous vote in the House. The unions had a great victory; the monopolies had overplayed their hand.

The case of monopolies is interesting in terms of free market economics when you consider the free market is supposed to adjust its own prices in self-organizing emergence style, and that's a good deal for everyone in the system. And if there are many actors in the field for any kind of product or service, it actually works well. But there is also a powerful tendency for the more powerful companies and individuals to get more and more powerful until they monopolize their area of business and then set their prices to their own enrichment first, instead of letting the market set more justifiable prices. Thus the market, without regulation, tends not to thrive because it's free, but instead gives preferential freedoms to the large and powerful, putting an end to competition.

What should be obvious is that the market is *both* free *and* regulated. This brings into serious question how anyone could believe the market ever would control itself, so powerful is the monopoly tendency. This also means regulation is as natural to markets as "freedom." The freedom part is all those physical people, products and services milling about and the regulation part is the natural pattern of transaction in the mind of the cultures and individuals that determine the action, something like noun and verb in language, matter and energy and once again a dimensional pair.

It wasn't until 1911, twenty-one years after the Sherman Antitrust Act was passed that Standard Oil was finally broken up into 34 separate companies. But what is particularly worth noting here is that the US Federal Government in that long, hard process, constantly corrupted and harassed by the monopolies, finally did act, as did Franklin Roosevelt's government during the Great Depression. Acted in what way? Ironically some might think by preserving the self-regulating competition of the market in tune with the basic observation about market dynamics identified by Cantillon and Smith so long ago, by keeping the market place from its own worse habit of tending toward monopolies.

Shortly after the Antitrust Act forced the dismemberment of Standard Oil and many other monopolies, a world war muddled the picture, being more than a little distracting and causing the economy to fall into patterns that were complex and hard to analyze in economic theory. But all that was becoming more stable and amenable to the student of economics in the 1920s as things settled into what in America looked like steadily and strongly rising prosperity. The world of economic theory settled comfortably back into its self-regulating market navel gazing. In fact, outside the other bubble, the economists' bubble of separation from the real world, it was back to the bubble of desire for unearned wealth, way beyond investing in or making reasonable loans for worthwhile ventures but deep into risky business, often "on margin" meaning using borrowed money so that if you failed the money lost wasn't even your own. Then I'm outta here and try to catch me!

The first sign of real trouble was anything but subtle yet roundly ignored: the Florida Real Estate Crash of 1926. It's an intriguing story from which nothing was learned at the time, such that the crash of three years later seemed a shocking surprise.

The side story of the Florida boom and bust has an oblique tie to Standard Oil and environmental issues too, in that an early partner of John D. Rockefeller who joined his firm as an investing partner in 1867 built a railroad deep into and eventually all the way down the length of Florida. Henry Flagler was a principal in Rockefeller, Andrews and Flagler even before it was called Standard Oil. On a trip to Florida with his wife in 1876 and greatly enjoying his stay there in tropical breezes and local hotels – nice but a little "rustic." Flagler was mightily impressed with the potential and shortly after decided to build a hotel or two of his own. His vision was to create "the American Riviera" linked to the rest of the country by railroad, his railroad. With money from his family connections but mostly his wealth from Standard Oil, he built the Florida East Coast Railway. It's locomotives ran on wood – that's the ecological disaster story – and propelled deep into Florida the country's first Pullman cars – a new idea for sleepover trips celebrated by scenes in the popular movie "Some Like it Hot," with Marilyn Monroe, Tony Curtis and Jack Lemon. The first Pullman car train arrived at Flagler's St. Augustine Ponce de Leon Hotel in 1888 for the hotel's grand opening celebration and the land rush was on. Little noticed was the wave of open space rolling out from the tracks as the forests fell for the wood the locomotives were burning, (biofuel!) until, distances needed to be covered by the wood cutters spreading out farther and farther from the tracks added to energy costs to the point where coal was cheaper. Eventually, his line went from near the Florida border with Georgia, 560 miles all the way out over the Gulf of Mexico to Key West where Flagler dreamed a major US port – which turned out to be extremely minor. For one thing he didn't have Jane Jacobs' insight that, in commerce and properly understood economics, it takes a city to be a decent port and you couldn't build much of a city at tiny Key West surrounded as it was by the Straights of Florida on one side and the Gulf of Mexico on the other. And second thing: he didn't take nature seriously. Though he was long gone by then, a category 5 hurricane in 1935 stripped his railroad to Key West right off the water. It was never replaced. Or more accurately said, a causeway for cars and trucks was built over its bones.

By the end of World War I the automobile was coming on strong and highways were connecting warm winter Florida to cold New England and Midwest. By 1920, with the war two years gone, anyone with a little money could lounge on a beach and dream Henry Flagler's dream. Never mind the swamps to be drained, mosquitoes and hurricanes. I remember my first visit, 1974, West Palm Beach. I stepped out of my friend's two-story apartment complex condo onto the back lawn adjoining the golf course with its water traps – no fence – to be greeted by a ten-foot long monster covered in hard pointy scales and yawning fangs. An alligator had hauled up from the water and was slowly crawling toward me. Needless to say, I went back inside. It wandered around a while then disappeared.

But by the time the land rush, or more accurately, the money rush was on, thousands of people were buying lots unseen and selling them on down the line, "flipping" them in the language of 2000 to 2008. President Warren G. Harding helped it along by lowering taxes at the federal level to stimulate spending and investing while the State of Florida got in the grove eliminating its income and inheritance taxes to lure emigrants. Henry Flagler died in 1913 but his dream lived on and many times larger. "The Florida boom," said Galbraith in his book *The Great Crash of 1929* "was the first indication of the mood of the twenties and the conviction that God intended the American middle class to be rich. But that this mood survived the Florida collapse is still more remarkable."[92]

Through the early 1920s speculation continued spiraling upward. The case of Charles Ponzi, enshrined in the English language for his "Ponzi schemes" – close cousins to chain letter frauds – was all too typical. After spending jail time in Montreal, then Atlanta for bilking people in several different ways, he found himself in Boston where, writing home to Italy, he discovered something called international reply coupons designed so that people in one country, Italy in this case, could pay for family members and friends to send them letters and packages going the other way. He noticed that to send a letter to Italy cost four times as much as sending one to the US from Italy, so when he got international reply coupons from Italy he could buy US postage and sell it at 400% mark up to anyone wanting stamps. He sent money to friends in Italy to buy the reply coupons that they mailed to him and he was in business. He convinced investors to put money into his "company" and promised – and delivered – double their money in 45 days. Investors were stunned, delighted and word spread fast. The money going out was based on new money coming in, large numbers of late comers paying off smaller numbers of early investors while Charles Ponzi peeled off millions of dollars for himself, buying houses, swimming pools, bringing his mother over from Italy in a luxury state room on a classy passenger ship, which was kind of touching.

Caught in just a few months it was off to jail again, this time in Massachusetts. But after more jail time in a story too complicated to get into here, he appeared in Florida to sell sight unseen swamp land as wonderful real estate ripe for development with infrastructure like roads and electricity ready to go with nearby towns providing great convenience – none of which but the soggy soil existed, including the towns. Some who bought his worthless property sold it for a higher price if they flipped it fast enough, but of course the great majority lost almost all or all the money they put into his deals. In all his schemes there was a small business core from which dreams were magnified – ad absurdum. Just as in the stock market boom and crash of 1929, Bernard Madoff's Ponzi scheme and the financial crisis of 2008, real property was at the core, but its value, all by human agreement, was wildly inflated, called by most people "paper wealth." It just didn't connect with the real economy and investors cared far less about what was actually being built than about dreams of glory. As to the real total economy, no one was thinking about resource flows, ecology and certainly not the limits of a finite planet.

The Florida Real Estate Crash, three years before the Wall Street Crash, was a terrible wipe out of tens of thousands of people's investments and savings affecting people all over the country. And yet, like joy riding in a new car, well, third gear was fun, but hey! let's jam it into fourth and floor it. And by the way, has anybody tuned up the breaks since the Sherman Anti-trust Act? To emphasize the point

[92] John Kenneth Galbraith, *The Great Crash of 1929*, Mariner Books, Houghton Mifflin Harcourt, Boston and New York, 1954, p. 6

that reality has a way of catching up, two hurricanes hit in 1926 when everyone was down, and the one of September 18 killed 400 people, destroyed 30,000 homes and left luxury yachts scattered about the desolate streets of Miami. Said Frederick Lewis Allen quoted in Galbraith's book, the 1926 hurricanes showed "what a Soothing Tropic Wind could do when it got a running start from the West Indies." [93]

Needless to say there wasn't much regulation in the market at that point, neither in the real estate market in Florida, nor in the Stock Market in New York City, where somehow the enthusiasm had shifted seamlessly from castles built on Florida sand to stocks built on the air of greedy dreams.

When the Crash of '29 did hit, though, some interesting things happened. First: nothing. It happened that, President Hoover, being a friend of the self-regulating market, held the theory that the market would just correct itself. It didn't, unless you count millions of people around the world losing their savings, jobs, dreams, future and in some cases lives in the slow down and cool out as some kind of God-induced "regulation" or "correction" of an overheated economy. That's like calling a car crash a healthy means of slowing down a car; a crash is not a very reasonable "adjustment" for either car or market. Four years later as the country and world sunk deeper and deeper into the Great Depression Franklin Roosevelt was sworn in. Then rather amazingly, things happened fast in the next 100 days because somebody other than just the market did something.

Franklin Roosevelt, a muddled economics? – but what got built

Herbert Hoover, who must have been one of the world's most unlucky men to have taken office of President of the United States just before the bottom fell out of the market, was still presidential timber and haughtily advised Roosevelt, "When you've been in Washington as long as I have, Mr. Roosevelt, you'll learn that the president calls on no man." So four days after his inauguration, hearing about a small party honoring retired Supreme Court Justice Oliver Wendell Holmes on his 92nd birthday, FDR called on Holmes for a surprise visit. What's somewhat historic about the event, if a bit muddled and unfortunate, is that a conversation came up discussing the two Roosevelts, Teddy and Franklin, during which Holmes was heard mention that it was nice to talk with Franklin and by the way, it was Teddy who nominated him (Holmes) to the Supreme Court. He was then overheard to say, refereeing to which Roosevelt no one was certain, "A second-class mind but a first-class temperament." Accurately rendered or misquoted, it ended up sticking to Franklin.[94]

---

[93] John Kenneth Galbraith, Ibid., p. 5

[94] Jonathan Alter, *The Defining Moment, FDR's Hundred Days and the Triumph of Hope*, Simon and Schuster, New York, 2006, p. 234

The "second class mind" comment didn't seem to make sense to me. My initial thought was he probably thought things out better than his critics while not letting them in on his thinking process and it was their minds that weren't quite up to his, not vice versa. In any case it seemed he came up with one idea after another by gathering trusted advisors with a wide range of good ideas and just tried out the ones that he thought were best. At the core of this strategy was more likely a sense of proportionality than randomly picking out serendipitous advantage. In any case the ideas that didn't work out, he dropped and moved on to try something else. "I'm like a cat," he said, "I make a quick stroke and then I relax."[95]

Jonathan Alter in his biography of Roosevelt focusing on his first 100 days in office, *The Defining Moment,* wrote of people thinking he was "contradictory to a bewildering degree." Eleanor Roosevelt once said, "…he doesn't think, he decides." But first he played the role of convener of people with best ideas, which is what good conference organizers do, but in his case he put the good ideas to work – on the largest scale imaginable. Elmer Davis, journalist, author and Director of the United States Office of War Information during the Second World War said Roosevelt's method, reminded him "of a farmer with too many new born puppies on his hands. He took them out in a boat, dumped them in the water, and kept those that could swim back to shore." In fact, FDR was in some cases quite explicit about what he was likely to do, if not a "plan" or attempt to accomplish something according to an elaborately described "philosophy." During his first campaign for President, speaking at Oglethorpe College, May 1932, he said, "The country needs and, unless I mistake its temper, the country demands bold, persistent experimentation. It is common sense to take a method and try it: if it fails, admit it frankly and try another. But above all try something."[96]

The first trip out the door of the White House, the day after his Inauguration, FDR was stuck in a traffic jam at one of those Washington circle intersections, stuck among people trying to flee town after the celebration. With characteristic spontaneity he told the driver, "Pull out and drive on the grass. You won't hurt it." (I like the homey "you won't hurt it" part.) Said biographer Alter, "The Secrete Service man took this as a sign that things were going to be different."

Yet Roosevelt had some long-standing ideas that looked like if not plans, at least solid core notions plans could be built around. If a plan has a bad core idea, better never to develop it. All the planning around such a core only makes things worse, and worse yet if implemented. It was his core ideas that were often so helpful. The advisors and heads of departments he gathered around could then shape the ideas into plans. As he said, if it ends up not working admit it and try something else.

[95] Jonathan Alter, Ibid. p. 238 – most of my quotes about FDR are from this book

[96] David M. Kenned, *Freedom From Fear: The American People in Depression and War, 1929-1945*, Oxford, 1000, p. 104

Core idea in waiting: Early in 1932, almost a year before his inauguration Roosevelt had discussed the idea of a corps of men employed to execute major conservation and rebuilding work for the country. Then five days after the drive on the grass he convened a 9:00am emergency meeting at the White House that produced, another eleven days later, a bill to create the Federal Emergency Relief Administration (FERA) to run the Civilian Conservation Corps with the goal of immediately putting a quarter million unemployed young men to work. Get them producing, get them paid, get them spending. It wasn't quite shovel ready, being brand new, but was shovel ready in two more weeks. The speed was stunning. For the somewhat older more skilled men, there was the Public Works Administration (PWA), the first of the agencies for intensive larger projects: dams, bridges, airports, schools, post offices, murals in post offices, studies of American ethnic crafts and music… Republicans immediately started carping. Roosevelt was trying to be Santa Claus. The larger projects would take years to build and more years to pay back. But that's another good reason why establishing the CCC made sense: it would be an immediate start and inform the other programs that would take longer, some of which later on would be abandoned but the overall thrust was to get moving, invest, produce, learn, keep moving.

But lest we think it was all liberal, traitor-to-his-class as many of the elite claimed, or that he was even a socialist to establish the larger government-run public works projects or even radical as some people would claim of his Eleanor Roosevelt-influenced civil rights oriented programs later in the Depression, despite all that, Roosevelt cut veterans' benefits a full 50% for all those who didn't have service-related injuries and he vetoed legislation that would give World War I veteran's bonuses. In this, Congress was more liberal than he was, overriding his veto. Some chinks in the armor of his charming smile emerged in his making fun of his faithful son's lack of hair compared to his own enduring quaff, to the hilarity of the press corps which seems a trifle more than cold, and after a visit to Roosevelt by psychologist Carl Jung, said Jung, "…impenetrable mind, but perfectly ruthless."[97] Also, though widely credited after the 2008 financial crisis with establishing an admirably strong, bubble resistant banking system, FDR was, like Hoover and the mainstream capitalist economists, originally against the banking regulations in discussion that might help repair the damage of the 1929 Crash. He was not in favor of Keynes' idea of deficit spending – he was initially against relief but for job creation and he did put people to work almost immediately coming around to deficit spending later. But… working for the CCC for just a dollar a day? Even with housing and food, that sounded unsympathetic. Many who took the jobs were not that happy with the pay and called it a form of slavery, but they were at that point on the way back up.

Moreover FDR was changeable, and observed closely as some puppies sank and others swam. He hired Marriner Eccles, an apparently conservative Mormon from Utah, to head the Federal Reserve Board in 1934. Eccles went through the

[97] Jonathan Alter, op. cit., p. 241

same changes he led FDR through, but for FDR it would be a couple years later. Eccles was a notably successful banker and owner of numerous thriving companies. When the economy turned south he called in loans and restricted new loans carefully, recovered as much as he could in cash and successfully built up reserves to prevent runs on his banks. It worked. For him.

But he noticed the negative effect on the public in general as operating funds and capital for any new business investments, among them some very good ideas, were withheld. Jobs were lost and others not created. People failed to spend so companies couldn't sell their products and so they let more people off. How to get around this downward spiral? No one was there but government charged directly with the overall public good. So it was government that should be involved and stimulate the market. Maybe it should even go into debt selling bonds, borrow to raise money to kick-start the economy. Who else could do it? Government could provide insurance on bank loans financed partially by the banks themselves, encouraged by government, so why not try it? If this approach, even if incurring or expanding a deficit, managed to build up the economy – one of Keynes' strategic prescriptions – the government could, at a later date, tap into the new prosperity thereby created with reasonable taxes, pay back the debt and go happily on its way covered by new tax revenues. If the people were just prosperous enough, the taxing might not even have to be that high. Which is exactly what Eccles suggested and what FDR later changed his mind to adopt.[98] He was essentially "...a free thinker, unencumbered by economic ideology."[99]

Somehow his exact kind of mind seems a little beside the point as I'm busily writing this book and contemplating my own Social Security check and wondering what my faith in my own future success brought me: not much! At least not much in terms of savings. How many people like me thought we'd do just a little better in the money making department than we did, who, responsibly following exactly what we thought was most important and with seriously good prospects, didn't make a nice solid nest egg and now realize their condition would be far worse without Social Security? A savings account tied in with the tax system, whether we wanted it or not, turned out to be a good idea for millions of us. Maybe FDR's polio taught him the vicissitudes of fate and surprise can set people back and he believed he could help us prepare for such reverses.

[98] Background on this from Robert B. Reich's *After-shock – The Next Economy and America's Future*, Alfred A. Knopf, new York, 2010, p. 11 through the first chapter

[99] John de Graaf and David K. Batker, *What's the Economy for, Anyway?*, Bloomsbury Press, New York, 2011 p. 187

27. Yoff Village plaza with Atlantic Ocean in the distance

This village is built on sand. Kids don't skin their knees when they fall. The distant roar and murmuring of the sea is always in the background. Host town for the Third International Ecocity Conference and anchor for the book "Village Wisdom / Future Cities," the conference report, 1996.

After the Crash of 2008 it was almost universally acknowledged – even by many economist themselves – that the deregulation craze of the 1990s was a disastrous string of policies and activities. The banking reform and genuine social security (lower case letters) created during FDR's administration was the source of stability and created a more economically just country than existed before.

The genius of whole systems economic thinking

Second-class (political/economic) mind? Maybe Roosevelt grasped the dynamics and did a masterful job in extraordinarily difficult times. Or maybe a more important conclusion from all this is that economic solutions are not so elite and complex and hard to get at. Maybe they are actually fairly comprehensible even if complex because of patterns that make sense within the total natural resources, human organizational pattern – and you get there not only by good information, inductive thinking leading to principles but also by personal experience, "feel," intuition and well tuned sensitivity to the emotions and moods of the times. Maybe the moral sense is sufficient to understand those trying to get rich fast in 1926, 1929 or 2007 might just be something of a problem? Maybe open eyes and FDR's privileged information were delivering the obvious that a war with Hitler couldn't be avoided. But his job was to get the strategy right and convince and drag along the people he was supposed to both represent and lead.

Maybe Roosevelt also had a sense of nature's role, that her economics were at the base of human economics. She was there cranking out solar powered food and fiber from farm and forest, providing the usual flood of minerals and oil through a fast growing set of industries far from the falling bombs. Knowing what to plant and what to build, how to reclaim soils and forests in Dust Bow times needing to press nature into service for the war effort – in the larger picture it may have been hard to get it more right. As far as nature and resources were concerned it hardly mattered if the money was from savings or loans or maybe even a little secretly printed new money the conservative economists didn't know about, just so people were working, focused and knew what to build. The Administration's theory was that prosperity after the war would more than repay the debt. Keynes must have been smiling at his correct proportionalizing of economic needs of the times thus endorsed. He died in 1946 righteously living long enough to savor the victory of deficit spending in winning the war for democracy.

Lester Brown likes to point out Roosevelt's grasp of the larger situation in his "Plan B" talks, that is, *not* going along as we are in the 2010s on the momentum of our present course, Plan A, business as usual, leading toward depletion of resources, global heating and growing societal problems heading toward what he calls "failed states." He claims our problems are as severe now as if we were entering a world war, in this case with the people vs. planet war. Brown points out, that with a unity of purpose, Roosevelt went to the car companies and said, "Stop building automobiles and start building bombers. You'll get paid." Not wanting to relinquish the profitable habits of their car making, the car companies preferred to ease off some on cars an add some planes and tanks, but the Administration was firm. No cars from February 1942 to, as it turned out, the end of 1944, and not just increased but massively increased production of bombers, guns, military trucks and so on[100] and on a unified front that involved almost all aspects of life: the kinds of jobs available, limits on recreation, encouraging repair and reuse of old things, growing food gardens called Victory Gardens, encouraging the practical, staple and subsistence items on the American artifact list while discouraging the luxurious, silly and superfluous. Quite quickly people knew the difference. Plus in the background, anchored in soil, the plants with their chlorophyll kept changing massive amounts of solar energy, air, water and minerals into the basis of production down at the foundation of the total

[100] Lester R. Brown, *Plan B 4.0 – Mobilizing to Save Civilization*, Norton and Company, New York, p. 260

economy with first New Deal then War Effort investment boosting material production of the necessary sort, with the Administration, in its reforestation and soil conservation programs, recruit nature to the recovery and war cause.

And building was a gigantic chunk of the action in the New Deal and War Effort. His administration built bridges, highways and airports, post offices, hospitals and federal administration buildings while reclaiming soils and replanting forests. In brief: Roosevelt knew (or learned well) what to build for the needs of his times

Lester Brown says we need to mobilize for saving civilization *now*. But can we find the resolve in the 2010s to plan for a better future and literally build it? Can the economy stand the investment in such activity – or can it stand much longer *not* investing in and building a new type of infrastructure, attached technologies and life ways? The threat is even more grave for the future of life on Earth now than when we were entering the Second World War. But the threat is fuzzy and targets others first, poor people, endangered plants and animals, the seemingly abstract "climate" instead of us the richer people, at least in the short term. So in comparison the all-important resolve, based on the proportionality factor is far, far away from cultural consciousness and resolve at this time in the 2010s. None dare call it stupid, but what is it about those who refuse to think about evidence, experience and the proven best of our science? They stand between us and realizing the true scale and nature of the war against nature we are wandering deeper into every day. But, in all cases, as Brown points out, there is much we can do about it and some are doing fairly well even if operating without a clear notion of what to build.

So now, retuning to the historical perspective from the years of the Great Depression and the Second World War, we have some conditions, patterns and initiatives which could be thought of as eventually leading to the post war period of prosperity. 1. Banking laws were improving, 2. along with other forms of reinvesting in real productive work. 3. Confidence was being inspired by the sheer character, positive enthusiasm and leadership of the President and his team, and 4. there was a death threat to reinforce resolve and promote hard work, sacrifice and postponed gratification like few other things could accomplish.

We could add some other major factors too: 5. The role of higher taxes and serious investments, which produce increased prosperity and easier payment of taxes at a later date, 6. the gift of America's vast natural resources, 7. The fact that war was never on American soil, and finally 8. spoils of war, frankly stated, meaning the many advantages that came to the US when emerging in the position of control, influence and ability to effect all aspects of reconstruction globally, including taking advantage of economic wealth to build up infrastructure fast and make advantageous loans and investments in the rest of the world. This led to very profitable deals, low cost resources and basic products for American businesses where "percale down" actually worked for the great majority of US citizens, as tends to happen when a country becomes exceptionally rich.

Finally I'd say number 9. would be the approach of America exercising what in many ways amounted to generosity to the peoples of the former enemy countries and others devastated by the war through the Marshall Plan for rebuilding, the opposite approach from the settlement of the First World War that many including John Maynard Keynes thought ensured new disasters: the massive reparations demanded of Germany and the Central Powers that essentially flung tens of millions of people into poverty and intensely frustrated resentment.

Lets get back to the issue of proportionalizing. The generally improving employment rates, growing GNP and productivity of the economy from FDR's arrival in the White House to the end of the Second World War were proportionally big factors to take into consideration. But let's also look briefly at taxes, which after all are where most money in Government hands, i.e. the citizens' collective hands, comes from. If we think seriously graduated income tax is a major part of the solution today too, here are some of the reasons why.

Before the First World war, taxes as a percentage of the wealthiest tax payers annual incomes was approximate 7% but by the end of the war they were up to about 78%.[101] By 1925 their rate was down to 25% and stayed there for four more years while Hoover and his economists and political strategists waited for the overheated market to adjust itself. Then the Crash of 1929. Still, Hoover and mainstream economists just waited for the market to adjust itself. But things kept sliding away until after approximately two more years, and the Administration finally got impatient and decided to jack top taxes up to approximately 62% for the highest bracket. Roosevelt, too, was a little reluctant to raise taxes even though he was starting a vigorous building campaign through his various agencies. Not until more than two years into his first term were taxes raised on the wealthiest, then in steps over the next three years, up to 90% on the highest brackets upon entering the Second World War. With minor perturbations the high tax rate lasted until 1963, eighteen years after the war was over which would amaze forgetful people today who can't imagine anyone would ever dare raise or keep taxes so high in anytime but war years. It is even more amazing to contemporary ears in the 2010s with the tiny increments offered up as serious "new taxes," a term to strike fear in the hearts of supposedly everyone, that the country was prospering so well for almost 20 post war years with seriously high taxes.

Then it was under a Democrat, Lyndon Johnson, not the Republican presidency of Dwight Eisenhower, that the rate dropped to approximately 70%. Under Ronald Reagan, the wealthiest got a real windfall: down to 28%, plus Reagan did all he could to launch the deregulation frenzy that promoted much higher income to wealthy speculators and contributed to a growing disparity between rich and poor that has run all the way through to as I write today, as well as being the largest cause – deregulation – precipitating the Crash of 2008. Taxes for the richest category went up very slightly under Clinton, and dropped slightly under George Bush II and Obama to approximately 27%. (This doesn't include adjustments from capital gains

[101] Need better info here... "Wealthiest tax payers" should be explained, perhaps as the top 10%? 1%? Plus I seem to have lost the reference. Find replacement figures.

that make for a lower percent tax when averaged out, and doesn't include non-profit tax deductions for various causes, and other loopholes but it does give a basic proportional sense for the pattern).[102]

The lesson seems to be that medium high taxes were helpful in the Depression era when employment and productivity in the US improved and high income taxes were crucial in winning the Second World War and enhancing prosperity and equity through the period generally regarded as exceptionally prosperous from the late 1940s into the late1960s. Then, over the three decades that started under Reagan, with the very significant drop in taxes on the wealthy, both prosperity and equity steadily eroded. It is hard to be certain of a strong direct correlation, because as just pointed out, there are a fair number of other factors including improved banking practices in general. In any case, the large money flows of taxation to active government programs for stimulating production and establishing security look like they were significantly successful.

Proportionality again… If we scan the list quickly: 1. Banking laws like Glass Steagall and the usual regulations and stimulations applied by economists to mellow out excesses and reduce risk, 2. investing in productive work, 3. confidence in the system 4. pressures from outside the system from a threat, 5. high taxes, invested for higher yields later on, 6. rich resources, 7. peace and hard work in the homeland 8. advantages of winning a war, and 9. generosity to other nations in rebuilding paying off. Let's add one more to the total economy picture, number 10. investing in ecological services through bolstering nature's productivity. Similarly, related intimately to ecological services, we should include generally reliable climate to provide proper temperature and moisture regimes for, lets face it, all life on the planet.

[102] Wikipedia://en.wikipedia.orgwiki/File:Chart_1.png

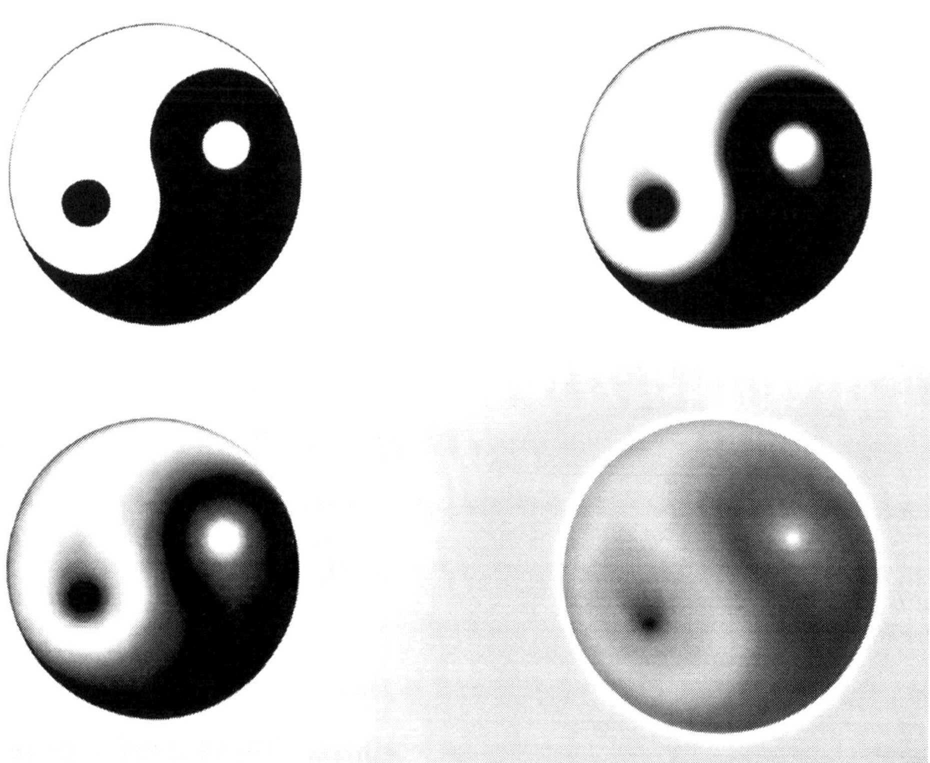

28. Dimensional pairs

One of the more novel ideas presented in this book, is actually a different version of the ancient East Asian "Yin-Yang" graphic illustrating the dualistic nature of reality. But Einstein's formula E=mc2 demonstrating that such solid dimensions as matter and energy turn out to be one and the same thing is an amazingly different twist on that whole construct. It adds "fuzziness" to the graphic. If a dimension of reality is one of more than one "thing" that without another, nothing exists – like time and space, say – this helps explain why some generalizations and powerful intuitions can get it right when faux precision, such as claimed by many economists get it disastrously wrong. Analogies are seldom if ever perfect and the same for graphic representation of concepts. So which of the above four expresses the concept best, which degree of "fuzziness" to the laws of the universe staring us in the eye? Not enough space in a caption to explore, but the text tries and doesn't have an answer.

CHAPTER 9

Current Events

Cars and the emerging real economics of our times

"Our times" I'll define here as pretty much my times, the times of a reasonably oldish person – I'm starting my 70s – and imagining I'll last another 15 to maybe even 30 years. My grandmother lived to 102 so who knows, I could live into the era when a better notion of economics becomes operative, just maybe. Keynes saw his ideas successful.

"Our times," so defined, is a time in America when we woke up to see, after the cowboy movie gun battle – times hundreds of millions – just who was left standing, who was wounded and what cards the players had in their hands after the shootout. Proportional information, you might say, for the student of economics, was that for all the efforts to rally the nation in the Depression, the War summoned the resolve to spend six times as much money on building something than did the New Deal. But the money was spent in about half the time. That's a real time multiple of twelve. Twelve times more spent per person is what a lot of people would call "real money" and makes one wonder what spending twelve times the inflation adjusted money of the New Deal era might accomplish today if someone were not, on behalf of one economic theory or another, preventing spending on developing a prospering ecocity civilization. Time travel deeper into the early 21st century and maybe it would be dramatic enough to solve our climate destabilizing, environmentally violent and potentially world civilization destroying ways, though we'd have to know in addition how to build something "sustainable" as then we had to know what to build for victory in depression and war.

In the Second World War much of the product produced literally self destructed – the bombs exploded – and a lot of other material product was torn to pieces and wasted too: airplanes, ships, bridges, buildings, whole cities and 53 million human bodies left dead and many more wounded. And the US came out of it prosperous – preposterous! How could anything so bizarre actually happen? But, speaking of thinking proportionally, that vast expenditure on job creation must have meant a lot and "paid off," as they say. But in the War Against Nature, today's World War, who gets the spoils if the resource base can't be coaxed again to give us massive floods of cheap food, fiber, minerals and energy, if the climate is ruined and if the species list ends up short, weak, and ineffectual at delivering "ecosystem services"? On the other hand, if we knew how to proportionalize well and we knew what to build and spent on *that*...

But again I digress and now will instead rejoin our flow of economic history by looking at two men's careers that tell quite directly of the times we inherit, Victor Gruen, "father of the shopping mall" and Ken Schneider, a planner and generalist thinker with powerful insights whom I had the privilege of knowing well, a friend and major ecocity theorist. Anyone in planning or architecture in the period from then to now knows Victor Gruen. A few detective researchers among the seekers after sustainable, green or ecological cities know Kenneth Schneider. Gruen and Schneider came together, in a sense, around 1960 at the downtown pedestrian Mall of Fresno, California. The Fulton Mall replaced an everyday downtown main street filled with cars. Gruen designed it and Ken worked there as it fell apart, or more correctly, was abandoned and eviscerated.

Gruen, born in 1903, was a Viennese architect, Jewish and had barely started his practice when Hitler's swarm of heavily armed robots marched in. Not your everyday young architect, Guren also co-organized a cabaret where he and friends satirized the Nazis. Fun, but a little dangerous if... And "if" happened when he arrived at his office he'd recently established and found his Nazi-sympathizing employee with a gun sitting in Gruen's chair saying, "if you cooperate you can be my partner some day." Running for his life, not figuratively speaking, he first sprinted to his theater, picked up a Nazi uniform used in plays, made it to a small airport, which was an open field among farms, and arrived in 1938 in New York City with eight dollars in his pocket. There he started working his way up through set design, to small architecture jobs and by 1948 modest sized commercial shopping facilities. In that year he met the owner of a major department store chain in Detroit, Michigan called Hudson's, made a deal to design a car-oriented shopping mall. By 1954, the job was built, the largest shopping mall in the world, called Northlands – surrounded by a parking lot for several thousand cars appropriately in a suburb of Detroit. It proved to be Gruen's launch pad to fame as the father of the shopping mall, American style.

My friend Kenneth Schneider, born 24 years later, joined the US Marines, made it through the flying bullets and friends' body parts on the islands of the West Pacific fighting the Japanese. He was studying city planning at the University of California at Berkeley, 1952-54, while Gruen was sketching out Northlands, pencil in hand. When Ken got out of college, he took a planning job studying and advising on cities in California's Central Valley, cities including Modesto, Bakersfield and Fresno. He immediately noticed and started commenting disapprovingly about the rapid spread of low-density development beginning to push back against the rich agricultural lands, even then. But before he could settle into the groove there, in 1961, he took his wife and children off on three years of working first for Cooperative for American Relief Everywhere (CARE), the privately organized international aid group based in the US. Shortly after he worked for the United Nations, first to the Philippines, Jordan and Sierra Leon, and then back to the states, to Hopwell, New Jersey. There he wrote his first book stuffed with generalist theory called *Destiny of Change*.[103] In the late 1960s he became somewhat obsessed with the impacts of cars, their incredibly rapid take over, and he dedicated a long trip, again with his family, to a small Mediterranean town near Barcelona in 1968, to crunch through a new book: *Autokind vs. Mankind*.[104]

Now he was radicalized, that is, firmly opposed to the radical shift in development toward car dominance that was becoming the planning dogma of the day, but nonetheless somehow landed a job in Fresno, California on the city planning staff just a little more than a decade after he left the Valley farm towns.

By then Victor Gruen had designed a mall for downtown Fresno, the Fulton Mall, that kicked out the cars and converted six blocks of Fulton Street into a pedestrian environment, completed two years before Ken arrived.

Here's what else was happening. Gruen loved the pedestrian centers of cities and towns he had known in Europe. In the US he discovered there were few opportunities for such centers in already built up US city centers and all the new architecture jobs were out on the flats, scattered about the city centers in ever more automobile-oriented low-density areas. The significant buildings to be designed and built were just that: buildings. He wanted to build environments people could walk around in with lots of space, other people, plazas with sculptures.... Voila! The answer was the shopping center in the middle of a parking lot, something like the town square with long-honored market that was traditional in Europe but instead of being *in* a center it would *be* the center, the only center around. Instead of at the core of

---

[103] Kenneth R. Schneider, *The Destiny of Change – How Relevant is Man in the Age of Development?*, Holt, Rinehart and Winston, Inc., NY, 1968

[104] Kenneth R. Schneider, *Autokind vs. Mankind – An Analysis of Tyranny, A Proposal for Rebellion,* A Plan for Reconstruction, Shocken Books, New York, 1971

and sharing in a vibrant mix of different activities – living, working, buying, learning, socializing… it would be almost wholly commercial, supplemented by a little art, maybe some adjunct "community services" and surrounded by hundreds, even thousands of parking spaces for cars.

Gruen never liked the compromise with the car. But to be practical, how else to assemble people in the happening development pattern of the America of the times? One suspects he didn't like the near complete commercial profit justification for the investments in his shopping centers either, but again, America had been his rescue and here he was. He wasn't going to be overly critical of the source of his money and growing success. But about the car, he went so far as to suggest that automobiles along with cigarette packages should have labels warning that the item is hazardous to your health, may cause death. The first two images in his book *Centers for the Urban Environment* are photographs of a pile of crushed and junked cars and a contrasting lovely forest scene – images of cities wait until later. To write his rants against the automobile when he had been building enormous asphalt deserts for them must have been something of an act of mental gymnastics to win Olympic gold medals of the mind. He should have been getting profoundly depressed. Probably he was.

His first generation shopping centers were in the middle of nowhere, but as soon as Gruen could find clients, he was designing malls in downtowns, closing streets and adding facilities for as wide a mix of activities as he could get away with. The idea was to make convenient, commercially successful environments while augmenting the natural centers of the city, enriching the lives of the people who lived near and could walk or get there on transit or by car. In the American context, that meant lots of parking lots. That was just the way it was. Worth noting is the economic and political difference between the cheap land and already existing large areas of simple zoning in the case of the suburban mall development site and the expensive land in the midst of a variety of smaller area zoning designations and many competing political goals and financial ambitions in the city centers. In other words, it was by far a more difficult and politically charged project to build a pedestrian shopping mall in an existing city center.

Ken Schneider arrived seven years after Victor Gruen's Fulton Mall was opened and by then the downtown was well on its way to being abandoned. In a report Ken wrote for the City of Fresno while on staff there, called "On Planning In Fresno," 1971, he lamented the many growing forces against the pedestrian mall. You can almost read between the lines, "People will start to wake up any day now. They will realize that this car-based fad is wrecking the conviviality and other good things of the city and leading to disasters painful, lonely and numerous. Soon the tide will reverse back to beautiful pedestrian city centers. My writing will be part of that returning tide of happy civility and sanity." But they actually liked sitting in their suburban isolation in front of their televisions for social contact for thousands of hours a year. After all, they could drive anywhere, no? Here we see the partnership of cars and TV in producing sprawl among a population thinking good fences make good neighbors, as Carl Sandberg cast the American character.

The Fulton Mall's timing in the history of planning in America could hardly have been worse. It was just the beginning of the trend that carries on with Walmarts still, *approaching half a century later* destroying downtown vitality with Americans racing to get more stuff cheaper, driving there on their ever more expensive gasoline, in their ever more expensive and (collectively as their number rise around the world) destructive cars, now turning slowly into hybrids and electrics. Not only was Ken Schneider's adopted city gaining population in 1971, but, in step with the whole country, in the worst manner – very scattered low-density – and with the worst expectations: that there would be ample free parking for all those – the strong majority – who could afford the wonderful convenience of the automobile.

About the time Ken Schneider arrived to work in Fresno – I met him five years later – and started work, a large hotel near the mall was closed and a new Veterans Administration Hospital was opened far away. Then in quick succession the new Internal Revenue Center for the western states was built three miles to the east. The worst blow was two at once: the new campus of Fresno State College was built a full seven miles to the north and a new large shopping center, already inspired by Gruen's earliest profitable suburban sprawl auto malls, called Fashion Fair, was located almost as far away as the college. Victor Gruen must have felt a little peculiar that his fast success with his downtown-destroying suburban commercial magnets sucking the life out of city centers all around America were ironically beginning to wreck his slightly later and much less emotionally conflicted attempts at vitalizing downtowns. You might say he had poisoned his own pond. In fact, he may have seen the disaster for his higher hopes coming, his past success wrecking his future in America so he went back to Vienna shortly before Ken even arrived in Fresno. You can almost see him slipping out of town as quietly as possible before his American friends of downtowns caught on. In Vienna he actually succeeded in establishing, with sympathetic collaborators, a large pedestrian district in the center of the city. I've been there. It works. It's beautiful. But then the cathedral, the buildings and open spaces there already, if invaded by cars in the decades just before, were great urban features going back hundreds of years and begging just to be rid of the cars that he and his friends successfully banished.

Meantime, back in the States, central Fresno died such a depressing death with shops closing, buildings demolished for parking lots, people thinning out until they seemed to walk like the living dead, that it lived on in the infamy of the US planning legend that "downtown pedestrian malls always fail in the US." I remember in my three decades of trying to make progress on behalf of ecologically tuned projects in Berkeley, California, a town without a single block of a street dedicated to pedestrians, hearing that refrain over and over from merchants and NIMBYs from up to almost 40 years after the collapse of the Fresno Mall. They'd say, "Pedestrian areas are a real disaster; remember the mess in Fresno," with no reference to the great differences between the two cities and the two times. NIMBYs, for a brief historic aside, is a term from Not In My Back Yard opponents to development and physical problems, real and imagined, of all kinds. It was coined at Love Canal near Niagara Falls, New York in 1978 where industrial dumping was causing cancer and birth defects. The tactic of local opposition has since been used to try and often succeed in thwarting healthy as well as damaging initiatives. A double edge sword you might say.

Seven years after arriving in Fresno, and essentially black listed for his stance against cars, Ken gave up the planning profession entirely and started a business called Beauty Way, making actually rather beautiful oversized post cards of scenes of the Southwest USA: desert scenes, Monument Valley, high mountain aspen forests, Grand Canyon, sunsets, exotic animals, the colorful people from cowboys to Indians... He did this for a living – he had to do something – and he loved the countryside. The cards did well at hotels, tourist spots and up and down Route 66 now Interstate 40. Meantime, from his new home in Flagstaff, Arizona, and later near Sacramento, California he continued to write books on city design, planning and theories of democracy and economics until he died in 2005. I remained impressed with his ideas throughout; he seemed to me to represent the best thinking I could find linking the physical structure of the city to economics.

February 27, 2014: the Fresno City Council decides to dismantle Fulton Mall and let the cars back in to Fulton Street, paid for by a US Department of Transportation grant. And just when more and more people are beginning to return to city centers craving more pedestrian conviviality. A fitting twisted end to two lives of pioneers of positive ideas into the land and times of cars, contradictions and dysfunction.

Victor Gruen, Kenneth Schneider: their nemesis wins

Something else going on in the times when Gruen was hitting his shopping mall stride and Schneider was a young idealist planner just starting out: society was prosperous; everything was possible. But, as Ken pointed out in his book *The Runaway Economy*, there is only so much one can eat. You might be able to make ten times as much money, as you build up your wealth, but can you eat ten times as much food? Can you actually use ten times as much house to knock around in? Does it make sense to drive ten instead of one car? "Unlike the advances in times past (especially from 1900 to 1950) which introduce totally new and very useful household heating and air conditioning, refrigeration, washers and dryers, microwave ovens, steam irons and even radio and television, new consumer technologies are now increasingly exotic rather than basic, improvements rather than new products." [105] What he's missing of course is what we tend to call greed. It was once the birthright of the elite back in the days of the preindustrial city, their splendid conspicuous consumption helping enforce control and command, and it still proves you are something special today. You don't eat, live in and drive ten times as *much* but rather ten times as *expensive* for each, plus some amplification of scale, too, plus the symbols of it all, plus the "freedom" of impulsive action: you can do whatever the hell you feel like; forget everyone else.

But let's stick with Schneider's democratic thinking for the moment. He also pointed out that the suburban house on cheap land, of cheap materials, often with garage and driveway, financed by the GI bill, with a tax deductibility of interest payments on the mortgage, was the affordable and perfect container for more and more stuff. Those who live in small apartments in city centers or in medium density to dense neighborhoods where land is expensive and jobs and amenities are in close proximity couldn't possibly have four cars in the family of two, small power boat on a trailer in the driveway (what driveway?), private basketball backstop, lawn furniture, swing set and trampoline, rubber swimming tank for the kids – or actual real pool – storage space in the double garage for cars, tools, big boxes, overflow clothes, board games and on and on ... For all that, the suburban house with yard and garage was a natural encouragement to consumption, the supreme, democratized mass consumption magnet. Said Ken in that regard: "Together with promotional advertising, the forces creating inefficient and chaotic urban environments are now assumed to be resolved with further increasing production and consumption. However, the greater reality is that they generate the radical runaway economy, the most audacious irony of our modern economic development."[106]

Schneider makes an emphatic point, along with Galbraith, that the productive might of the country and its big companies had saturated the sustenance market soon after the war – the Depression was over. The economy moved beyond sufficiency into real comfort and by the 1960s and 1970s had moved from one that was chiefly physically productive to one that was chiefly for stimulating consumption to keep productivity going, an economy that was more and more service oriented as well as production and sales oriented. The big companies themselves were planning this, as Galbraith's observed. They weren't waiting around for the invisible hand of the market place to lead. *They* were the invisible hand, hiring psychologists – studied propagandists – and using massive advertising for the first time, in the 1960s up 40 times over by money spent since the 1920s according to Schneider. That, in those

[105] Kenneth Schneider, *The Runaway Economy – The Rhetoric is Growth, The Issue is Freedom*, iUniverse (essentially published by his daughter Leslie Schneider after his death) Lincoln, Nebraska, 2004, p. 24

[106] Kenneth Schneider, ibid., p. 6

post World War II years, was just the beginning of the service economy in which the United States and recovering Europe were becoming the office to the world, assuming the higher paid management functions, while shifting more and more basic production, meaning the lower paid labor and raw resources exploitation, to the poorer countries.

At home in the US, Schneider contends, the power of the corporations, "...penetrates human behavior to its quick, so much so that it is assumed in behavior and hardly recognized; it is included in the purpose and content of the public schools, the mind control by the mass media, the structure of urban form, and increasingly the base support and directive force of higher education and cultural institutions."[107]

Add the energy flow. David Lilienthal, Chairman of the US Atomic Energy Commission, convinced the futurist in all of us, at least until the 1970s, that nuclear power made it possible for people to soon have electric energy so plentiful and cheap that it would no longer be necessary to meter and charge for it. At the time there was an enormous sense of human destiny among many Americans including Kenneth Schneider, based on the perceived technical achievements, including high flying airplanes, the awesome invention of the atomic bomb and men on the moon, including rapidly expanding industrial output and the reality of high consumption levels and dreams of ever more: *that* idea of prosperity.

Said Schneider, again in his book *The Runaway Economy*, "Once basic material affluence is reached and household appliances are absorbed, the good life logically shifts from material and current consumption to activities and long-term interests founded upon personal leisure, social stimulation, cultural opportunity and public support."[108]

Well, that's what he imagined it should be like, and certainly more people did become involved in leisure activities at that time. But in later writing he agonizes over the fact that serious reflection on human destiny and the ultimate purposes of prosperity did not seem to emerge from material prosperity, certainly not in America. In fact, four decades after he'd formulated his idea that with proper progress we'd have near infinite choices and therefore needed a powerful philosophy with which to make them, he was complaining no such cultural conversation was heard outside small subsets of New Agers that made more mainstream folks fidget and blush and among some futurists, middle aging Hippies and academics studying specifically ethics, values and the altruistic individual. Maybe some French existentialist philosophers obsessed on the question but certainly no American opinion leaders or followers in noteworthy numbers.

Meantime one-income families morphed into two income families with the homemaker having to enter the job market to attain even close to the "standard of

---

[107] Kenneth Schneider, ibid., p. 4

[108] Kenneth Schneider, ibid., p. 24

living" people were used to just a couple decades earlier. Instead of assessing the directions and meaning of civilization, which would even sound a little pretentious and embarrassing to most Americans' ears, they began to simply become more resentful and the pattern continues in the present. Now, instead of vision, anger and reaction are the best the Tea Party can summons and those concerned with maldistribution of the usufructs of prosperity, maybe most of the "99%" featured in the Occupy Wall Street movement, just want more for those who have less and less for those who have obscene quantities of more. The truth of the matter is that's not much of a vision for a civilization.

There were a few, so few Ken Schneider stood almost alone, who saw the role of the automobile and design of the city as essential to understanding what was going on in the economy. (Soleri, on the other hand, who saw the design of the city as crucial to understanding *everything*, didn't paid much attention to economics.) It was general knowledge that General Motors had bested Ford's, cheap, useful, no nonsense Models T and A expressing the values and philosophy of the times with its yearly new models in flashy colors and constantly changing styles and options, establishing a new approach in business, as noted by Galbraith, manipulating the market instead of vice versa. But in economics, what that meant in mass flows of energy and material – the creation of the truly gigantic infrastructure of the car/sprawl/paving/ cheap energy city form – was completely ignored as an issue by the mainstream – while being lived enthusiastically.

29. Bicycle City

An idea for an early stage in the development of an ecovillage starting around a plaza with a view to ponds, valley and countryside, with stage. You might note a "T" intersection slightly above and right of mid picture where you'd be lost in an "urban" world yet in the country – about the smallest scale where "urban" and "rural" can come together in a small area.

Takes a death threat to get us moving?

In looking at what most economists seldom publically analyze, what about the psychology of the serious death threat? Economists do not talk, at least publically, much about its influence on promoting certain companies and development projects.

It wasn't that obscure either, in the duck and cover days when I was in grade school in Albuquerque, New Mexico, downwind from the nuclear test sites in Nevada. That was the era of the early cold war, surmounted by the image of the mushroom cloud towering five times higher than any cloud you'd ever seen. My sixth grade teacher would pull out his Geiger counter to see if we were in the radiation cloud this time... If the bomb were dropped in late twilight you'd see it in full sun in a nearly black sky with the brighter stars around it, as if in the solar system, not the atmosphere. While America was busy being prosperous and economists were as usual concerned with the self-guiding all-powerful market and whether it was dominantly demand side or supply side and so on, what about the Cold War in the 1950s and the American War on Vietnam in the 1960s and early 1970s? Early in that period, not only did we have to crouch under our desks when the sirens went off but the country was being rebuilt around not just the car, but the National Interstate Defense Highway Act's new and creatively named "freeway" system, which was very expensive in terms of tax dollars, hardly "free." If you read the rationale it wasn't all for commercial and citizen prosperity but justified largely as a system for evacuating cities under nuclear attack and for moving weaponry about the country. Or did cars and oil have effective lobbyists?

The G.I.s knew and remembered well violence, and everyone had some inkling of what a World War III might bring. It was a little schizophrenic, threat of an incinerated world on one hand and happy-go-lucky prosperity on the other with a car in every driveway, a television in every living room and an appliance to make every chore fun, or so it was in television advertisements. What I was hearing in my childhood that you don't hear much any more, was that more concentrated cities are better targets for bombing attacks and scattered ones harder to "take out" because they cover such large areas. That was another rationale for sprawl. The real deal was in the psychology of the Cold War, an element in the economy that pumped through immense sums of capital, transforming the money into probably the most expensive machines the world had ever seen, military weaponry. Something in that should have been debated as a real economics. That is, the militarization of the economy is very big business and as most businesses like to stay in business; so do the defense contractors.

Meantime, said Milton Friedman, economists "...do not have and should not have... public responsibility outside profit making."[109] President Dwight Eisenhower begged to differ and warned us in his goodbye speech in 1961 about the "military industrial complex." As influential people economists have a moral obligation, a "public responsibility" no less than Eisenhower, that even us much less influential every day sort of people share, to improve things or try our best in that direction.

Not long after his warning the death threat took another twist leading into the American War in Vietnam. Its dynamics flowed from the threat that unified world Communism would pour down through Vietnam, and somehow hop the Indonesian Islands to Australia and who knows where after that. The "domino theory" I've mentioned here before. What did happen was the US invested massively in the war there only to admit after nearly five million deaths, according to then Secretary

[109] Kenneth Schneider, ibid. p. 41

of War Robert McNamara in the documentary film "The Fog of War,"[110] that it was a "mistake" and then withdraw. When the Vietnamese Communists drove the US out, did they swarm through Singapore and Darwin to Sydney and thence to Lima and points north? What fantasies rationalized that war? None at all said a rich and amazingly frank investor I once met. "We won," he said. "You should have seen the profits our companies made, including some I invested in."

The system is still very much with us as Chalmers Johnson has pointed out, as I've mentioned earlier, in his three books reporting on over 730 US military bases in 130 countries[111] plus fleets "afloat." He worries that we have lost the Republic already and are likely in an irreversible oligarchy that controls most of the money, the media and electoral process so almost totally it could be called close to totalitarian. The fear of losing our democracy might wake up people – he hopes.

Similarly fear does work, as Pinker indicates, for environmentalists, too. For fear of the consequences if we don't do something positive, recently those concerned about "nature" range as far into economics as to encourage green businesses even sustainable cities, though to date with relatively random approaches and with more success with business than with city design and planning. Those concerned in this business-like way sometimes get their proportionality right and hone in on the essentials. The green business owners convince millions of people to buy one product rather than another by rating it "green" and there is enough concern around that it often works fairly well. Businesses developing reputations for their good ethics are netting more and more customers into the 2010s because of, if not necessarily the death threat, the threat of loss of health, damage to admired indigenous cultures, loved countryside, wild animals and so on. The point here is that the market is following once again, as in after advertising by the big corporations, rather than leading, but in this case following moral convictions. Adam Smith's social values are here leading the market, not vice versa, just like he wanted it despite his invisible guiding hand. Ecocity promotion with fear – I have to admit in the face of climate change and other problems, I hope it works. I hope something will work! But here comes the issue of exaggerated gamesmanship. Be careful the exaggeration on "our side" doesn't lead to what Chalmers Johnson calls "blowback."

And something of a conclusion: the large and growing amount of money moving through ethical business is certainly worth noting and accommodating in theory. In fact, there is even the potential that boycott and buy lists could bypass much more expensive advertising in the long run, saving guess what? More money for consumers for one thing. Such lists often consulted and acted upon imply much

---

110 *The Fog of War*, a film by Errol Morris, Sony Pictures Classics, 2004. Eleven international film festivals selected this film as best of the year, according to credits on the cover of the DVD.

111 Chalmers Johnson, *Dismantling the Empire – America's last best hope*, Metropolitan Books, New York, 2010, p. 30. At the time of Johnson's writing, he cited a 2005 Pentagon official survey reporting 373 foreign bases.

less advertising and top-down manipulation in the functioning of the market. In participating in the market's classical capitalist traditional unseen guiding hand largely self-regulating self, the buyers armed with the boycott and buy lists are then free to cut loose the manipulation and join the good old capitalist market as it should be with minimal interference – but in this case free of corporate control rather than government regulatory control. This is a form or regulation by the people themselves.

An actual evil in "our times"

We are still with "our times" as I've earlier defined as around the time I've been alive from approximately the end of the Second World War into the 2010s. That's the period Pinker calls the "Long Peace:" quite a few small wars but no wars between large countries and declining violent crime in general. This has been a period of economic trends with a certain pattern launched largely by the Franklin Delano Roosevelt Administration with its separation of community banking and investment banking (largely though the changes required by the Glass Steagall Act) and the assumption of the positive value of government acting effectively for the common good, a time generally viewed as prosperous and sometimes considered good, relatively stable capitalism.

About half way through this cycle of the Long Peace (world declining deaths per 100,000 people due to violence) things began to change in economic philosophy and practice. Launched in the Reagan years, safeguards that kept capitalism buzzing along powerful but under reasonable control, were step-by-step stripped away by deregulation. Now at the end of this circle we are back to a confusing time with some parallels to the 1920s before the big crash in 1929, perhaps with our 2008 financial crisis being somewhat parallel with the Florida real estate bust in 1926. Many things have been deregulated ("modernized" in the names of the bills that did much of the deregulation) to give big speculators a free hand at making money much faster and gave the market a fee hand in freeing millions of people of their savings, houses, jobs, small businesses and personal security. We are, as I write, still in the pattern of the last half of "our times" in which the idea that government was powerfully helpful for a healthy economy gradually transformed into the idea that it should stay out of economics and business, let the market regulate itself (please ignore government bailouts of large banks and car companies when thinking about this). The anti-government idea is now embraced by a vast number of angry people who feel entitled, whether rich or poor, to ever *more.* The mantra of the economist, the 2008 Financial Crisis notwithstanding, is still growth, growth and still more growth or else the economy is in trouble.

Let's turn now to economic theory – in action. What's this about value free being good? Good and evil are value judgments based on something going on in what we think of as our best understanding of reality, that is, what's actually the truth of the human condition and the state of the world we seem to be part of. What makes religion powerful, and much of philosophy, is its delving into what is good or evil, compassionate or cruel, creative or destructive, reverent regarding God's Creation or impiously oblivious to its worth. Value-free means the absence of what we generally call values, values of good or evil. If absent values, how could anything be good? Or for that matter evil. Let either one come rolling in! Random uber alles. Not a good idea. Remember Milton Friedman's comment that economists "...do not have and should not have... public responsibility outside profit making." But a question: How can science or economics be good?

When you get what you expect because your plans are effective, you tend to think the means to get there were... pretty good. In this case, "good" is not a values or moral conclusion but simply a statement about the reliability of some thing or activity, that it works, gets desired results, targets we set up are successfully met (such as cleaning the air in Los Angeles – and getting climate change, not to sound too cynical about that one). That some thing or activity is "good" in this usage only in the sense of effective in a cause and effect chain, "good" therefore also at predicting with some better than mediocre chance at accuracy. Science is great for this and therefore tends to get "good" results when applied within the parameters of some sort of activity heading toward some sort of objective. But a gangster good at deception, stealing and killing isn't so good in the sense of healthy, friendly and moral to have around your neighborhood. It is not so healthy if we conflate the two meanings of good.

The word "value" has two meanings also, and also often conflated. There is the quantitative sense, which may be where yet more confusion reigns for the economist. More, a larger number of something and or bigger in scale of each in that number, generally *seems* to be good when it comes to money and the economist advising the capitalist definitely is talking about more being good from the capitalist's point of view. And when it comes to prosperity, that's what most people would like to have: a larger quantity of *it*. But values, with an "s" on the end, is a different concept, a moral concept that has something to do with life values, health, happiness, peace and creativity, and justice – just like "good" in the moral sense. However, even quantitative good isn't such a good idea as in eating ten times as much food for dinner doesn't translate the quantitative value into qualitative that supports health. Not so good for beauty either or justice if you take the food away from nine other people. Some extremely significant things just aren't translated into higher value by quantitative measure, much less higher values. That's the value of the values underlying Bhutan's Gross National Happiness standards.

But most of conventional economics isn't even that good or of value in the "effective" sense outside of very narrow limits, that is, in the non-values meaning of the word "good." With Alan Greenspan, perhaps the most influential "applied" economist in the entire country being blindsided by the 2008 Crash he helped create, we have a good solid example of something just plain wrong. Hence economics is far from good science, extremely far. That's the case largely because of the utterly unpredictable influences of the emotionality of the key actors – us people. The economists doctrine that people are predictable, like billions of atoms bouncing about at a certain temperature and therefore applying an exact amount of pressure on the inside of a container because of their heat-induced movement, the mainstream economists call the "theory of rational expectations." They theorize that investors and buyers and sellers with good information will always act in their own self-interest and this can be averaged out and relied upon as basis for sound economic theory.

Speaking of theories, what's with the Nobel Prizes for the theory of rational expectations, and why a high regard for the economists' belief, applied to economics, "in the beautiful language of math," in the words of economics Nobel Laureate Thomas Sargent?[112] There is a higher rationality that brings the logical, emotional, instinctive and resilient together, more often called wisdom. It operates with the messy, fuzzy edges of ecology around various basic general principles and admits that in such a world dogmatic certainty often fails to work and often math and logic do too. Uncertainty and certainty, random serendipity and precision – maybe two other dimensional pairs? Existence can't exist without both?

Then there is economic theory as an article of faith, or a whole matrix of dogma to in fact support good in the moral values sense – or evil. When capitalism or Communism or most likely any other –ism is used to commit what is almost universally considered destructive, deceiving, cruel, greedy, thieving, murderous – all those things that end up on "thou shalt not" lists from religious books to books of law, how could the exponents of these -isms begin to claim they were good "-isms" in the positive moral values sense? We have here a double failure to achieve anything "good" in both senses of the word.

Yet this is precisely what Milton Friedman's Chicago School has been all about. Its notion of pure Capitalism as a moral good that does a good job in its application and produces an economists' version of paradise requires a particularly harsh form of regulation, not of the market's excesses but direct regulation by violent suppression of the people themselves and their practice of democratic rights, a double failure of horrific consequences in both senses of value and values and both senses of good. It "works" at all only when the state applies police and military power to regulation of the economy – and the people. Contradictory, too, that a set of economic ideas that is anti-regulation would require regulation so severe as to round up thousands of people in the soccer stadiums of Chile in 1973 at the point of the gun and execute hundreds of them for being on the side that won the last election. Strange an economic system "working" through government regulation that killed or "disappeared" more than 3,200 people, imprisoned 80,000 and was "free" enough to send 200,000 people fleeing to find freedom somewhere other than in Chile's new "free market" economy directed by Friedman's "Chicago Boys." Strange also it doesn't quite dawn on those setting up Friedman style systems that

[112] New York Times, "How Two Quiet Economists Reached a Profession's Peak," by Jeff Sommer, December 4, 2011, p. 1, Sunday Business section.

this is even a form of regulation when it is regulation in its strongest and most ultimate form: "Be regulated – or I'll spray your blood all over our football field."

Meantime, Augusto Pinoche, the General who murdered the democratically elected Salvador Allende in his successful coup, and applied Friedmanesque economic management as best he could kept most of the rest of that country in a state of shock and terror for years while over the following decades many economists including Alan Greenspan held the sacred texts of Friedman's economics in high reverence until finally the disaster of the 2008 close encounter of the Crash kind. And what then was learned? Obama appointed many of the same people who ran the economy into the ground in the lead up to 2008 to positions responsible for managing the country's economy.

It seems obvious from overwhelming evidence that this truly moral issue of the "good," or in this case the evil of what Chicago School economists accomplished in Chile, has been well established. CIA Director Richard Helms was even convicted of lying to Congress in 1973 saying the CIA was not involved in assisting the overthrow and killing of Salvador Allende when it in fact was.[113] He got a suspended sentence and $2,000 fine. But all that history got the silent treatment in economics debate because American companies invested in Chile were making very high profits there and sending money home while the economists themselves were receiving grants from USAID (US Agency for International Development) and the Ford Foundation,[114] among other sources, for this work leading up to the coup and through much of the time that followed.

The relative silence on the part of the press, also partially beholden to large advertisers with some of those advertisers making money on Chilean deals, looked much like a pre-Reagan era version of the "percale down" theory – money from foreign countries coming in at the top and spreading through and down to practically all in US society. Here again the "don't look a gift horse in the mouth" percept prevails and the voters just didn't want to rock the boat. When immigrants send money home to their relatives and friends it is called "remittances," a term with a condescending, disparaging cast, and you will find a good many economics studies on this flow of capital and its benefits to its recipients. We find less information readily available on another kind of "remittances" that are considered, not gifts or charity from relatives and sympathizers, but as just earnings to companies making large profits and sending them home, but in much larger quantity, to the wealthy countries where most of the investors live. Shades of mercantile positive balance of trade… Also, it is vindication of the good but mostly ignored insights of John Kenneth Galbraith's "technostructure" doing an effective job (for profits anyway) of planning outside of and manipulative of (instead of vice versa) the "free" market.

[113] Thomas Powers, *The Man Who Kept Secrets*, Knopf, New York, 1979, p. 347-353.

[114] Naomi Klein, *The Shock Doctrine – the Rise of Disaster Capitalism,* Henry Holt and Company, New York, ps. 73-75

Chile, Milton Friedman's big chance

In contrast to the Friedman faith, the Keynes approach and New Deal economic policies would be considered evidence and experience based. Not being faith based, it's Keynesian capitalism, lower case "c". With no pretentions to absolute and pure math at its core or dependence on miracles and revelations, in contrast to Friedmanism's grounding in the high laws of the universe faux-built on physics and math, Keynes' system muddled forth like the engineer with the inductive method, checking out, like FDR, what actually seemed to work in the physical world, then making a system around that.

When I started digging into ideas of economics and commenced my scan of its history looking for meaningful patterns, following my intuitions and attempting as much good logic as possible, I early on ran into apologist statements about Milton Friedman traveling to Chile emphasizing that his trip was a year and a half after the coup and he only briefly saw Pinochet. He was not that involved – don't worry about it. But read a little deeper and a great deal more appears.

Friedman considered himself a Keynesian as a young economist but by the post World War II years became committed to a radically pure notion of capitalism. His Holy Trinity was 1. privatization 2. deregulation and 3. government cuts in social spending. Generally this meant getting rid of as many impediments to accumulation of capital in the hands of... capitalists as possible. Naturally, low taxes would also be part of his formula for a healthy economy. His ultimate cause, he emphasized, was freedom for the individual. But what that meant in practical translation was freedom of the individual capitalist to maximize profit and do whatever he or she wanted with it including imposing his or her will on poorer, less powerful people impinging on *their* freedom. The individual was highest form of life on Earth if it was the right type of very rare individual, specifically the kind able to be free because of accumulating capital, often the accumulated capital of parents or grand parents for starters. The good, normal, rational, well-informed human would reinvest in his or her business wisely and rise to the level of deserving freedom. Likewise the consumer would be similarly endowed with the Friedmanist gene for rational self-interest and knowledge of comparative prices, would wisely discern which products were best and invest in those, and also would find the cheapest of the type of the best to buy for personal use. Thus would come into existence, as part and parcel of the machine of progress moving through time, the best of all possible economic worlds.

If the individual free capitalist produced a product not so popular, it was, as quoted earlier from John Kenneth Galbraith, as part of the "accepted sequence," a signal to redesign the product so it would be more useful to society or come up with a new product and place it into the market as another initiative. It was all very conscientious, hard working and it harkened way back to Adam Smith, if not in fact deep into our genes and origin of our species. Maybe Milton Friedman thought he had really hit upon it: the combination of God given and directed market from religion and complete proof from the sciences of math and physics manifest in the workings of his brand of Capitalism, absolute belief from religion and absolute proof from science, the ultimate formula for highest truth. But as far as I know, he never said quite that.

A little background for Friedman's times is in order. Coming out of the Second World War, Britain and other European colonial powers were exhausted. The economic and political vacuum immediately became something of a tabula rasa for US capitalism and Soviet Communism, albeit the Soviets were reeling from horrendous wartime losses of 23.4 million dead, 13.9% of the population, as compared to US dead at .418 million or .32%.[115] Proportionally speaking that was more than 42 times the human death toll relative to total national population of the US that was suffered by the USSR. And, much of the agriculture and industry in the USSR and many of its villages and cities were crushed, burned and smoldering. In the former European colonies, other than the few in the wealthy elite, the people there were, not too strangely, not too interested in some new form of colonialism. With rather sudden withdrawal of colonial administrations, they were caught between being manipulated in proxy wars and trying to manipulate aid from the Cold War US vs. USSR blocks.

The main economic models on the table at the time were:

1.) Soviet style Communism in which the state owned practically everything equitably distributed – in theory – with voting behind closed doors by a party elite, the only party allowed, the whole process under a dictator,

2.) Generally right wing dictatorships, being centered on a single person and supported by a powerful, wealthy elite, with no voting or meaningless voting, government decision making by the powerful and wealthy hidden from view,

3.a.) "Decent capitalism" based on private initiative and mildly regulated markets, one form of voting or another manipulated largely behind the scenes by the wealthy and also through advertising and lobbying, but also characterized by real public debate and public voting.

3.b.) Developmentalism, a brand of "decent capitalism," generally supported by the United States and western powers as against the Soviet Block, active capitalistic market working with policies to strengthen the development of nations with internal development of business and industry, protected by a certain level of tariffs. The idea was largely import replacement strategies of the Jane Jacobs sort but not necessarily with the city recognized as a major or perhaps *the* major economic organizing force. The notion was largely to help former colony countries become industrial and relatively independent, with attempted limits on the powers and concentration of wealth in local elites. Democratic elections attempted. In practice, many autocratic regimes were supported in their development by either or both western and/or Soviet aid and trade. In practice it might also have been noticed that

---

[115] Wikipedia: http://en.wikipedia.org/wiki/World_War_II_casualties

the kinds of development offered by West and East were, as Jacobs and Galbraith pointed out, not so different.

4.) Friedmanism – nobody wanted it quite yet in the two decades after the Second World War and what one might see as the spectacular success of a government-managed capitalism winning the war. With the unregulated market, with memories of the Crash of 1929 and the Great Depression still fresh in mind, it looked not just a little dangerous. People weren't yet so charmed by the idea that everyone could supposedly be a happy worker or a capitalist owner of some business, all paying very low taxes, a model in which money and power would obviously concentrate in fewer and fewer hands while more and more of the workers or "common people" would in reality own less and less. To me Friedmanism looked like National Tammany Hall for All, a set up for an all-depends-on-who-you-know-who-likes-you, patronage system. "The people" smelled a rat and didn't go for it.

And of course the people of Chile didn't vote for it. What they did vote for in the birthplace of Friedmanism's manifestation – was Salvador Allende and his government that was actively involved in efforts to distribute prosperity more equitably, taking property and capital from the wealthy and privileged, who had taken it initially from the mineral and agricultural riches of the country and low wages of workers.

When Friedman and his students in the Economics Department at the University of Chicago – the "Chicago Boys" – saw an opportunity to try out their theories in Chile as early as 1953, seventeen years before Allende's election and twenty years before his murder in Pinochet's coup, they became Los Chicago Boys. They began collaborating with and being funded by USAID and American foundations in a project soon to be called "the Chile Project." Phase one saw 100 students from Chile brought to Chicago to study Friedman's free market economics.[116] Back to Chile they went and by 1963 12 of the 13 full-time faculty members of the Economics Department of the Catholic University were graduates of Friedman's program at the University. They were by then famously anti-socialist and less conspicuously anti-developmentalist, real messianic missionaries. Walter Heller, economist to John Kennedy's government made fun of them: "Some are Friedmanly, some Friedmanian, some Friedmanesque, some Friedmanic, and some Friedmaniacs." But, said Naomi Klein in her book *The Shock Doctrine*, "As a form of intellectual imperialism, it was certainly unabashed. There was, however, a problem: it wasn't working."[117] For the great majority of the Chileans anyway. But for US companies and investors…

By 1969 US mining interests had invested $1 billion in Chilean copper mining, sending home $7.2 billion and ITT (International Telephone and Telegraph)

[116] Naomi Klein, op. cit., ps. 73-75 – much of the historical information here is from this book, from these pages on.

[117] Naomi Klein, ibid., ps. 75, 76

had a 70% share of the Chilean market. Allende offered to buy out such foreign companies with fair compensation, but preferring to continue making similar and hopefully growing profits indefinitely into the future these companies asked for more backing from the US State Department. The Chilean voters seem to have figured out what was happening: by the 1970 election, the election that brought in Salvador Allende as President, all three of the largest parties were in favor of nationalizing the copper mines, which had majority ownership in American hands.

Then came the coup – and the milestone Friedmanist, Chicago School economists work producing a 500 page book of radical free market policies referred to as "the Brick," which landed on the desk of the Junta almost exactly 24 hours after Allende's murder, just in time for serious application.

Adoption of The Brick and placement of Los Chicago Boys in Pinochet's senior economist positions was by then long planned by highest members of the financial and military elite deeply involved with, and sharing profit and/or power with American investors. As mentioned above, Pinochet followed their advice 1.) privatizing numerous state-owned functions, 2.) deregulating: allowing loose new forms of speculation so that those *with* could more easily gain *more*, 3.) immediately cutting government spending on social programs – though expanding spending on the military plus 4.) lowering taxes on the wealthy and 5.) eliminating many price controls that had kept necessities like bread and milk from escalating in price due to inflation.

But these Friedmanistic reforms too were a miserable failure. In 1974 inflation was at 375% - twice that experienced under Allende, "free trade" was swamping local markets with cheaper foreign goods, which people bought because they were losing their jobs and their ability to spend money was severely strained... because their companies were closing down due to... the cheap foreign goods and around and around. Unemployment hit record highs and food costs for the poor were increasing to the point of growing serious malnutrition. Meantime capital continued to flow out of the real material economy to foreign investors and financiers, producing more wealth for them and poverty for the Chileans who weren't part of the local owners' class.

In March of 1974 Milton Friedman flew down to help out. That's when he had his meetings to ignore with Pinochet. Pinochet, who admitted he didn't know much about economics and was getting a little worried about his Chicago Boys, gave Freidmanism one more try. Friedman counseled moving faster with his free market reforms, and said the only problem was that the reforms had not gone far enough and fast enough. In follow up letters Frieidman urged "shock treatment" and wrote that it was "...the only medicine. Absolutely. There is no other. There is no other long term solution."[118] Another year and a half later the country's economy, already reeling, contracted by 15% and unemployment was at 20% compared to Allende's high of 3%.

---

[118] Naomi Klein, ibid., p. 98

A relevant side thought here is this: what was going through the minds of Friedman and the Chicago Boys? He and they clearly saw the human catastrophe everywhere around them. How did they rationalize what they were doing when they knew they were on the side that destroyed the democracy, when they knew hundreds, maybe thousands of people were being murdered and terror was being released throughout the country while they were preparing their experiment of shifting more wealth and power to the wealthy and powerful and, evidenced in the streets they had to walk to get from one place to another, violence too? They knew this was the price of their dogmatic experiment. Was the abstract point that the system they believed in fervently was worth such crimes against humanity? Was it a cultural perception Los Chicago Boys and Friedman himself had that good people would experience even worse if they did not write and push such economic policy, some enemy, presumably the International Communist Conspiracy, would do that "domino effect" to them or worse if they didn't strike first? Did they enjoy the results? Were they actually sadists?

In considering the times of decolonization after the Second World War and what was going on in economic theory, one might wonder about the formerly poor countries, most of them previously drained by colonialism; what was wrong with them emulating some regulated form of "decent capitalism" with a generous amount of "socialistic" sharing of services delivered through government economic policy? Should we make war on Denmark before it spreads? Though Allende's approach was stronger on the socialist side than most it also had numerous capitalistic elements, as does today's version in China.

But Chile was important as an object lesson for an international audience. Playing the gamers' exaggeration game, The Los Chicago Boys, with what looks like strong elements of paranoia, believed the countries newly created from the colonies and the many other established but sometimes precarious democracies, couldn't be allowed to have elements of moderate socialistic policy succeed in making them prosper lest the domino theory activate and lead to the defeat of… their brand of capitalism. To punish and exploit Chile would be a warning to other countries thinking of adopting any significant amount of socialist policy.

The Friedmanist ideas, it turns out, were guidance for the next 30 years growing since Reagan's administration until today when, despite the Financial Crisis of 2008, these ideas are still not thoroughly repudiated. Thoroughly repudiated?! Barely repudiated at all: notice who Obama appointed to run the US economy.

30. A pedestrian corner in Barcelona, Spain

Reagan to approximately now

It took a while for the US to shed its New Deal protections for social values and to slowly build up to the deregulation frenzy leading into the Crash of 2008. As mentioned in these pages, the first big blast was from Ronald Reagan's time. It started with deregulation advisors like Wendy Gramm – Reagan called her his favorite economist. Robert Sheer named a whole chapter after her in *The Great American Stickup – How Reagan Republicans and Clinton Democrats enriched Wall Street while Mugging Main Street.* He called Chapter 2 "The High Priestess of the Reagan Revolution."[119] Alan Greenspan, originally appointed by Reagan, served as Chair of the Federal Reserve from 1987 to 2006 (a long time), was a powerful influence too. He knew Ayn Rand personally, spent many an evening debating economics with her at her New York apartment kitchen table and assumed much of her "Objectivist" capitalist philosophy. He saw much of Freidmanist Capitalism as a guide for application

[119] *Robert Sheer, The Great American Stickup – How Reagan Republicans and Clinton Democrats enriched Wall Street while Mugging Main Street,* Nation Books, 2010, p. 25

in the real world. In Rand's books, *The Fountainhead* and *Atlas Shrugged*, the creative, hard working hero individualist prevails against all the herd instincts of the lazy, unimaginative, conformist, slob masses and their self-serving leaders – "parasites," Greenspan calls them in a letter to the Editor of the New York Times defending Ayn Rand. Those parasites who "...persistently avoid either purpose or reason perish [in her novels] as they should."[120] But later for more on Greenspan and the roots of deregulation.

31. Barcelona – the same corner by night

The Big Meltdown of 2008, by whatever name historians eventually use, is a case in point, of exaggerated differences, and brings us up to date in my outline dash through economic history according the themes I think most important. The main exaggerated difference in this case is the enormous disparity between the very

[120] Alan Greenspan, New York Times, Nov. 3, 1957, Letters to the Editor

wealthy and the not so wealthy that resulted from deregulation, and more specifically, a suite of changes rolling back the economic reforms of the New Deal and associated prudence in the economy. The Roosevelt era reforms constituted something of a middle course attempting to utilize the best of the two competing sides, right and left, that were amplifying their differences and battling for victory at the time of his election. With the collapse of the Soviet Union the victory was to the Friedmanists – *they* thought – now to consolidate gains and take over for the cause.

The Friedman Free Marketers, leading up to and through the Reagan time, went for the extreme and vilified the regulators and the policies that had delivered stability from 1933 to about the 2007/2008 period. In their more extreme pronouncements, the Free Marketeers accused their opposite camp as fomenting class warfare – blame the other side for exactly what you are trying to accomplish, foment exaggerated gamesmanship.

It was the ascendancy of doctrinaire deregulated market, thought the doctrinaire deregulators, over the extreme, state ownership of practically everything version dictatorial "socialism" in the USSR that collapsed in 1991. I mentioned Wendy Gramm bending Ronald Reagan's ear. He later appointed her chair of the Commodity Futures Trading Commission in 1988 where instead of regulating the newly designed, potentially very profitable (for lucky or insider informed few among the wealthy) and highly risky trading instruments, she could neglect to regulate them. Or she could – and did – actively work with her husband Texas Republican Senator Phil Gramm to support explicitly making them legal, in fact making deregulating these dangerous instruments illegal. That's exactly what they accomplished.

I could add, Reagan was already working for the rich and powerful and serving their desire to become more rich and powerful long before the two met. One of his early roles was as a well-paid actor promoting General Electric products on television and in hundreds of personal appearances around the country from 1954 through 1962. For her part, Gramm encouraged deregulation in a market place where the wealthy could amplify value through trading astutely on the ups and downs of the market, producing no valuable product or service for anyone but themselves, if they made money, and some made a lot.

Simply stated, with deregulation investors could have more opportunities to sell when the dollar value for the real things or services was agreed contractually to be high, cash out and buy things or services (including shares in companies that provide them) in more quantity when such shares' value was low, wait for the value of that to rise (while busy doing other things), then sell again, and so on, playing the market. Maybe buy and sell some short. Plus, buy some asset with good return (dividends), that is to say, with a high percentage on the original investment coming back in regular payments, as compared to a low percentage, when dividends are paid out. Another approach is to try to get in on high growth in stock value hoping it continues up… to the time you sell the stock itself, cash out and do whatever you want with the money including buy physical property of value like real estate or gold to be almost primordial about it. Or send your daughter to college. Or start a small business. Whatever.

The most lucrative of these investments are often in companies with another kind of deregulation, not of the financial system itself, but of the companies' unregulated or simply ignored impacts on their workers and the environments in which they operate via low pay and low costs for environmental clean up – they just dump in the river – and remediation; none if possible. This is a tactic for not paying for "externalities," the costs in human and natural problems that are not paid for among the costs of doing business, costs caused by but said to be "external" to the business. Economist and futurist Hazel Henderson calls people making money by this strategy "bottom feeders."

Add to approaches like those even higher profits that might be made by convincing people by the tens of millions to borrow money in many ways they struggle to afford or just plain can't, from real estate to credit cards, bundle those loan agreements into packaged "financial products" known as derivatives that give an even higher percentage return on investment simply because parties to the transaction write up legally defensible contracts saying who owes whom how much, increasing the value on paper, and you have even more opportunities to make money investing, investing beginning to look ever more like high stakes gambling.

Why buy such bundled derivatives? Because they pay higher dividends as a percentage of the invested amount, checks arriving regularly. Why would anyone enter into a deal at the bottom, the physical source of the money flow, for example buying a house that's beyond their means with payments they can only endure a short period of time by borrowing from family and friends, working overtime, holding moonlight jobs, dealing drugs, cheating someone somewhere, skimming at their job and so on. The desperation of the over extended bottom is what the profiteers exploiting such financial instruments know they are dealing with, which is not different in all ways from exploiting child or greatly underpaid labor, stripping landscapes without following up with soil reclamation and so on. The desperate at the bottom, say a couple buying a house that's way too leveraged, in the hopes of flipping it and walking off with a windfall profit are the source of the financial flow through in this case. Sometimes at the working or cheating bottom they are the small time greedy or just gamblers taking a dangerous chance. They at the bottom of the money flow are often desperate to pay off debts or improve their community standing with a little money and therefore willing to take the chance. Any way you look at those purchasing such instruments as derivatives, knowing there's a serious case of over exploitation going on at the source of the money flow, or having petty greed at the "bottom," you understand what Hazel means by calling them "bottom feeders."

In more general, less personal terms, as learned in many depressions before, most notably in the Crash of 1929, the tendency with minimalist regulation is for the economy to expand into enormous bubbles – that proceed to burst, damaging the entire economy and all the people in it except the lucky ones who bailed just before the collapse – unless the crash gets so big as to sweep them away too.

As my Republican father used to say, "It takes money to make money," meaning the big money is in investing and finance and buying large quantities of stock before or on the early upswing, or selling short anticipating a down market, in either case smart gambling or inside knowledge in a volatile market is where the money is. (Actually, being a high executive or trader at the top these days just plain pays pretty well too.) One might add to that that the biggest money is when the risks are highest for all, including the whole society. To allow such extreme trading, incurring obligations that can't be paid, is to tempt destabilizing all of society, which is exactly what Friedmanism advocates, and advocates on the part of those hoping to make – and making – truly vast amounts of money.

Reagan's old client for his advertisement acting, General Electric, is a good case in point. During the Depression, GE created a division called GE Capital to provide credit to customers so they could take out loans and spread payments over time, thus empowered to buy GE products. That way the company could not only sell more physical product, it could make money on the loans' interest rates as well. In the 1980s when Reagan had placed his full force as President behind deregulation, GE Capital decided to expand into loans more vigorously, getting into credit card property and other loans much more broadly distributed than before. By 2007 GE Capital amounted to 55% of the income of the entire company. After the Crash of 2008 it was saved only by a $100 billion loan guarantee package from the US taxpayers, a socialistic rescue of a business one might say.[121]

It is somewhat surrealistic that a gigantic physical facility of many parts – factories, distributions networks, office buildings, fleets of company trucks and cars, not to speak of the homes of the workers paid for and in that sense built by the company – and an immense material collection of products spread around the world such as power plants, wind turbines, home appliances, light bulbs and LEDs, aircraft, train and ship parts, military products of many kinds, blood glucose monitoring machines, silicone bathtub calk and on and on and these purchased by thousands of companies and hundreds of millions of individuals, that all this that the company has created end up with the company making less money on physical product than on the interest on loans and other strictly financial transaction income. Amazing.

Multiply that amazement 1000 times and consider this: "Whereas the financial sector accounted for about 16 % of domestic profits in the mid-1980s, in the past decade it counted for 41% of those profits" in the whole United States. So says David Sirota, author of *Back to Our Future: How the 1980s Explain the World We Live In Now*.[122] We are now talking about the profits made off of all transactions in the United States. That 41% goes to those simply collecting interest and dividends on loans and investments speaks to an economic system radically out of balance relative

[121] Robert Sheer, *The Great American Stickup*, op. cit., p. 44

[122] David Sirota, "Back to Our Future: How the 1980s Explain the World We Live In Now", in a San Francisco Chronicle editorial in December 2, 2011.

to its "real economy," the production economy, which is based in turn on Nature's Economy, which is mostly what we build and most of that is organized by and *is* our cities, towns and villages.

The outlandishly high percentage of profit in the US going to finance was made possible by Reagan, Bill Clinton, George W. Bush, Wendy Gramm and an enormous cast of regulators who failed to regulate, Congress Members passing laws to deregulate finance, the so-called "revolving door" between government office and financial firm's executive positions. Claims on that profit were mainly by the maximum profit seeking business community, especially Wall Street financial firms.

At the base of much of the destabilization of the economy going into the Crash of 2008 was the subprime mortgage "home owner" who actually didn't own the home – the bank did – but for innocent dreams, petty greed or desire to give something to the children, was manipulated by real estate agents and brokers, developers, neighbors, friends, relatives, and the insecure conformist ego within to join the rush to buy a house as a fast turnover commodity with high profit potential "almost guaranteed."

I'll digress a little... "Derivatives" is a term I've already used as if we all understood it, and most have, but I'll explain just a little more anyway. They are loan instruments like mortgages or agreements to pay credit card obligations that "derive" from some real productive product (a house for example), work or service by way of providing financing to said item or service. These loans can be sold, for example by the bank that made the mortgage to the "home owner," can be bought by other institutions or speculators and are often bundled together and resold for higher amounts if they bring in yet higher interest rate payments relative to their cost than other investments might bring in. What you are buying if you buy a loan is the income stream paid by the person taking out the loan at the base of the transactions, Hazel's "bottom," say the home owner sending in a couple thousand dollars a month to have a little skin in the game, for example. The home "owner" may not even know the checks he or she writes are transferred to the person or institution that paid the bank money to buy the rights to the income stream. Whoever or whatever bought the derivative "bundle" may also have no idea exactly where the money is coming from – or care to find out.

Some people, a little worried their derivatives might suddenly run dry if at the bottom, the source of the money flow, people are starting to go bankrupt and defaulting. Then checks would stop coming. These worried derivative buyers can buy insurance and pay interest on those insurance policies so that if the money source does default, the insurance company instead of derivative holder pays out. That's a derivative too! Even such insurance policies can be sold for the income stream they represent, which adds yet another layer to the derivative bubble. So you have derivatives deriving from derivatives from derivatives on down the line, everyone taking a cut as they buy then sell jacking up the supposed value (legally backed paper value anyway insofar as contracts are honored) and claims on whatever and whoever is the physical and services basis for the real value in the real economy which is anchored in the real resource based, physical economy, the function value of the property at the origin of the stream of money, the place where the derivatives derive, and the labor or personal borrowing or whatever is going on at the base where someone writes a check for the monthly mortgage or car payment, to the credit card company and so on.

Notice the investment with an extremely high return. It is almost always based on unfair treatment or serious exploitation of people or environment at its basis. As the saying goes, for every great fortune there is a great theft. Then there is the dental receptionist I mentioned earlier making 30% interest on her holdings in munitions manufacture during the American war on Vietnam. Think also of the investors' returns based on Sir Francis Drakes ventures expecting he'd simply pillage a few Spanish gold galleons, an overblown example I know. But still an investment with certain moral implications.

But what if the people at the bottom just plain can't pay any more? When suddenly the bottom drops out – the bottom of the income stream, down in the real material and energy economy, supplied and powered by nature remember – there is just no way to generate as much real economic value where things are made and services rendered relative to the agreed upon inflated values up on the top. Then in George W. Bush's words of wisdom, "...this sucker could go down."

The Curse of Tricky Wendy Gramm

For a quick tour through this build up and collapse period, Wendy Gramm's career is telling. As a Ph.D. candidate in economics she met her future husband Phil Gramm applying for a position at Texas A&M University where he was a Senior Professor in Economics. Later Phil Gramm was a House of Representatives Member then a Republican Senator. Through Gramm's connections Wendy met Ronald Reagan.

At about that time, in the early years of Reagan's presidency, the Administration had hit upon the idea of placing enemies of the regulatory system in leadership positions in the regulatory system. Thus we had the Secretary of the Interior James Watt trying to lease drilling, mining, logging and ranching rights in national parks and trying to sell off as much of these properties as possible to private bidders. Small government Reagan was building up the military and expanding its budget big time – and the whole country's – so much that he needed all the help he could get to get closer to what looked like a more balanced budget. So part of the game plan was to sell off the national treasures created by guys like Teddy Roosevelt.

James Watt was trying to help a little. He was almost as famous for his Christian fundamentalism as Reagan was for his comment, "If you've seen one redwood you've seen 'em all," and he unadvisedly talked publically about (what amounted to) letting the Earth go to ruin (while in private hands temporarily) because he was convinced when the Lord came back the world would be destroyed anyway. And he talked about it. Then the good people were going to take rapture rides right past death to the place of streets of gold and no more of these creepy crawling eco-things that go bump in the night down here on planet number three. His attitudes and attempted policies demonstrated clearly the confluence of two fundamentalist perspectives – religious and economic – flowing harmoniously together in the country of separation of religion and state. Unexpectedly, however, the public, and among them many wealthy conservative conservationists who actually believed in defending God's sacred creation, got nervous and he was out of office much faster than Reagan and many political observers had anticipated. Ever the optimist with a sense of humor, shortly before Watt resigned under pressure, Reagan bestowed on Watt a plaster sculpture of a foot with a big round hole in it. For those international readers not informed on American figures of speech, that means he shot himself in the foot and thus he was his own worst enemy. He'd pushed extreme ideas a little too far, even for Reagan. Essentially fired in 1983 he was unrepentant: said he in a dinner talk to the Green River Cattlemen's Association in Wyoming in 1991, "if the troubles from environmentalists cannot be solved in the jury box or at the ballot box, perhaps the cartridge box should be used."[123]

Later in the course of the Administration but in similar anti-regulatory, free market promoting strategy, in 1988 Wendy Gramm was appointed by Reagan to head the Commodities Futures Trading Commission (CFTC), the very regulatory body whose mission she was more than a little inclined to subvert. This body was charged with regulating derivatives such as credit default swaps and collateralized debt obligations, financial instruments two or more bundles and transactions down the line from the real financial instrument, or up from the base in the way I've been describing them. You can stop regulating by getting the regulators to sit on their hands or by passing laws. With Wendy Gramm, you got both, with a little help from her husband. That's exactly what they did: pass laws to contravene the banking safety measures put in place by the Glass-Steagall Act of 1933 under Roosevelt.

But, revolving door style, Wendy Gramm bailed on her government job in 1993 and joined Enron, of all companies, as a member of the board. That's the company, incidentally, whose employees provided George W. Bush's Texas Governor and US President campaigns with $600,000 in contributions, the most contributed to Bush by any company in America.[124] But Ms. Gramm didn't jump ship at the CFTC until she and her husband had gotten through Congress a bill that specifically exempted Enron from some of the most risky and lucrative types of financial transaction Enron was enthusiastically pursuing, including ultra-fast and difficult to follow electronic transmission transactions. Then within five weeks of passing this

---

[123] New Scientist magazine, "Feedback," September 21, 1991

[124] Amy Goodman, "Enron – the Bush Connection," Democracy Now!, May 26, 2006

deregulation bill, she was working as a director and an in-house auditor for Enron.[125] The company made millions in profits on illegal trades as well as the newly-legal electronic transactions while Ms. Gramm had access to and significant authority over the financial records of the company. With such information she nonetheless rubber-stamped accounting gymnastics that siphoned money to executives in violation of company rules and national laws. Later, having earned an estimated $2 million personally, maybe one of the worlds best escape artists, she bailed on Enron too, in one of those last minute speedy strategic moves, shortly before its $90 billion in paper valuation collapsed leaving its investors broke.[126] Also victimized: 21,000 people out of work with $2 billion in employee pensions evaporated with the bankruptcy. The company's Chairman and CEO Kenneth Lay and CEO and COO Jeffery Skilling were convicted of securities and wire fraud. Skilling got 24 years but Lay died of a heart attack before he could be sentenced.

Some unexpected more personal punishments materialize sometimes for such greed, lying and theft: Skilling's 20 year old son John Taylor Skilling committed suicide in February of 2011, despondent about a breakup with his girlfriend but as the senior Skilling himself said of his conviction, it was extraordinarily hard on his family too.[127] One wonders what Skilling Senior thought of his business activities at the suicide of his son. Such unexpected punishment was visited upon Bernard Madoff while aging away on his 150-year conviction for his Ponzi scheme that lost $17 billion for his investors: his son Mark committed suicide in December of 2010 in a state of shame and depression, Mark Madoff himself stating it was due to the fraud catastrophe. The suicide date was the second anniversary of his father's arrest. In September of 2014 Andrew, another son of Bernard, died of cancer. As reported by Reuters news service on September 3, 2014, "Andrew Madoff told the magazine People he 'would never forgive his father for his crimes' and blamed a recurrence of his cancer on the stress caused by his father's arrest and conviction."

Wendy Gramm didn't end up in jail and no one I've heard of died for her sins, for the cooked books at Enron or other more legal but destructive activities she engaged in. Remember, she'd co-written legislation with her husband making what would have previously been illegal legal, so those activities at Enron didn't count against her. That she too wasn't convicted on corruption charges speaks to the failure of regulators and prosecutors to regulate and prosecute – she knew all about *that.* It is what she used to do herself when she was head of the CFTC immediately before joining Enron. While Enron was thriving it was providing Wendy's husband with

[125] "Blind Faith - How Deregulation and Enron's Influence Over Government Looted Billions from Americans," Public Citizen's Critical Mass Energy and Environment Program, www.citizen.org

[126] Gary Lamoshi, "Wendy Gramm has no Regrets," article in Salon online magazine, January 28, 2004, http://www.salon.com/2004/01/28/wendy_gramm/

[127] Daily mail reporter, Mail Online News, February 4, 2011

big campaign contributions for his political campaigns as well as big contributions for George W. Bush's.

But all that was just the warm up. Here comes her master stroke. In 1999 and again in 2000 Phil Gramm, with his wife's collaboration, engineered more legislation, this time designed to destroy the banking security and dependability holy grail of the New Deal, the Glass-Steagall Act of 1933, which they had eroded to some degree earlier. These bills would make it explicitly illegal to regulate some of the most dangerous, bubble-inflating OTC (over the counter) derivatives by then concocted for maximizing potential investor profit. The Commodity Futures Modernization Act of 2000 was spectacularly close to the line. Approaching Christmas, one day before adjournment of Congress, and after last minute maneuvering to secure Bill Clinton's support, the Congress passed the bill into law and Clinton signed it. George W. Bush had already been elected President of the United States by one vote in the Supreme Court on party lines and in less than two months Clinton was out the door, but the deregulation frenzy was just warming up, going full speed ahead with derivatives based on wilder and wilder real estate subprime mortgages, very sub-, and primed for accelerating all the way up to the Crash of 2008.

Now, building up to the recent past – a few short years before the publishing of this book – in our tour of economic history according to what I believe are some of its most important patterns and lessons, there is the track running along beside if not quite parallel to that of the Gramm's, namely the track of Alan Greenspan and his career.

32. Bicycling Auroville

Auroville, India, city for the world citizen, hopefully promoting our higher evolution. It's off to a good start on bicycles. Note the beautiful posture…

Alan Greenspan: Ayn Rand's man

Some called him their economic guru, some The Wizard. What's most important to note? When in 1987 Ronald Reagan appointed Alan Greenspan to Chair of the Board of Governors of the Federal Reserve, Greenspan had served as a member of the President's Economic Policy Advisory Board. When Reagan fired Paul Volcker for lack of sufficient deregulation enthusiasm he knew from whence Greenspan came. But, in the craft of the economist, in the position as head of the Fed in the next few years, he seemed to be competent and effective. In fact, within two months of his appointment Greenspan oversaw policies that dramatically helped the economy recover from a downswing that included the largest single day collapse in the Stock Market in US history. That was Monday, October 19, 1987, when the market lost 22.61% of its total valuation. [128] The job of the Federal Reserve is largely to control interest rates, money availability through backing loans, and serve as "lender of last resort" to banks in trouble (if enough of them or if big enough to be "too big to fail" – from medium sized on up they are all "too big to jail."). This averts pandemic runs on banks. In fact, the Federal Reserve was created in 1913 for exactly this purpose: preemptive regulation I might be bold enough to call it, keeping the irresponsibility of the banks and investors and lemming-like reactions of the public in panics from causing disastrous bubbles and collapses, designed to moderate Recessions and Depressions. The Fed is supposed manipulate the whole economy in this way to create jobs and keep employment high, check inflation through indirect price controls and otherwise intervene as government for the public good.

The economics craft Greenspan executed at the Federal Reserve, starting with the "Black Monday" of 1987, he did well enough to be endorsed by Republicans and Democrats alike, appointed and reappointed to the Chairmanship by Ronald Reagan, George H. W. Bush, Bill Clinton and George W. Bush.

In such work Greenspan seemed capable, a wise elder, even mysteriously transcendent. But in the days when complex derivatives were being deregulated into massive flows of capital some observers were beginning to get nervous. Billionaire investor Warren Buffett called these instruments "financial weapons of mass destruction" as you will remember from an earlier reference worth repeating. When Greenspan explained these financial devices to Congress and alluded to the complex math assuring their wisdom, everyone took his word as if the pronouncements of a clairvoyant with inside knowledge of a more fundamental universe, some commentators calling him "the Oracle" meaning he must have had a mystic connection with the gods if not God. He exuded absolute self-confidence. In trying to explain why so many Congress Members took him at his word, said Arthur Levitt, ten-year Chair

[128] Encyclopedia of World, "Biography on Alan Greenspan," 2004

of the Securities and Exchange Commission, "I always thought that the titans of our legislature didn't want to reveal their own inability to understand some of the concepts that Mr. Greenspan was setting forth," he told the New York Times. "I don't recall anyone ever saying, 'What do you mean by that, Alan?'"[129]

The more important item to note here is that Greenspan himself didn't understand what he was saying, or at least that's what he said, and this is extraordinarily important to a much more real economics built on what we build. How'd he get that way?

There was a deeper strain of beliefs that illuminated Greenspan's path into the darkness or the blinding glare of revelation, depending on which your economic school. He shared that path with the Gramm's, that path leading toward… Ayn Rand, his close personal friend.

However practical and helpful his early work at the Fed might have been, in his attitude toward regulation he could hardly have been more off base: that the profit motive always works for the higher good when it works for the highest profit for the self-interested individual. The higher good in service to the higher greed? People know what's good for themselves and buy accordingly, which in typical capitalist thinking transmogrifies into the Common Good. Conversely the producers and the financiers have reputations to protect and so regulate their activities for the collective good voluntarily as part of their strategy to stay competitive by way of producing *whatever* to maximize profit. So the thinking went, though that was what Galbraith considered the outdated "accepted sequence" uneducated by the more real "revised sequence" in which the large corporation rather than the market was the "invisible hand."

But things unraveled in 2007 in the real estate market and crashed in 2008 in the Stock Market and finance with a spreading wave that swept the planet. This is where Alan Greenspan confessed – before the US House of Representatives with television cameras recoding for all to see – that his world-view had crumbled.[130] "I made a mistake in presuming that self-interests of organizations, specifically banks and others, were such as that they were best capable of protecting their own shareholders and their equity in the firms," he said in answer to questions from Congress Member Henry Waxman. "I have found a flaw. I don't know how significant or permanent it is. But I have been very distressed by the fact."

Mr. Waxman: "In other words, you found that your view of the world, your ideology, was not right, it was not working…" Greenspan replied, "Absolutely, precisely. You know that's precisely the reason I was shocked, because I have been going

[129] Robert Sheer, *The Great American Stickup*, Op. cit., p. 97

[130] Greenspan's remarkable admission of flawed thinking appears in many places on the internet. His words before House Member Henry Waxman at this URL is typical: http://www.youtube.com/watch?v=lGYtnW_1lUU

for 40 years or more with very considerable evidence that it was working exceptionally well."

It's worth thinking through where such an idea came from and what it really means, so serious have been the repercussions and so enduringly and damagingly persistent is the notion still, even after its spectacular failure. It's important to note also that gigantic as the economic disaster was for so many it remains something of a smoke screen for something much larger going on, a distraction from the larger disconnect from nature's economics and human economics, the symptoms of which are degrading soils, growing ocean dead zones and world scale acidification, rising seas, climate change… you know the rest…

But considering Greenspan's role in this major problem, it goes back to meeting Ayn Rand when he was 25 years old. If his more everyday manipulation of the economy was not so destructive, at least maintained a reasonable keel, or so most people thought, his notions of human nature and the nature of business and the workings of the market around self-interest were not so good and deserve some attention. Hint for the time being: the market doesn't regulate itself – it only regulates prices – and only then when it is free of monopolistic forces and controlled by reasonable regulation from the Leviathan or reasonable ethics.

Rand was born in Russia in 1905.[131] When she was 12 years old the Bolshevik Revolution succeeded and shortly thereafter her family's pharmacy business was confiscated. She and her parents became refugees within their tumultuous country, sometimes nearly starving. One can imagine and sympathize with her enormous resentment. She rejected Russia's ancient mysticism and hated its new government's collectivism. With permission to leave Russia to visit relatives in Chicago, at 20 years of age she traveled on condition of returning in six months. Instead, she stayed in the US and settled first in New York, then worked in Hollywood as a scriptwriter, then moved back to New York for most of the rest of her life. She launched her own career as a writer of novels and philosophical explorations while holding various jobs in the motion picture industry and later presiding over an institution to promulgate her "Objectivist" philosophy.

Said Greenspan about that philosophy: "She was a devoted Aristotelian – the central idea being that there exists an objective reality that is separate from consciousness and capable of being known. Thus she called her philosophy objectivism. And she applied key tenets of Aristotelian ethics – namely, that individuals have innate nobility and that the highest duty of every individual is to flourish by realizing that potential."[132]

In her own words in 1962 she outlined her ideas at a sales conference at Random House, the publishing company.

[131] Biographical material on Ayn Rand mostly from Wikipedia and the Ayn Rand Institute/Center for the Advancement of Objectivism website: www.aynrand.org

[132] Alan Greenspan, from his autobiography, *Age of Turbulence*, as cited at the website noblesoul.com

"Metaphysics: Objective Reality
Epistemology: Reason
Ethics: Self-interest
Politics: Capitalism"

She added for good measure: "If you want this translated into simple language, it would read: 1. "Nature, to be commanded, must be obeyed," or "Wishing won't make it so." 2. "You can't eat your cake and have it, too." 3. "Man is an end in himself." 4. "Give me liberty or give me death."[133]

In her novels, the heroic character – Howard Roark, architect in *The Fountainhead* for example – is ferociously individualistic and focused on his creative work and life trajectory. Roark is a modernist, though would see himself as too unique for any label, building in stone, steel and glass as they erupt through the sod and into powerful transformation of nature's hard, strong material in beautiful human-forged form. Wood would be a little sentimental. Roark coldly rejects imitation, tired out traditional styles and silly surface flourishes of decoration and esthetics to please lesser tastes. He will only take on a client who allows him to create the most powerful realization of what the program of the building and its unique place on planet requires, the function and materials demand and what Roark himself can rise up, hammer, mold, compress, rivet, weld and explode with dynamite into existence or oblivion through the medium of the mind and pencil over matter. I rather like all that. But…

Rand's favorite word: violence. It's the violence of "man," the violence of burning iron out of the mountain, blasting and cutting the stone, melting glass with flame to erect and dress out glistening towering skylines. Rand's heroine is even raped by the Roark of early in the book only to develop an obsession with him and 400 pages later rapturously and subserviently commit to him happily ever after, which is a little odd for an author advocating self-fulfillment rather than finding in subservience highest calling of life.

Roark has the force of relaxed natural conviction and disposition to focus on that and that only. He's a monomaniac who would be disdainful of all the fuzzy, furry, cozy things and sentiments around him if he even noticed them at all. He compromises, if very little, and only to survive which he often barely manages so uncompromising is he with his clients that he loses most of his prospective jobs. He never compromises in his real work, his own designs. His critics can level withering sarcasm and insult – he moves ahead as if they weren't there. All he needs is the appreciative client happy to work or live in a work of art and power. Other architects ostracize him while stealing his ideas piecemeal with no sense of a larger order or

[133] Copyright 1962 Times-Mirror Co., why, I'm not sure! Can't find the source right off…

meaningful integration in the whole design. They know he's a driven genius and they can pick up some of his crumbs and accept that it's the architect's lot more commonly and securely to just copy styles all the way back to Rome, Greece, for god sake even Egypt or if you want to be really funky, Polynesia or Hollywood. Normal architects fight over money, prizes, acceptance, nice reviews in the papers – he could care less. He's coolly satisfied with himself as any force of nature might be just doing what it is supposed to do. As all great artists, he's just doing his destiny providing enormous pleasure to those few, or maybe many, who can appreciate his creations, but their appreciation and enjoyment doesn't warm his heart or caress his ego. Like the profit maximizing financier, Ayn Rand and Alan Greenspan would agree, he benefits society with the results of true creativity but that's not his direct objective; Roark is above all else true to himself like every capitalist individualist and a few other driven types – and literally above all others: the book ends with him standing victorious on his, the tallest building in the world, with his heroine's arms wrapped around him, their hair tangled together in the powerful winds of such heights.

Ayn Rand has been criticized as viciously angry – humorless too – and you feel it in her disdain for the common person in their swarming numbers and welfare cheating, in their rabbit like reproduction rate – she in real life and her main characters have no children. You feel her anger for the pettiness of the "successful" people who parasitize the real artists. In "The Fountainhead," with the exception of two or three clients who understand and see authenticity in Roark, they all got their success by pleasing others, selling them crap, or stealing from the truly creative few to make themselves look good.

One wonders how, if the vast majority and often their efforts to help people in community and/or family values ways, is as demeaning to human potential as she implies, this squares with humans as the pinnacle of creation and almost god-like creators in their own right, or how there could be only one such person in the whole book. And the hero, heroine and actual author don't even reproduce and neither has Alan Greenspan – the lonely cold world dies with them in their genetic line. Could a philosophy, namely here Objectivism, promoting self-interest over all other values, be the one thing to lead toward more personal integrity or higher civilization? Or would self-interest simply turn to greed while I'm alive, small greed tending to laziness and satisfaction in conformist comforts and security or swell up to grand theft and even murder and war on the large scale? To my reading it looks like the welfare cheat, that Rand sees in almost all of us, is pretty self-interested too, if embodying a lower life form.

I think the real deal is the authenticity, the integrity, the courage, the creative energy, not the self-interest. You have to have self-interest to get there, but you don't get there alone and to be self-interested is not the goal. If self-interest were the goal you wouldn't feed your children – or like Rand and Greenspan – or just don't have any. Now the subtlety appears on the part of the free market purist: "But your children would make you miserable if you didn't feed them so you feed them not for their sake but to defend yourself from their harassment." So to keep from having to split such ideological hairs, Ayn Rand had no children in real life, as just mentioned, neither in fiction nor in the philosophical construct she spins in her books. Here, the obvious makes more sense: though we are all individuals who need to take care of ourselves, and ourselves first so we can be an effective part of a community – social and ecological – we all need each other too. Simple! "Place the oxygen mask over your own mouth before helping others..." Then what?

Needed: total economics now!

You've noticed my theme in the foregoing pages: we need both a relatively free market and sensible regulation, private motivation and energy, and public vigilance and course correction for the common good, the positive essence of capitalism plus the collective management traditional socialism has strived to enable and execute. My overriding conclusion is that we need to devise an economic system that has balanced forces from self-interest and from interest in the common good. We need to stop this game of exacerbating differences, exaggeration gaming, as if "the other side" were hogwash or evil, and need something seen simply as an inclusive or maybe called mixed human economics.

And, we need to acknowledge nature's economics as the basis of our human-created economics at the same time. And so, that all embracing economics needs to be that combination of nature's economy and ours. Of course new terms sound awkward – I invite other submissions for the same meaning. By whatever name, that whole systems economics would be the economy of material/energy physical resources and products and the services we humans deliver to one another standing upon and harmonizing with nature's economics.

In a formula of sorts that would be:

Nature's Economics + Human Economics = Total Economics

Understand that human economics is comprised of gifting and monetized exchanges – predominantly monetized – all mixed up. The monetized part has two emphases that should be in dynamic if ever changing balance: the good in capitalism and the good in socialism. Get used to it. Life goes on. But don't get overly extreme in the competition, the "finding the balance" knowing that it swings back and forth being its normal self. The percept here (to use Jane Jacob's term): Eschew exaggerated gamesmanship.

33. Cow grazing in Auroville town center

Also in the city inviting world citizens and human higher evolution, India.

LAST CHANCE FOR A HAPPY FUTURE – SECTION 3

CHAPTER 10

Rescue the World

Design yourself

My short review of the history of economics and major trends and basic principles within, from the point of view of emphasis I believe most important – remember proportionality – is now complete. Now begins a treatment of my ideas about strategies and tools for proceeding into a healthy future based on an ongoing assessment of that history.

This chapter I'm calling "Rescue the World." Its background question is, "Would we really rather go on sacrificing the future of our children's world in our exaggerated gamesmanship or try out an open-minded and thorough search for powerful solutions?" That thoroughness has to start recognizing patterns and principles, then move on to the everyday details of application, starting with each of us. Let's get along, in both sense of the term, get along with one another so we can get along down the road to difficult, essential, solid solutions. Gandhi proved it could work. The long time between his time and ours shouldn't prevent us from understanding that universal logic, that non-violence and the sense of human kindness behind law and reasonable governance can still be operative. All that made him stunningly successful. We could be too.

So what's the dynamic here and how to move forward once we do know the stakes and have a pretty good idea what the terrain looks like? A good start is exercising our powers of self-design as warm up and practice for redesigning the human enterprise here on Earth. It benefits each of us personally too. We can redesign and rebuild ourselves, each of us. Start at home, with our own bodies and minds. Why me? Because our lives depend on it. Collectively, that's all we are, lots of "mes." That's all we have, each one of us adding up to the total – total success, total failure or muddling through with collateral damage and wounded and dying by catch strewn about our dusty path.

I had a dream a couple months ago. On a blue sky day of light breezes I was visiting a small city in the country with a friend, rolling hills, beautiful views all around. I said, "There is a really nice neighborhood around here somewhere, in a small town, with this bustling little center. It had a couple rooftop restaurants, really good food… I'm hungry – how about you? But where was that?... These warehouses and empty streets aren't familiar. Everything's changed. Even the color seems to have dried up and drained away." At the edge of the town was an abandoned quarry, bare cliffs, a couple lonely whirlwinds scuttling about the floor. I was saying to myself, "Can't we do something about this?" Without thinking the words came out of my mouth. "Why me? Because our lives depend on it." My friend grinned and pulled his fist down from above, elbow to the side like a locomotive engineer pulling the cord to the whistle. "Bang!" he said. I woke up saying to myself things don't get much more basic than that. I got it! The starting gun goes off and the race is on.

We design ourselves, an idea I introduced earlier, in rather pedestrian intentional ways by, say, taking a series of courses at school, getting a higher degree at college, taking piano lessons, going to the gym. We design ourselves by learning about history, deciding on a hobby or who to hang out with, whether to buy the golf clubs, skis or chess board making the implied commitments, study yoga or maybe we buy a car so we can take spontaneous trips or engage in longer distance commuting. Our everyday actions, books we read, even food we eat set in place personal and social patterns that play out as adjustable habits that "in aggregate" define individuals and whole societies. In a way that seems a little shallow but reflects deeper currents: we design ourselves by selecting our clothing, putting on jewelry, make up or these days getting tattoos. As Jane Jacobs has reminded us, often the things we buy and do are rather paltry – or less sympathetically named, sometimes actively pathetic – devoid of any socially or personally redeeming qualities yet adding up to immense economic forces. Meantime we billions of people who are varying degrees above subsistence acquire and fill our lives with little things sometimes barely considered by our minds, sometimes agonized over as rationally as we can as in coming to a major career decision. All the while, if we wake up to the process, we are in varying degrees of awareness designing ourselves.

Like everyone else I have some habits I seldom think about that largely shape my daily life, eventually my total life, maybe not in a big way but definitely there. On the career level, self-designing mission-establishing decisions of a very conscious sort serves as an example here. The almost mechanical outline of the process is that it goes from decision to training to competence to some level of pride, satisfaction and pleasure, as well as producing a benefit to oneself and society. Things you might not have thought would be fun turn out to be. Surprise!

My own personal example was that in the mid 1970s I was happily making sculpture. It was a very gratifying occupation and preoccupation in which I enjoyed the material and tools, was delighted with welding – flame, sparks, flowing metal and all that. To hammer and chip away at stone seemed to be capturing and shaping time itself into the deep future. If stone lasts as long as it preserved the shapes of the Burgess Shale soft-bodied animals – more than 500 million years – that was eternity enough for me. It was a thrill to see wood in carving into the body of once-living trees turning into three-dimensional human form with the characteristics of pose and expression I wanted. But also there appeared in the sculptures some personality that I had not created that came as a permanent surprise, as if from another parent, almost like sex producing an absolutely related but unpredictable offspring with a life of its own from two sources, oneself and some mysterious other, the sculptor and the medium. Even the more abstract sculptures had that aspect of myself and something else coming together in something new and truly exciting to see and feel.

In fact my sculptures felt so good I began making them primarily for the sense of touch and often displayed them in the dark. I noticed touch was a blending of several senses able to register not just form and surface texture but also temperature, pressure, vibration, moisture and dryness, even electricity (at low voltage of course). Exploring this almost unknown art form was as thoroughly delightful work or play as I have ever experienced.

The world of artists was exciting too, filled with searching, motivated, often inspiring people, fascinating eccentrics, seething with more or less free love shortly after birth control was more or less well worked out, percolating with ideas bubbling out of the soup both great and insufferable – a constant entertainment. The work and the social flux was so pleasurable it was often, late at night, hard to stop working – or hard to stop partying. But I decided to leave the "fine arts" scene, gallery openings, and the cavalcade of stimulating experiences, tasty hors d'oeuvres with people much more open minded than most, leave the delight in my own hands making gratifying things, I thought, of beauty or valuable insight. I left that world behind to relegate whatever talents I might have to the discipline of illustrating ecologically healthy cities, making almost no sculpture for the rest of my life up to the present. Only rarely and only since then for my own small pleasure do I engage in "art" for sheer enjoyment or for, as they say, art's sake, much less fall into the ego trip of "trying to be a great artist" or if "successful" to use art to make lots of money. And when I "do" what is conventionally thought of as "art," it's only small sketches for nothing but a little pleasure. I traded one world in for another in which writing and public speaking to promote ecological cities, including speaking before City Councils, had to play a big role. City Councils I always found difficult and unpleasant. Genuinely curious audiences always a pleasure. The artist doesn't normally try to convince anyone of anything quite so directly as the politician or the activist or the developer trying to get something done, or in my case and the developers', built.

Why'd I do it, why the change? I decided, around 1973 or 1974, the world of healthy biological and cultural diversity was in clear danger, which I believe is still the case but in an even far more dangerous state today. By coincidence of growing up in a world of building as the son of an architect, having worked on constructing two of the family's houses, having met Paolo Soleri with his very basic and promising ideas about cities, befriending a number of straight talking environmentalists who loved nature and realizing I was one of them, and having some talents I thought I could use like being able to draw more or less in perspective, I made the conscious decision to re-design myself for another trajectory through life, which is not so different in many ways from anyone else changing his or her career.

And what did I learn? That taking up a new life with different challenges, people and environments can end up as pleasurable as the earlier life and may even be more rewarding and fun later on. We can shift our ways and discover we actually enjoy many of the new things that come our way because of the shift, because of the discipline, hard work and satisfaction. And we can have pride in our new skills, insights, productions, services and whatever else good we help bring into being.

What I'm suggesting is that the great majority of us are wasting most of our time beyond our work for sustenance. In many cases our work for sustenance isn't helping sustain the health of our world either. We need to shift our attention, efforts and means to enjoy ourselves to something that actually recognizes where we are in place and time. With a little more effort and some strategic thinking we might be able to shift our means of sustenance, a few billion of us to something tuned to survival and thriving in a sustainable future. If enough of us shift focus there will come a time when the ecocity and related enterprises, perhaps a serious campaign for "natural carbon sequestration" for example take over and provide both serious satisfaction and satisfying remuneration; such transition strategies are equal opportunity employers. What I'm suggesting is that, as when an enemy is massing over the horizon with clear intent of invasion, you don't go about the same old thing. More subtly if you care to influence a healthier, happier future you may discover with a little reflection that some other course of activity than the same old thing, learning something new – or not spending time learning something useless or unhealthy – is called for. In either case, fighting the negative or trying to create the positive, the future now portends something threatening and we can either all roll over and play dead and accept it happening to us or actually engage the future and change our trajectory. And even if we see that the needs for changing that future are not what we'd ordinarily chose to do, we can understand that a new set of activities amount to designing ourselves for a future we can help shape and it is worth it for ourselves and others all at the same time.

Now is the time to do that. Currently, however, society is neither in appropriate learning mode nor have we many productive habits to meet the crisis. We are not yet in a mood much less a mode to design a world thriving in social/cultural and environmental health. We just don't take our crises seriously enough, not feeling the sort of death threat like our parents in the US did when they went from spending money on fighting the depression to spending 12 times as much per year when faced with the Second World War. We have to change ourselves individually and collectively from attitude through to personal goals and daily habits. The key is to realize there will have to be some postponed pleasures, invested efforts, deferred gratification until out beyond some period of learning and training and hard work, entering the unknown, prepared for roles in bettering the future, whether or not we actually get there, but knowing at least we are en route to more compassionate and creative times, ironically, whether they come about or not.

34. Detroit ecocity fractal neighborhood core

This is an "ecocity fractal," a fraction of a whole ecocity with all the essential components present and well organized, "like a complex living organism." Also known as an "integral project." This is imagined to be placed in the presently burned out low-density semi-open space of a former car-dependent layout Detroit, helping lead us all into a healthier, happier future. The term was created by Adelaide, Australia Paul Downton and is a key concept suggesting transitions from neighborhood centers to full on ecocity project: real ecovillages with restored nature and agriculture restored at the same time.

CHAPTER 11

Special Case Cities in Ecocity History

Car Cities: Detroit, Los Angeles and Brasilia

To go directly to building an economics on what we build, we'll need to thoroughly understand the radically healthier pedestrian oriented, highly mixed use, compact, energy and land conserving, assiduously recycling cities, towns and villages that build soils and restore and protect biodiversity, broadly labeled the ecocity. And to understand that it helps heaps to understand what's happened to cities historically in their transformation to, in effect, anti-ecocities, the Frankensteins we might jokingly call car cities and automotropolises.

I'll feature three special cases to contrast a number of points between our current general notion and actual built type of city dominating the world today and ecocities. The dominant city today, could be called the classic autocity, swamped by those body snatchers called automobiles and running on automatic, meaning, with only minimal and scattered deep reflection on the part of human beings. At this point in history they mainly run on habit, bad habit, our habit.

The three most archetypical cities in this history are Detroit, Los Angeles and Brasilia. To emphasize, they are "auto" in both those senses, automobile dominated and running on automatic, with little thought about it all on the part of humanity. We've barely noticed that of all the streets of the world's cities and suburbs, probably only in one in 100 or considerably fewer do people walk down the middle in comfort and impunity: pedestrian streets. Cities have been transformed from environments for people to environments primarily for cars. Amazing how few people even noticed so through has been the infection. In fact, when people list the causes of problems in cities, and even in the larger environment, for example when talking about problems with climate change, they speak of the "drivers" of such changes and don't even realize the most consequential of all those "drivers" is the driver – of cars. And the classic cities with the key roles in the story of that transformation of cities as built environments for people to built environments for cars are, as said, Detroit, Los Angles and Brasilia.

Motor City – Detroit – built cars by the millions, as we all know. For all those gasoline voracious, beetle shelled mechanisms on doughnut shaped thick rubber balloons, Los Angeles bought up and destroyed its excellent, cheap and efficient streetcar system, setting the pace for the world, all as advertised by Hollywood, as I've mentioned earlier. Brasilia, however, represented the city not kind of obliquely or half consciously reshaped for cars by our inner lust for mobility, sex appeal and dollar signs in the eyes of all steps in the supply line, assembly line and writing of advertising jingles, but it was the city to celebrate the car and be explicitly designed around its needs, way above the needs of humans. Oscar Niemeyer, Brasilia's chief architect, loved the flamboyant buildings as modernist sculptures in a park, each building an enormous monument with open space wrap around view lines for worshipful admiration. He was a futurist as well as an architect, laying out the street system plan in the swept-back wing and fuselage silhouette of a jet airplane, the city to be home to space age people in high-speed motor driven projectiles barely holding the ground.

How would people get around Brasilia? Driving. (Without knowing it they'd be drivers of climate change too.) North/south streets fly over east/west streets. Their crossovers function something like freeway interchanges right in the middle of the immensely spread out town center with open spaces serving no function but to provide the cinemascopic panorama and opportunities for driving in circles. If you are heading north and want to turn west, that is left, take a long looping curve to the right, not left, east not west. You then complete a 180 degree change in direction heading exactly in the opposite direction you came from. And you'd continue turning for another 90 degrees to complete your 270 degree ¾ circle passing under where you just were and finally headed west, the original left you had in mind. You had motored right through a long urban space-consuming loop to end up turning left. If in your northward drive you'd wanted to turn right, you did bank right 90 degrees. But you'd have to skirt around the big loop provided for people headed east who have to turn south then west to end up going north. Or did I make a mistake?... I know it sounds confusing, but you get used to it and traveling at around 40 miles per hour in the curve instead of stopping at a streetlight is ever so gratifying and modern. In the US we are used to it as part of the freeway system way of life, the everyday cloverleaf, but by design right in the very heart of a city and on all major arterials, not just freeways?

Through the middle of the whole arrangement is the Esplanados dos Ministerios, the two and a half mile long esplanade of brown sun-toasted (when I was there) grass more than a normal block wide, something like the Capitol Mall in Washington, D.C. but about half a mile longer. In addition, in Brasilia this strip of open space is surrounded by enormous parking lots near the government ministries' headquarters, which along with the open space of the clover leafs and the Esplanados, keep low profiles for respectfully viewing the swooping cathedral building, Oscar Niemeyer's Saturn-like conference and performance hall where I spoke once, the national library, museums, Supreme Court and other government buildings. There are parts of Brasilia that seem lively on the street, but not the parts designed to be leading the city into its true car speed, expansive sprawl and messianic propheteering. The idea was that in the city of the future one could drive anywhere without coming upon a street light or stop sign, a dream only a totally car-worshiping elite could dream. And when it became pretty much real in Brasilia it was discovered it didn't work.

I didn't fully grasp all that until I went there for a conference and must say much enjoyed the sculpture-like grand buildings set in clean surrealistic distances "held together" completely unsuccessfully by the wildly looping network of streets and clover leafs. It was like you could park your car then walk through a Giorgio de Chirico painting and out into a Salvador Dali landscape. As grand, absurd sculpture it was one sort of artist's wonderful. But though the esthetics were definitely stunning for those of us who like big sculptural forms, the ecological implications were disastrous. I hope we can learn that.

People around the world wanted the messy compromise that could include the car for personal reasons but skip the grandeur, throw in some malls and franchise restaurant/gas station/McDonald's corners for economizing and convenience and randomly something at the cozy scale. They decided not to adopt Brasilia's more purist car city mission and extend it but rather haphazardly mush together sprawl, big buildings, freeways, single family houses by the hundreds of millions, residuals of lively centers, immense parking lots and structures, specialized districts, struggling rump transit systems stuck in traffic jams, scattered parks and squares, a splashy, curvy, scurvy, off-balance starchitecture building or two… the city with enormous appetite for mass quantities of land and gasoline.

Meantime LA, hardly pretending to be pure about anything, especially its acquisitive mishmash of architectural styles thrown up close to randomly, designed in purity only for providing ample free parking almost everywhere… *that* proved very contagious.

Detroit's history is truly stunning (when you stop to think about it) with thousands of acres already cleared, new grasslands and moldering asphalt facing the sky just yearning for farms, nature and ecocity development. City of opportunity! But also city that played a key role in saving democracy.

But many people who live there, that I met anyway, say they hear so many suggestions they wish the do-gooders like me would leave them alone (though I was received in a very friendly manner – they were only referring to those other do-gooders). I understand their feelings. Everyone has a novel idea for fixing Detroit. Tourists watching the Tigers' games and conventioneers buzzing General Motors' flashy, big world headquarters Renaissance Center in the elevated light rail People Mover most welcome. Gawkers at their towering empty buildings and thinly dappled suburban rump houses, many burned or rotted out, roof fallen in, in waving fields of nodding china-blue chicory open spaces, with an occasional lonely tree, please don't. They have their pride despite or because of the ghost town empty streets and neighborhoods. They have their own ideas about what to do to solve their problems and thrive again. Hearing these ideas and looking around gave me a little cognitive dissonance, however, because what you hear at the same time is, "Just find us the jobs and start the economy going again." But how? What to make? What to build? Not very well thought through. To say somebody hasn't been doing a very good job in the last few decades while sending the work to distant low paid labor pools in foreign countries is an understatement.

Ecocities, as you might have guessed, is my answer of how to fix their situation. Which made me the guy from Mars. But the times they are a changin'...

Their Mayor when I began researching for this book and when I first went there was David Bing, a black man in a community that is about 82% black (10% white and 7% Hispanic/Latino says the 2010 census). Bing has been passionately attacked for his efforts to get a handle on the reality that the city has shrunk back to about a third of its glory day's population. The decaying infrastructure has passed that fine line between fear and almost relaxed fascination, hence the not very much appreciated gawkers – it's relatively safe now so people like me show up. No longer is the typical scene one of the unemployed righteously depressed and sometimes dangerous people hanging around run down squats with burned out houses crowded together between dead trees and rosebushes battling weeds. Having no work and hungry, most have left. Enough time's gone by that most have just plain died. Many blocks have only three or four occupied houses left, some none at all. Much of the town has passed over that thin line into what begins to look more like a kind of cheerful rural landscape, if you can ignore the occasional still standing falling down or heroically maintained holdout houses between the much more numerous vacant lots.

I have to admit my impression might have been of a place more welcoming than it really is since the whole week when I was there the sky was a bright summer blue with fluffy white clouds and a perfect temperature for bicycling in a short sleeve shirt, no undershirt, which is just what I did for three of my days there. I also timed the visit for the annual tour of some of the hundreds of food gardens that have appeared in vacant lots, though like Motor City in general, also very thinly scattered. Go to Google Earth and you will have a hard time finding gardens; there's room for thousands more, and some big ones too.

Mayor Bing said in early 2010 the city needed realistic "downsizing." The hostility of denial was deafening, if built on a sense of genuine loss, frustration and depression. So by the fall he was trying a George Lakoff-like spin, a different "framing" of the same thing and floated the term "rightsizing." It took the citizens at the planning hearings about .2 seconds to hear the content and get doubly insulted that maybe they wouldn't understand the same thing by a different term. Well, he tried and his ideas were not contrary to a beginning effort at an ecocity transition.

That's why I went there but discovered those who could activate a world-changing ecocity transition, though intrigued it seemed, not enough for forging a working relationship. Yet anyway. Those I met included a key development official under Bing, Al Fields by name, some imaginative developers, the architecture, planning and business writer for the Detroit Free Press, John Gallagher, and various activists and gardeners, planning and design students and professors. An imaginative developer I'm proud to mention was busy building something about half way there to a thorough-going ecocity project, her name Diane Van Buren Jones. Hi Diane! I hope being published in this nice book for those really in the know leads to you getting lots of fresh development money! I tried to get some said money at the local foundation said to support kindred planning work, that I won't embarrass here, that strung me along then suddenly cut off communications without explanation. So, onward with other approaches.

Meantime the potential is amazing, if they know what to build. As most people are aware, the city is immense, scattered over about 135 square miles, built by the car as much as the car was built by the city. There are tens of thousands of vacant lots and they had then, probably still do, a mayor when I was there with the unlikely sounding friendly plan for demolishing tens of thousands of houses in his term, which could only sound good where the houses in question look bad, really bad. That also means land values are at bedrock bottom. The downtown is a strange mix of deserted towers, a few cozy hotels, up-beat new businesses, micro arts areas, great farmers market (just to the northeast), ambitious cafes and night spots like glowing bubbles of light lost in a Medieval Black Forest of towering ghosts, energetic music and revelry enveloped in old musty urban darkness… waiting, and waiting and waiting… And the Detroit River – that was, to my surprise, a beautiful Bahamas turquoise. Apparently all the silt falls out in the upstream Great Lakes, not at all like the muddy Mississippi, Rio Grande or Sacramento, much less Ganges. There was the friendly bike rental shop and the elevated rail loop called the People Mover, which is as much amusement park ride as transit system that helps… but it does help, and in ecocity dense city design, flies right through several buildings about four stories over the ground. If it were a little more extensive and connected more places, if the central area were closer to fully occupied instead of about half empty, if the population it served were three times as big, not bad.

And the open space? So much of it just sitting there. Why not ecocity and farms? I dug into the history some on the public computers at the downtown library three blocks from my hotel. I learned that before the Midwest there was Southeast Michigan, Bread Basket of the Young Republic, in the days when the Erie Canal was the main link for commerce with the eastern seaboard. There were – still are –

deep rich soils, plentiful water, cold winters to set cherries, apples other fruits and nuts and warm summers for real agricultural bounty.

But what became ever more interesting as I explored its history was Detroit's potential trajectory from our past into our future. The city that gave us the car, that led to sprawl, that led to climate change and that contributed mightily to species extinctions was also the city that saved the world for democracy, not single handedly but was certainly in the star role. And now it can also just plain save the world – period. Not just the biosphere in its time of distress but the temperature regime, climate system, sea level position and ocean circulation. It could aim straight for leading the world into building the healthy, thriving ecologically rich and economically prosperous future, which is saying a lot. China these days says it would like to create the "ecological civilization," but such a destiny has a historic opportunity to start in Detroit. (Could happen in China but they'd need to change a few things, which I'll talk about soon.) Yes it would take a couple delightful surprises along the way including some people with stellar leadership qualities. The potential is not, definitely *not* for a few successful electronic firms in the auto industry supply line setting up there, a desire I heard several times during my visit. It would take something way, way beyond that, something of truly mythic proportions. A gross exaggeration? Well, let's see what history says about that.

Detroit: history past and future

Back to Detroit and 1941 and President Roosevelt dropped in and ordered the remissioning of the city's reason for being. He said stop making cars. Make tanks, bombers, guns… The auto companies insisted they could do that and continue making lots of cars too. Roosevelt said no. No cars. We need an intense focus on winning the war. And it came to pass that for two long years no cars were manifest in the land and city of automobiles. Begrudgingly at first Detroit took up its role as star of the "Arsenal of Democracy," that boiler under which, if you lit a fire, in Winston Churchill's words, could do anything. Then Detroit got religion enthusiasm and the weapons production approached the miraculous.

I referenced that history in my comment to the folks in Detroit whom I'd hoped to work with on future designs. I said essentially this: You (or your history at least) produced the car city that became the future, ready or not, and along with it came hamburger stands to cruise and drive-in movies to see what your early girlfriends and boyfriends actually feel like – which everyone loved for a while. But it also paved paradise and farmland, resulted in a non-trivial number of dead and injured in crashes and brought on climate change, and a number of other problems. But you could make a transition again, as once accomplished to win the Second World War, but this time to win the war for us all, the war that has inadvertently appeared between people and the rest of the planet, the War for the Future. It would be a powerful story to change everything.

Perhaps needless to say it was a message to make people feel a little uncomfortable: City Admits Leading Role in the World Disasters; Claims it can Save the World. It read a little like a religious conversion and around building a new kind of city, which people aren't used to thinking about. People could make fun of that, even if we need something like it.

To even begin in that direction, though, Detroit had a head start with Mayor Dave Bing who when I first visited in 2010 was already on the case proposing intelligent downsizing. That involved finding the areas most likely to succeed and investing in those sites while being frank that water, electricity road repair, police and fire services just could not be provided in many other places because of the vastly reduced tax base and overwhelming maintenance cost of long pipes and wires serving very few people, lots of miles between cases for cops in their cars and fires for firefighters in their engines. That's a problem the city has to face in any case, but the ecocity mission there would have to be part of that total picture and be part of raising the same issues and fears. Naturally people in the areas of thinnest density who had lived through the worst, though they were also beginning to see a little of the better side of nature coming back too, what with their actually pretty beautiful food gardens, many becoming volunteer urban farmers for some food and fun… didn't want to lose yet again.

The Bing Administration planners were talking about centers of vitality coming back along a new light rail line up Woodward Avenue from downtown out to 8 Mile Road right through Wayne State University. A few centers of activity there could be revitalized and become the cores of a new and better pattern of development.

I thought the thinking was off to a good start. But what would fill out the vision is this: the application of our ecocity mapping system for the city in helping establish and keeping with the identified future centers becoming real ecocities, ecotowns and ecovillages in the new Detroit Ecotropolis, separated but yet united by farms, waterways and nature corridors. For people, bicycle and foot paths as well and the new light rail line and the already existing transit system would be created or upgraded. Some new centers of mixed-use higher density along the People Mover extended to, say, three times its present geographic extent might work well too.

The strongest initiative that could launch this new stage would be two or several centers that were full-on ecocity fractals, or integral projects, introduced earlier in these pages. These would be neighborhood centers adjacent newly consolidated farming open space with housing for the farmers in apartment style. They would feature multi-story solar greenhouses, a pedestrian street or two, public gathering place, several shops serving the center with a variety of things approximating the old general store but not necessarily under one roof, and in more variety to serve people in the surrounding area coming in by transit or bicycle. There would be jobs and nearby space allocated for equipment for the farming and native habitat restoration integral to the constructed environment of buildings with their open spaces and features, linkages and networks. Because the architecture of clusters of buildings with best relationship to public open space and foot streets is so important, rooftop uses and above ground connections between buildings for circulation would be integral to the project. Most or all of these features would need to be part of the living, teaching, learning environment created. The absolute minimum size for such a project would be two blocks but preferably three to six or seven. At the very least, one block of a street would have to be converted from a street for cars to one for people and another street removed for farming, like this:

Acquire enough properties to remove a street, to depave it for creating farms while sending the development to the ecotown center/new neighborhood project immediately adjacent. In other words the project of two parts, new building in one part and new open space in the other would create a sharp edge between the new construction and the newly opened ground turning into farmland. The number of empty lots adjoining or close together and the low land prices provide a rare opportunity for reorganizing the land uses and depaving the street.

In Detroit it could be a historically large depaving project. I'm unaware of any large-scale depaving project for "shifting density" to an ecocity fractal or integral type of project. The depaving projects I know about are relatively small and I've been involved in several: a driveway here, a small section of a parking lot there, a number of concrete "planter strips" between sidewalk and curb. Removing two or three blocks of a street as part of an "integral" or "ecocity fractal" project would be a major advance for the ecotropolis, an occasion for celebration and media attention, a real public wake up call. "Four Blocks and Two Streets to Become New Farms, Village in City" a headline might read. Typically a block in Detroit features 30 to 40 lots with two thirds of their earlier houses missing and half of the remainder burned or rotted out, torn up by tree roots and vines or Swiss cheesed by termites. Consolidating 75 to 150 properties, the great majority of them vacant lots or derelict structures, would create the opportunity. People love tearing up asphalt as I noticed when I organized a number of such depaving projects to plant food gardens and street orchards in the San Francisco Bay Area. Especially teenage boys love working the sledgehammers and crowbars. The stuff cracks and comes up surprisingly easily once you open up a small hole in the surface and get the knack of leverage. It's a civic spirit lifting party of hard to surpass enthusiasm, a celebration of photogenic controlled violence – Ayn Rand would like the violence parts – and farming creativity that leaves a mark productive into the deep future: so long as the sun shine, soil produce and the trees fruit.

It would be a real milestone, a city intentionally trailblazing into the ecocity future to accomplish the sort of "density shift" that would be illustrated in the kind of depaving/development described above. Detroit, due to its history, is very different and with a much larger potential than any other city than possibly Los Angles, for meaningfully broadcasting to the world about what it all means. Real estate prices in LA would make such a project virtually impossible. But Detroit… It could be a massive party, and major educate-the-world event declaring it is time to roll back the asphalt and liberate millions of acres for a genuinely sustainable way of living.

35. Elevated artificial mounds

Building above the floods works for tsunami coastlines as well as hurricane corridors and any other flood areas.

New Orleans: Learning from Katrina and the Sumerians

It is hard not to romanticize New Orleans. It's about as close to objectively romantic as possible. Objectivity and romance in the same sentence seems a bit contradictory, but contradiction is at the city's very foundation: the contradiction of land and water. The city is almost literally waterborne, more like an island of the Caribbean that somehow floated north and got jammed into the US Gulf Coast. The geographer Richard Campanela at the Center for Bioenvironmental Research,

Tulane and Xavier Universities, in his richly detailed *Time and Place in New Orleans*, imagines flying into town saying, "...ten thousand feet below us lies the watery lithosphere and earthly hydrosphere by a great river flailing methodically at its terminus spilling sediments gathered from the western slopes of the Appalachians and eastern slopes of the Rockies into a gulf of a sea of a great ocean... We are now south of the South."[134] The directions there are no longer by compass but upriver and downriver. My own first glimpse of New Orleans was from an airplane on a trip from Rio de Janeiro via Maimi to San Francisco. All I could see looking south was water with the sun's reflection glinting through the haze, the water of Lake Pontchartrain, I learned later, the waters of the swamps and the waters of the Gulf of Mexico beyond all shimmering gray and luminous silver. At that altitude and angle, water was all I could see until I noticed the apparition of Oz rising through the water like an immense outcropping of crystals in the distance, a craggy island silently moving through the mist far away, its reflection pointing downward as well as the city itself rising upward and passing slowly along the horizon as the plane sailed west. It seemed to float in a miasma of neither or both water and air. Land didn't even occur to me.

Four months after Hurricane Katrina pounded and flooded New Orleans I visited for nine days to see what I could learn – and learn if I could help with my ecocity perspectives. A friend named Joell Jones thought I might have some ideas and paid my way. Born and grown up there, she thought I might be able to help. In the streets and on the streetcars, which had just started service again, through the muffled conversation the name Katrina emerged like a distant bell, tinkling now and again, everywhere. A pleasant sound, "Katrina," on a sunny day... for a real monster. Another contradiction.

The destruction was stunning, staggering even. Looking at some scenes froze my feet to the ground, took my breath away, then sit down and cry. A house floated up right off its foundation, moved over a few feet, turned about 30 degrees at an angle to the foundation and settled back down so that the walls crumpled and splayed out over the three or four points where the foundation now pressed up against the house's full weight. I had no idea houses could be so buoyant: the bolts anchoring the house to the foundation had torn their way clear through the bottom plates of the walls as the water lifted the whole thing rocking and twisting, wracking this way then that, up and over, leaving ragged holes through the framing wood. Many houses were folded like cards, cars stranded at odd angles on their sides, hoods, trunks and even in trees. A child's smiling plastic toy fish caked in mud. Several paces from a wrecked house was an electric wheel chair missing its battery pack. It was for a severely disabled boy about eight years old and was sunk a few inches into a field, also caked in white-gray mud, rust appearing in a number of places, with a sign clamped to the back of the seat, and a photograph of Josten Mason, 1318

[134] Richard Campanela, *Time and Place in New Orleans – Past Geographies in the Present Day*, Pelican Publishing Company, Gretna, 2002, p. 9

Jourdan Ave., 304-1518. The number was disconnected. What could have happened to him? Were they too poor to pay for batteries? The wheelchair looked like it was well rusted already before the storm.

I discovered quickly how strikingly flat the city was, a sprawling car-dependent city like so many, with a high-density business district called Downtown. Also the French Quarter, two to four stories of zero lot line development, meaning buildings up against one another along a continuous street edge, and also very dense for its limited height. In New Orleans a slight and gentle rise to five feet above sea level in its vast area is called a ridge – a city perfect for bicycling, yet when I was there almost nobody was and I heard seldom did. What other city would have a streetcar named Desire? that is, a real streetcar named after a street called Desire. Also, there's Architect St., Music, Painters and Miro St. How about the corner of Arts and Law 1½ blocks from Ideal Place? But I digress from the fact that they have a much loved streetcar system there, a long step toward ecocity solutions, something to work beautifully with centers of some real ecocity density and vitality.

I felt a little guilty while my friend from Oakland staying with me there in New Orleans, Paul Richards, who you might remember from my trip to the suburbs that got me feeling superior to Alan Greenspan, went about volunteering for a few days in plumbing and carpentry while I was studying the town, deferring real work until later, if ever it might catch on. I was meeting planners, architects, urban farmers, teachers, students, artists, permaculture practitioners and a couple lawyers who knew the zoning and the history of fighting the freeways, one that was planned as a two deck rumbling wall cutting the French Quarter off from the Mississippi, a plan defeated. One of those lawyers was author/activist William Borah. His book: *The Second Battle of New Orleans.*[135] Bicycling Earl Blumenauer of Oregon, the only Congress Member to invite me to his office, had made the contact for me.

I hadn't thought of this idea until the second day there, though I had come with the notion that ecological city thinking was bound to have some insights for New Orleans and its efforts to reconstruct. And that idea was something as simple as "elevated fill," or you might just call it building whole district centers and neighborhoods in ecocity style on "artificial mounds," mounds of the muddy, sandy soil. Heap them up, let them dry out and build above the floods. Nobody hurt. Sea walls of concrete about a foot think up against the outside slope would prevent destruction by waves. This could never be done for the vast sprawl of car-dominated New Orleans but with occupied real estate of 1/10 to 1/20th the land area in apartment style, with ecocity features, instead of thin sprawl, it would be imminently affordable. And the people love their streetcars there so public transit over automotropolis please.

Building on elevated mounds of earth wasn't my idea, but at least I remembered it. The Mesopotamians came up with it 4,500 years ago. Ur, the oldest city of

---

[135] William Borah, *The Second Battle of New Orleans – A history of the Vieux Carré Riverfront Expressway Controversy*, University of Alabama Press, University, Alabama, 1981

serious size on Earth at around 60,000 people, and the largest in the world in the period around 4,500 years ago, give or take a hand full of centuries,[136] was elevated about 20 feet above the valley floor of the Tigris and Euphrates River valley bottom. These rivers had the nasty habit of flooding every so often, especially after the locals cut the upstream forests down though that took hundreds of years to play out. But, the people of the Sumerian cities did build most of their cities high enough that the great waters parted for them and for a while it must have been dramatic. I'd even say it must have been just plain fun to see the fields turn into a broad moving sea of light brown water moving by, as if the city were a ship heading out across a vast, strange, alien ocean.

I also remembered Galveston, Texas and its catastrophic Hurricane of 1900, back in the days before Hurricanes had men's names, before they had women's names, before novelist George Steward wrote *Storm* in 1941 and gave the name Maria, pronounced "ma-REYE-ah" to the real hero of his book. The catastrophe in Texas caused more loss of life than any other natural disaster in American history – somewhere around eight to ten thousand known and/or presumed dead and missing in the town and nearby on Galveston Island. The toll was a difficult call as the boomtown, vying with Houston to be the port city for Texas and points west to the Pacific, had so many people newly arrived and just passing through. I'd read the spellbinding and terrifying *Isaac's Storm*[137] by Erik Larsen about the hurricane, Isaac being Isaac Cline the weatherman on watch when the Weather Bureau's Central Office in Washington, DC stonewalled the Cuban hurricane warning instead of passing the information on to Galveston. The Bureau Chief's egotistical condescending racism and anti-Cuban xenophobia left weatherman Cline on his own with winds that destroyed his anemometer somewhere way over the 100 miles per hour it was built to withstand.

What did they do for rebuilding? Jacked up the surviving houses as much as 20 feet, dredged up the mud and sand from Galveston Bay and the Gulf of Mexico and pumped the grainy slurry around and up to the elevated buildings. The water drained downward and evaporated upward leaving an artificial hill running behind and parallel to the beach. New buildings replacing those that were completely swept away were added on top of the mound thus created. "They raised the altitude of the entire city," said Larsen. "In a monumental effort, legions of workmen using manual screw jacks lifted two thousand buildings, even a cathedral, then filled the resulting canyon with eleven million pounds of fill."[138] The work was completed in 1910. Behind the new concrete seawall and above the waves, damage from hurricanes since

---

[136] en.wikipedia.org/wiki/Ur citing "Largest Cities Throughout History," by Matt T. Rosenberg, in about.com., geography: geography.about.com/library/weekly/aa011201a.htm

[137] Erik Larson, *Isaac's Storm,* Vintage Books, New York, 1999

[138] Ibid. p. 265

has been miniscule compared to that from the Hurricane of 1900. Why is it I was the only guy in New Orleans who remembered this? (Or so it appeared to me at least.)

We should learn from the past. But 4,500 years of experience in the Middle East could learn something from the natives of North America. It turns out they knew something about the value of natural levees in flood conditions, building on elevated fill. Going back 5,400 years the ancient Indians (beat you Mesopotamians 900 years!) were building mounds of somewhat mysterious function, starting in north east Louisiana at a place called Ouachita Ring, ring of two story mounds, that is. In all over 10,000 similar mounds were built, many of them in flood prone areas. Up and down the Mississippi they augmented their height artificially, carrying mud in baskets, mud that dried out and served as platforms for ceremonies and villages. The city of Cohokia not far to the east of present day Saint Louis housed 15,000 people and was the largest town north of the Rio Grande until Boston and New York, and built largely on an artificial mound made of more material by volume than the Great Pyramid of Giza, with a base 900 feel long and 659 feet wide, reports Charles Mann in his book *1491 – New Revelations of the Americas Before Columbus.* "There is little indication that Cahokia floods killed anyone."[139] Of course not. The people simply hunkered down up on their mounds.

Add in the insights of ecocities to artificial elevated mounds and New Orleans has the potential to take the sort of leadership role you just read about in my advocating for Detroit. From my perspective someone has to do it and I welcome all applicants. New Orleans has that potential without the positive historic role Detroit played saving democracy and the negative baggage of giving us the disasters of cars turned jujitsu style into a powerful statement about ecocities superseding car cities and ushering in real sustainability. New Orleans has neither the Greek tragedy for all humanity status like Detroit's nor the potential for glorious conversion and redemption. But it did have a Greek Tragedy villain called Katrina.

New Orleans has the charisma to attract far more attention than most cities. It has the Tennessee Williams quote, "There are only three cities in the United States: New York, San Francisco and New Orleans," and it has the sensuous, classy, wild and mystical Voodoo Queen Marie Laveau curing the sick and cursing the powerful and evil with spells – for a price. Actually she was a mother and daughter by the same name, historically undecipherable, to double the legend. She was two free women of color, homeowner/investors and probably true economicsts and the powerful allies of the kindly former head of the Spanish Inquisition for Louisiana, Pere Antoine of St. Louis Cathedral, who accepted her Voodoo ceremonies in his

[139] Charles Mann, *1491 – New Revelations of the Americas Before Columbus*, Vintage Books, a Division of Random House New York, 2005, p. 299

church while she charmed police and provided full congregations for Catholic services as well as Voodoo ceremonies. You had to be there – the book is by Martha Ward.[140] Recommended.

New Orleans could also turn the all too famous tragedy of Katrina into leadership and success in teaching many cities how to reshape themselves after disasters. The elevated fill message would be one of profound assistance to Bangladesh, flood zones of the Mississippi central valley and other costal and river flood plains all over the world and in addition, hurricane and tsunami coastlines and areas effected by sea level rise. In other words about a quarter to a third of all humanity. And tagging along with that, the ecocity design/elevated fill lesson would bring the ecocity story to the world. It would be a bright silver lining on Katrina's ripping, thundering, screaming even winds and surging black-green clouds. The same lesson applies in the wake of Superstorm Sandy for the low-lying areas of Staten Island, Manhattan and Brooklyn. The ecocity part of it: everywhere.

The key element is that elevated fill works powerfully with ecocity layout and design. The two fit together perfectly, swimmingly you might say of New Orleans. The compact city of some real density – and the French Quarter is a perfect example right there within city limits – places enough people close enough together that the dollars per square foot investment would be high enough, in elevating a destroyed section of the city, to easily pay for raising the future city centers, district centers and neighborhood centers. They could be raised, say, 25 feet becoming a model for an archipelago of ecocities, ecotowns and ecovillages: the new New Orleans Ecotropolis. Each community would be mainly pedestrian by design, perhaps to start, two in the Lower Ninth Ward, with open space of native wetlands with all their natural storm surge mitigating vegetation between and linked by bicycles and streetcars to each other and the rest of the city.

There is no way the whole thinly dispersed pattern of the flats of New Orleans could be lifted. There are far too few people per acre to pay for the earthworks and they are too scattered for effective transit or even bicycling, the distances are so great.

To conclude, in hurricane country there are three components to make the city safe: 1.) elevated "fill" or raised mounds, 2.) narrow and even labyrinth-like streets, and 3.) shell, meaning only the buildings on the outside edges need excessive shielding from the wind, a hardened "shell" for buildings within the elevated, compact, narrow, winding street district. Since in ecocity design there would not be buildings losing building materials-come-projectiles up wind, the arrangement would be many times safer than single family homes in the low-density, below-sea level mode. The closely spaced taller buildings would also dampen the wind whereas

[140] Martha Ward, *Voodoo Queen – The Spirited Lives of Marie Laveau*, University Press of Mississippi, Jackson, 2004

thinly scattered taller buildings provide ammunition for flying projectiles to be dislodged and shoot at other buildings. Dampen the wind by diverting it down relatively narrow pedestrian streets.

Another ecocity element that at first glance might seem to be out of place at this point in our discussion is this: who needs all the streets in a city, town or even village center to be bathed in sunlight when ample sunlight is available a couple blocks away or "upstairs" or "up elevator" on the sunny breezy terraces and roofs? Narrow streets like the covered Grand Bazaar in Istanbul with its dramatic beams of light falling through many windows, larger gallerias or larger yet cathedral interiors and "Portman building" interiors – hotel lobbies – with cathedralesque interiors are built precedents and proof you don't need direct sunlight on all streets – when streets then become car-free, pedestrian semi-interiors. The lobbies designed by architect/developer John C. Portman have been jokingly called "Jesus Christ" interiors because when people look up at the walls and ceilings of the bobbies typically 15 to 20 stories high they've been know, with head leaning back and eyes to the heights, to gasp, "Jee – Zuss Christ!" Narrow streets and enclosed spaces with dramatic skylights or side windows can be great interiors at the same time they function either with enormous vitality as in the Grand Bazaar or in quiet almost deep forest contemplation as in San Francisco's John Portman designed Hyatt Regency. Its lobby has one inside wall stepping inward one balcony and floor at a time like an inverted ziggurat rising upward 19 stories with Hanging Gardens of Babylon-like vines reaching down into the air, with murmuring voices muffled by the shisssshing sound of a smooth sheet of sculptural water – a kind of fountain in the center. No honking horns, roaring engines or acrid nostril-stinging car exhaust.

Not that all the above at once have to be in the Lower Ninth, though even on a very small scale, some streets might be covered – say with canvas on hot days as in many tropical and hot desert market places – and you would be only a short distance from the enfolding natural land and waterscape and a pleasant streetcar ride to the next center or downtown. Such development could be the beginning of the New Orleans Ecotropolis. Add that all up and we have another golden opportunity – or perhaps better said – silver lining on a dark gray-green cloud.

China – Steroids for Ecocities?

As typical around the world, ecocity progress in China is spotty. The costs to benefits ratio (depletion, pollution, damage to landscape, waterways and biodiversity to services for people) can be added up on both side of the equation, but does it balance in any way other than subjective preferences? The urbanizing enterprise there is explicitly seen as part of the effort to raise people from rural poverty and

36. Peace and Ecology Museum

Berkeley, California was once a leader in peace and ecology innovation. I once proposed an eco-peace museum for the shoreline that looked like this from the inside, a large solar greenhouse essentially with view straight out the Golden Gate to the Pacific from the San Francisco Bay.

there is a justifiable pride in having largely succeeded: in the last twenty years about 400 million people actually have been elevated from poverty and freed of the age-old fear of famine by moving them to cities and creating jobs. The national government and some regional governments are exerting great efforts to try to serve both people and nature in attempting to further "eco-city" development, inserting a hyphen into the word as I prefer not to do. But to my heart's delight, including at the Ministry of Housing and Urban and Rural Development in China, they even give me credit for coining the word.

To say I'm an expert on China isn't quite right, but I have taken 23 trips there at this writing with another invitation pending. I've given one to six or seven talks on each trip and have met with ten or so planning department heads. So at least I do know something about their cities.

There as elsewhere, car dominance assumption is the unquestioned norm. But to their credit, their eco-city promotions, solar and wind energy systems, co-generation of electricity – the "co-" being waste heat used to warm buildings in cool and cold weather – geothermal or sometimes called geo heat exchange to use the stable temperature of the earth under buildings to help cool in summer and heat in winter, and on a district basis that pumps temperature stabilizing water between many buildings at once. And they promote transit and bicycles, the latter after a decade of being discouraged, now supported with new bicycle lanes, racks, and cheap rental programs with the largest bicycle sharing program in the world, the Hangzhou Public Bicycle Program with 61,000 bicycles and 2,400 stations.

They have the density but little of the fine tuned ecocity mix of functions supported by ecocity layout and infrastructure that I emphasize here in this book and few of what I call ecocity architectural features, though some: the keyhole plazas I frequently mention I haven't found. There are some rooftop mixed uses with gardens and accessibility, bridges between buildings, exterior glass elevators, beautifully designed natural waterways through vitality centers and so on, but not many. The gigantic plazas they have everywhere, designed to impress in imperial tradition, are not so pedestrian friendly. Blocks and streets are usually lined up with the cardinal directions unrelated in the massing pattern – three-dimensional basic design – to wind direction, people-friendly open spaces and views. The scale and arrangement are about the opposite of the intimate, narrow winding streets of old European cities though a few historic districts are very "fine grain" and planners are starting to pay close attention to their growing popularity as many tens of millions are rising in prosperity and realize it's nice to have nice personable environments.

The more massive newly built development generally contrasts also with old Chinese urban areas, not so different from compact areas of European cities, and the famous one to three story pedestrian *hutong* neighborhood districts, as they are called, a few still hanging on. Most of them though have been destroyed and replaced with dense coarse grain development in cities exemplified by most of Beijing. "Modern" areas are characterized by enormous buildings and very wide streets with blocks twice or three times as long as the US average and about twice as wide. The result is a street environment daunting for the person on foot or bicycle and tempting for the car driver to gain speed, for the longer distances involved and appearances of a larger scale world seemingly appropriate to fast, big machines. That's America-pioneered low-density development and cars; China, paradoxically figured out how to adapt high-density to cars too, leading to some of the world's worst traffic and smog. Those features of typical recent city design in China fit well the current mania for cars generally strongly supported by government there despite some serious ecocity efforts that are supported by other elements in the government, notably the efforts of recent Vice Minister of Housing and Urban Rural Development Qiu Baoxing, also long-time President of the Chinese Society for Urban Studies.

There are historic reasons in China for the large, often personally unfriendly scale of urban features, the imperial past for one, but also we in the US have to take some responsibility. It's the legacy of Detroit and Los Angeles. Most convincing about that was an incident in which I was taking a taxi from the Beijing Airport to my hotel speaking with a Chinese businessman in the back seat. "What do you do" got back to me and I explained I explored ecological city design. I mentioned ecocity people like myself were generally in favor of better pedestrian infrastructure, rails and bicycles and saw cars as a problem, so we promote cities with as few cars as possible. "But then," he said, "If I can't have a car how can I get a wife?" That hits home. We've modeled, in the US, an idea that has caught on. Also, "You've had cars for a whole century. Now it's our turn." Plus I have to admit that if I didn't have a car when was a teenager, how was I supposed to pick up the girls at the hamburger stand?

Overall, their ecocity efforts are as serious as I know of anywhere. They even have a city in construction as I write with the word "ecocities" in its official name (plus hyphen): Tianjin Eco-city planned to soon house 350,000 people. Apropos the main themes of this book, do they know what to build? Does the United States? Who is getting closer to an ecocity trajectory? Can we find anyplace where we get beyond tacking a few ecocity features glued to a car city layout? Can we get anywhere if we can't get everywhere, that is, to a complete ecocity design, a whole town, a whole neighborhood or an ecocity fractal?

When I first went to China in 2000 I landed in the Shenzhen Special Economic Zone, (SEZ) the first in China, and I was amazed that a Communist country in official ideology had such a district of rampant capitalism. I knew, naturally, that there were several other such SEZs as well. Shenzhen was so wildly successful with its opportunities for significant individual financial gain, that they had to build gates around it on the roads and issue passes to avoid having their capitalist experiment be swamped in enthusiastic prospective workers and young potential entrepreneurs. My hosts from the Chinese Academy of Science, Wang (pronounced Wong) Rusong by name who became one of my best friends, had to show passes so that we could enter and leave.

I wondered if the leaders of the country were nervous about such an experiment. Coming from such an intensely centrally planned governing arrangement and one-party-determined economic policy, I wondered if the leaders there were more than a little fearful things could get out of hand in the SEZs and result in yet another horrific revolution. Old folks there could remember early in their lives when warlord, communist and capitalist armies roamed the land, millions dying in the fighting and famines. Plus there was the chaos and atrocities of the Japanese invasion before and during the Second World War forcing alliances to form and break up, including with the United States and the Soviet Union, shifting through a spectrum of confusing, unpredictable, painful, often violent and profound changes until Mao finally got control of what is now China in its current borders.

In China it goes way back through those authoritarian family lines of the sort we've traced in these pages from Big Men redistribution systems of Gift Economics societies to patriarchy allied with their god-like mythic ancestors and to hereditary monarchies and empires. The last empire of the many going back 3,000 years, the one controlled by the Manchu people from the Manchuria area in the northeast, called the Qing Dynasty, ended in 1912 with the partial victory of Sun Yat-sen's Republic transforming over time into Chiang Kai-shek's military government not too easily distinguished from an out and out dictatorship. Meantime different warlords ruled in various parts of China and until the Communist victory in 1949 was China unified – or almost unified since the Mainland Chinese government believes it should control the island of Formosa – Taiwan – as well as the mainland but doesn't.

The Qing dynasty lasted from 1644 to 1912 but by the middle of the 19th century it was suffering exploitation by European powers. By the early 1800s, the Portuguese had long had a colony city at Macau and the English traded out of Canton, today's Guangzhou, in an uncomfortable arrangement with the Dynasty under Emperor Daoguang. He was trying to maintain the traditions of China against westernizing changes while allowing a modest amount of trade. The Chinese could offer fine silks, cottons, porcelain and other items, notably sensitive artistic creations, many of them on nature themes, going one way, away from China. The Chinese insisted on payment in silver, headed the other way. They didn't find much else from the west to be that desirable. Not that European traders didn't make money, in their transactions on down the line, but in mercantilist balances of trade it was becoming obvious that much of Britain's treasure, if treasure was to be measured in silver, was heading to China.

Victorian England decided it needed something mass-produced to sell to the Chinese to reverse the flow of precious metals so they supported growing opium in large quantity in India, shipping it to China and aggressively encouraging addiction. The Chinese in self-defense made trade in opium illegal and smuggling punishable by death. But the high value of the trade and armed protection for smugglers by the British made smuggling so profitable, for many it was irresistible. Meantime the rapidly growing numbers of the addicted in China began having a debilitating effect on the whole country. When the Chinese government interdicted a large shipment of opium and destroyed large quantities of the drug, England invaded starting the First

Opium War, 1839-1842. In the resulting treaty China was forced to agree to "legalize" opium but continued interfering with the trade, harassing it, from the British point of view. Using multiple excuses, Britain now joined by France, invaded again – the Second Opium War, 1856 to 1860 – which ended with the "Unequal Treaties" that forced China to open several ports to foreign commerce. These became known as the concession cities.

By the beginning of the next century, in 1900, the Boxer Rebellion broke out initiated by a mystical secret society, the *I-ho ch'uan* (Righteous and Harmonious Fists), called the Boxers. They were attempting to preserve old Chinese values against the West but provided the excuse for no less than nine countries (Indian's under British command included) to gang up on the Chinese to pillage as much of the country around Beijing as possible in a short cheap attack, then establish more trading sites and concessions from the Chinese. The invaders called themselves the Eight Nation Alliance: Britain, United States, Russia, France, Germany, Austro-Hungarian Empire, Italy and Japan plus India. The waning power of the Qing Dynasty and the "Century of Humiliation" wound up leading into a home-grown Chinese revolution attempting to regain the country's history, pride and power. That revolution established under Sun Yat-sen a national government in a republic governance format, but left much of the country under regional warlords and with uncertain borders.

Two things to be noted here: first that the Chinese Imperial system was weak and spread over a very wide area considering the transport and communications technologies of the time, with weak taxing policies and powers. They were unable to put up serious military resistance to well-armed aggressors hungry to make enormous profits. Second, they came out of the three wars noted above with those small but very economically active concession cities along their coast where foreign governments and trading companies set up highly profitable operations.

These concession cities were foreign bodies, you might say, inside China itself with enormous economic impact and functioning mostly to the benefit of foreigners, though some Chinese merchants and producers, a small proportion of the population, got wealthy as well. Not on my first trip to China noticing the SEZs and their capitalistic activities, but around 2010, I thought of Lynn Margulis and her idea, now widely embraced in biology and evolution theory, that early simple cells became more complex and advanced rapidly when invading bacteria broke through their cell membranes or walls… and stayed. I've mentioned this notion earlier but it's important and well worth emphasizing in the Chinese context. Here's what she had to say in her own words:

> It may have started when some sort of squirming bacterium invaded another – seeking food, of course. But certain invasions evolved into truces; associations once ferocious became benign. When swimming bacterial would-be invaders took up residence inside their sluggish hosts, this joining of forces created a new whole that was, in effect, far greater than the sum of its parts:

> faster swimmers capable of moving large numbers of genes evolved. Some of these newcomers were uniquely competent in the evolutionary struggle. Further bacterial associations were added on, as the modern cell evolved.[141]

The microscopic biological invaders became something like parasites, but relatively quickly in evolutionary time, ended up adding new capabilities to the host cells, creating a new hybrid kind of cell. In biology the simple earlier cells are called "prokaryotes" and the more complex later-to-evolve cells called "eukaryotes." It had long been wondered, among biologists, how the eukaryotic cells that make up the bodies of higher plants and animals could have had time to evolve such a complex set of special functioning "organelles" – Lynn's bacterial would-be invaders – settling in for the long haul. The organelles were something like special purpose organs within their invaded "host's" cell membranes (animals) or walls (plants). Lynn Margulis' idea was that the eukaryote didn't evolve in the usual sense. They were really something new and far more complex and capable of all sorts of new function – emergence in the biological realm of new material form and function from originally hostile, eventually peaceful living forms. Her term for what was happening in this new alliance-come-new kind of cell was "endosymbiosis," meaning internal living together, to the benefit of both, a new whole. Thus Lynn Margulis added to the study of evolution the principle of accommodation of differences and new synergies – cooperation – to create more complex functions, balancing the competitive mechanism identified by Charles Darwin and Alfred Russell Wallace with their "survival of the fittest." (Remember, that's "fittest," not most powerful or violent, meaning able to "fit" well into the particular organism's total environment.) This new combination occasioned the possibility of synergy, that is, a combination of parts together much greater in possibilities than simply bringing the two together. Some compare simple joining together to addition and synergy in that coming together to multiplication.

All this began to seem familiar as I looked around and saw that somehow Communism and capitalism appeared to be thriving, the invading "cells" of the old concession cities becoming the new SEZs lending capitalistic virtues of individual initiative to the host "cell's" virtues of sharing for the common good, in their case through central planning. The combo seemed to be thriving. Not very democratic, but the people were becoming more prosperous all the time. Will Margulis become as important to economic theory as Charles Darwin, Alfred Russell Wallace and she herself are to evolution theory?

How did it happen? China's paramount leader at the time, Deng Xiaoping, while contemplating a way of advancing China while hopefully ending its isolation

---

[141] Lynn Margulis quoted in *The Third Culture: Beyond the Scientific Revolution* by John Brockman, Simon and Schuster, 1995 (where in the book I don't know; got the quote from: http://news.discovery.com/earth/lynn-margulis-pioneer-of-evolutionary-biology-dies-at-73-111124.html)

under Mao Zedong, delivered his remarkable "building socialism with Chinese characteristics" speech on December 13, 1978 at the closing session of the Chinese Communist Party Central Work Conference. That was a mere four days after the death of Chairman Mao. In the speech he called for a "responsibility system," "...allowing some regions and enterprises and some workers and peasants to earn more and become better off before others, in accordance with their hard work and greater contributions to society..." This, he said, "will inevitably be an impressive example to their neighbors, and people in other regions and units will want to learn from them. This will help the whole national economy to advance wave upon wave" – which is exactly what happened.[142] The product of his new idea was the establishment of policies creating the Special Economic Zones, "organelles" of invading capitalism within the centrally planned socialist "host cell" called China. But this time China, not the invading powers, was in control.

The location of the first SEZ, Shenzhen, inland from Hong Kong about 20 miles to the north and about 65 miles east southeast of Guangzhou, was in other words right in the trader, we might say, capitalist heart of China. It was also 1,200 miles to the south of Beijing, the administrative center of China. "The mountains are high and the Emperor far away," as they said for thousands of years down south...

Shenzhen, incidentally, was the host city and location of my own organization's Fifth International Ecocity Conference in 2002, organized mainly by the Director of the Research Center for Ecological and Environmental Sciences at the Chinese Academy of Science in Beijing. That would be the main organizer, Wang Rusong, my friend who I just mentioned, with myself in the role of assisting him and his efforts as co-convener. Our roles were reversed in 2008 when Ecocity Builders hosted the Seventh International Ecocity Conference in China's favorite American city, San Francisco, with myself, our Executive Director Kirstin Miller and Rusong sharing co-convening responsibilities.

But my point in all this, as you will see building up, is that Galbraith, Jacobs and myself are getting ever closer to seeing something effective as a hybrid between various elements of socialism and capitalism being better as collaborators giving rise to new hybrids than as battling Titans from fun comic book fiction and real life horror shows. Hey!

China's ecocity design progress to date

I was hired by the Sino-Singapore Tianjin Eco-city Administrative Committee, the jointly controlled agency of the two national governments, China's and Singapore's, to tour, study and report from my perspective on the project as it was

[142] Thomas J. Campanella, *The Concrete Dragon – China's Urban Revolution and what it Means for the World*, Princeton Architectural Press, 2008, New York, from page 27 forward several pages.

progressing in March of 2012. I found my earlier critique of the layout with its typically Chinese superblocks changed somewhat, having more potential than I had thought based on my impression from my earlier trips to China.

I have to admit I was didn't like the super blocks with very large buildings and wide streets that looked like they would encourage considerable automobile ownership and discourage people from bicycling or walking outside the "eco-cells," a term the eco-city builders, meaning planners of Tianjin Eco-city in this case, had bestowed upon their superblocks. Remember they are about four to six times that land areas of typical American blocks. I thought the term "eco-cells" looked like a transparent euphemism for… big old blocks of overwhelming big buildings. Then there was crossing those forbiddingly wide street intersections to try to enjoy the rest of the community, the next superblock or "eco-cell" over. Obviously the density was there even if the close-in variety of functions (complexity) and friendly urban design seemed weak.

Certainly in many regards the project's designers and leaders were working hard to implement good, ecologically informed detailing of the sort of technical systems I've already mentioned. They were also planning a fairly wide corridor of open space running a sinuous path about seven miles long through the length of the project which they had dubbed their "eco-valley," a route for bicyclists and pedestrians in a long linear park. Heavy emphasis was on public transit with a goal or reducing automobile trips to a small percentage of total mobility. Perhaps I was weighing the layout and street pattern too heavily in the total picture? Or maybe through various changes it could be modified in some way over time as I advocate doing to American sprawl utilizing the ecocity mapping that guides transition from automotropolis to ecotropolis.

Studying these streets and blocks more carefully I realized that the interiors of the blocks were in fact pedestrian areas with considerable potential and their "eco-cells" might with some serious redesign even become my "ecocity fractals." They may have been laid out using the country's present massing and street pattern consensus with automobiles setting the standards, possibly as the only possible way to get their eco-toes in the door. But these big blocks of big buildings surrounded by their big streets had more potential than I initially thought if a little flexibility could be retroactively squeezed into the system. For example, adding crosswalks midblock for pedestrians and bicyclists would break up and calm down the long stretches of cars tending to accelerate down the length of the streets corner to corner and would create a much more human environment. Where the street looked like it gave all priority to drivers, a crosswalk or even two dividing the street into shorter segments would create a whole different set of experiences favoring the human over the machine.

This is an interesting and complex problem in that with the streaming stuffed streets, the "solution" has been to build a considerable number of pedestrian bridges over the automobile hoards. The people seemed to accept this way of getting from one super block to another without looks of exhaustion or resentment after climbing stairs high up to the bridges and over the traffic, something I've done dozens of times myself. But the base assumption seems to be, "Move those masses of cars and trucks as fast a possible," though often clogged in jams, of course, rather than declaring that the street level should be primarily for people on foot and thus traffic should go slower and people have the right to one or two street crossings along the super blocks' sides, stopping the cars with traffic lights set on not longer intervals than about 25 seconds.

But what I began noticing was that some of the interiors of the blocks in Beijing and other cities are in fact very nice compact neighborhoods in which cars are present but not so dominant and in which there are such features as small food shops and repair garages, nursery schools and mini-parks and playgrounds and occasional sculpture gardens and stages for arts and social events. I've seen a few weddings on such stages in the middle of superblocks.

An interesting detail: the extra wide streets create the opportunity to make the streets much more narrow as well as slower. Imagine this: at one end of the street, as you begin walking the length of the block, on the right side as you are walking along, the street has been shifted closer to the buildings so that the sidewalk is narrower than originally planned, but still you have plenty of room to walk. The other side, however is extremely wide, surface captured from the overly wide street for cars. Then, mid block as you walk along, where you approach the crosswalk, suddenly your side of the sidewalk gets extremely wide while on the other side of the street that sidewalk becomes narrow. The motorized traffic heading along in your direction has to swing over to the left as it goes through the intersection mid block with the cross walk. There is all this enormous amount of wasted space for cars after all, lots to work with. The added area on the widened side now provides enough room for some new buildings and open spaces for intimate mini–plazas and parks, socializing spaces and the mixed commercial users of a lively community that augments the quite interior of the superblocks just one minute's amble away. Not too bad!

In the interiors of the super blocks, too, there would be many opportunities for pedestrian scaled features. At Tianjin Eco-city there are multi-level shopping areas with bridges connecting levels above grade. Overall what can result from putting these features together would be an infrastructure of "superblock interiors" with pedestrian and bicycle paths instead of streets for cars holding it all together. In any case, one important implication follows from this: the potential exists for retrofitting much of the recently constructed infrastructure of China in the superblock mode to a much more fine grain and pedestrian oriented pattern.

In my report to the Sino-Singapore Tianjin Eco-city Administrative Committee, funded by the World Bank, I suggested that there appeared to be some areas as yet without firm designs in planning that still had time to follow a more thoroughgoing ecocity design process from the ground up, not just modified in the ways proposed in the last few paragraphs. For such places I proposed the building of a powerful ecocity fractal or two and given the canal that winds its way through the project site and the nearby Bohai Bay of the Bohai Sea, which connects with the wide open Yellow Sea and Pacific Ocean beyond. There would be a great opportunity for a keyhole plaza or two, as earlier described. Such a project with its large pedestrian street-like interiors with beams of sunlight streaming though skylights, with terracing, rooftop uses of a wide variety, solar and view orientation, exterior glass elevators plus the usual "green" of best insulation, recycling and water and air quality… such a project would be like a searchlight illuminating the future of city building everywhere.

37. Shade cloth and trees for street market

In hot climates, shade cloth is an old and traditional way of creating a pleasant environment. Here I've also added trees on the roofs, admittedly a little large, but you get the idea. Shimmering shade in the streets – what not to like in that.

CHAPTER 12

Of the Six Big Ones, the built environment first

Holistic generalizing, and "It is important to start"

Our best way of dealing with our condition in evolution as human beings is to think both with reason and with "feeling," good assessment and intuition for general patterns that are actually fairly true representations of what's going on. Call it holistic generalizing. Plans need to grasp the conditions we find ourselves in at this time in history in this general sense, understand the underlying principles. If in addition such plans are good at integrating many things that influence one another, that is if they are aware of "ecological systems" of cause and effect and networks of cross influence, they become crucial to solving our present enormous global problems. In fact, no other approach ever will.

And one other note of caution: we don't need more studies that postpone forever moving forward. In trying to work with Berkeley, California I've seen dozens of excellent projects killed by postponement through yet another study, committee, commission or new process going over the same old material. The citizens there are proud of their open public process but use it to keep the city stuck in place on the big issues that could take a modicum of ecocity leadership, such as zoning for opening creeks, facilitating increasing the number or size of community gardens or moves to create pedestrian streets. There is not a single such street for even just one block in the city and the citizens think they are "green." The people there are educated enough to use its endless public process to accomplish some meaningful steps in the right direction toward genuine progress toward a sustainable society, but they don't. They are proud of their solar energy systems on a few houses and their high percentage of Prius automobiles. But they don't realize, because they won't think about, that these two items perpetuate the land use conditions at the base of many environmental problems and problems of public access to the city's gifts. They again and again stuff up serious progress for another few years, more studies, more meetings, more studies, more meetings.

Jaime Lerner, the charismatic mayor of Curitiba, Brazil's famous ecocity leader emphasizes that, "It is important to start. Planning can be a flexible process; you can learn and adjust as you go. But you will never have all the facts so you must start."

If we are not swamped in enough good information at this point in history to solve anything we find in our present conditions we never will be. Just separate out the meaningful and relevant from the infoglut and deception, the seed from the chaff. Decisions based on the best of what we have already is key and the first step in making good decisions should be correct proportionalizing for scale and importance, quantity and quality at the same time. The second step is prioritizing based on that good proportionalizing. The third step is designing what we need, and the fourth step is resolving to move and to start. Back to our mainstream…

No one in any media or among scientists, government officials, NGOs, religious communities or general social critics as far as I have seen have made a serious approach at proportionalizing and prioritizing for what to do to rescue our world. There isn't even the accepted word "proportionalize" meaning to put things in proper proportion. It's most firmly rejected by my computers spell check application. It's not in my old Webster's New World Dictionary of the American Language and neither is it found at Wikipedia nor in the on-line Encyclopedia Britannica.

But understand "proportionalizing" and four big physical issues loom into urgency: #1. overpopulation, #2. our very destructive agricultural/diet nexus and #.3 the disastrous built environment of automobile dominated cities, #4. the climate emergency calling for aggressive sequestering of carbon in our atmosphere and placing it in the planet's soils and sediments, an approach I call natural carbon sequestering.

Overpopulation and the problems with agriculture and diet are being broadly addressed, if so far with support, commitment and effectiveness short of the challenge. But the fact that cities are disastrously conceived to maximize waste of land, energy, money, time and lives in accidents while contributing the large majority of air pollution and climate changing gasses is barely dawning – it needs the full glare of mid-day light.

The two big mental, psychological or spiritual issues are #5. generosity and #6. education. Regarding generosity, we need to invest in the Big Ones #s1. through #4. above and in someone other than just "me," other than "our generation," other than "us humans only." That's what I think is most gracefully addresses as generosity. A dimension of this is taxing ourselves and investing money well in building a healthy future, and not insignificantly, in cutting back the greed factor at the top: seriously graduated income tax needed as if we have a new war to win, the war to save destruction of our planet. Sounds like a science fiction story and unfortunately it is on that dramatic scale. Another dimension of generosity is not stealing and killing others for material wealth: we need to put an end to war as our great grandparents did to dueling and we need to invest in all efforts to grow human understanding and peaceful resolution of conflicts. In the tradition of disciplined non-violence from Jesus though Gandhi to Martin Luther King, Jr., there is an international history with considerable instruction that uses yet transcends politics, religion and all other manner of cultural, racial and belief system to work for compassionate resolution of human conflicts.

#6? Education, but vigorously emphasizing the above Big Five.

Finding the money – the three sacred golden cows

Next, where do we find the money? When governments say we are in difficult times and don't have the money to solve our problems, they are failing to see the treasures right before their eyes. Remember the success in increasing worker loyalty and recycling money into Ford Motor Company that resulted when Henry Ford doubled his workers' pay. He spent more in payroll, money he could have claimed he couldn't afford for one reason or another, but it came back in purchases of cars by his own workers. He was, like Franklin Roosevelt two decades later in government, engaged in deficit spending.

But most people, including myself most of the time when asking, "where's the money," would mean it more in the present tense: where are the existing hoards and flows? And if those claiming no money available are politicians they usually refuse to touch or even talk about the conspicuous resources plainly in view, which congers the image to me of sacred cows in India wandering about in full view and treated almost like ghosts, holy ghosts. Utilizing them is taboo. Specifically they are the very wealthy – more like the top 20%, not the top 1%, and if the 20%, we are beginning to talk real money for immense good.

Then there's the military – again an immense pool of capital. Third, the assets of the automobile world.

Even talking about these sacred cows where resides the real money has been taboo until as recently as the Occupy Wall Street movement violated the taboo regarding income disparity and the issues of accessing wealth from the wealthy and until the Tea Party – good for them – said the military budget should not be regarded as sacred – "Cut their budget too." Still, few dare violate the law of silence, keeping society from getting to the sources of the real resources of capital. At least the conversation that we need new and different taxes has been raised. For example California Governor Jerry Brown even got reelected in 2012 for his fourth term when he articulated clearly that we needed new taxes for fiscal responsibility – and people listened and acted. Nice to take some first steps but so far the increases are very far from sufficient to address our truly epochal problems.

Taboo? Said before and worth it again, if we open our eyes we can see that never has society had so many good tools and ideas, so much energy and capital to turn into good things, never so much wealth to build and shape a healthy world. Ever. So much energy and material is flowing through our world economy we could build almost anything we set our minds to, even a world that cut its energy consumption 90% and material waste 80% while leaving us more prosperous in terms of satisfaction and "standard of living" and Gross National Happier than before. Why be immobilized by glum hopelessness in a field of riches? (Though it won't stay rich forever if we don't move fairly quickly now.)

What a paradox that we think our economy is in bad shape. It's our thinking that's in bad shape. We are just too intimidated, spooked and frightened. Or are we too lazy to do what's obviously needed which is to take the money from where it is doing so much damage and place it where it needs to be: rescuing the world by building an ecocity civilization and regenerating a vital natural world.

Getting our proportions right gets us off to a good start.

38. The three sacred golden cows

Vast resources for building a far better future are available if society taps the very wealthy, the military and the wasted resources of the car dominated city.

Big One #3 – Why ecocities make sense

I'll start with #3 instead of #1 because this book is after all about building an economics, on actually building something. Also I know more about ecocities from 40 years of practice in the field – I'm an old field hand by now. About population and agriculture only recently have I made those subjects a serious study.

We are all familiar with the cities we live in now: car dominated, gigantic and, world wide, growing rapidly. The ecocity, in contrast, is an ecologically healthy city. The health is for everybody, including all other life forms, and the "city" is more comprehensively, as generally used in this book, the city, town and village: the "built environment," the "human habitat," our "collective home," the "built community" of humanity. It is not a collection of green buildings only but of much more, including open spaces like plazas and parks, networks like streets and electric, gas, water and food supply networks and organized as a whole living system, each city, town and village.

I use this definition to emphasize the importance of understanding the design and layout of the built habitation as a whole living entity. I call this the "anatomy analogy" because the city, town and village have so many useful comparisons with complex living organisms. They are actually built *environments* in literal fact, but as built, they also compare in form and function admirably in many and important ways with living *organisms* called plants and animals. There are many comparisons from both those great kingdoms of life. Built environments of cities, towns and villages are grounded in their layouts and foundations of the buildings like plants with their roots. They are also conscious and pulsing with internal intelligence, communication and transportation systems, like animals with their brains, nervous systems and circulatory systems.

Then again maybe the city *is* an organism, an organism of many organisms: mainly us. Both plants and animals are basically three-dimensional, like cities should be and ecocities will be – if we build them – to bring parts and functions into close well arranged relationship. Ecocities are not conceptually, nor if we built them would they be, flat and sprawled out in the way of automotropolis described here by now several times. Ecocities would also be like species of creatures different according to climate, terrain, local sun angles, associated bioregionally-tuned biota and so on. There would be the larger category of cold climate ecocities with large solar greenhouses and hot climate cities with shade structures and "massing" of built structures, mainly buildings, collectively angled into the cooling prevailing breezes or otherwise arranged appropriate to their bio-climatic location. There would be coastal cities, island cities, cities on flat ground and cities on steep slopes. There would be mining and farming ecocities, forest economy cities, manufacturing cities, college towns and on and on, many of them specialized but also with many normal community living functions complete and well tuned. There could even be the floating water ecocities, of which we have a large number of small scale precursors right now, boat cities linked to land with docks, bridges and causeways which often relate to fishing, port-to-port trade and tourism, we humans tend so much to love water. Some would be island, coastal and interior flood plane cities constructed on elevated fill, safe from flood.

But all will have, if ever built, those basic functions of complex living organisms: architecture like the bones; energy, transport, water and recycling systems like veins; communications systems like eyes, ears, nerves and brain; finite edge with nature like skin, fur, bark and so on in the anatomy analogy mode.

In addition cities – and especially ecocities – can be seen as like individuals further distinguished from one another by the people themselves and their cultural, racial, religious, political, economic histories, their themes in architectural ornament, love of certain kinds of plants and public spaces and desire for a certain look of their built environment, tastes in food, clothing, music, art and on and on.

When talking about the ecocity here, or any city really, we are not talking about single farmhouses, caves for a hermit or even a near hermit family. We are not talking about the lonely yurts of herding Mongolians, though we might be talking about the ever-shifting tent capital of Genghis Kahn moving about central Asia in the 12th and 13th centuries, with different parts built and functioning for specialized purposes, like organs of a living organism in this case moving *like* an animal. Well organized motorcycle club encampments and the one-week-every-year town called Black Rock City of the annual Burning Man arts and wild freedoms bacchanal in northwestern Nevada, mainly a ribald flash colony of San Francisco, have most of the elements of a "city" but not quite and certainly not very ecologically healthy.

That is, all constructed habitations including and beyond a very small cluster of simple houses that include a small number of structures for commerce, business, socializing – whatever makes the small village tick – is generically herein a "city." If they are healthy for those who live there and contribute to regeneration of the natural world, they are also ecocities. That village, with all the components of a living organic system, is the basic smallest "city" in our general usage here. We might think of it as "complete."

A hamlet of twelve houses with no special structures for the community's social or economic life is not a "city" in my expanded sense. It needs a little specialization of structures as complex organisms need organs. The city's essence is the mutually beneficial arrangement of different parts functioning differently, but all contributing to the life of the whole in indispensible ways. Among living organisms, as an analogy, the smallest village to fit the definition would be comparable to a very small multi-cellular organism with parts for ingestion, digestion, internal filtering and recycling, excretion, movement, coordination with environment, internal coordination, reproduction and a semi-permeable protective covering separating inside from outside: a membrane, skin, bark or shell.

Movement: open spaces through which people can walk or actually built for that purpose being then streets or rail lines. Elevated walking and bicycle ways on bridges linking buildings and elevated mini plazas, and elevators, escalators and moving pedestrian conveyor belts also count for movement.

Protection from environmental, external harms: cell walls, skin, bark, etc. as mentioned above.

Selective connection with environment: openings in walls, borders to keep out predators, enemies, illicit weapons and other destructive things, providing for controlled comings and goings like mouths and nostrils.

Excretion: sewerage systems, compost toilets, organic matter recycling and composting building up the soil.

Reproduction: places for learning and teaching for continuity into the future and chief among what is taught, how to arrange the city, town and village and its structures so that they can feed, protect and renew themselves and spawn healthy offspring long into the future which compare of course with our much apprecated reproductive organs.

James Miller has written a self-confident tome called *Living Systems* that identifies 19 subsystems that all complex living organism (whole systems) possess. Each subsystem, or organ, is linked with connecting tissue to other organs or subsystems or supported, protected, and fed by such other tissue. That's the way our bodies are, and all complex living organisms. I mention only five subsystem analogies immediately above, but you can imagine others, such as muscles and the bones of the skeletal system – and their connectors such as tendons connecting muscles to bones. [143] I say "self-confident" tome because Miller sees the parallels so close between, say, the living anatomy of an animal and an ocean going ship, or regional governmental facility, or a larger corporation with all its interlinked functions, that he can go on for over one thousand one hundred pages detailing the parallels with text book authority. We don't have to be as thorough and scientific as he actually is, but we can get his general idea most clearly.

Specificity and rather obviously the city is composed of buildings for residence, manufacture, commerce, office, school, eating, etc. and streets, rails, bridges, staircases, elevators and other means to move about. It is arranged around open spaces such as plazas, parks, playgrounds, food gardens and sports fields and all this in some relationship to local geography and climate. There are specialized places such as hospitals and recycling centers, sewage treatment plants and energy works from power plants and reservoirs nearby for electricity and water, to storage places for vehicles: parking lots and parking structures, bus and train yards. There are grocery stores and other stores large and small for an enormous variety of things; places for entertainment, music, dance, art, sport, relaxation, strolling, swimming. Manufacture is provided for and if unavoidably noisy or requiring a buffer to guarantee pollution can be cleaned up, located close by if not in the city. Limiting the wrong kind of ingress and egress from the whole these days, walls have been replaced by police, and to control the enemy within, cities needs, more or less, a Leviathan within: police, courts and jails. All this is familiar and serves social, cultural and economic purposes quite well. Working environments and trade places and portals have to be provided and all this in good relationship with the basis of food, other resources and nature's ecological services.

Among resources delivered by nature, a special interest of ecocities of course, education and inspiration are amply available and the structures of the ecocity need to be built to provide for people's awareness of them: permeable edge with nature, arboretums, menageries, viewing points, observatories, research centers of a wide variety. Nearby: actually close to natural nature.

Ecocities themselves could be described as cities built on the human measure and designed to advance consciousness and conscience, creativity and compassion. They further the civilizing process, whereas it's dubious cities built for cars do. Ecocities are cities for people, pedestrian cities, feet first, not wheels. As those who are excited about "biomimicry" might point out, wheels are not even present in nature to serve as some sort of model. Today the city is designed around our high-powered machines like cars and trucks. But an even higher-powered machine like the intelligent brain suggests wheels for bicycles and streetcars – not so bad. Streetcars and ferries are something like moving architecture, for efficiency that really

---

[143] James Grier Miller, *Living Systems*, McGraw-Hill Companies, New York, 1978

counts. They work because they serve far more people than they displace in the city for pedestrians. Cars push people off streets; streetcars, metros and trains get people to car-free streets. Ferries connect citizens with their waters in a wonderful way. Bicycles? Great wheels. They are a wonder of efficiency. On a flat surface they use approximately one eighth the energy required for walking, extending the person's non-motorized easy to walk or pedal range about 9 times the urban land area over walking[144] which, with good city layout and planning means almost everything should be available without motorized transport, except for some elevators, escalators and, in some higher density areas, conveyor belt "people movers" as we see at airports. Higher density center to center: streetcar probably best.

As to the basic structure, the ecocity is compact, generally tall on a small footprint – remember that the ecological footprint is largely proportional to the physical footprint of the city. The much dreaded-by-Americans word "density" works beautifully, but in association with a diversity of functions close together. In any case, that word is ever more showing its helpfulness as we begin to face the facts of sprawl, lonely suburbs, foreclosures on the fringe and lively, convenient places to live "close in."

To provide what is called "access by proximity" (instead of access by transportation machinery) the various city activities have to be provided for within a short distance. For example, housing near jobs, shops, food, entertainment and even much closer to food production and natural features than is common in today's car-dominated cities. You should be able to bicycle out of the city and into rural agriculture and natural landscapes. Or hop in a canoe and paddle out. The rule here, expressed in the formula "access by proximity," is that the shortest route from point A to point B is not a straight line but designing the points close together.

The finer details make all the difference

Then there are the finer details, the relationships of parts to one another and the function of the whole such that they become mutually reinforcing. "Synergistic" is the term most useful, meaning: when considered together the parts multiply their benefits, not just add. We have in this category, at the larger scale, the design of public open spaces surrounded by buildings and other infrastructure. Probably my favorite in this category is what I call the "keyhole" or "view" plaza. From above on a map this plaza would look something like an old fashion keyhole with an open space in the middle – the plaza itself – and a slot out to one side. The keyhole slot conventionally points downward under or above handles and door knobs. The "slot" in the keyhole plaza layout is actually a gap on one side of the plaza or at a corner

[144] If walking at 3 mph and bicycling at 9 mph.

so that a view to something special in the natural environment is framed by the buildings that surround most of the plaza, opening up and conspicuously highlighting the view, thus the alternative name, view plaza – we will see which name catches on eventually. The view might be a mountain, a coastline, the curve of a river. But there should be a clear view without city structures in the way. Such a plaza used to be Jackson Square in New Orleans from which in the earliest days one could look out over the Mississippi River, but as the levee was built up higher and higher over the years, now the "view" is the blank slope of the dry side of the levee wall. But you get the idea. The idea is to celebrate nature, brining culture and nature into a clearly acknowledged, even revered relationship.

Another large scale feature is the system of avenues, streets, alleys and other ground level means of moving about. For ecocities generally, that means narrow streets – and curving and complex is good, since all this fits with the more intimate and active scale of the person on foot as compared with his or her bottom uneventfully pressed to automobile upholstery. But some wider and straight streets for a sense of orientation are called for and some hallways through blocks, or the use of very small blocks for maximum pedestrian permeability. The wider streets do work with vehicles such as streetcars and taxis and provide views toward special monuments and out into the surrounding natural or agricultural environments – think the boulevards of Paris, which city also provides the narrow pedestrian scale winding streets of Medieval times. Small alleys or hallways through city blocks provide for show and sale of smaller items and lots of face to face between people in trade, eating, drinking, promenading – think the intensely commercial Grand Bazaar of Istanbul with its ceiling no more than three stories over the street, beams of light dramatically streaming through skylight windows. Passageways through the middle of blocks could actually be rather large serving as what are often called gallerias. On the largest scale they are covered streets like the famous Galleria in Milan, but could also be largely enclosed and like both grand cathedrals and the smaller Grand Bazaar lit by changing angling sunbeams and points of artificial light. The rule here is that a diversity of urban features, including different types of streets, like biodiversity in the natural world, is healthy, vital and worth celebrating.

Then at the finer grain and smaller scale there are attached solar greenhouses, rooftop and terrace gardens, restaurants and the like and bridges between buildings. The greenhouses, up to many stories high, provide heat in cold weather, passively delivered by sun and natural convection currents – warm air rises – at no expense of energy other than invested in the building materials and arrangement of architectural elements. Plants in the greenhouses provide fresh air. Glass in such structures can be seasonally removed for cooling in summer. Glass can also be positioned and hinged such that should fire break out, the usually connected open interior along the sunny side of the building could be rapidly sectioned off into separate cells like the separate water-tight compartments of large ships that allow one or two compartments to be flooded in accidents without sinking the ship. Accessible rooftops give us beautiful views, fresh air and all sorts of uses including gardens, restaurants and cafes, shops, meeting and party rooms, mini plazas and parks, even elevated plazas of the keyhole type. I helped redesign a building in downtown Berkeley for "live roof" access. It's known as the Gaia Building, third tallest in the downtown and so elegant and popular with its spectacular view of San Francisco Bay, Golden Gate Bridge and the infinite Pacific horizon beyond, that people get married up there on the roof ten floors above the streets.

In the more dense parts of the compact ecocity and ecotown, even mainly for sheer enjoyment of the close-in environment in medium density areas, bridges between buildings can provide many services to pedestrian permeability, more variety of safe means of egress in case of fire and provision of enough people moving about to make a big difference in the viability of commercial uses in the sky, that is, on the various terrace levels and rooftops. Critics say bridges between buildings take vitality off the street, but that's a function of just how active and dense the centers actually are. The higher the density the more vitality on both ground level and elevated levels. In earthquake territory bridges between buildings can be equipped with shock absorber-like devices to do double duty and stabilize buildings, breaking the harmonic sway that can be catastrophic.

At the Embarcadero Center in San Francisco's intense downtown, sixteen city blocks are united on the third and fourth floor level by bridges. The environment on the rooftops between the towers is light and fresh with views to the bay and sky, not to speak of the buildings themselves for those who enjoy them. There are parks with big trees and lawns on five of the blocks and the whole third story level is landscaped with decorative tress and bushes that could, with a slightly different program, be natives to attract birds and fruit orchards to attract snacking or harvesting by the municipality or another institution. On most of the rooftop/terrace level it is lively at lunch and dinner. Being the main business district and featuring generally high end shopping this level is busy during the week though only a few shops are open on weekends. The bridges connect food and entertainment with office space and housing, but the ratio of offices to residential units in that part of town must be about 10 to one. With a mere 100,000 more people living within a ten block walk, the rooftops there would undoubtedly be busy on weekends too. Immediately to the waterfront side of the Embarcadero Center is a busy plaza – weekends and weekdays – and a foodie paradise in the old Ferry Building, farmer's market and Gandhi statue where I like to meet people then go out to lunch or have a drink on the water. The Embarcadero Center is almost like an ecotown in a city.

In Montreal we have what they call the "Underground City," linking many blocks of downtown with 20 miles of tunnels over an area of four and a half square miles. The passageways are roomy and some quite large connecting movie theaters, offices, condominiums and restaurants, museums, colleges and transit stations along the way, all below grade and linked to what feel like open plazas with generous natural light from glassed in domes and ceilings between surrounding buildings. These really are plazas since they function that way centered on fountains or art exhibits.

Benches and tables around these underground courtyards, that don't feel like they are underground, are places for people to gather. And all of this in several locations is surrounded by food courts with cuisine from around the world. The regular street system is about 20 to 35 feet above that pedestrian system and stuffed with automobiles and their usual noise, smells and hazard. Purists scoff, braving sub-zero winter weather snow and slippery icy streets emphasizing, well, it's not *really* a "city." Others scurry about on foot and lounge 30 feet below, with easy access to the metro system connecting to much of the rest of the city. Light, not cold, penetrates their world.

Bridges between buildings could include elevated bicycle freeways. The High Line in New York, a long-abandoned elevated rail line converted to a very popular footpath and 20 block long linear park above the busy streets flies through the air down much of the western edge of Manhattan. The view stretches from way up the Hudson River in the north to the Statue of Liberty in the south. The designers have retained some of the native plants and celebrated local flowering weeds and grasses, even trees originally planted by bird droppings or brought in as fluffy wind-bourn seeds. It is wide enough for plants, pedestrian paths, benches, some of the rails as historic reminders. Not quite enough room for bicycles. Seoul, South Korea is well into planning it's own version of a High Line called the Seoul Skygarden converting an old section of a freeway with several feeder ramps into a looping pedestrian promenade 50 feet over the streets below and connecting several neighborhood centers and the Seoul Railway Station.

To my surprise and delight, since I had drawn pictures of elevated bicycle paths threading four stories high through dense downtowns and out to surrounding open hills and landscapes almost 30 years earlier, I discovered by accident that such an elevated bicycle routes had actually been built. I was delving into the history of the Pasadena Freeway only a year or two ago. Coincidentally it was the scene of one of only two automobile accidents I've been in – no one hurt too badly. That stretch was the first freeway in the US, and opened in 1940 linking downtown Pasadena and downtown Los Angeles. There in dependable old Wikipedia I learned an elevated bicycle path called the California Cycleway was built along the same route, if not the full length, one and a quarter miles in any case, made of wood and shown in a picture provided in the Wikipedia article.[145] It opened for use, in 1900, 40 years before the car freeway, but unfortunately at almost precisely the moment enthusiasm for bicycling was beginning to be pushed off the roads by the rapid growth of car culture, another – and very significant – automobile fatality. The cycleway builders, hoping to see increasing popularity and extending the cycleway around town, instead saw it start losing riders almost as soon as completed. Unfortunate timing. I'd even say disastrous in the history of city design and layout.

[145] http://en.wikipedia.org/wiki/Arroyo_Seco_Parkway

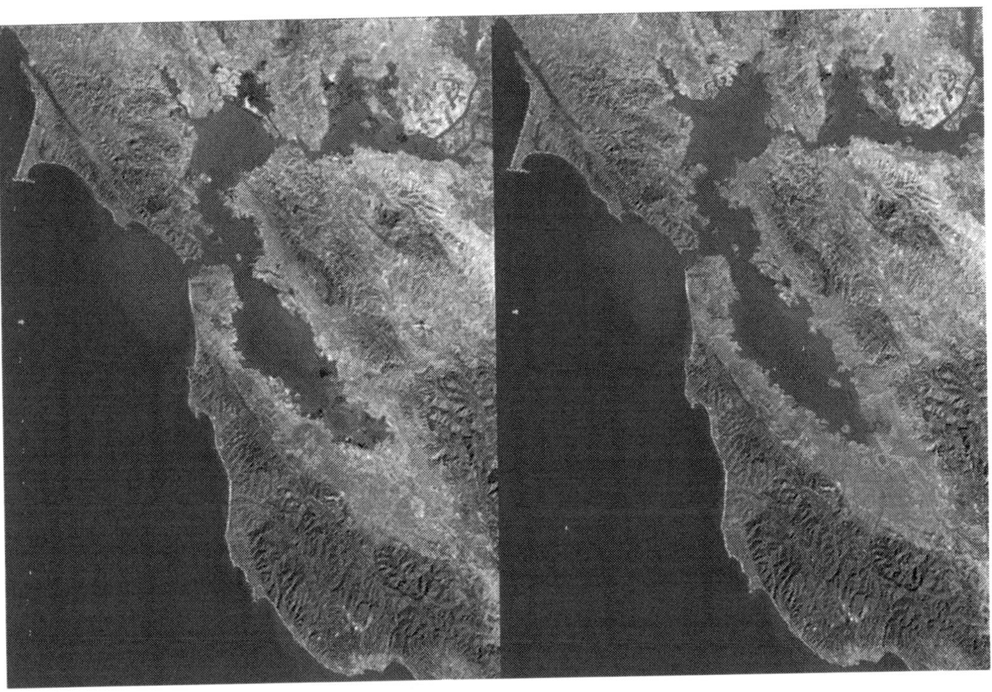

39. From metropolis to ecotropolis

The NASA satellite photo of the San Francisco Bay Area on the left is transformed in the right hand picture to a set of ecocities, ecotowns and ecovillages where formerly were central business districts, major district centers and neighborhood centers cinched together with asphalt and concrete. Nature and agriculture moves back in, as sprawling automobile infrastructure is steadily removed over the decades – illustrated in the "future oriented" ecotropolis map on the right. Call it "centers-oriented development" with restoration, transit, bicycles and renewable energy systems established.

Ecovillage, ecotown, ecocity and ecotropolis in bioregion

To best imagine what the geography of an ecocity civilization might look like, imagine your typical metropolitan area in the American experience. Almost all cities of the world, following America's lead, have been contaminated by thousands to millions of cars each, so if you are in any metropolitan area you'll get it. Most likely in earlier times the area was a few small towns, often with a larger one, the main city there, in an area linked by one or a few rail lines and small country roads through farmland, up valleys and sometimes winding through forest or along coastlines or rivers. Then in the 1950s cars began rapidly expanding the land area of the towns way beyond the more close-in, compact streetcar suburbs. Single-use housing developments punctuated by occasional shopping centers with surrounding parking lots became the new standard. By the 1970s and 1980s the pattern in the US and many other countries was supplemented by sprawling "back office" complexes and occasional big box shopping centers. The suburbs filled the space between the towns and continued to spread over natural and agricultural land while once lively centers grew together as one physical carpet of development which, if deconstructed to a pile of building materials, would be no more than a foot or two high in residential areas.

This thin veneer we can, with a little imagination, rather easily transform from automotropolis into an ecotropolis with its ecocities, ecotowns and ecovillages tuned appropriately to its bio-economic region. If we decide we want to. We have the zoning tools and can rewrite them for a serious transition. We can hire people to accomplish the change, shifting jobs step by step from one kind of city support system to another.

Imagine the metropolitan areas filled with today's car-dependent, low-density development. There are nonetheless existing centers of higher density too in our conventional metropolises. There are downtowns and major district centers, usually with some functions serving areas larger than just their own centers. Regional transit hubs, hospitals and colleges perhaps appear in major district centers as well as in downtowns. Most of the infrastructure in this metropolitan area has been created by locking waterways in underground concrete pipes, by paving over farmland and covering the once scenic higher places – hills and ridgelines – with the more expensive houses with good private views that clutter the formerly good public views *of* the hills and that displace places for the public to enjoy the views *from* the hill tops and ridgelines. The high places are now "keep out – private property" places. These houses on high, with their steeper streets, forcing cars to climb hills as well as move out long distances from urban centers, are among the most car-dependent, energy consuming, transportation infrastructure intensive areas of the metropolis.

But we are not thinking metropolis anywhere anymore, even anti-automotropolis. We are thinking ecotropolis somewhere very definite and from now into a future we can influence its creation. It has its own soils, geography, climate, ecology, economy and human history placed properly in our own changing times placed snugly in its bioregion context. The metropolis is transforming into a matrix of ecocities, ecotowns and ecovillages where, respectively, city centers, major district centers and neighborhood centers today prevail. Bits and pieces of nature come back, as farms instead of replacement housing appear where aging infrastructure dies of beetles, termites and dry rot. Don't build again there in automobile dependent places. Recycle the building material, chip and compost the wood with other organic waste, build soil. When buildings burn down or collapse in earthquakes do not replace them with the same old car-dependent farm- and nature-exterminating housing. Instead create the open space of community gardens and actual commercial farms. Or, depending on location, replace the low-density development with restored creeks, shorelines, ridgelines or noteworthy geographical features like rock outcroppings and monumental trees that might be lost in dull neighborhoods but could last another few hundred years growing in open landscapes magnificent for people's appreciation and usefulness, for birds seeking nesting places and food. Productive farms and natural environments return and along with them, education for the children about Nature's Economy and food.

Public plazas replace the parking lots of big box stores and the big boxes are torn down for vital town centers surrounded by medium or higher density housing in ecocity design. This started happening in the 1980s – Mashpee Commons on Massachusetts' Cape Cod is an early example where a mall in a large parking desert was replaced by a semicircular plaza surrounded by 80 various shops and new medium density housing where cars used to park. Changes in this direction need to accelerate if we are going to solve, among others, climate change problems.

In our ecotropolis scenario, office and commercial downtowns gain new residential buildings: apartments and condominiums adding variety to the former daytime-only business busyness. District centers might get a balance of new shops, offices and housing all at once, plus an upgrade on transit and bicycle facilities – they turn into real full spectrum towns in their own right. Everywhere schools for younger children appear close to housing old and new, and the kids can walk or bike to school safely because better transit and people living closer to centers or in them mean fewer cars, and fewer cars mean streets can be opened up for people on bicycle and walking more and more as the years go by until many are designated completely car-fee streets and whole car-free districts.

Neighborhood centers turn into real villages, ecovillages eventually, as nature and farming return. How does that happen? It happens there is some good recent history to work with in the form of many successful creek daylighting projects, restoration of coast lines, bay shore trails and the like bringing back natural features and public access judiciously so that both can thrive side by side. There has to be enough room for both the returning natural environment to be basically natural in its complement of species and for development of public access, but not everywhere. In some places people stand off far enough to give regeneration of native habitat a chance. Areas for wild species and public access have to be given the proper amount of room. Property by property, as people are willing to sell – "willing seller deals" – for comparable prices to land trusts and various levels of government, houses of no particular distinction can be disassembled, the materials recycled and small waterways restored, public parks expanded, community garden and actual commercial in-city agriculture transformed into serious local food production.

That's a good start and there are creek restoration projects now happening all over the world as people grasp that these are new, magnificently biodiverse areas rich in education and sheer pleasure for children and adults alike. In a pinch, for very high priority for the community – and for the larger community we are protecting in the effort to build ecocities, which includes the biosphere and climate system – eminent domain might be applied to condemn and purchase critical pieces of property to, say, complete a creek opening project, finish a bicycle and foot path or expand the area of community food gardens for "food security."

As time goes by and more and more waterways are restored where low-density development used to be, as parks expand and streets and vacant lots are replaced with bicycle paths and orchards, as fewer and fewer people drive and hence no longer need parking, farms appear between the centers. And the centers themselves turn into ecologically tuned, socially and economically vital cities, towns and villages. The entire metropolis, out of whack with its bioregion, now transforms into an ecotropolis of ecologically healthy communities of a variety of scales, each one surrounded by natural and agricultural lands, each one linked by transit and bicycle and foot trails. The streets and roads that remain are much smaller, much cheaper to build and maintain, and more friendly than today's freeways and surface arterials where you wait for more than a minute for the light to change, idling and breathing car exhaust at the many major intersections.

Once the general pattern of the ecocity in its ecotropolis and in its ecological and economic region become clear, that is, once you know what to build, strategies of transformation clarify too. A few things immediately materialize and fit the picture perfectly. One is that we can begin to see, when we have an ecocity infrastructure to help give order to everything else, a transportation hierarchy appears. Because the human comes first, it's only logical that feet come first. The top priority is to design for the pedestrian.

A "transportation hierarchy" becomes evident and should be a major guideline for ecocity design. Next after feet in the hierarchy comes the magnificently energy efficient bicycle. A bicycle can carry a considerable weight with no use of fossil fuels at all – freight bicycles serve beautifully in more compact city centers and would work well for all ecocities and towns with the possible exception of towns in extremely cold and snowy areas – and even there if sheltered streets were provided. Some Zen warrior type bicyclists don't even need that and use steel studded tires and very warm clothes. As the saying goes, "There is no such thing as bad weather, just inappropriate clothing." (Eskimos probably invented that one.) Presently the main hassle with bicycles of all sorts is that they can barely work at all in the higher speed, far more dangerous car dominated traffic.

So we have feet first then bicycles second. After that, third down on our transportation hierarchy list is the streetcar, or maybe the elevator, in medium and higher density areas. It would be interesting to know the lowest energy per person forms of motorized transport delivering the highest utility to the most people, streetcars or elevators. They could be compared for getting people from where they are to where they want to be next when going by foot. In a city of buildings more than three or four stories tall, this means elevators are moving enormous numbers of people. I suspect the elevator may well turn out to be next after bicycle, and first motorized mode down our transportation hierarchy list. Streetcars (small vehicles as rail transport goes and covering shorter distances) and Metro rail (larger and covering longer distances) would undoubtedly come next, then busses. Next to last we'd have taxis and various City CarShare and other automobiles from rental companies for occasional errands or drives into the country. And finally, last, private cars, eventually banned from most or all of the city. Think Venice, Italy and Zermatt, Switzerland, Gulangyu, China; Avalon, Catalina Island: *very* enjoyable places and along with a few others, car free. If it exists it is possible.

The eventual ecocities, though, like many old town centers in Europe, Nepal and other places where cities first developed as pedestrian environments and where they still exist to some extent, would have similar narrow streets and well loved plazas and parks that cars would not fit into even if allowed. These pedestrian zones would feature large areas completely absent cars and in most areas, absent all motor vehicles.

Electric cars? The better the car the worse the city.

The better car perpetuates and promotes the sprawling form of the car-dependent city, every purchase a commitment to keep driving for another few years maintaining a destructive land and energy hungry infrastructure, postponing dealing with the basic layout of the community when it is most crucial to confront. Remember that Los Angeles improved the car considerably with the "smog device" only to influence city development such as to give us thousands of car cities turning into the automotropolis world about 40 years later, the anti-ecological civilization the Chinese have recently said they want to create as an "ecological civilization". Ironically, as chronicled earlier here, LA's smog device, a massive improvement from the local perspective, gave us climate change.

Something else is becoming conspicuous: if the densities are going up in the centers and the low-density areas are being converted to productive agricultural land and natural habitat with recreational uses included in the ecotropolis transformation scenario, that must mean single family houses in low-density areas are being replaced in centers of more vitality by apartments, these centers becoming higher density.

Yes indeed it is very important to pay attention to the simple truisms that mean big changes in the right direction, and this is one of them: the single-family house has many times more negative impacts on our world than the apartment, whether in a city center, suburb, smaller district center, neighborhood center or ecovillage surrounded by open space. Apartments to the rescue. Or if you own instead of rent, condos in the physical apartment arrangement.

In most of my public talks I show a picture of a house that an aspiring green architect was most certainly righteously proud of, got lots of attention for and probably won an award or two for green architecture. I hate to make him or her feel bad but trying to make a single-family house function better only perpetuates a destructive overall pattern of development. You've seen similar ones, no doubt; they represent a popular idea about how we can go green without changing anything significantly in lifestyle or infrastructure. In fact the most eye-catching versions of "sustainable houses" appear in large format, all color glossy coated stock paper coffee table books as luxury green houses with three times the floor space of the average suburban American house. A word to the wise: green luxury is a contradiction in terms, an oxymoron.

The eco-house I use in my slide show is more humble and sincere than luxury green. It is two stories tall with smallish yard, plants on the roof, gutters and downspouts conveying rainwater to a cistern under the house for later use. It has permeable paving for a driveway to reduce storm runoff and return water to the soil, an energy conserving car on that driveway, along with recycling bins, all on a modest sized lot. Truly it's not bad; it would be as good as it gets in a dictatorship with storm troopers that outlawed apartments. I've drawn into the image two adults and their toddler, three people, about average for a house this size. Then in my presentations I compare it with the small apartment building I live in in Oakland, California that takes up about three times the land and is four stories tall, five with basement unit, laundry room, bicycle storage, utilities, etc. It serves 45 residences. Just for fun I've drawn in everyone who lives here – a Photoshop job – having a party on the roof, nice colorful clothing, the downtown skyline in the background.

When you do the simple math you notice the apartment is serving five times as many people for the land area and probably around three times the number of people relative to amount of building materials, but that's only the beginning. At this location on the edge of downtown Oakland we are within five blocks of practically anything we'd ever need on a daily or even weekly basis. All that is within easy walking distance, though I sometimes bike. At three times the speed of walking that expands my area nine times over for the same period of time moving about. The regional metro system, BART, short for Bay Area Rapid Transit, is only four blocks away making access to places all over the San Francisco Bay Area very convenient. Living here I gave up my car twelve years ago. It's a pleasure walking around the corner and less than two blocks to two small grocery stores, three blocks to a selection of four or five cafes, fifteen or more restaurants, a beautiful urban lake with resident and migratory birds flying, diving, fishing, paddling, courting one another, some raising babies and it is only a block and a half to the office of the organization I work for, Ecocity Builders.

As said, five times as many people served for the land area and three times as many for the building materials is just the beginning. But how much is saved by not having a car? You might have thought I was going to refer to energy saved, but I'm thinking about the $10,000 a year right off the top – times 12 means I've saved $120,000 not having a car here (where'd it all go?!). Actually, transit costs around 1/5th as much as the car so I've saved *only* $96,000 here so far. Not to minimize the value of not burning the US car driver average of about 500 gallons of gasoline a year, however, which is the equivalent of more than 12 filled to overflowing average American bathtubs (42 gallons) of gasoline, and making the proportional contribution to climate change. Imagine just burning 12 tubs of gasoline every year and putting all those gasses including CO2 into the air.

In terms of energy savings for heating and cooling, the apartment shares heating and cooling energy between units whereas the single-family house loses the energy to the outside after one use, sharing with no one, and that's a large amount of heating energy lost, paid for in money and more CO2 emissions.

There are many other ecological savings and social, cultural and economic services close at hand worth mentioning but that's enough for now. The conclusion: the benefit of simply moving from a single-family home with car to an apartment without, near a decent town center, is so enormous just as a starter, even without those ecocity features like rooftop uses, bridges between buildings, solar electric and/or hot water systems, expanded parks, keyhole plazas, community food gardens, restored creeks, street orchards and so on. Imagine adding them to the well located apartment house without car. And now we are well on our way.

There is, after all, a silver bullet

That term is common for meaning one solution solving many problems all at once, a "cure all." There's low consensus that silver bullets exist; smart people think the idea simplistic. Yet some do exist and the ecocity is one of them. And a reminder to stress the importance of this line of thinking at this point in our book: cities are by far the largest of human creations and we must absolutely proportionalize and prioritize for basic understanding – Ecocities 101 – of their negative impacts and potential positive contributions if we are to have a decent economy and civilization. Back to our line of reasoning…

You have now a starting introduction to the idea of the ecocity. Now to make the point that it provides many solutions for many problems but none are more important than that it simply provides room for everything else, both as a "town" inside its skin or city limits and by opening or preserving open space around. That sets up the conditions for a close to cure-all set of solutions.

An example of the "internal" effect first: I was one of a number of people engaged in debating what should be done with San Francisco's military base at the south end of the Golden Gate Bridge, the Presidio. The Army was about to move out. I was a speaker at three conferences on the subject in the early 1990s, invited to two of them by the great American environmentalist David Brower. There were people who wanted to see the old base converted into an artists and poets colony. Others wanted it to be saved exactly as it was deep into the future as an Army history museum and record of the architecture there with the rolling eucalyptus studded landscape of Australia, with the grass lawns of wet Europe and open views to the bay and Golden Gate Bridge. Others wanted low-income housing. Some spoke out for a campus of the United Nations University. What finally prevailed: the buildings and landscape stayed almost the same while dozens of non-profit civic organizations and some governmental offices moved in with a smattering of cafes and curio shops for those working there and visitors. Lawns and trees the same. An interpretive center was provided for better appreciation of a marsh and beach system that was restored where a small aircraft landing field was located on the edge of the bay. A small number of new buildings were added in very similar style and one large facility replaced a military hospital known as Letterman Hospital. One proposal wowed the decision makers: Star Wars film maker George Lucas' new offices. Those got built in a tasteful design one might call Faux Old Presidio.

What I said at the Presidio base conversion planning conferences was that the world needs ecocities for all the reasons you are seeing here in this book and the location deserves something unique in the world to compliment the iconic view of the Golden Gate Bridge. In this magnificent location we could have, simply, a regular town but one with extraordinary features to match and enhance the location. The everyday functioning of the town is precisely what is so important about it: it would provide room for pretty much everything everyone was calling for: housing, work, offices, shops, arts, education, recreation, celebration of location, provision for the disadvantaged if simply designed for that. What every town should provide and very normal.

But in addition we need a thorough going model for the towns we need in these times, a town-sized ecocity, in its own right a Golden Gate to the future, an example of how to shrink (physical infrastructure) for prosperity. A full functioning car free pedestrian town is a start, transit connected to the rest of the city, using one fifth the land per person and one tenth the energy, fully functioning and optimally designed in the ecocity sense. That would be a beacon to a better future, a new version, new vision of a "complete" town. The location with the view to the Golden Gate and the bridge by that name actually anchored on the Presidio property is one of those iconic to the whole world already, with the great vermillion bridge sweeping north to the mountains of Marin. It would be the perfect harmony of nature and human engineering to celebrate with a keyhole plaza design framing the extraordinary panorama. At that particular location, with the potential of 1,480 acres of mainly open space in San Francisco it represented nothing lest than a fantastic attention getting, education producing, potentially world leading opportunity for a model town for the world and the future. It would be a prime destination for the serious public interested in such things – as Curitiba, Brazil was already at the time – and for your everyday tourist come to see the spectacle as... "The fog comes / on little cat feet."[146]

If it had happened you would have heard about it by now but...

They must have thought, "Who invited *him*?!" Instead we have a statue of Yoda greeting people near the east entrance, the same scattered military buildings upgraded a bit and a nice restoration of a kind of inlet and small marsh with pleasant public access. Once there was a small airfield there where the Army used to fly in GIs who just 12 hours earlier were horribly mangled in Vietnam to the now gone Letterman Hospital where the Lucas team now works their Industrial Arts and Magic. The civic institutions are a generally good thing but could be joined on the site by many more normal town functions including housing for most people working there and nearby all in a design to address the needs of the real future rather

[146] Carl Sandberg, "The Fog"

than the reel future of Yoda's world. No history was written there, no wake up call and down to earth sci-fi vision of a healthy future – opportunity missed.

Location-aware green jobs and the economy

"Green jobs!" is a great battle cry; better is "locational relevance!" The consensus green job list is far too short. What's on it mainly is solar and other renewable energy systems, better recycling, conservation in general and jobs in installing insulation. The list has to be much longer and, my main point now is that where the pieces of the city go is the most important first step – a sense of the whole. Electric cars, like outright toxics, should not be on the list – they promote sprawl just like any other car.

Solar energy, like every other technology should be thought through in relation to its location, its full context starting with how it relates to city design and layout. Real estate agents say "location, location, location" meaning the most crucial element in the value of the property is where it is located: the neighborhood, the part of the city it is close to, whether it is quiet or lively, has good views, fresh air, easy access to this or that, is likely to increase your equity, has important people living there and so you should buy there too. In my world, though, it's more like, "At least it's affordable."

This place-conscious perspective needs to take a step up in sophistication now. If you know where buildings of particular sorts should go, serving what functions, which planners usually call "land uses," then you are well on your way to the most powerful approach available to solving the great environmental and biological problems of our times: getting ready to build ecocities.

The most basic guidance again is the anatomy analogy that specifies "mixed uses" and the basic three-dimensionality that is the form of complex living organisms and healthy cities, towns and villages. And, we need the synergistic relationship of parts within, those 19 subsystems of James Miller's living systems such as skeletal system (buildings), nervous system (telephone wires and cell towers), circulatory system (streets and rails), etc., that determine the functions of the whole built environment – healthy or pathological, depending on layout and design. By layout I mean placing the parts in best relation to one another on the land and by design, integrating all that rising up in the third dimension like a complex living organism (or town) in its supporting environment.

When we get used to thinking location, location, location we realize the waitress in the pedestrian neighborhood where people just walk around the corner has a green job. The waitress on the edge of a suburban parking lot? Not so much. In fact, not at all. The ironworker building a 12 story apartment building in a core city area that has little housing has a green job adding to the diversity there, providing "access by proximity." His job helps people get out of their cars and off the thousands of square feet of paving every single driver requires as his or her fair share of suffocating agricultural land and natural habitat while heating the planet. The student or professor who lives on or next to campus, the professional who can walk to work... In other words practically any job that does not directly produce poisons and is in the right location for helping an ecocity economy function smoothly and grow in a healthy way is a green job.

Back to solar for a moment, a technology case in point. As an urban design person I've seen many cross-sections of street and building layouts where solar access to each structure is the bottom line. This is starting with the technology first, placing the solar electric and hot water panels on buildings as we conceive of them now when we should start with the understanding that compact urban design is what the energy system should fit into, not vice versa. The illustrations starting from the idea of maximizing solar gain, the cross sections, tends to spread the city out to avoid each building shading the other. This approach, like adopting the automobile as a design element, also spreads out the city, if not as much.

But some of the world's most well loved and economically successful streets are in shade most of the time – and notice that it's shade from trees everyone finds wonderful yet shadows from buildings that are said to be a problem. In fact, the pleasantness of the environment is a complex thing of many factors and categorical thinking and thinking from one detail at a time – maximum solar gain for example – can lead us astray. It is not whole systems thinking, not "organic," not relating to anatomy analogy 101 lessons. Add two variables, say taller buildings *and* trees, and you get a new effect many people find just fine.

If the basic form that works for living organisms and saves enormous amounts of material and energy is three-dimensional and not scattered out, if we start our thinking from seeking a harmonious whole, rather than a green technology, we find maximizing isn't as good as optimizing. Thus should look for solar's best place in the built environment rather than building the wrong overall environment so that solar can be everywhere on all buildings. Some of it fine, but where most of it should be is out on the flats nearby and shipped in as electricity. For a modest amount of energy delivery, on rooftops is fine but relatively speaking, smaller as a fraction of urban landscape covered as population density and city or town average height increases.

Also it may be your town's locality might not be in the sunniest place. Maybe it's a more cloudy and wet location, but might have good hydropower from mountains and rivers. The idea with both hydro and solar is to reduce the demand by building cities that run on 20% to 10% of the energy now consumed. Then a smaller amount of energy can be covered from more reasonably sized sources. For a particular example, in the San Francisco Bay Area, the sun is not too powerful in somewhat foggy San Francisco itself, better in Berkeley, better yet in Oakland, but over the hill and 20 miles east – excellent sun and wind both.

Says Siemens, the German high tech company: "The most economic solution for long-distance bulk power transmission... is transmission [over wires] with

High Voltage Direct Current (HVDC). A basic rule of thumb: for every 1,000 kilometers the DC line losses are less than 3%.)."[147] That's about 32/1,000 x 3% and means a loss of energy that amounts to about one tenth of a percent of the energy going over the hills and into the cooler and less sunny and windy Bay Area from the California Central Valley. Not much loss at all. Even at 300 or 400 miles the losses are small compared to spreading out the suburbs one and two story infrastructure to gather solar on all buildings, requiring all that automobile infrastructure. And, solar electric is perfect for transit and far more efficient than powering cars off your ranch style rooftop.

Moreover, there are many pedestrian alternatives I've mentioned earlier, such as narrow streets and gallerias – the excellent Grand Bazaar, Hyatt Regency in San Francisco, cathedrals, the Galleria of Milan, some existing thoroughly pedestrian malls and whole compact cities like Venice that are strictly pedestrian and very pleasant with little direct "solar gain." So we need to start our thinking in the proper sequence.

I call that the "builders' sequence": you can't just drive up your flat bed truck and dump building supplies at a construction site then start nailing shingles on plywood. You have to start with a plan, drawings, digging the foundation, pouring it, putting down sill plates, raising the framing, sheltering the interior with roof and siding, finishing out in various details and so on ending with installing the built ins, painting and carpet. The city builders sequence starts with the general layout and design of the city, plus its more complex because it is changing over time. The sequence progresses from that land use base and mixed use design and spatial arrangement out from there – in living organisms something like starting with the DNA – then assembling the technologies and lifestyles, filling in the detailing for proper functioning.

Now back to the jobs to get the whole job done. The DayGlo green jobs, you might call them, are not the ones that are green by placement alone, though those are quite helpful – the waitress and the ironworker earlier mentioned – but the ones that do relate to those things already considered green, like delivering solar or wind energy, engaging directly in recycling, running a bike shop and the like, and *also* in the right place. DayGlo green is double green. They would include rural farming and farm supporting jobs in the organic, low or no meat, low chemical mode based in or on the edge of a city. If the farmer or support person in his or her supply or distribution chain also lived in an ecovillage or ecotown and walked, biked or drove in one of the much smaller number of car-equivalents running on solar electric power, say, or work truck – or rode a horse – all the better. I know a farmer in Iowa, for example, who has a big farm but lives on the 16th floor of a Des Moines condo.

147 http://www.energy.siemens.com/hq/en/power-transmission/hvdc/hvdc-ultra/#content=Benefits

Finally, and this is precisely why I have the "job" I have writing, drawing, building demonstration projects and giving talks in support of ecocities, I'm now talking about the whole battery of things to be done to promote the very design and layout of the ecovillage, ecotown, ecocity and ecotropolis that I think is about as positive and high leverage as any kind of work I can imagine. Call it the green light bulb job, triple green. That's exactly why I chose it. Anyone engaged in full-on efforts on behalf of the Big Six I've mentioned, in an ecocity context – perfect! That too, triple green job.

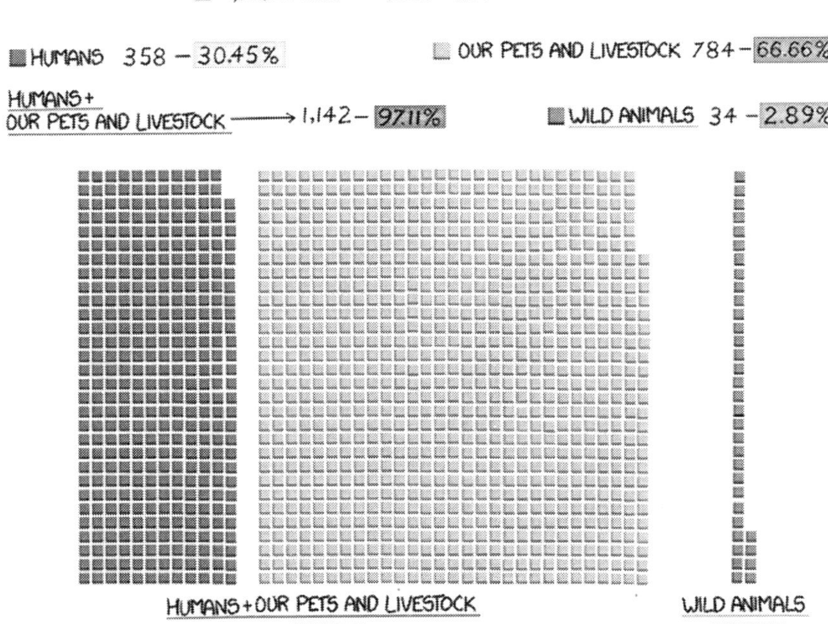

40. Land mammals on the planet by weight, approximately the same as "biomass"

Dark gray us humans.

Light gray our food and pet animals.

Green, wild animals.

This must be the most frightening chart I've ever seen. That any one species among millions should take over and appropriated 97% (slightly over) the mammalian biomass of the planet is about as horrifying as I can imagine and the most basic indication of overpopulation I have ever seen. I'd understood from E. O. Wilson's writings from around 2002 that we humans were leaving only about 6% of the mammals on the Earth wild. Now it is down to less than half that.

Source: University of Manitoba's Professor Vaclav Smil, extensively published polymath in basically all the sciences.

CHAPTER 13

Population and Agriculture

People, sun, land, food, natural carbon sequestration

We now have something of a model procedure for solving our larger problems in a process of proportionalizing and prioritizing, for getting to the most promising solutions to our most pressing problems. As something of a conclusion of that proportionalizing and prioritizing we arrive at the "Six Big Ones" that clarify what to deal with now, what not to postpone. In embracing the Big Ones we decide to take the harder path that insists on placing less important tasks in second priority – leaving the low-hanging fruit for the children. We've decided not to procrastinate until it's too late.

The Six Big Ones approach gives us a simple outline easily grasped, for the things we have no choice but to deal with if we hope to successfully pursue some sort of a world rescue operation. Undergirding all this we have a strengthening foundation in some ideas about economics we might distill from the kind of economics history I've provided earlier in this book and which we will wind back to in our conclusion, a non-violent economics you might call it in which the sides do not go extreme in a game of greed, power or ego dominance. We've even seen a powerful addition to evolution theory reinforcing the idea of joining the best of capitalism and socialism: Lynn Margulis' endosymbiosis theory, which in studying ecology and evolution, seems also to be fact – which in fact adds her to the other great evolution theorists Darwin and Wallace, rounding out the dynamic duo of competition (survival of the fittest) and cooperation (endosymbiosis). Add that to similar indications of finding the best from left and right in the economics spectrum as suggested by Galbraith and Jacobs. Ask mainstream economists if those above five are leading thinkers in economics and they'd probably say, "Who?" with a qualified slight exception regarding hardly in style Galbraith. But I think those five are profound in terms of economics *and* ecology.

In addition to recognizing the importance of the Five Big Ones, the issues rather than the people immediately above, we now have a fairly clear idea of what to build: #3, the ecotropolis, ecocity, ecotown and ecovillage with their many appropriate technologies and lifestyles. These built communities can stand essentially whole and complete like everyday natural living organisms in their natural and agricultural contexts, connected to other similar centers by transport and communications networks. Or they can form in the ecotropolis pattern in various sized clusters in their bioregions. So of the five – #1 population, #2 agriculture, #3 built environment, #4 natural carbon sequestration, #5 generosity and #6. education – we now have checked off #3.

Now we turn to population and agriculture, both of which I will handle in the same chapter, so intimately are the two linked ecologically and in the planet's energy system. Given the complete dependence of life on Earth on the steady flow of solar energy, the large but finite surface area of the planet and the specific capacity and limits of chlorophyll in converting solar energy to chemical energy to run the entire biosphere, the basis of population in agriculture is a kind of irreducible constant we have to bear in mind. This sets the ultimate limits on our finite planet that most economists pretend don't exist. If humans want to appropriate all of the solar energy flow into the ecological system, aka biosphere, for ourselves and leave nothing for the wild species, our children face a bleak and lonely future, ironically crowded at the same time – crowded with people and a narrow range of food animals and plants in vast quantity of each single type.

The graph I start this section on population and agriculture with two pages earlier, is truly horrifying. University of Manitoba's Vaclav Smil, one of the most thorough of all researchers and writers on subjects scientific, says we humans now comprise about 30.5% of the biomass of mammals on the planet, with our food and pet animals representing 66.66% - 2/3rds. Together one species has appropriated a little over 97% of all the mammal biomass on the planet. Already we have only the tiniest dribs and drabs of the wild ones left among us, less than 3%.

Never have I seen a graphic image to show just how overpopulated the planet is with humans as this one that show us how a single species among millions has appropriated so much for itself, only one of those millions, and left so little for the other mammals. Stunning and I maintain, quite frightening. The delicacy with which those other species hang on is something like us stomping on their fingertips while they clutch at the edge of a cliff with a drop of thousands of feet into oblivion. Never have I seen a representation of such unconscious, near total collective greed

– yes, mainly unconsciousness but here we have created the situation all by ourselves with 100% of the responsibility. We are already very close to "last man standing" – with our cows and pigs anyway – with a lonely evolution's future extending out into the desert to come. Leaving only slightly less than 3% of the animal biomass on the planet wild is well on its way to complete biocide of our closest natural companions on our home planet.

After that shock, to start off saying trends toward more organic agriculture and farmers markets and a certain fresh enthusiasm among young people for small scale, richly diversified farming are good signs seem encouraging, doesn't seem all that great. But it is. So we will take a breath and continue. This is relevant. Agriculture is an absolutely immense enterprise that includes deforestation and forest harvesting for building materials, paper and energy (and a little food as in pine nuts) that has transformed those lands that used to support the wild ones, for starters. We need to develop the positive alternative more organic, less energy, chemical, machine and land consuming approaches and push it farther, faster. Thousands now call themselves permaculturists: students, advocates and practitioners of a "permanent agriculture," which takes a design approach to the homestead and agriculture and is a whole systems approach very similar to ecocity design in many of its principles. Agroforestry too is a powerful set of ideas to utilize knowledge of healthy forests and food production in coordination.

These disciplines feature and emphasize components of the productive system that reinforce one another with reciprocal services while minimizing chemical, energy and machinery inputs and maximizing knowledge of the synergies of living things in both nature and agriculture. Biodynamic food gardening is a variant seeking highest production of widest ranging nutrients in healthy food by preparing soils and planting plants that associate optimally with one another. The Native Americans of the United States Southwest had their "three sisters," a version of such an agriculture strategy, in which corn, beans and squash work together complementing each others "skills and needs" you might say. Corn would provide stalks for the beans to grow upward while the beans would fix nitrogen in the soil to benefit the other plants while the squash would shade the ground retaining moisture in the soil and the corn would benefit the squash too by lifting the beans into the air to leave a large surface area for the squash to maximize solar gain.

Another interesting synergy: farmers are shunting their waste stream to builders in promoting and selling wheat and rice straw for bales for a relatively novel way of building that saves wood from the forests. These and other new agriculturalist practices indicate lower fossil fuel, highly productive, minimal chemical, maximum ways of producing food and fiber from the land. The practitioners run from conservative farmers looking at conservation techniques for higher efficiency to nerdy science buff back-to-the-landers that look a lot like Grateful Dead fans but sometimes with advanced degrees. Those who love growing things and enjoy working with sophisticated ecological knowledge in producing food and fiber are a very large part of the answer and should be honored and supported.

Many people realize this already as shown by the growing CSA movement: Community Supported Agriculture in which people buying fresh foods subscribe to the program and in so doing provide something of a more dependable income stream to the small farmers. Many I've met in California and rural New York are women it turns out, nurturing the soil as traditionally they've nurtured the family. The customer/CSA members in these arrangements often appreciate the farming process enough to volunteer to help in various stages of farming, especially when a larger crop is coming in and could use more hands in the harvest.

The growing realization that going local and planting more food closer to home is a very good development. It fits perfectly with reshaping the city to consume radically less land, opening millions of acres for close-in farming. Often this land was farm country earlier – which is why cities were built there in the first place – people need food; how basic can we get? – only to be paved over for suburbs. The land is still there, but just under gasoline-demanding asphalt and concrete and botanically monoculture lawns. The benefits of coordinated ecocity and essentially organic and ecologically informed agriculture is enormous: depave as the suburban fringes molder away and don't rebuild there. Send the new development toward the centers in the evolving ecotropolis and where the asphalt used to be, freedom on the soil for farmers and even where in some places, "...the buffalo roam, and deer and the antelope play" – as well as the farmer's children.

I recently met a man named Tom Newmark who certifies organic farms and owns one himself in Costa Rica. I mention him because, along with rancher Alan Savory – I'll introduce him just a couple more paragraphs – climate scientist James Hansen and myself he is one of the four people I have ever heard of say we need to expand our thinking to using natural processes to sequester carbon out of the air and into the soils and sediments of the Earth and if we do this in a systematic and thorough way we could actually start drawing carbon out of the air much faster than it is now going into the air. As Einstein says, we need to change our way of thinking. Newmark deals directly with high production farms, not just community gardens and he's convinced that organic approaches can impress millions of square miles of the Earth's present agricultural surface in the enterprise of reversing global heating, while replacing a high production high energy, machine and chemical agricultural system with a high production, low energy, chemical and machine system – with a secondary effect that we solve our climate change problem while producing particularly nutritious food.

But generally, I want to wake up to the positive side of the solar/chlorophyll/soil story in lots of people's minds and, when going into writing this section of my book, I was hoping for such an opening in my research, one of the those surprises I think might just be out there to counter my generally gloomy planetary prognosis. To be considered is that all the habitual, traditional and religious determinates of diet, as with population, need to be tested against the limits of the Earth's life systems and we need to pay attention to the likely results of such diets, the demand side of agriculture, if we are to successfully deal with the planet's limits and further our own healthier evolution. But I'll let you know now, viewing agriculture as broadly as to include forest production and the other results of chlorophyll such as producing ocean algae, sea weed, krill and fish, that I surprised myself in coming up with something of a novel track that will look like a diversion off the subject of agriculture and diet into very broad territory, as you will see. As to the diet connection with agriculture, of course they are connected – intimately.

My glum prognosis looking for positive surprises did indeed stumble across one such very happy surprise: herding large herbivores properly can restore grasslands (and provide beef and milk) to sequester stunning quantities of CO_2. Could there be other places on the surface of the Earth that could also serve in that way, maybe places in the ocean too? The unlikely very positive clue was that zebras and wildebeests herded by lions bring back degraded lands, cultivate extremely rich biomass and biodiversity and render the grasslands managed in this manner to soak up not only massive amounts of CO_2 from the atmosphere but sponge up water that otherwise, with typical agricultural herding practices, runs off instead of soaking into the soil. When it does soak in it replenishes aquifers, raises the water table and brings back dried up springs and streams.

The story starts when Allan Savory, white ranch owner in Ian Smith's severely racist Rhodesia, led the white opposition party and, for sympathy with the blacks, had to flee the country – to return later when it was rechristened Zimbabwe. His keen interest in wildlife, growing up on the family ranch as it would be called in the United States, farm in Zimbabwe, led to observations of the way predators cause herbivores to cluster in defensive tight clutches of up to hundreds of animals. The result: their dung and pee mixed by the action of thousands of hooves drives seeds into the earth/fertilizer mix that vastly enriches the entire grassland landscape.

The predators – lions herding the African herbivores in Zimbabwe and wolves herding bison in North America – find it hard to attack their prey from directly behind. The large muscles that carry the herbivores forward with enormous power also power hooves as deadly weapons in kicking backward, able to deliver devastating blows as mentioned earlier discussing the hand ax. The objective of the predator then is to separate out an old, injured or unprotected young victim and attack at an oblique angle. From the herbivore's point of view, the clustering offers the protection of providing no good angle of attack to the predator and clustering to protect one another and especially the young. Savory points out that the horns on the other end of many of the prey, such as the wildebeest, are for tussles of strength to win mating rights, not for fighting off predators.

Looking a little more closely we can see that the action of the hooves creates an amazingly varied environment for sprouting seeds. With soil and fertilizer mixed perfectly in small crater like depressions of hoof prints in the moist soil/manure mix, water can accumulate during rains to soak some seed thoroughly while on the elevated ridges between the hoof's indentations, less water means drier soil/fertilizer mixture. The variety of what we might think of as micro-geography moisture regimes thus created provides a wide range of conditions guaranteed to make many just perfect different kinds of conditions for many different kinds of plants to sprout. The result: very high biodiversity as well as maximum primary photosynthetic product (PPP) and biomass. The action of hooves also cracks the hard shells of many of the seeds making it easier for them to germinate. When the vegetation grows back and rain falls, very little water runs off, instead soaking deep into the soil where the roots – made of large amounts of carbon – soak up the moisture and transpire a large part of the water back into the air. But in balance, more water penetrates deep into the soil and does not run off. The result is a steady build up of water in the soil and rising of the water table. On Savory's land, when he managed cattle in the same general style using the local ranch labor, called cowboys in certain countries, he saw that the water level rose so high that long dried out streams returned. Photos of his property with dense growth, streams and ponds compared to neighbor's farms with sparse shriveled plants and sandy dry wash bottoms look pretty convincing.

Now think of flying in an airplane over the landscape of the Earth and looking down at all the soil down there. It's like a sponge, thin in some places and very thick in others, 10,000 feet deep in central north east Australia's Great Artesian Basin, the world's vertically thickest aquifer plus immensely large in area undergirding one fifth of all Australia's land surface. Notice that from the airplane the rivers all over the world are narrow glinting silver lines of reflected sun. Everything else is, or almost all of it could be, soil saturated below a certain depth in water and the water capable of holding various gasses from the atmosphere. Only impermeable layers of rock and tightly packed clays prevents water from soaking deeper…

Surface soil is like a saturated or moisturized sponge that lets gasses in and out. Every root of grass, bush or tree is a tube plugged into the earth pumping gasses, chemicals and moisture downward and upward. The dead roots, stems and leaves of the plants – and even moldering bodies of animals if in about 1/1000th the biomass of the plants – fluffs up the soil to accept more moisture and hold the gasses delivered downward by the roots of plants and the mycelium of fungi. There is a colossal volume of loosely packed or porous soil capable of massive buffering for the atmosphere.

When you think of the soil's water-saturated gravels, sands and even sandstones that can be thousands of feet thick all the way down to impermeable layers of clay or tightly fused igneous (generally lavas or basaltic) stone or metamorphic (melted, squeezed and compacted sand and other) stone, you begin to picture an immense reservoir of moisture and capacity for holding carbon, mostly in various chemical combinations, that the crust of the Earth actually has. Remember also that the atmosphere holds gasses in such thin concentration you can see right through it. But the soil concentrates all sorts of gasses by absorption, adsorption and chemical combination with the elements and molecules packed much closer together, basically solids, not gasses anymore, hundreds of times more concentrated. Though I don't know the exact numbers involved, it looks like very large capacity for carbon sequestration provided by nature in the permeable layers, starting at the top with soils and sediments.

I began to get some feel for this when I asked myself a few years ago, "Well, cities may be the largest creations of humanity in terms of things we build, but farms and managed grazing lands and forests are yet much more immense in terms of acreage carved out of the natural environment by human activities for human purposes.) It then follows that agriculture and forestry for production must be so big as to be one of the Big Five at the time, turning into the Big Six. Also, it is no small consideration since we all need the food or we die, not an insignificant variable in our list of needs and wants, *the* bottom line *sin qua non*. We also need the shelter of buildings, millions of them of wood, too. Lacking shelter we are hard pressed to be comfortable, or often to survive at all and fatally compromised in our own strivings for self-fulfillment in any complex culturally and economically specialized society. For example how could I be writing this book on this electronic machine buffeted by gusts of wind and cold rain?

About the potential for total CO2 sequestration available from nature with very minimal management by people? Crudely stated it might be called "tweakable natural sequestration." Allan Savory maintains that the grassland soils constitute a gigantic part of the solution. He says in addition it is not the grazing or even "over-grazing" (when meaning intensive grazing) that has been the problem and given the herding people of the world a bad reputation for the damage their flocks have done, but the wrong methods of grazing. Heavy grazing, he says, is good if it is in the pattern just described, "mob grazing" as one soil scientist I know called it discussing the topic with me recently, temporarily appearing to beat down the grasslands but preparing seed and soil for rich production as soon as the next rain comes

In Allan's own words in a May 10, 2012 e-mail to me, "No technology can ever replace billions of organisms in the moist gut of large herbivores cycling billions of tons annually dying plant material while also laying soil covering litter. And why should we ever try to do this with such machines as were developed, all using fossil fuels, when animals do it free using solar energy and feeding people?"

His work reminded me of a quote I remembered form Alfred W. Crosby's book, *Ecological Imperialism – The Biological Expansion of Europe, 900-1900,*[148] To set the scene, Crosby's talking about the temperate regions of the world, similar to Europe in the planet's mid range for moisture levels and temperature and in places with relatively clearly demarked seasons. Europeans colonized not only with their bodies but also with their animals, plants, pets, pests and diseases. "...these animals are self-replicators," wrote Crosby, "the efficiency and speed with which they can alter environments, even continental environments, are superior to those for any machines we have thus far devised." To the point Savory mentions about the animals running on solar energy, as compared to machines on fossil fuels, add that in most technofix approaches to CO2 sequestration we would need even more machines powered by

[148] Alfred W. Crosby, *Ecological Imperialism – The Biological Expansion of Europe, 900-1900*, Press Syndicate of the University of Cambridge, New York and Melbourne, 1986, p. 173

energy from somewhere to pump CO_2 into (hopefully) impervious layers deep below, every machine needing to be manufactured whereas the animals "manufacture" themselves and multiply enriching the very soil they depend on for their own food as well as ours.

And then there are the plants too, self replicators also, that for Charles Darwin on a riding excursion from his voyage of the Beagle found himself in a field of artichokes in Uruguay – a plant introduced only 20 years earlier – that rose higher than his rental horse's shoulders and extended from horizon to horizon.

Allan Savory speaks of millions of square miles that can start soaking up CO_2 while refertilizing the soil and adding instead of subtracting ground water. So his "holistic management" takes care of large areas of the grasslands and semi-dry brushlands. What about the wetter landscapes? We are all familiar with the role of forests in producing oxygen and moisturizing the air, drawing in enormous amounts of carbon and storing it in woody tissues. That land area is immense too.

And what about the marshes, the swamps, the fens and bogs and the coastal brackish or salty wetlands? Do they also hold the potential for absorbing or otherwise storing great quantities of carbon?

Bogs: rain fed wetlands, acidic, mostly in cold climates though some in the tropics, build up peat by hosting sphagnum moss that lays down layer over layer and can host some other organisms, low in oxygen, slow decomposition or no decomposition and no CO_2 outgassing at all if under water.

Fens: wetlands fed by slowly flowing water, mildly acidic to alkaline, more diverse life than bogs.

Tidal marshes: fresh, brackish, salt water.

Non-tidal marshes: by ponds, lakes, streams, rivers, mineral rich with sand, clay and silt often covered with grasses and reeds swaying in the breezes.

Swamps: forested wetlands with bottomland hardwoods, shrub swamps, mangrove swamps.

All of these sequester carbon but in different ways and different rates of accumulation. According to the Irish Peatland Conservation Council bogs contain more carbon than the rainforests of the world. The deeper layers of peat accumulate layer after layer of carbon-based organics in an ever-growing deposit.[149] Most soils together with their biota accumulate carbon to a certain point then, reacting chemically with oxygen from the air, start to out-gas it after a certain point as CO_2 and methane, CH_4. But with peat bogs accumulation can go on and on with much of

[149] John Couwenberg, "Methane emission from peat soils (organic soils, histosols)," Greifswald University Wetlands International, Ede, the Netherlands. This paper on page 9 features a graph showing not only methane release (fluxes) to the atmosphere but methane sequestering (fluxes) to the soggy soil. The author notes, "Negative values denote net uptake from the atmosphere by the soil." He also says, "The actual amount of methane emitted to the atmosphere depends on the balance between methane production and consumption and the mode of methane transport," indicating the bog is taking methane out of the atmosphere in some cases – need more information! Important inquiry. http://www.imcg.net/media/download_gallery/climate/couwenberg_2009b.pdf

the carbon never released as CO_2 or CH_4, essentially indefinitely. The moss called sphagnum can grow on the dead material of its earlier generations, taking in nutrients from the air, dust and the few other plants and insects that live and die in the medium the moss creates powered by sunshine. Don't forget bird poop, which also brings in the fresh chemical magic and serious diversity of wide ranging seeds.

The notion then emerges: would there be here in these peat-producing wetlands the potential for the light but intelligent hand of society to leverage great areas of the Earth's surface into biological factories accumulating carbon and supporting biodiversity like Allan Savory's "holistic management" herding techniques for grasslands?

Ron Freethy in *How Birds Work – A Guide to Bird Biology* mentions, "Much of the vegetation of northern Britain consists of heather moorland which is not a natural situation, but artificially maintained in order to support a high population of red grouse"[150] for those loving hunting and eating grouse with the wine jelly he mentions. (Liking wine I wonder what that's like.) Could this be a very promising clue that much larger and better management techniques could be similarly created, such as small check dams to hold water at the surface over immense areas of peatlands, natural and artificial, preventing chemical decomposition of the organic matter that's accumulating? Carbon in this location can go on accumulating deeper and deeper, which is a version of the accumulation of carbon that produced our fossil fuels. In the peatlands literature you see plastic "piling" dams that fit together interlocking slabs to stop streams that drain water on slightly steep slopes and dams made of peat itself for very slight slopes. Some peatland areas are immense. The Western Siberian Swamp, a very flat veritable sponge, is almost as large in land area as all of Mexico. What could be their total area that could be impressed for service in carbon sequestration?

Add in the forests too, that deposit carbon that can build up from leaf, twig and rotting wood litter creating soil. Some forests contain most of their carbon in their living biomass, rainforests for example, because of constant dissolving and washing the chemical products of decomposition out of the soil by rain. But an enormous amount of carbon is stored there in trees. So on the surface of the Earth we have powerful potential for carbon uptake in a variety of mechanisms where, in some locations, carbon uptake could be cumulative, essentially forever.

What then about the oceans and the other large bodies of water and ice? The planet is about 71% covered in water. Can these waters or some large portions of them function like Allan Savory's degraded lands have for two or three decades under his management similar to the way ancient natural grasslands did for tens or hundreds of millions of years? That's a case of what Janine Benyus calls biomimicry, or might be more accurately called ecomicicry. That is, are there methods for encouraging whole natural ecosystems that safely take carbon out of the water or air

---

150 Ron Freethy, *How Birds Work – a Guide to Bird Biology*, Blandford Press, Poole, Dorset, England, 1982, p. 192.

in large quantity arriving at a high maximum sequestration or even a constant build up as in the case of peatlands? Are there biological processes in the oceans, shore areas and depths, that can remove CO2 and perhaps methane from the atmosphere and harmlessly store carbon in their depths like peat building its mass indefinitely?

Could human technology tweak such processes into massive service to the atmosphere and biosphere? Could we imagine partnering with nature, while learning how she does things, so that we could reverse the climate change we've unconsciously unleashed like a nuts Doberman pincher, but not bring back too quickly the ice ages we were scheduled to begin entering about now but rather let normal evolution take place in the immense swings of time but not catastrophically fast, adjusting our activities and total population and list of demands on nature to modest and much more natural change, educated by looking at these changes and, as said, partnering with, instead of forcing nature one way or another violently as we tend to do socially and economically in our wars?

Back to a more intermediate scale: there is a considerable literature on the damage caused to the ocean by the fact that it absorbs CO2. Research papers from the Monterey Bay Aquarium Research Institute say that, "In the long run 85% of all mankind's CO2 emissions will be absorbed by gas exchange across the air-sea interface."[151]

But CO2 absorption in the oceans mostly leads to acidification, which, along with general warming, is causing big problems for coral reefs and all the life they support. As the waters become more acidic, their acids attacks coral and other shell-forming life forms. The acidic waters damage other organisms at the base of the food chain, too, that leads right up to the largest fish and marine mammals plus land animals that eat seafood like us humans.

Meantime the sequestering efforts seem headed in the wrong direction. The May 14, 2012 New Yorker had a disappointingly loose and undisciplined article on the subject called "The Climate Fixers," by Michael Specter. Ideas that were floated there – literally in the following case – included littering the oceans with trillions of tiny dandruff-sized floating mirrors to reflect sunlight out into space cooling the ocean and ridding the planet of a little pesky planet warming sunshine. Another sunshine rejecting idea: spreading mirrors across millions of square miles of deserts in the same solar energy reducing strategy. According to another idea given serious ink, the world's largest fountain – forget Switzerland's 500 foot high extravaganza in Lake Geneva – would spray salt water from the ocean high into the atmosphere to increase Earth-cooling cloud cover while another fix would rocket up a stream of sulfates to create the sort of shading provided by massive volcanic eruptions (reducing the potential of solar energy technology). A last one, though the list goes on, would force ocean currents to push cold lower level water toward the surface, in

[151] Peter G. Brewer and Jim Barry, "The Emerging Science of a High CO2/Low pH Ocean," Project Overview, Monterey Bay Aquarium Research Institute, Moss Landing, California, 2012, http://www.mbari.org/default.htm

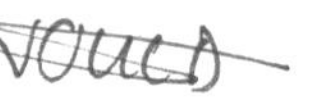

other words mixing the ocean to cool upper layers with water from the bottom and hence the atmosphere and land eventually (while, not mentioned, warming the depths slightly – enough to perhaps release methane from the cold mud on the bottom – methane being a more active climate "forcing" gas than CO2. Warming the methane clathrates which are frozen methane ready to sublimate into gas down there brings up some truly apocalyptic possibilities, but that's more detail on the subject than I will tackle here).

All of these "solutions" look incalculably demanding of materials for metals, chemicals, machines and energy to the point of causing likely larger problems in mounting the effort than solved with the effort. Some sound wildly silly, completely impossible with no back up detail and one wonders how they ever get attention, much less serious ink, at all. Plus it doesn't take exhaustive expertise and Jules Verne imagination to picture some stunningly disastrous unintended consequences. I can think of a few for each of the above proposals.

Still I couldn't help but think something people could do involving sophisticated technology would help. For example by building ecocities outfitted with all the technologies, some simple, some complex, that actually fit. Thereby we'd radically reduce energy demand – with the ecocity itself – while shifting to renewable energy systems appropriate to the basic structure of the best-built urban environment. Why aren't scientists talking about that? Such building would have some elements of a technological fix, and on a large scale – maybe there would be other such positive alternatives.

Then there's ecocity building itself – that is, literally the buildings. Getting back to wood, much emphasized earlier in these pages, much of the mass/material and most of the energy/fuel for building pre-coal and oil civilizations, the material some call fiber from the agriculture perspective, also called silviculture from the managed forestry perspective.

The interesting thing to note here is that wood that stays in the building and doesn't burn or rot away does not put its carbon back into the atmosphere. Wooden buildings are carbon sinks so long as they stand and continue serving. Architecture firm Waugh and Thistleton in London specialize in very heavy wooden buildings – think super plywood, plywood so thick it barely burns, the charred surface resisting the penetration of oxygen deeper into the wood. Andrew Waugh lives in one, a mixed-use seven story structure. Says Andrew whom I met sharing turns speaking at a Chicago conference, the solid sheet "cross-laminated" composite boards are typically six inches thick that serve as both floors and ceilings at the same time, and four to five inches think that serve as walls. No studs or joists, posts or beams needed. Paint or sheetrock finishes out the interior surface, a thin layer of insulation on the outside, a film of breathing but water impervious material over that and whatever siding desired outside that. Whitmore Road, the structure Andrew lives in, is mixed-use with two stories of offices including one double story photography studio and residences above. The firm has designed and built a nine-story apartment house called Murry Grove as well. Whitmore went up in five weeks with a crew of four skilled workers and a crane. The speed of erection and the longevity of the buildings are truly remarkable. And if we protected them well into the deep future, and if they began to replace energy and CO2 intensive concrete and steel we would have a very significant case of carbon sequestering in the wood itself and a contribution to planet cooling. Designing around bicycles as well as foot traffic this scale of vertical structure could produce some very dense and interesting ecocity small city designs indeed.

In my ruminating about ecocity designs I can imagine practically every possible spectacular and functional, culturally and ecologically healthy and pleasurable design in up to 20 maybe 25 stories, but it is hard to imagine why we would need to go much higher than that. Andrew says that's about max for wood of his type. The 50 to 150 story chamber of commerce advertising devices designed to be expensive lures for derivatives investment money in *our* best of all possible cities and designed for giant corporate or nationalist branding, the super talls that are going up all around the world in the early 21st century take so much in building material strength at the base it would seem a profligate luxury squandering precious resources wasting the time while neglecting working out the finer details and qualities of future cities.

Soleri called for lean and frugal, if very dense and complex, pointing out that that's the way living organisms are designed: for enormous efficiency. I'm sensitive to the frequent complaint from admirers of European old cities that anything over four stories is useless and inhuman, not to "human scale." But that seems to me to fail to get to the densities and flamboyant designs to, as they say, stir men's souls. Also European: cathedrals, castles, monuments, museums, skylines if not Manhattan, are often dramatic, beautiful and many times taller than four stories. Christopher Alexander also says in his book *A Pattern Language* that no buildings (but rare towers for special views *from* the towers, views called "prospect") should be over four stories. If your child is playing on the ground below your window you can't throw down a sandwich wrapped up for lunch without it exploding in the child's hand, a colorful expression of "human scale design." So height limits? It all depends on many things. One can build with terraces so that environments of smaller scale can step up four stories at a time for more variety in designs and taller total height, with some dramatic "cliffs" and towers in some places but stepped slopes in others, say again, four stories at a time. Bridges spanning between buildings from terraces and walkways on the terraces create more intimate spaces.

When it comes to higher density centers, my intuition is to taper off after about 20 stories. It's rather like setting speed limits. We need to work out what is just a little too slow (to function well) and a little too fast (to step over into the dangerous or absurd) and strike a balance. Probably that is more experience, art and common sense than science and strict measurement. In any case, Andrew Waugh says 20 to 25 stories passes muster with the engineers for his heavy plywood and thus for carbon sequestration we have the potential in the realm of normal everyday but dense living of adding something we build to planting forests and restoring grasslands, peatlands, marshes and healthy oceans.

So now, as there is the very recent idea of big massive wooden buildings to sequester carbon, so there is the ancient "black soil" or "tera preta" of some ancient South American indigenous peoples. In areas in and near much of the Amazon Basin the native peoples have, starting hundreds of years ago, been building carbon-holding soil by mixing in carbon charcoal from fires, along with broken pottery, and food waste like bones and fish scales producing a rich food-producing soil that in many areas is now up to around six feet deep. The solutions for carbon sequestration go on and on – and probably always have. We need to pull them all together, as we need cities that pull all the elements and features of ecocities together for a truly complete vision of a healthy future we can build.

Now all this above might seem like a serious diversion from the usual approach to discussing agriculture, and I guess it is. But says Allan Savory: "Agriculture is not crop production alone, as commonly believed. It is the production of food and fibre from all of the world's land surface and waters."[152]

It's us – all of us – in the most literal sense

Following this trail through a kind of expanded notion of agriculture I think might lead toward planetary balances, something was bothering me. We all know that in many places there has been a long history of rapid population expansion, so I looked up United Nations figures on population expansion all over the world and in Allan Savory's part of Africa, the southeastern part of Africa, in particular. Other than in just a few Moslem countries, we are seeing the fastest growth on the planet there. UN population researchers assembled a 100 year set of figures that looked at the last approximately 60 years and projected into the next 40 years, with the assumption based on trends, that population growth in Africa as well as most of the rest of the world would gradually slow.

Specifically these figures were looking at the period from 1950 to 2050. Zimbabwe would see a multiplication of population 8.1 times over, Sudan 8.3 times over, Rwanda 10.2, Ethiopia and Somalia 10.4, Kenya, 14.0 and Uganda 17.0. I said to Allan that it looked to me that these figures would absolutely overwhelm any kind of range management, what did he think? He wrote back:

> Population is of course serious and yes we very much bring it into our work - just do not talk about it because it aggravates the situation - something I learned long ago in Africa if a white talks about it then it turns racial tragically. This is dying out slowly. We point out that almost all the strife here is due to deteriorating land and rising population - the two collide with tragedy

[152] Alan Savory, from his talk entitled "The Future of Range Science to Meet Global Challenges" at the 47th Annual Congress of the Grasslands Society of Southern Africa, July 16, 2012 at Western Cape Province.

as we see repeatedly. To deal with it our mainstream NGO's have three kneejerk responses - put in boreholes and dams to provide water (and the situation gets worse), feed starving mothers and children and treat diseases (and family size gets bigger and problem gets worse) and the third thing is to improve the economy with micro-banking, access roads to markets, etc. (and family size gets bigger and problem worse).

> I gave a talk on these lines in Northern Kenya not long ago and a woman from USAID came up to me after and said, Oh how right you are. We have done all that for forty years here and now there are five times as many people killing each other.
> So to deal with this we stress - put in your projects but make sure that some money is always going to two things - teaching people to reverse the land degradation (as we demonstrate here [at his ranch in Zimbabwe]) and educating and empowering women. Only the latter seems to lead to family size balancing with resources.

How in fact can we realistically approach the problem of overpopulation? Step number one is acknowledging there's a problem at all. Famously we find people promoting large families in certain circles among Catholics, Muslims, Mormons, ultraconservative Jews, rural tribal ancestry traditionalists in many parts of the world with high infant and childhood mortality rates and in families with strong family-first traditions of celebrating in-close accumulated power under a patriarch. Reality has a way of slapping people in the face, as Rwanda's grizzly holocaust precipitated largely by overpopulation, land scarcity and hunger demonstrated. In such places instead of a slowdown of fertility, increased mortality through violence reduces population in terrible waves oscillating over the decades.

On average, the good news is that by 2009 the UN Millennium Development Goals established in 2000 of halving the poverty rate, a measure of average percentages, by 2015 are better than on track. Moreover, after citing South Korea, Taiwan, China, Thailand and Viet Nam as countries that thrived economically after very significant slowing of their birth rates, says Lester Brown in his book *Plan B 4.0*, "except for a few oil-rich countries, no developing country has successfully modernized without slowing population growth"[153]

The further bad news is that this growing prosperity has come at the cost of many growing environmental and resources problems. The solution is largely people simply looking those facts in the eye and trying to inform themselves about the facts of the situation. Maybe most helpful would be making the information into the kind of digestible package that if some interest were cultivated, in-depth further exploration of solutions would follow, the objective of the short outline provided by the Six

[153] Op cit., p. 185

Big Ones: to provide an accurate but brief outline around which to structure a comprehensible set of solutions that can be grasped. The overall pattern is helpful.

Two things about the population issue: the impediment is usually religious or simply not taking population as a serious factor. I've already tried to make it clear that there are limits of support for large populations in terms of something as basic as acreage for food and that such demand for land to feed us has already almost eliminated (proportionally speaking) wildlife on the planet, a significant and I should think existentially very meaningful point to make about what it means to be alive on this planet. To put that in religious perspective – isn't life on the planet the work of the Creator? The non-religious might call it "just" the wonder of the way things work here on the Third Planet from the sun, but the religious should have at least some pangs of conscience realizing that their insistence on large families doesn't extrapolate to a healthy future for God's creation, doesn't adore it, doesn't celebrate it, doesn't even respect it. Albert Schweitzer's "reverence for life" is the exact opposite to "blind eye to overpopulation." Evidence is conclusive that such – aggregate population demand, along with destructive built infrastructure, damaging agricultural practices and rising average consumption rates – is destroying said creation, and if you comprehend that, you should be doing something about it. As Alan says, education of women is a very good start.

Italy and Iran provide interesting stories relating to the issue of religion and population. In Italy, where the Pope lives, the population is very slowly declining, people happily continuing with the famously romantic and passionate Latin ways of living and loving. What's happening? An Italian man who I found myself in this conversation with said, "Oh we're good Catholics and the Pope has a lot of good things to say. But what does he know about birth control? He's celibate."

In Iran between 1980 and 1988 Ayatollah Khomeini "wanted large families to increase the ranks of soldiers for Islam. His goal was an Iranian army of 20 million," as Lester Brown reports in *Plan B 4.0.* "In response to his pleas, fertility levels climbed, pushing Iran's annual population growth to a peak of 4.2 percent per year in the early 1980s, a level approaching the biological maximum. As this enormous growth began to burden the economy and the environment, the country's leaders realized that overcrowding, environmental degradation, and unemployment were undermining Iran's future."[154] He adds that the religious leaders approved of the resulting changed policy to reduce population growth, which means that eventually the limits have to be faced no matter how ardent your belief system. The physical is basic. Once on board, the national leaders pulled out all the stops setting up 15,000 "health houses" to give family planning services to the rural population, supporting the new small family policy on television and even becoming the only country in the world requiring couples to take classes in contraception before being issued marriage licenses. By 1994 Iran cut its population growth rate more than in half, bringing the new families' average size from seven children to three.

[154] Op cit., p.182

A last note on population in addition to just say we need to pay attention and shrink in that particular for prosperity too, and that is that the spread of ideas is very helpful in repairing the world. Paul Ehrlich and Anne Ehrlich predicted famine in the 1980s or 1990s given the trends when they wrote *The Population Bomb*, which was in 1968[155] Population growth slowed somewhat after that time and the "Green Revolution" in agriculture pumped up production such that those two factors didn't just add to one another but multiplied and thus staved off the predicted catastrophe indefinitely, only smaller numbers of people starving to death and vast new areas of land "falling under the plow" (to the deficit of natural species in many millions of acres). The Ehrlichs ended up admitting their dates were off and certainly we have not seen the disasters they predicted. But they cheat themselves of the very mixed success that they helped bring about. That is they did in fact help wake the world up, stimulating more interest in "population control" as it was forthrightly called in the 1960s, precursor to the rather more benign sounding "family planning" of today. Whether in the long run a success, given the massiveness of the agricultural enterprise that has resulted with its many detriments, is or is not really certain, and whether their prediction was just 50 or 60 years too early for an even larger scale famine should we have a general collapse, is hard to say at the present time. But it is worth considering that the concern they raised was taken seriously enough by enough people and ones in influential positions that a real catastrophe was at least postponed. Good ideas can spread, even if in an environment so complex that even those at the source of those ideas can't see the connections and give even themselves the credit they deserve. But in any case, the principle is encouraging: sometime facing the difficult truth communicates and actions with healthy results can follow. I'm hoping that applies to this book too.

But, as a last comment/addendum a question: after the destabilization of the Middle East and western Islam in general by the Bush-Cheney invasion of Iraq, plus the pressures of let's face it overpopulation (and exploitation of Africa), is the terrible flood of desperate immigrants trying to get into Europe as I write the beginning of the period the Ehrlichs predicted two to three decades too early?

[155] Paul and Anne Ehrlich, *The Population Bomb*, Buccaneer Books, Catchogue, New York, 1968

41. Shade cloth cooling a street market in Istanbul, Turkey

In the pedestrian city it is a very simple thing to replace mechanical/electrical cooling with simple shade.

CHAPTER 14

Generosity and Education

Putting it all together

We've now concluded four of the six "Big Ones," issues we can't afford to postpone at this point in history, *not* the low hanging fruit for the children. Now, of the two Big Ones I think of as the mental, psychological and spiritual Big Ones, we will next touch on generosity, then education. Generosity is very big, very important. We will need lots of it. And we will need that master virtue, courage, to follow wherever generosity leads and to master whatever it means. I'll be writing about the generosity of investing in the long-term future, something of an economics theme. But it begins much deeper than that.

Some say if we want to help, it's love we need and we, in some ultimate state of being, to love our enemies as well as we love our selves, our friends and family. I tend to think we have to be honest and admit we don't, can't and likely shouldn't pretend we love a real enemy, but acknowledge that for everyone's benefit we should try to understand others' perspectives including and maybe especially our enemies'. Maybe Gandhi and Jesus really did love their enemies, but that's like an advanced post-doc degree in existential self-design: not many of us can concentrate on that career track and get there while doing other things in our lives like dentistry, plumbing, selling shoes and counseling high school drop outs, staying reasonably informed and raising the next generation all at the same time. Religious dogmaticians who cast the extreme idea that we need to actually and genuinely love our enemies, not just metaphorically speaking, as a first step to peace, reconciliation and cooperation, present an almost inhuman mystic goal that makes them look as wise as to be beyond questioning, requiring we take their word on faith, not moving according to our own experience. They cast an aura of cosmic paradox around an inflated version of a basically very good and much more practical idea which is that the vast majority of us, almost all of us can, in reasonable frame of mind, consider other people's perspectives and make serious progress toward better mutual understanding.

We need most basically to be generous in providing opportunities to consider one another's reasons, different habits of being and historic backgrounds so that we can coexist successfully and thrive as best possible. Probably most important in this is presenting such generosity to the "enemy" as a mutual option important for him or her to take seriously too, the option of taking generosity seriously. He or she doesn't have to acknowledge loving you any more than vice versa (guaranteed to be phony at the beginning) to recognize the utility in mutual generosity that can greatly benefit the children of both and begin some sort of conversation. Giving someone the benefit of the doubt is providing a conceptual framework for understanding, and it is a form of giving, of being generous. It's like giving anger a count to ten to cool off some and time to summons more reasonable thoughts and emotions. That too is a "giving," a generous act.

Is giving in this regard, in communications about things of consequence, kindred to the origins of economic exchanges too, as in the gifting economics of early complexifying cultures? Is it accompanied by expectations of some return at a vague later date determined in timing and content of the gift by the other side? Yes, and that's good the gift is not seen as a one way act that stops with the receiving of the gift because the expectation of cycles within an expanded community continues the relationship in a mutually beneficial, friendly cultural pattern. One gift is a challenge to the other to also be generous and thus multiply generosity, take the expanded society into a virtuous cycle of getting to know the players more distant as well as in the circle of friends and family. Ultimately such generosity is indispensible to make real the old notion of "the brotherhood of Man" and probably especially in communications the purpose of which is to solve conflicts non-violently.

"A long time ago in a galaxy far, far away..."

Entering this subject is something like leaping onto one of the rockets illustrated by Chestley Bonstell back in the 1950s[156] to explore deep into space, but down on Earth, inner mind space rather than outer physical space. The two converge in what I call the Star Wars Myth. You might also call it the Star Wars Problem. It all starts (or finishes, or ever continues?) with a line in the opening "crawl" (written words that move across the screen) for the movie expressed in this way: "A long time ago in a galaxy far, far away..." The scene is, right at the beginning, a battle chase with one space ship filled with bad guy aliens chasing and shooting at another space ship filled with good guys.

Its message: war exists at the heart of consciousness and pervades the universe in both time and space. "A long time ago" means forever, it has always been thus, and "galaxy far, far away..." means everywhere in the whole firmament. Find conscious life anywhere and it's battling its inner and outer demons by way of outward violence rather than understanding and resolving conflicts for inner peace and for mutual benefit, or most basically in very active creativity that is also compassionate. When "this town isn't big enough for the two of us" and one or the other western movie gunslingers has to be killed and eliminated from competition forever, have we seen a collapse of both compassion and reason? Is one person 100% evil and the other 100% good? Is 51% good vs. 51% evil justification for the killing the 51% evil guy? Is this heart of war the permanent state of affairs for creatures with brains and complex cultures as well as highly evolved complex bodies? Is this really the case? And if it happens to be, would it even matter if we took responsibility for designing a future with compassion and creativity despite the tendency to dehumanization and destructivity somewhere deep inside us, the reflex to preemptive strike due to never having 100% assurance that we aren't perpetually synched in by the Hobbesiasn trap, the advantage in striking first?

There's the special case, all too often coming about in history, when a Hitler arises and takes a vast number of people with him over the line into 90%+ bad guy world, into an situation irreversible with any reasonable approach and that we have to judge as requiring legitimate defensive violence. What the situation indicates more than anything else is the failure of understanding far short of the point of irreversibility, ultimately, the failure to call a halt to the Star Wars Myth before it goes too far and becomes a real disease of the species.

Cultural mythologies are powerful stuff. Positive myth might even be able to overpower the Hobbesian trap and bring out our creative, compassionate inner self, making our violent, destructive inner self look a little ridiculous. Like the stiff old gentlemen pacing off for a duel soon to be forgotten as the younger generation just

[156] Odd, interesting note – he, Bonstell, was an architectural designer and painted renderings of buildings for architectural firms. He and a colleague designed the look and surface treatment of the Chrysler Building in New York City, which looks very much like his rocket ship designs.

laughs at them for the antiquated problems their egos refuse to solve, perhaps our inner selves can wake up to more highly evolved real solutions with the help of updated myths of the helpful kind.

Myth has the power of story – we can see ourselves and our friends as the main characters, or failing that, in the supporting (or opposing) roles as a narrative unwinds. There is always a place for us in the drama. It feels democratic even when it's manipulative from above because we can participate and change things. Think patriarchs come-priesthood elites, come-kings, their bards, their priests and cultural DNA. Think early Christians saying, "OK, you get what Ceasar gets, but we get God's Total Creation and are just as good as you:" democracy! Creation myths are the most powerful of all myths, explaining where we came from, what we should be doing, where we are now and where we are headed if we do this or that.

"Shoulds" are important in creation myths, New Age liberalism that says, "You should never say 'should'" not withstanding. And as you notice, that sentence uses a nicely contradictory "should" in its own wording. To cap it all off, there is guidance for proper direction, moral duties hinted at if not made explicitly into threats of death and permanent suffering the fires of Hell: perpetual destruction should you not heed "shoulds." Creation myths express basic values backed by force and violence just like laws (enforcement), the object of which is to help the culture maintain continuity into the future. Such myths deal with the very real struggle for life and means to resolve disagreement and conflict in the culture in which they were written. Creation myths often take no particular position relative to nature, taking it as a given at the Beginning or in the creation process, always there and dependable. Usually as in the Christian religion there are directives for the relationship between culture and nature but all too often seeing everything in the universe as made just for people, if to be used with some care since after all it is God's Creation. It takes a long time to develop consensus as powerful and all-pervading as a good creation myth, so most that we relate to at this point in history came from a time well before science cast some interesting new light on the fact that nature isn't so steady a given but changes very substantially over time. That's called evolution; for any newer creation myths, basic assumptions on which the myths might be built need to be revised. Also it turns out nature is not in steady state because one of the species on the planet is doing massive damage to it at the moment, that is, nature turns out to be vulnerable and not always powerful, serene and dependable after all.

As said, in these myths violence is always in the background, survival the objective, thriving in the lessons of the myth the eventual goal. The mysteries of birth and renewal are there too, including, in many creation myths, the birth of all and everything. And throughout there are contradictions as well as explicit lessons, serious inconsistencies presented as mysterious and wise cosmic paradoxes. There are also vague innuendos to provide the believers in the myth opportunity for personal interpretation, thus leaving room for people from all habits and educated persuasions to be part of the community, the drama.

The Star Wars myth isn't a creation myth. It is more of a steady state of the universe myth obsessed with destroying things. But still it expresses some very basic values and attitudes of the culture it comes from. It doesn't deal with The Creation or origin of things nor does it deal with the creation of the things represented by the sets, the props, the robots, aliens, actors and the planets, artificial and otherwise, in the story. Nobody actually makes anything in these movies. But boy does a lot get hurtled about, evaded, chased and destroyed. One might note it hasn't the slightest interest in creativity other than the cleverness in out smarting, out flanking and out gunning the enemy. Who makes the Starship Enterprise and all that other stuff anyway, or cares? Its endless battles are programmed to be fun as surely as Pavlov's dog was keyed to salivate at the sound of the bell. No wasted footage at the Intergalactic VA Hospital where the grievously wounded waste away the last of their lives for decades in ghastly condition with wounds that took a split second to deliver; that would tend to dampen audience identity pleasures and box office returns. Denial of the honest results of violence skips that part that lasts so long and sucks up so much of national budgets while nobody is supposed to notice.

What American presidents learned about waging real wars, as compared with Star Wars, from the Vietnam disaster on into the future was to never, ever again show the gory truth on television or in newspapers and magazines. Since Ronald Reagan's invasion of Granada in 1983, which banned reporters, there has been a policy to keep the graphic, bloody truth from the people. The media has complied like a chastised puppy dog curling up at the foot of the bed, bedding down with the military, "embedded" in their terminology. Citizens, for their part in the consensus tactic of avoiding guilt and hard work, make little protest. All that to say the fun at the core of the Star Wars turns the myth to a lie.

It's a lie we'd prefer not to confront. While writing this part of this chapter, a "madman" calling himself the Joker after one of the characters in the Batman movies murdered 12 people and wounded 58 in a Colorado movie theater premiere of a new Batman movie, ripping them to pieces with several guns. The moviegoers were enjoying simulated killing of people for entertainment on the screen when the attack occurred. I'll be writing more about No War Toys later, my idea of what an obscure youth like me at the time could do about the American War on Vietnam. At that time, probably in 1966, I ran across an idea in the current psychology literature called the "culture pattern model;" certain psychologists were so confident that it represented "the way things really are" they abbreviated it to CPM, as if it was self-evident or so generally accepted as to become a culture model in itself.

The idea was that the basic meaning and values associated with a particular pattern finds expression in many forms in any particular culture. The suggestion was that entertainment means more than "getting out your aggressions" vicariously and in theory mellowing out in the cathartic aftermath. Instead, CPM suggests, pretend, copy-cat or symbolic violence actually tends to connect with real violence and real violence tends to infect fiction as not completely fictitious after all.

My own experience as an artist has always been that the whole point of the most important fictions in my own brain was that they could be translated into physical realities: the artworks I produced on a normal, daily basis, drawings, paintings and sculptures. For me and the other artists I knew, fiction translated into realities and more generally speaking, things in the imagination and realities were for us closely related. Similarly I was struck in my first visit to Brazil in 1992 that the generic term for any violent movie at the time was "American movie," no matter what country it came from so consistently were American movies more violent than the run of the mill non-American ones. Here in America they aren't really violent. They're "action movies" of course. But such movies, said the CPM psychologists in the 1960s – and I tended to agree with them – actually did have a mutually reinforcing relationship with actual violence. That most likely remains the case today as the culture pattern model that has seen over 334,168 Americans killed by guns by fellow Americans since the 9/11 catastrophe at the World Trade Center in New York up to this time in writing this book.[157] The culture pattern model suggests large patterns of consistency exist in cultures that find expression in multiple ways, thus violent entertainment is consistent with actual violence. The culture pattern model suggests that imbibing lots of entertaining violence acts as informal training for actual violence in a culture, the general gestalt of the activity settling into other forms of expression. The psychological counter theory is that the fiction violence – "get your aggressions out" – is cathartic and actually makes the society more peaceful. You can guess I think that is nonsense. The culture pattern model suggests a more peaceful society would have less violent entertainment, and such entertainment would tend to more peaceful addressing of frustrations and conflict. CPM awareness in society might even encourage creativity instead of destruction. Maybe pretend = pre-tend. It is interesting to note the word "pretend" suggests tending to do something in advance (pre) of actually doing it.

The good news relative to this bad is that nonetheless and in an even larger pattern over the centuries, somehow, and in some ways even in America, the general "civilizing process" noted by Norbert Elias has been toward less violence.

But for our consideration here, a little discipline and awareness of truthful meanings that isn't turned off by endless gun battle chase scenes with 182 explosions and 1,500 bullets per hour on the screen, so popular these days, would suggest we might better be doing something else more productive instead. My "designing ourselves" theme then suggests just that: don't waste your time with the pre-tend violence. The whole world is soaking itself in such imagery and hoping for positive change. Simply put: that's contradictory.

Relative to thoughts on economics and ecology it is also interesting to note the larger patterns that become themes in the complex biological environments and economic environments. They turn up as powerful patterns of consistency discoverable from the swarm of details, all of which require considerable knowledge of the

[157] Andrew Cohen, "Under a Blood Red Sky," The Atlantic, July 21, 2012

various "environments" – social, ecological and economic – and the basic principles within those environments. Then apply a little reasoning and some intuition and the results have a chance at wisdom and some guidance for a better future.

So if I'm saying screw Star Wars, what would be a myth for our times, seeing that our times will determine evolutionary times here on this planet? Thomas Berry, Catholic priest and theologian, who somehow got away without being defrocked while at the same time being an influential bard for evolution advocated for *The Universe Story* (which is one and the same thing as the evolution story). He proposed that science has given us a tale that is gloriously beautiful and substantially accurate if we are serious about gaining true knowledge about our world from experience, evidence and experiment. But he told his friend Brian Swimme and coauthor of their several books together, "You scientists have this stupendous story of the universe. It breaks outside all previous cosmologies. But so long as you persist in understanding it solely from the quantitative mode you fail to appreciate its significance. You fail to hear its music. That's what the spiritual traditions can provide."[158] Seeing that swath of cosmic time and our universe changing can be and should be the basis for a new vision for humanity from now on, Berry believed, one infused with the reverence and awe appropriate to its infinite to infinitesimal presence we humans share somewhere between the nothingness of the small and the everythingness of the large and the change that goes on eternally, eternity being maybe the only thing that never changes.[159]

Another myth for our times seems to distill from the many American Indian myths reported in a book by Eskimo Willy Willoya and author and publisher on many American Indian themes, Vinson Brown: *Warriors of the Rainbow*.[160] In simple outline, people of all colors and belief systems come together from around the world, put their conflicts to one side and unite to defend the Earth from destruction. A new era then leads to peace and understanding. Greenpeace, in its early days, already peopled by activists from around the world of several nationalities and races, thought this described them well and named three of their ships over subsequent years the Rainbow Warrior. The first was sunk by French government terrorists for trying to stop the country's nuclear tests in the Pacific Ocean, killing a New Zealand photographer. Rainbow Warriors II and III were later launched by Greenpeace.

I tend to think of this book World Rescue as a myth builder of a practical sort, not attempting to create characters we can identify with – I'm not a fiction

---

[158] Brian Swimme, *The Universe is a Green Dragon – a cosmic creation story*, Bear and Company, Santa Fe, New Mexico, 1985, p. 19

[159] Thomas Berry develops his ideas in several books co-authored with Brian Swimme, notably *The Universe Story – from the primordial flaring forth to the ecozoic era – a celebration of the unfolding of the cosmos*, HarperCollins Publishers, San Francisco, 1992

[160] Willy Willoya and Vinson Brown, *Warriors of the Rainbow – Strange and Prophetic Dreams of the Indian Peoples*, Naturegraphic Publisher, Indian Camp, California, 1962

writer – but to at least provide some specific ideas of what could be a healthier future than what we are seeing developing now, lending some particulars to what us "rainbow warriors" might actually do to build our new world: rainbow builders? This book, then, is something like an "applied Universe Story" hinting where we might go if we sought to harmonize our trajectory, each of us and all of us collectively – averaging out (aggregating) anyway – within nature's trajectory.

42. Space age comes to home to Earth in a city

Fanciful of course but we actually do need an Earth-based, back to the earth vision of the future for a creative and compassionate species. Bring back the space age recognizing we are already sailing through the great cosmos. Then cultivate the cosmos within to explore humanity's full long-term potential to make peace on Earth, peace WITH Earth. Ecocities: generous city, city of the future…

To love – or just respect, converse with and understand?

Regarding cultural myths, emphasis becomes important. That emphasis might lie in basic principles or it might be expressed as the larger more important flows of ideas and activities in a culture. Life's dimensional pairs include love and hate, good and evil, compassion and indifference but we can choose emphasis to shape what comes next. What to say about the emphasis on violence in the myth of forever-and-everywhere-war-is-inevitable? Is it in our genes? Is this self-image for consciousness in the universe overdone, not just in Star Wars and the like but in everyday nationalism, and destined to make us more destructive?

Mohandas K. Gandhi, the *Mahatma* or Great Soul in the eyes of those who loved him, believed in disciplined non-violence and together – Gandhi and his philosophy – led India to independence from England. His grandson Arun Gandhi wrote an insightful book not on Gandhi directly but mainly about Kastruba, Gandhi's wife, Arun's grandmother. It was called *The Forgotten Woman – The Untold Story of Kastur, the Wife of Mahatma Gandhi.* To give you an idea of the power of small things, though, I'll state a few words about our great soul when he was a young student in India trying to get a scholarship to go to England to study law. At that time the British would allow local princes to run things so long as they agreed with overall British objective to profit greatly on their relationship with India. One Mr. Frederic Lely was the British administrator of Porbandar, the princedom in which Gandhi lived. Said Arun, "with high hopes, Mohan [Gandhi's first name abbreviated] went by appointment to Mr. Lely's residence to present his case. Upon approaching Mr. Lely, he bowed politely as Indians would to an elder, palms together. But even before he could explain the reason for his visit he was curtly interrupted, 'No help can be given to you now.'" Said Arun Gandhi's account, "With that Mr. Lely turned his attention to weightier matters unaware, as the British historian Geoffrey Ashe put it, 'that he had just stood face to face with the ruin of the British Empire.'"[161] I love that story.

Arun was interviewed by Amy Goodman on the radio and television show Democracy Now on the 100th anniversary of Grandfather Gandhi's gathering together of 3,000 Indian nationals in Johannesburg, South Africa to announce his philosophy of non-violence and to ask for support in fighting the racist laws of that country. That was, by coincidence, another 9/11, September 11, 1906. Gandhi called his idea and his method of dealing with injustice and issues of violence "Satyagraha" meaning roughly "truth force." Asked the definition of Satyagraha, Arun Gandhi had the following to say.

---

[161] Arun Gandhi, *The Forgotten Woman – The Untold Story of Kastur, the Wife of Mahatma Gandhi*, Ozark Mountain Publishers, Huntsville, Alabama, 1998, p. 36, 37

> ...Satyagraha is the pursuit of truth. Truth should be the cornerstone of everybody's life and we must dedicate our lives to pursuing truth, to finding out the truth in our lives. And so this entire philosophy was a philosophy for life. It was not just a philosophy for conflict resolution but something we had to imbibe in our life and live it all the time, so we can improve and become better human beings. ...
>
> I believe non-violence is our nature. Violence is not really our nature. If violence was really our nature we wouldn't need military academies and marshal arts institutes to teach us how to kill and destroy people. ...the fact that we have to learn the art of killing means that it's a learned skill and we can always unlearn.
>
> My grandfather said violence will prevail over violence only when you prove to me that darkness can prevail over darkness. We can never overcome violence with more violence. We can only overcome violence with respect and understanding and our love for one another. [162]

Herman Goering, Hitler's Deputy Fuhrer, during the Nuremburg War Crimes Trials, probably as exactly opposite to Gandhi as is imaginable, a genuine believer in and practitioner of war, more than ironically agreed with Arun Gandhi about the resistance to war in the normal human's character:

> Why of course people don't want war. Why should some poor slob on a farm want to risk his life in a war when the best that he can get out of it is to come back to his farm in one piece? Naturally the common people don't want war: neither in Russia, nor in England, nor for that matter in Germany. That is understood. But after all, it is the leaders of the country who determine the policy, and it is always a simple matter to drag the people along, whether it is a democracy or a fascist dictatorship, or a parliament, or a communist dictatorship. Voice or no voice, the people can always be brought to the bidding of the leaders. That is easy. All you have to do is tell them they are being attacked, and denounce the pacifists for lack of patriotism and exposing the country to danger. It works the same in every country.[163]

For those in countries with the draft who don't believe in the war, they join and fight nonetheless, or end up in jail, or get ostracized, or become the victim of

---

[162] Arun Gandhi, Amy Goodman and Juan Gonzalez, Democracy Now, September 11, 2006, http://ia600302.us.archive.org/26/items/dn2006-0908_vid/dn2006-0908_512kb.mp4

[163] Gustave Gilbbert, Nuremberg Diary, Farrar, Straus, New York, 1947. This Herman Goering quote is as recorded in a cell during the Nuremburg War Crimes Trials after the World War II German defeat. Recorded by Gustave Gilbert, April 18, 1946.

other forms of social violence, or escape to another country, or… summons the courage to resist and take risks, hopefully in intelligent ways. For the middle class when war is remote but nonetheless happening "in our name" or when the draft does not exist, it takes some courage too, though of a lower order, the courage to face social pressure, incur the wrath of "patriotic" family members', maybe lose a job – many possibilities – but still to oppose requires courage. In many cases there may be a real problem in not knowing what is going on, either because we don't want to know – maintain lack of courage and an excuse for inaction – or just can't find out. There may be a problem also with our own self-discipline that allows us to be manipulated for the manipulators' purposes: advertisers selling us something, movie makers seeking fame and money preying on our weaknesses, politicians seeking power over people – a real opportunity for exploitation and greed, even war.

The rationales soak deep into our cultural being and blind us to something as basic as learning what to build for a decent life on this planet, even what to build as *ourselves*. A brief story is told in the book about Frank Oppenheimer, brother of J. Robert Oppenheimer, head of the project that built the atomic bomb, which illustrates this bridge between thinking and the reality of conflict and violence. (Frank was also the founder of San Francisco's science museum called the Exploratorium that featured my tactile sculptures built in 1974 long before the museum moved to a new location in 2012.) The first explosion of an atomic bomb had just taken place in the desert of New Mexico and people were awestruck, aghast, humbled, profoundly worried – had a lot of various comments. "In some ways the most touching remark – perhaps because it was so understated and also so ultimately true – was made by one of the guards: 'The long hairs have let it get away from them.'" [164] (Perhaps that term isn't used so much any more: long hairs here means scientists and compares with military crew cuts.)

So a nasty racist or jingoistic remark here, a war toy as a gift to have "fun" there, a little fear of foreigners cultivated, a promise from a politician to protect you from danger when a little understanding or diplomacy would go a long way, a seemingly abstract vote for someone who says extreme things "but he wouldn't really do it"… who knows how all this adds up and when to step in and stop it? It may be hard to know where the ideas connect with real events in ways that turn out a little out of control and tragic. But step in we must, which is the code of the non-violent and I should think a beacon for non-violent economics.

At issue here is whether our mind sets can accommodate cooperation and compassion over competition, anger and the adrenalin rush of violent action and instead set up peaceful, if very active and creative patterns in mind, then reality.

Lynn Margulis with her endosymbiosis shows that in the wisdom of evolutionary time the two antagonists, sharing complementary traits, host cells and invading cells, realized mutual benefit so intimate that their combined life efforts were

[164] K. C. Cole, *Something Incredibly Wonderful Happens – Frank Oppenheimer and the World He Made Up*, Houghton Mifflin Harcourt, Boston, 2009, p. 61

fused in one new whole reality, the eukaryotic cells of complex life forms, both plant and animal, all over Earth today. True, the principle of survival of the fittest meant some killed to eat and survive, but survival of the fittest was also smart enough to cooperate and take things to the next higher level of well-integrated complexity, which led, among other things, to consciousness in us humans. But will our consciousness recognize this gift of most basic cooperation, quite irritating no doubt in the first cells becoming eukaryotic, in the normal advance of evolution, as at the opposite pole to the Star Wars Myth?

If love for the enemy seems a little mystic, paradoxical and even occult, generosity to provide room for understanding might be closer to common sense and the sort of compromise for progress by which nature seems to genuinely attain Progress. My point is that both competition unto death and cooperation unto higher life do pervade the universe but not mainly in terms of good and evil to support "our side" and destroy the other, but in terms of whatever it takes to keep evolving in a healthy manner. Remember, it's not survival of the most powerful and violent but of the creature that best fits its total environment.

What it seems to have to do with generosity is this: generosity is giving to life as much or a little more than life has to give each of us, leaving, to say it again, Rome more beautiful than I found it. But it doesn't depend upon magnanimity in the material world. One does not have to be rich to give. The poor can uplift with a smile, giving perhaps more of what smiles can give than a very rich person can give in philanthropy.

Stealing is the opposite of generosity and stealing the life of another – killing – the ultimate endpoint on the sliding scale polarity from generosity to highest greed. When I was trying to proportionalize and prioritize, before I even thought of the process in such terms, I was wondering how to talk about greed in the economy, leading to injustices and even war. Just calling the egregiously greedy "greedy" and citing that the 1% has 30% of the wealth in the US (necessarily in a somewhat angry voice) would just lose me the more conscientiously fairly wealthy who invest in good things and give some back because they actually do care about society and planet. Many of the very wealthy do have children they love and do want to leave them a better future in terms beyond just private property. So I don't want to accuse, insult or embarrass those I hope to communicate with and hopefully work with to make the world a better place. In some important ways we are all very similar.

Taking the inverse approach, the positive side of the coin, seemed a lot better than harping on greed, real though it is in many people. Harp on generosity instead. It's more constructive, more conducive to actually buildings a better economics, infrastructure and reality going into the future. The expression of the problem has come down to us as a moral issue. Said Jesus, "It is easier for a camel to pass through the eye of a needle than for a rich man to enter into the kingdom of heaven." That was recorded in various similar wordings in the different translations of the Christian Holy Bible (Matthew 19/23-26). The quote expresses the superiority of the spiritual over the physical while giving us a prescription for actions that might qualify one worthy of ultimate honor and happiest experience, which I take to be the essence of heaven. In any case it implies that hoarding is at minimum a minor sin, maybe major, a real personal and social problem.

Manfred Max-Neef, Chilean economist, has worked with the poor all over South America. Among his stories is the following, bringing us into the discussion of greed and generosity and the notion of "enough," of balance and limits.[165] Max-Neef worked training Peace Corps volunteers in the US and sent them off to Peru where he often worked. To help the poor people in the typical way of small capitalist loans and start up gifts the "lovely young people" of the Peace Corps, in Max-Neef's words, who were "well-intentioned," acquired a weaving machine for helping a women make ponchos. Hand weaving produced two ponchos a week. With a machine a woman could produce 20. The volunteers come back a few months later to see how production was going. Said one of the your Peace Corps members according to Max-Neef:

"Oh, how do you like the machine?"

"Oh, very nice."

"And how many ponchos are you making?"

"Well, two ponchos a week."

"What do you mean? You could make much more."

"Well, but I don't need to make more."

"But why do you make just two. Well, what is the machine then for?

"Well, I make two, but now I have much more time to be with my friends and with my kids."

Manfred Max-Neef continues: "In our environment, you know, you have to do more and more and more and more. No! There, instead of making more, they have more time to enjoy themselves, to have a nice relationship with friends, with family, etc. You see? Lovely value which we have lost."

Max-Neef goes on to say there is no greed among the really poor. You might think from the point of view of living in a capitalist country poor people would be greedy because they must be focused on acquisition for sheer survival then want much more to feel secure. But a strange thing happened on the way to greed: in poverty enough is pretty good, and getting to "enough" is helped largely if a social enterprise rather than a loner's. The real objective is the "enough" that lets you go directly to feeding your family and enjoying your friends. Greed is a condition of those who have much more than enough says Max-Neef.

But interesting and confusing things happen that need sorting out with those new things in evolution such as human imagination and creativity, desire for power and mastery, maybe over one's skills, maybe over other people. Humans can produce surplus which they can turn to all sorts of uses some real treasures for the collective culture, some strictly personal, some megalomaniacal, some to blow life right

---

[165] Manfred Max-Neef, interviewed by Amy Goodman on Democracy Now, November 26, 2010, http://www.democracynow.org/2010/11/26/chilean_economist_manfred_max_neef_on

off the face of the Earth and through good fortune and maybe nothing else, said Robert McNamara who was in the decision room at the time, we just missed Armageddon by a hair's breath once during the Cuban Missile Crisis in October of 1962. The documentary film by Errol Morris, The Fog of War, includes the chilling experience of being there as we barely slipped through the crack of annihilation into continuation of the living, as John Kennedy, Nikita Khrushchev and their political and military strategists frantically worked against the clock to diffuse the end of civilization possibly even life on Earth as we had come to know it. [166] How to save face, rethink pride and its relationship to force, back off like the honorable gentlemen from dueling in the 1800s, the art of the reasonable compromise. When will we apply it in conflict one down from war? Up from dueling, down from total war – where in both places we learned our lesson, now we just need to clear out the small and middle sized wars too with some of the same restraint and disciplined non-violence.

Disciplined non-violence, empathy and altruism

All that takes incredible discipline and the intelligence to know the cultural context very well. It will take even more of the same if we hope to "rescue the world." Exactly the point and exactly what Gandhi required of his Satyagraha (truth force) shock troops: disciplined non-violence. Martin Luther King, Jr. saw the wisdom in the approach and realized it was all about not only rights delivered in the theory of law but responsibilities delivered by our very existential condition of being, reproducing and carrying on the ever-evolving species. (I added that last part.) We are here, therefore we must. Must what? Take up responsibility as a member of the community of life to defend life. Each individual's, as each animal's responsibility, is first to itself, and next and absolutely rigidly to the other – "...when the oxygen mask falls from the overhead, place the mask over your own mouth before helping others. The oxygen will start flowing..."

Assume the "capitalist" self-interest as a duty to yourself first, but in proper sequence and with equal dedication serve the other person in "socialist" mode immediately after – we are all in it together. Sequence like proportional thinking and prioritizing is crucial too. The sequence connects with others and becomes a cycle, the cycle of normal social "solidarity," a term I noted is used with all due solemnity in a village I got to know in Senegal, West Africa. Capitalist "me" first but *necessarily* next, much that would be considered socialist. The village picks up on the cycle on the other side, starting with solidarity being good then for the individual.

---

[166] Robert McNamara in *The Fog of War*, a documentary about his life, film by Errol Morris, Sony Pictures Classics, on DVD.

All this every day helping self, then other, then self, then other, then self, etc. is not very exotic, doesn't involve a lot of game theory, doesn't get you Nobel Prizes, doesn't provide chances for heroic victories over the vanquished, requires calm and cooperation – and it's very... helpful. If we all play by those rules (and have the sort of insights that guide to the right things to build) we'll do just fine.

Discipline is one of the key elements here, non-violent discipline. When rotten laws are written and we know in the heart of justice they are rotten, it becomes our duty to engage in peaceful disobedience, to resist the injustices. Even democracy isn't a grant from God to do whatever the politicians or voters want just because the votes establish something. Democracy is no better than the values – which can be constructive or destructive – of the people exercising the policy-making of democracy and the follow-through actions. It often takes real courage to exercise non-violent disobedience against authority, democratically established or otherwise or to face the hostile attitudes of prejudiced people who may be the great majority or even in your family. The Highlander Folk School in Tennessee trained many civil rights activists, helping Martin Luther King, Jr. and Rosa Parks among many others. It was severe training including role playing in which trainers would shout racist insults and rough up those in training, giving them a harsh experience in what they might expect from the bigots. The connections from Jesus to Gandhi, to Tolstoy, to King, to Mandela is a history in serious discipline all the way. Legend has it Rosa Parks was a young woman who had had it with moving to the back of the Montgomery, Alabama buses and she was certainly a courageous and dedicated woman. But not quite. In fact she was 42 years old, a hard working seamstress, respected citizen and Secretary of the Montgomery branch of the NAACP (National Association for the Advancement of Colored People). She and her associated civil rights movement comrades were planning the action with the organization for months.

Rosa Parks was preceded by nine months by a courageous 15 year old who had had enough, refused to give her seat to a white person and was carted off to jail, which may be how the story about Parks being a young innocent got started. That was March 2, 1955. That young lady's name was Claudette Colvin, her case, not Parks', went all the way to the Supreme Court and put an end to segregation on Alabama buses.[167] As two cops drug her from the bus she was shouting, "I paid my fare... It's my constitutional right!" Ms. Colvin was terrified – that's what it took. After her family's minister bailed her out of jail that evening she was afraid she'd be killed and her father and neighbors kept watch with guns all night in case the Ku Klux Klan might come riding over the hill. Even her protest, that of a 15 year old, didn't come out of nowhere, required intelligence and a certain type of training called everyday education: in school it was "Black History Month" and she'd had enough of injustices, got the context down with history about the Underground Railroad, studying the lives of Harriet Tubman and Sojourner Truth. But in all cases

[167] Phillip Hoose, *Claudette Colvin – twice toward justice*, Melaine Kroupa Books, Farrar Straus Giroux, New York, 2009

when a society – democratic or otherwise – institutes policies and laws on the side of injustice and violence, it takes knowledge, serious commitment and courage to make a peaceful difference.

What about when push really comes to shove? Joan Baez has spent a large part of her adult life – and teen years too – trying to further non-violence. She had this to say when asked about a situation when someone attempting the non-violent resistance gets killed: "Generally the public reaction is, 'Aha, I told you it wouldn't work.' I think I was in Granada, Mississippi and in one of the churches there was a list of people who had been killed in the Civil Rights struggle. It must have been four or five years into the struggle and there were only four or five names on that list – as opposed to 3,000 or 50,000, or whatever it might have been had it been a violent revolution."[168] Interesting thinking that had never occurred to me. In a book on economics it's in order to point out the loss of productivity those 3,000 to 50,000 killed, plus injured, would have cost the economy. And her thinking represented a good solid sense of proportionalizing, as well as the power of non-violence for changing the terms of conflict. Though there were a number of high profile murders and assassinations after that time, still the point demonstrates how there must be some almost unspoken respect for the non-violent approach considering the successes of the Civil Rights movement.

And what about empathy and altruism? – do they really exist, as Arun Gandhi would imply, or are we lost in the conundrum the two sociologists noticed earlier in these pages? That was the conundrum the Christian philosophers were picking to death because to do a good deed helps get you into heaven and thus was a selfish and therefore not charitable at all. Or are we always destined to self-serving actions intrinsically leading ultimately to violent resolution of problems, war forever into the future, the Star Wars Myth?

In the book *The Brighter Side of Human Nature – altruism and empathy in everyday life* by Alfie Kohn many studies are cited. He starts off, "The only species to invent for itself judgments of good and evil has frequent occasion to use both." And continues a paragraph later, "There is good evidence to support the proposition that it is as 'natural' to help as it is to hurt, that concern for the well-being of others often cannot be reduced to self-interest, that social structures predicated on human selfishness have no claim to inevitability – or even prudence. In short, the cynical consensus about our species is out of step with the hard data."[169] An author Kohn quotes, Leon Eisenberg, comments on the negative assessment of human nature, as if it were the dominant state of things, "Pessimism about man serves to maintain the status quo. It's a luxury for the affluent, a sop to the guilt of the politically inactive,

[168] Catherine Ingram, *In the Footsteps of Gandhi – Conversations with spiritual social activists*, Parallax Press, Berkeley, California, 1990, p. 64

[169] Alfie Cohn, *The Brighter Side of Human Nature – altruism and empathy in everyday life*, Basic Books, La Vergne, Tennessee, 1990, p. 4

a comfort to those who continue to enjoy the amenities of privilege."[170] Pessimists simply re-label "cynicism" as "realism." Kohn's book was rejected by one publisher who said, "It is too well meaning to be engaging," not pessimistic or negative enough. He didn't care much about the "hard data".

Among many signs that a brighter side does indeed exist in human nature that Kohn cites, here are just a couple.

Military analyst S. L. A. Marshall who was appointed chief historian of World War II and later served as a General in the Korean War said, "Fear of killing, rather than fear of being killed, was the most common cause of battle failure in the individual."[171] (By "battle failure" Marshall meant the unwillingness of a soldier to actually use his weapon in battle, shoot the enemy. His estimate from exhaustive research and personal experience is that fewer than 25% of the combat soldiers in his studies actually shot at the enemy. That sounds startling to the point of highly unlikely – surely he exaggerates – but he was certainly in a better position to know than an armchair peacenik theoretician like myself.)

Regarding the neoclassical economics idea of "economic man," basis of most neoliberal economic theory, who is rational in his actions, calculating, consistent, and fully informed "bears little resemblance to people in the real world," a nice comment I once overheard.

Another item: in many situations wealthy people give to charities because they want to help others – to "improve the world" – and want to remain anonymous so that the good they do is not credited to them, is not a cause for acts of thanks or some other reciprocal benefits from the receiver, kudos from society, etc., purely a gift. That this might really be so and not just anecdotal experience shared by millions but somehow inaccurate, Kohn points out, "In 1982...when non-itemizers were first permitted to begin deducting charitable gifts, there was no discernible increase in generosity [to take advantage of the money they could save]. ...tax deductions appear not to have been the primary concern. ...There have always been, and presumably always will be, people motivated only by natural kindness or a sense of social justice or religious conviction."[172]

From my own observations I would question that the economist's idea of self-interest at the core of all human behavior and human nature from the simple observation of people delighting in the delight of babies and toddlers "as if" and actually *because* they are appreciative of the experience of the other person, a baby in this case, is having. I see a baby gazing intently from a stroller and think of what the baby must be seeing and wondering. I'm not doing that because I want to have the pleasure of receiving happiness from that baby myself but just simply because there

[170] Op cit, p 40

[171] Op cit, p 50

[172] Kohn is here using a quote from Melvin Lerner, Op cit, p 222

is a genuine empathetic connection happening. I really do wonder how the baby is seeing things with such fresh new eyes, things never seen before. Conspicuously people are able to feel for another whom they love. People are also able to "get lost in" the lives of characters in novels and movies. One wonders in fact, with such intense feelings around such things, with so much concern for other people's lives and rights how a theory of self-interest lurking behind everything in the complexities of life, could be reduced to something that simple: economic man. The whole idea seems a little disrespectful to the amazing richness of it all, a poverty stricken construct somewhat insulting to something of beauty: us.

Generosity, more equality – an economics solution

Perhaps a more conventionally understood "generosity" could be seen in the way we invest for the common good through taxing and spending. For most people this is a little easier to grasp in economic terms than talking about strategies to give back to the future through peace and rights activism, though obviously war is an expensive waste of money averaging victim and victor costs, though the victor often thinks it's a profitable business.

From this perspective we can first consider the private gift, doing good deeds, helping in small ways, contributing personally, private individual to private individual. This could be seen as taxing ourselves and giving to others – and ourselves at the same time as members of the "common good," participants in the community – as in the economics of the gifting economies of many early societies: gift, obligation, gift, obligation, gift, round and round = more variety for all in the exchanges and an expansion of the overall community involved, broadening of horizons.

Second and intermediate between private personal generosity and government is supporting groups such as charities and non-profits and policy oriented non-partisan groups like League of Women Voters that are organized to support groups of beneficiaries, including disadvantaged people, "the public" and other living things or even the climate system of the Earth. Business associations, professional institutes like the American Institute of Architects and workers' unions organized primarily to benefit their members are set up to be generous to others in their particular group and indirectly themselves as individual members of the group while paying modest taxes called dues and by implication and sometimes rendering a service to the broader benefit to the whole community of which they are part. Usually they strive to serve the general good mainly through agreed upon ethics and standards of quality work. Generosity in this structure is mostly directed toward the group in which the giving individual is sharing in the benefits of the generosity, but also remember that in the gifting societies there was always the expectation, even the obligation, of gifts coming back later. Thus we see reciprocity working now as then as the relationships of people in a community of co-beneficiaries. In addition many give gifts of time, skills, efforts and services that no one bothers to monetize and try to keep track of.

This is all as it should be and really quite conventional when we think we are working for the common good – so our lives can be better too. It's "community oriented" and part of "good citizenship" with expectations of reciprocity everywhere evident. Even the capitalist leaning hard toward Laissez Faire often believes his or her work and investment is for the betterment of all with profit the main tool for reinvestment and supporting the capitalist to live better and do ever better personally... and in this way being a contributing member of society. If we are talking about a capitalist business, the most direct benefit to accrue to the whole community is by way of the value the buyer gets from the product or service and with all capitalists contributing, this leads to general benefit throughout society. If it doesn't work this way nobody buys the product or service and said capitalist with slow moving product has to start over with a different product or refinement of the old. That's the "accepted sequence" described earlier herein by Galbraith. As governments gather taxes to invest in improving what they govern, capitalists essentially self tax by foregoing personal use and enjoyment of some of their capital to instead reinvest in the business, or perhaps give to a non-profit that is supposed to improve the community, transfer to a family member as a gift such as paying for a child's college tuition and so on.

What about the fact that more equal societies in terms of the spread between the lower income and higher income are healthier in almost every measure? We might think of that as the pre-tax condition of income and wealth in the community. What happens if tax policy and other policies shift the spread from wide to narrow, from high inequality to low inequality?

There are many ways of measuring "income inequality." One system reported in the book *The Spirit Level – why greater equality makes societies stronger* is to compare the top 20% in terms of income with the bottom 20% and note the difference. Income isn't every measure of wealth, but it's good enough to get started in understanding what is going on. We could throw in the value of real estate, insurance policies, stocks, jewelry, art, gold hidden away and on and on, but many, if not most, of these generate income in some ways that gets counted.

The conclusion backed by enormous quantities of data from around the world is that the more unequal the society in terms of income, the worse almost every measure of health of the community and most of the individuals in it. Some countries with relatively low income have very good health measures and some with very high average income, most notably the United States, have an abysmally poor record in relation to health and well-being. To get a sense for the span, to cite a sampling, the US and Singapore each have a very wide gap between the top 20% in income of their populations and the lower 20%. Respectively the income of the top 20% in those two countries are 8.6% and 9.7% times higher than the bottom 20% in each of those countries. A middle cluster on the chart sees France, Canada, Switzerland and Ireland with their top 20% having 5.3 times as much income as the bottom

20%. At the end where there is the most income equality we find Norway, Finland and Japan clustered on the chart with their top 20% having around 3.5 times the income of the bottom 20%.

Say the authors, Richard Wilkinson and Kate Pickett in their introduction, "Rather than blaming parents, religion, values, education or the penal system, we will show that the scale of inequality provides a powerful policy lever on the psychological well-being of all of us."[173] The book is replete with graphs showing the results of their compiled studies. As a sampling, their graph for life expectancy in years shows that over around $20,000 per year income in 2010 dollars average in a country, there is very little difference in longevity. Costa Rica and Chile, the first a little below and the second a little over $10,000 a year average income have about 20% 25% the average income in the United States, but they all have an almost identical life expectancy: about 77 years for Costa Rica and Chile and 76 for the United States. (All statistics cited here and presented by Wilkinson and Pickett are from United Nations various agencies available in 2010.) Countries with lower income but higher longevity than the United States include Malta, New Zealand, Cypress and Greece, hovering around half the average income of the United States. Countries between half the average income of the United States and almost as high an average income with longer life expectancy include Greece, Germany, Finland, Netherlands, Israel, Italy, France, Austria, Spain, Sweden, Canada, Australia, Switzerland, Iceland, and Japan with longevity of around 82 years.[174]

Some of the other charts they provide record child well-being, literacy, CO2 production per capita, violent crime and an averaging of several health and social factors. The United State figures very high in income inequality in all of these and worst or close to the worst in most of the health and well-being measures. Poor health and violence are more common in unequal societies.

Wilkinson and Pickett average out the UN derived figures for general health and well-being including 1.) levels of trust, 2.) mental illness, including drug addiction, 3.) life expectancy and infant mortality, 4.) obesity, 5.) Children's educational performance, 6.) teenage births, 7.) homicides, 8.) imprisonment rates and 9.) social and economic mobility rates. They make no effort to weight the nine measures for importance seeing such a selection as too subjective and just count on the very general idea getting across.

The authors present many intriguing facts and draw important conclusions but I think possibly this particular observation is as important as they get:

> The health and social problems which we have found to be related to inequality tend to be treated by policy makers as if they were quite separate

[173] Richard Wilkinson and Kate Pickett, *The Spirit Level – why greater equality make societies stronger*, Bloomsbury Press, New York, 2010, p.5

[174] Op cit. p. 7

from one another, each needing separate services and remedies. We pay doctors and nurses to treat ill-health, police and prisons to deal with crime, remedial teachers and educational psychologists to tackle educational problems, and social workers, drug rehabilitation units, psychiatric services and health promotion experts to deal with a host of other problems. These services are all expensive, and none of them is more than partially effective. For instance, differences in the quality of medical care have less effect on people's life expectancy than social differences in their risk of getting some life-threatening disease in the first place. And even when the various services are successful in stopping some reoffending, in curing a cancer, getting someone off drugs or dealing with educational failure, we know that our societies are endlessly recreating these problems in each new generation. Meanwhile, all these problems are most common in the most deprived areas of our society and are many times more common in more unequal societies.[175]

In other words we have another situation here, a "silver bullet," similar to the multiple solutions that descend from the one enterprise of building ecocities, with its solution for land conservation and habitat restoration, energy conservation, transportation efficiency, partial solution to climate change, provision of in-close agriculture, radical reduction of death on the transportation system, supply of convivial public spaces for social and commercial gathering and many other advantages from one created condition. If these two things – greater general equality and ecocities – are not at the foundation of a much healthier economics, I draw a blank on anything better, except maybe commitment to nonviolent solution of problems. With more income equality we see a set of many solutions flowing from a single very major factor that we can "build" by policy – and guess which policy works most straightforwardly to do that? Graduated income tax… if you know what to spend it on.

In fact, I'd consider taxing to equalize wealth to a reasonable range with knowledge of what to build the foundation of non-violent economics, an economics to make peace: "Peace on Earth, peace *with* Earth." Some ideas reduced to slogans are definitely worth it.

---

[175] Op cit., p. 26

43. Solar power tower

This is a research concentrated solar power station owned by BrightSource Energy in the Negev Desert of Israel. It transforms solar energy to steam, then to electricity in a generator – a solar technology that fits ecocities and transit.

Education, coma, conventional

Now we consider education, seen in relatively conventional terms since we understand that it goes on in both formal and informal contexts. My thesis here is almost painfully conventional and obvious from any more or less objective ecological/physical perspective, though many will resist going there tooth and nail. They will do this for reasons of prejudice, that is, having made up their minds before assessing evidence or evaluating experience, much less trying out experiments. But throwing out the best information of science, as the right wing of the Republican Party in the United States is doing right now, is very dangerous. Many books harp on the dangers we are in now and we've heard some of that in this book. But you also now have the above first Five Big Ones to think about as a program for confronting our problems with powerful solutions via education. Put them in a context of a World Rescue campaign and there you have the core of a powerful formal curriculum for schools and a guidance for the individual in life ways decisions, an essential component of informal education that anyone can pursue in family, alone, in community non-profits, in special study groups – just do it.

One particular institution is missing though, and could easily exist in a very conventional format on a campus that would be in itself an ecotown or an ecocity fractal in a city, and such an institution could be founded and become a built and function reality come fairly soon. That would be an ecocity university – or a number of them racing to see which one appears first and how well its "campus" matched some very educational "ideal" physical format, testing and shaping the "ideal" itself.

City planner author Ken Schneider said, and I will lift his quote from my earlier book *Ecocities* and use it here regarding ideals because it says something so important. Writing in 1978:

> Both the faith and the sense of historic suddenness were vaguely with me in 1952 when I chose to join the relatively new profession of city planning which I felt could be a renaissance profession destined to help shape human history and maintain the faith. A few years' experience taught me that the profession was far from performing acts of renaissance. Alas it became clear to me city planning was destined to push paper for the established way of exploitation… Planners operate without a conception of an ideal city… We look vainly for a social ideal. Despite a 50-year debate about the neighborhood unit, the concept remains incomplete and exists only partially in a few locations. Urbanity, the quality of environments that stimulate a rich cosmopolitan life, is almost absent in the literature except as a reflection of particular architectural settings …. While medicine operates with a vision of health

and law with a distant image of justice, city planning exists without such a goal.[176]

I mention ideals to clarify that they are something worthwhile to help guide us if we think we might have a means to build ecocities, comprehend our total economics, nature's and human's, and even deal with a serious, ordered means to rescue our natural and built world. As crucial as building right is in physical solutions to our very physical problems and as crucial as building right is at the foundation of economics linking Human Economics with nature's, I believe formal schools for helping us along the way are crucial. If there is general consensus on the ideal, the core concept, the vision sits out there over the horizon drawing us onward, and actualities end up being very different than if that ideal and vision did not exist. But the point is that actualities often end up better than what would have happened if the ideal had not been there to help and schools of higher education can clarify the entire enterprise of evolving the ideal and the reality both, and both of them in constant feedback to one another. That is, as far as I can see, one of the most important processes behind any good educational enterprise.

What would be the content of the Ecocity University's teaching, the departments and courses clustered around the mission to build ecocities and help usher in an ecocity civilization? We'd need these subjects to be covered in detail, all helping us better know what to build deep into the future.

• City layout, design and planning, architecture and landscape architecture, in other words the physical description of ecocities from ecovillage to ecotropolis.

• The "Five Big Ones," an Ecocity 101 set of intro courses featuring Proportionalizing for a healthy future, the "movement" and "World Rescue" – like approaches (Plan B, Global Marshall Plan, etc.), in other words the total context for ecocities

• The history of the subject itself from ancient models (as in this book but far more detailed), through Garden Cities and Soleri's work, etc., through to present cities and ideas for the future

• The theory, cosmology, evolution and current events that are context for the ecocity study and building enterprise

• Renewable energy technologies and all relevant science and engineering

• Transit, bicycle, elevator, escalator systems, design and technology

• Restoration sciences for bringing back natural environments, high biodiversity

---

[176] Kenneth R. Schneider, *On the Nature of Cities – toward enduring and creative human environments*, Jossey–Bass Publishers, San Francisco, 1979, p. 255, also used in Richard Register's Ecocities

• Restoring agriculture to areas relieved of the mattress of asphaltic, concrete and lawns

• Land use law with emphasis on city zoning, land trusts, TDRs… all in a three-dimensional context;

• Biological/ecological/evolution studies beyond what's covered in the 101 courses, real physics, mathematics and new cosmology with back up by astronomy

• Economic theory refining and improving whatever I have going here (or something very similar), from Total Economics through Nature's, Human's, gift and capital economics to theories about capitalism and socialism, complete with game theory (potentially exaggerated) to simple economic craft of reasonable management of economies.

• Weather, climate, soils and oceanography with an objective to cool the earth among more general knowledge on those linked subjects

• Social justice and peace studies to help guide the entire enterprise and lead the World Rescue movement

• Carbon sequestration science, emphasizing the "natural" means that can be aided by high leverage human engineering, "tweakable" natural carbon sequestration

• And to best assess the immediately above, resources inventory science and library science to figure just what is renewable and how much are recyclable and how much is left on the planet that is economically recoverable and how to get at such information…

And that's a partial list.

All these stated and implied subjects, departments and courses would revolve around the mission to build ecocities and help establish the place of ecocities in the context of a World Rescue movement, but even more than that, a society-wide effort to build the best and most beautiful we can. All these subjects and departments would have connections to the others and be conceived to see themselves as part of a complex living, growing, shrinking (in mass/energy terms), wisdom cultivating, well ordered whole.

Crucial to the concept also is that the university be part of a designed and built ecotown or ecocity fractal with "all the essential components present and well organized." All this would function in a three-dimensional physical framework and the total intellectual flux therein would constitute the consciousness, psychological, spiritual connections within the ecocity fractal or ecotown such a university would help replicate around the world.

44. Hurricane Katrina, New Orleans, Louisiana.

I took this photo three months after the hurricane. Is climate change evidence adding up slowly, this plus Superstorm Sandy? In low lying areas part of the answer for living there is to build compact towns on artificial raised mounds of earth, an idea that has worked for 4,500 years that almost nobody pays attention to. And if the new communities are dense and mixed use you can bring on the bicycles and streetcars, skip the cars and stop pumping most of the CO2 that gets dumped into the air, reducing severity of future storms.

CHAPTER 15

Economics Roundup

$$Pr\ [T_A<1, T_B<1] = \phi_2\ (\phi_{-1}(F_A(1)), \phi_{-1}(F_B(1), Y)$$

Capitalism got some things right and some things wrong. Socialism too. Now's the time to sort them out for our own survival and thriving – and the surviving and thriving of most of life on Earth.

First, every day assumptions of what it takes to do honorable trading is a very good start. Remember that in the very bones of exchange in the market it is not the overall "me first" attitude but the "fair price for everyone." No agreement, no trade, no sale. As in outright conflict, if both parties to a would-be exchange insist on strongly off-balanced self-interest because each wants absolute maximum, no exchange happens – and bad blood develops too, which may lead to conflict.

Both parties have to be satisfied enough to actually trade, either goods or services, quite rare as barter, or money for goods or services, much more common in complex society. As we've learned from Mauss and Polanyi in the gift exchange of goods there is ceremony, time lag and social obligation that holds the extended community together for mutual benefit, not the benefit of only the guy who cuts the best deal for himself and worst for whoever is on the other side of the exchange. Basic satisfaction of all parties to the exchange, in gross numbers of participants and normal expectations, is so natural as to be required or transactions could hardly be expected to occur at all – other than at the point of a knife or gun of a bully, Mafioso or despot. How so many economists got the idea that it was all for self-interest is truly bizarre when you stop to think about it. By ignoring context, they seemed to think, they'd arrive at a more abstract and more certain truth than by paying attention to the more messy human world with all its social "ecological" complexities and connections that the market has always been part of.

But at the same time self-interest is the individual's perspective in the above context, but as part of that context, not as if everything was one exchange to a dead end in someone's treasure chest. Healthy self-interest makes for a healthy individual – so that he or she can participate fully in society, not so he or she can "win" and "die with the most toys," becoming the dead end capitalist. Remember the airline stewardess again: "...place the oxygen mask over your own nose and mouth before helping others..." But, necessarily then *"help others."*

The next thing to consider is that a lot has to do with the values held by large proportions of people in the particular society, societal norms they are called, and whether people internalize respectful conduct or not, whether they are highly evolved along the vector of the civilizing process or not so much.

So all that is very basic and it seems to me not that well understood in classical economics, despite the core of the functions of the marketplace revolving around fairness in exchange and general benefit for the entire society, not maximum benefit for the fanatic for self-aggrandizement.

Reminder of another principle here, one of my dimensional pairs – each, without the other, nothing. And that dimensional pair seen as a "unity" or "phenomenon" or whatever else you might call its existential being, is conventionally called wisdom. It is a pair, made up on one (theorized half) of reason, logic, evidence, experience, experiment and creativity in the physical realm and on the other side (other theorized half) just plain intuition that is sensitive to values, feelings, emotions and so-called spiritual insights. One might also say it is the factual obvious (if one bothers to look, and science extends the senses to look deeper in time and space) and the pattern that explains what can be quite subtle and not necessarily evident to scientists. A good example of what they miss, mentioned earlier, is the massive difference between the city built on the human measure and the one built for the 30 times as heavy, 10 times as fast, and 50 times the volume automobile. The intuition part will seem vague to many who think of themselves as methodical, effective, practical, rational and well informed. But it beats the faux precision of the formulas of economists.

Let's look at one of those formulas. This one is called the Gaussian Copula function: $\Pr[T_A<1,T_B<1] = \phi_2(\phi_{-1}(F_A(1)),\phi_{-1}(F_B(1),Y)$. I won't try to explain its detailed contents. It was invented by a man named David X. Li, "Gaussian" for the kind of bell curve pattern on graphs that show probability in large number samplings and "copula" meaning, in Latin, "coupling" things together, or you might say "copulating" as in "that fucking formula that screwed us royal in the Meltdown of 2008." [177]

It looks impressive to the layperson trying to figure out high finance and was one of those economists' "if-then" game theory formulas. It looked impressive enough to allow investors to enter the usual dreamland of desire that something extremely unlikely could make fast money. I don't know if Alan Greenspan brought up the Gaussian Copula function in the Financial Crisis Hearings at the House of Representatives or not, but it was the sort of thing the Congress Members, not wanting to appear a little dense, wouldn't have the character to ask, "Alan, what *really* do you mean by that?"

The idea was to gather together many variable possibilities for defaults in various very different financial instruments into a pooled collection – mortgages, bonds, bank loans, insurance policies, etc., known collectively as collateralized debt obligations of CDOs – and price them correctly for the risk involved. Certain hedge funds were all over this formula since after all they were based on the notion of "hedging your bets" by having a wide variety of investments so that if a few lost, some very different ones were likely to remain strong and so your total hedge fund should remain solid. The formula was supposed to help assess the possibility that those owing the money, paying off their debt and supplying the income stream that would be purchased when the package of debt was acquired, would not default – or might. Generally the larger the income stream relative to the cost of buying a share in the package of debts, the CDO, the more risk that those at the bottom, where the real economy money left for the gambling sector, would find it impossible to pay into the system and those holding the instruments would end up with a bad debt, no income stream (or much reduced) and having paid out a lot to buy into the arrangement in the first place, would have what is commonly called a loss. And such loss could be gigantic and spread through the whole world banking system – and did.

Felix Salmon in his March 2009 Wired Magazine article, "A Formula for Disaster" said thousands of "quants" – people who engage in quantitative analysis for assessing probabilities of profit and loss on Wall Street – rushed to apply the new Gaussian Copula formula. "The effect on the securitization market was electric. Armed with Li's formula, Wall Street quants saw a whole new world of possibilities. And the first thing they did was start creating a huge number of brand-new triple-A securities... The CDO market, which stood at $275 billion in 2000, grew to $4.7 trillion by 2006 [multiplied 17 times over]... Li's approach made no allowance for

[177] David Li, "A Formula for Disaster," Wired Magazine, March 2009, p. 74

unpredictability: it assumed that correlation was constant rather than something mercurial."[178]

This formula was supposed to correlate vastly different things as if apples and oranges were the same, which is to the senses, experience and intuition not so. But people were making their money siphoning off money from the typical expanding bubble famous forever in economics history, pretending this time was different because they were making so much money. The real correlation was that as a few people at the bottom defaulted and, regarding a very big and important sector of the market, real estate prices started to drop, more people sensed something was wrong, more defaulted while others stopped buying and house value declined more. Suddenly the correlation was so pervasive among things that were similar, all headed down – not different – people by the millions walked away from their now impossible-to-pay mortgages and collapsed value real estate. At that point, as usual in the history of bubbles, prices across the economy collapsed and defaults spread to other sectors and everything fell apart fast.

Everyone knew it would be amazingly difficult to figure out how such different kinds of loans could be "correlated" to each other to come up with a reliable simple number at the end that would make the CDO look irresistible. In the case of this formula, the number was the "Y" at the end. The "if" in this case was "if Y actually did mean something other than what it intuitively looked like, that is, impossible to achieve by treating things that are greatly different as if they were the same, then it would be most excellent indeed." Like the "if" in economists' "if-then" game that says "if the Earth were an infinite storehouse to pillage then growth forever would be healthy" so with the impossibility that one could dependably correlate all those very different loans of wildly varying levels of risk or that bundled loans of different risk levels would be rescued by the thought-to-be dependable ones making up for the risky ones. As when the all so historically well-recorded past bubbles were ignored long enough, this one too exploded in 2008. The results were stunningly destructive.

What's my point? Faux precision of mathematical formulas based on desire for profit and fake "ifs," that is assumptions that are concocted as part of game theory separate from the real mass/energy flows of the universe, are strictly illogical and dangerous to planet and people. It turns out that wisdom, which is facts and reason + sensitive intuition, works far better and one might say, though apparently more vague and fuzzy, far more accurate. Call that (F+R)+(I(S)) = 2W ("W" for Wisdom and Works!). Now is the Nobel Prize for Economics Committee impressed? The 2Ws Formula actually connects with the real world.

[178] Op cit. p. 79 continued to 112

Capital Economics – FDR a man for the future

My conclusion as an economics outsider, as most of us should be glad to be, is that we need to imagine a basic economics structure that looks something like I've described a couple times by now: Real Economics made up of Nature's and Human's, human's in two broad categories of gift based then historically later, as the artifact list grew and grew, monetized. Within that Human Economy imperfectly rough polar opposites called capitalism and socialism came to be a battle cry tending to exaggerated gamesman ship though both have their positive elements and are needed for a well integrated, dynamically but oscillating balance in a so-called, more or less "free" market with reasonable regulation.

Nature's and Human's Economics

Meantime nature's and human's economics are a continuous whole in the world of human cultures, the most powerful two links in connecting being: plants' capture of solar energy – you could justifiably call it the source – and the ever so consequential way we build our largest creations, which could tend to the automotropolis or the ecotropolis. The particular kind of city we build is most of what we build and shelters and orders most of the rest, the design of which therefore causing or solving most of our serious major problems.

Real economics…

… not capitalized, is what most people mean when using the term already, that is before I start playing with the words, meaning the economics of productivity, trade and utilization of resources, products and services. These services can include financing services short of usury and dangerous gambling – religions were on the right track but were typically too pure about it vilifying small reasonable loans as usury.

Capital economics…

…is simply "socialism with capitalists characteristics" in China's famous formulation, aka, "capitalism with socialistic characteristics" working for market stability and generally fair distribution, security for all, including the rest of the biosphere. This can exist and does seem to exist in varying variations in various countries today. My wording here in quotes I see taking off from Deng Xiaoping's "socialism with Chinese characteristics" which ushered in the hybrid of today's communist/capitalist economics of China in that rapidly changing country. It was effective in any case in raising 400 million people out of rural poverty and into urban jobs and lifestyles in about 20 years. As John Kenneth Galbraith and Jane Jacobs said, there is more benefit in utilizing elements of both capitalism and socialism than gained by doctrinaire antagonism based on their differences and, as I would add, thereby made dangerous and destructive by the gamers' exaggeration. The exaggeration of those differences led to the nuclear-armed fears, resource waste of the approximately 45 year "Cold War" with its real war spin offs such as the Korean War and Vietnam War and still contaminates economic thinking and healthy economic maturation to this day. Reflecting again on Lynn Margulis' discovery in evolutionary biology would do us a world of good in integrating rather than exacerbating differences. Make dance, not war.

Building right

That is, building in a resources-conserving, renewable energy, recycling, healthy nature-restoring way with an eye to creating environments that attempt to support human compassionate and creative evolution. If we tried that with serious dedication, I'd predict the "success" that Buckminister Fuller use to offer up as the potential of a cleverly thought up technology, and most certainly, ecocities would be a very intelligent technology of many technologies united in common purpose, a sort of metatechnology.

World Rescue – Built on non-violent economics

And, we need a theoretical framework like the one suggested above while actually pursuing a world rescue strategy addressing the Six Big Ones at its core, funded largely by our three sacred golden cows.

With that you have the outline structure of most of the essentials in this book. And it is actually hardly radical, more so it is like a practical set of compromises and adjustments required of the kind of active, disciplined non-violence that seeks understanding and that gives serious credit to underlying the important basic principles. It would be "radical," that is fundamentally different at its roots (from "radix," Latin for root) only in eschewing the gamers' exaggeration, which polarizes for conflict and clear victories in human political and economic games whose objective is growth and dominance by a small elite like the super rich in the United States and their "class" mates in a few other countries, and the clique that ran the Soviet Union. The operative principles behind what is "practical" in the above basic "framework," "construct," "theory outline" or whatever might be the best term for it would include principles we get from ecology and evolution, or "ecoevolution" in my terminology for that continuum in time scales.

This approach double checks frequently with how things are going for accurate information, not preconceptions including belief in capitalist or socialist doctrine. Most of *that* came out of 18th century basic capitalism, tuned up and rechristened for battle after capitalism lost whatever subtlety it had to monopolism, to be reigned in some by trust busting and unions as "neoclassical" capitalism and Soviet style, centrally planned, anti-capitalist Communism shaping up in the late 19th century and established for most of the 20th century. It has been characterized by historic episodes like Milton Friedman's fight in Chile that cost thousands of bloody deaths and Soviet vilification and rejection of everything capitalist including the healthier aspects of competition and open market non-planning (unseen guiding hand) that actually works for China but was rejected by the Soviets as too close to admitting the designated enemy had anything to offer. That antagonism should be considered just a bit dated by now it should be thought of as, as young people tend to say these days, "Oh that's so last year." When Republicans call people who want to tax the rich "Communists" the proper response should be, "Oh how 1950s of you! Come on, learn something in 75 years." Actually the taxes were very high then. But people forget.

I'm reminded again of Franklin Roosevelt's New Deal experiments and pragmatic assessment of what was and wasn't working and the willingness to admit one or another particular policy or project wasn't working... drop it and move on to try something else. The pragmatic core here is the opposite of faith-based action that thinks it knows what it's going to get before starting, even before noticing the proportionalized big issues and relevant facts. The pragmatic I'm talking about is the approach based on evidence, experience and, because we should remain ever vigilant in a democracy (or anywhere else) experiment to test out how things actually work, gaining new evidence and experience in the process.

We've covered Roosevelt and a number of his policies earlier, but here I will feature what I think we need all over again:

Glass Steagall

The "firewall" against community banks and savings and loans going into risky market transactions and other regulations to keep the greedy disempowered and the honest honest. And, elimination of all those gambling-encouraging economics "instruments of mass destruction."

High taxes, serious investment

For the wealthy and conscientious, and transparent debate around how to invest for the common good – with a long term horizon and common good seen as benefiting nature as well as us humans. The United States flourished with a stable banking system for about 75 years after the Roosevelt administration instituted high taxes (admittedly it flourished for other reasons as well, like winning the Second World War – but a salubrious economic system helped).

Deficit spending when strategically sensible

On investments that return a healthy future with an active economy, as encouraged by John Maynard Keynes. It's a good idea and FDR did a fair amount of this, borrowing from the American people by selling war bonds and through other means.

Knowing what to build

Crucial here is knowing what to build with the tax money – and private investment too for that matter – and in that regard building the ecocity civilization is absolutely crucial, its broadest design guidelines being the concept of the ecotropolis well tuned to its bioregion. As far as I can see, it is the physical link between Nature's Economy of resources and "ecological services" powered by the steady influx of solar energy and human "real economics," lower case. In FDR's New Deal his Administration showed a serious interest in building soils and restoring forests as his distant cousin President Teddy Roosevelt pursued similar goals preserving biodiversity and large areas of natural habitat. We need to go way beyond that, though the two Roosevelts were off to a good start, to an integration of soil and habitat regeneration with building the land, energy, and resources-conserving ecocity.

National insurance programs like Social Security

Also founded inFDR's government, and not forced purchase of private health insurance. What about the option to invest in the Social Security System itself to draw out more later in retirement if desired, citizens investing in the Social Security system voluntarily for a larger benefit at retirement time? So what if the government would be in "competition" with the insurance industry? It could be a far more reasonable and affordable system.

In addition to what we could learn from FDR, which lent considerable stability to the world economy in the many decades following him and what should be considered most seriously all over again, there are other economics moves to implement that would help enormously.

Greater equality

Closely connected are high taxes for the wealthy, in Roosevelt's time and until the early 1960s, mentioned above and in earlier chapters, rationalized more for the war effort than earlier in the New Deal. In most countries we need greater equality and less real poverty, closer to models like Japan and Norway.

Protective tariffs

Large economic blocks like nation states are like living organisms in some ways and one way is that they need a protective skin, fur coat, if not in some cases, scales like an armadillo or shells like a turtle. Skin provides some protection from cuts and sunburn and keeps out diseases but lets in a certain amount of air and moisture, and provides cooling and heating depending on season and functions in other helpful ways. Globalization of the economy has gone too far with the dogma that investment capital should be able to go anywhere even where it does damage to exploited economies, people and nature. Global understanding… we can never get too much of that and people who buy fair trade product have some of it. Like the subtle breathing of the pores in our skin, understanding should pass in and out of countries, city-states and other economic units. A kind of regulated globalism that utilizes mild tariffs is, like skin, is a good idea.

Understanding and talking clearly about growth

And finally, a healthy economics has to understand that mass/energy growth has gone way too far and needs to shrink back to something that conserves, recycles and treats people and other living creatures fairly so we can *all* enjoy our lives. Growth in terms of understanding, cultural explorations in art and science, growth in compassion and creativity all just fine, not to say growth in wisdom essential for survival at this point in history. But we have to stop conflating the two types of growth. For that I'd suggest the slightly awkward convention of simply saying every time we are talking about what most people think they are justifying in the use of the term in capitalistic economics circles: "mass/energy growth." Call it that. It has to reverse. The slogan "Shrink for Prosperity" applies only to mass/energy growth. Where economic growth is equated with mass/energy growth we have a serious economics misunderstanding because we can have economic prosperity with more money being exchanged and far less mass/energy growth going on, in fact with great mass/energy shrink. The electronics industry sweeping the world in information technology, genetic profiling and the arts of the small should provide hint enough that making a living as well as advancing positive human cultural product is in tune with miniplexion.

The above in sum seems overly simple in a way, but I think it is actually the basic structure of a genuinely decent capitalism, or conversely, a decent "socialism with capitalistic characteristics," honoring the creativity of capitalists investing in "job creation" and making products available to more people for the collective good, creating green jobs for the long haul. And that takes us back to the Six Big Ones that need money: the economy should as highest priority shift capital there, that is, to deal specifically with overpopulation, changing the agricultural system, building the ecocity civilization, taking carbon from atmosphere to lithosphere, investing generously and educating about it all. Generosity as said: "Peace on Earth and Peace *with* Earth."

Talk about reducing mass/energy growth while increasing growth in service jobs with much less physical impact on the Earth, imagine shifting defense workers and the military to a wide range of jobs in support of developing world understanding through education, cultural exchange and communications with international treaties agreed for all states to reduce defense budgets – on pain of sanctions by all other states. That relates specifically to directly working for a more peaceful world, but also we could use the money to build the whole ecocity civilization, literally build it. Overall the strategy would be more like backing off carefully with substantially reduced military budgets around the world every year and with real resolve and imagination.

I hate to say it – after years in the peace movement it sounds at first counter intuitive – but it may even be worth keeping a small number of nuclear weapons aimed at each other for some time yet until we are absolutely convinced we wouldn't use more "conventional" weapons against one another in wars of any size. It's one of those things I think I might just agree with against my own usual inclination simply because it looks like a lot of evidence suggests something rather undesirable – finally, *really* unthinkable – may have worked to beneficial end, since there have been no gigantic world wars since such weapons were developed. I say that because the perverse logic of MAD – Mutually Assured Destruction – is likely the most important reason we did not slide from the Second World War into the Third. Not only is the issue that the stakes in fighting finally got obviously and insanely high finally but the logic of the "exchange" meant something to subvert the Hobbesian Trap, to wit: The shoot-first-or-die logic of dueling that comes with the trap, and it does make sense in a horrible way, no longer applies when it takes 20 minutes instead of a 20th of a second for the bullet to arrive. That gives the person who sees the approaching attack time to attack back in a well prepared system that assures both die. This changes things a great deal and moves shooting from logical in the circumstances to suicidal and flatly stupid, which is even worse than outdated "honor" that looks anachronistic to people who decide they love living. But the point of vastly reduced military budgets, in the context of a world rescue strategy actually is thinkable and would provide massive resources for building a better world.

It is especially thinkable – peace is – when we realize that we have brought it to one aspect of individual violence, dueling, for the absurdity of not saying, "Well, let's just agree we disagree and we can avoid each other now" and we have stopped largest of wars due to the outright insanity of launching a nuclear attack in a MAD context. So we are already well on our way, with the two extreme cases of violence, personal and world war scale, finally, after many centuries, under a strong degree of control, a major advance in the civilizing process.

Eliminate the "Nobel" Prize in Economics

When Thomas Berry was in Berkeley three or four years before he died he phoned up early one evening, told me he was attending a conference but wanted to take a break and have a drink or two with me. It was the last time I saw him. I forget if he imbibed alcohol or something else instead. I don't know if the Passionist Order of the Catholic Church permitted or if he in any way needed or enjoyed it for his lithe and compassionate mind to move along its insightful thoughts more happily. I probably had a beer or two when we met at the Hotel Durant bar. His last friendly rant to me was about terminating the enormously misleading Nobel Prize for Economics, which was actually financed by the National Bank of Sweden, not part of the Alfred Nobel fortune. The prize is not only misleading, he told me, for appearing to be what it is not, but also because the abstract game theory of economists disconnected from the real universe is extremely damaging. People take the Nobel Prize very seriously, almost an ultimate Good Worldkeeping Seal of Approval, the apex of credibility.

So the prize should be eliminated. Hardly anything could be more important, he said, than to stop giving credit to the economists who are continuing the falsehood that infinite mass/energy growth on the Earth is healthy, that ultimately we are all in it for self-interest. Thomas went on emphasizing how crucial a cog in the deadly machine the prize in economics was and what a victory it would be for healthy ongoing evolution to put an end to it, a very public consensus of the damage it causes, a real wake up call for reshuffling the deck for a better chance at surviving and thriving into the deep future. What a rant! From my point of view getting rid of the economics "Nobel" might be a powerful opening to the kind of economics I'm dealing with here in these pages.

Looking up the history of the "Nobel" prize in economics and you find it has changed its name many times, trying to make more legitimate the initial mistake that the Nobel Foundation should admit and simply correct by publically repudiating the connection. You know the bank always had a problem with legitimacy as they struggled to settle on an appropriate name, so inappropriate was the idea in the first place: 1968-1970: "Prize in Economic Science dedicated to the memory of Alfred Nobel." Then they must have felt guilty about it or the Nobel Foundation was getting nervous because the actually dropped the Nobel name in 1971 and left it at, simply, the "Prize in Economic Science." But in 1972 someone decided, what the hell, lets go for the association with the real Nobel Prize after all and called it the "Bank of Sweden Prize in Economic Sciences in Memory of Alfred Nobel." For reasons abstruse and unknown to me from 1973 through 1975 they tried out the "Prize in Economic Science in Memory of Alfred Nobel." Then in 1976 and 1977 they decided to add the plural-making s to "science." And I won't bore you with the next seven name changes.[179]

As millions of people know, Alfred Nobel invented dynamite and eventually was aghast at the destruction it wrought. He hoped it would be as disastrous in war as it was useful in mining, tunnel-, bridge- and road-building and thus would help end war, as something just too terrible to continence. That notion had to wait for the atomic bomb to become even an arguably plausible idea and in the meantime dynamite just amplified the violence of war. As something of a karma balancing effort he decided to use his enormous wealth largely derived from his invention – he had many others, running to over 350 patents – to endow the Nobel Prize to encourage healthier, far more humanitarian results. He hoped to provide in particular a prize for people making very strong contributions to the movement toward world peace.

---

[179] Wikipedia article "Nobel Memorial Prize in Economic Sciences," http://en.wikipedia.org/wiki/Nobel_Memorial_Prize_in_Economic_Sciences

With his death Nobel established his prizes in 1895 by way of his will. Specifically money – 94% of his net worth – was to be used for honoring people making extraordinary progress in physics, chemistry, literature, physiology or medicine and for contributions to peace. I haven't yet discovered who convinced whom or how but in 1968 on the 300th anniversary of the Swedish National Bank's founding, the bank created the many-named Nobel Prize in economics. Opponents of the prize in economics contend that its purpose is further legitimatizing, even mystifying the craft of economics and role of banking in determining what is true in society and by association with the other Nobel prizes, what is true in virtually all else in the universe.

Some members of the Nobel family opposed the economics prize in their name energetically. Swedish human rights lawyer Peter Nobel, nephew thrice removed from Alfred Nobel, has been among the most severe critics of the Nobel economics prize. According to him no member of the Nobel family has ever had the intention of establishing a prize in economics.[180] Even free market capitalist Friedrich Hayek, godfather of the Austrian School closely related to the Chicago School of Milton Friedman stated that if he'd been consulted he would "have decidedly advised against it" (the establishment of the prize) because "the Nobel Prize confers on an individual an authority which in economics no man ought to possess… This does not matter in natural sciences. Here the influence exercised by an individual is chiefly an influence on his fellow experts; and they will soon cut him down to size if he exceeds his competence. But the influence of the economist that mainly matters is an influence over laymen: politicians, journalists, civil servants and the public generally." [181]

And with that idea – to clear out of the way a big impediment to far better economics – we would have a good transition to what to do actively about actually building an economics built on what we build.

[180] Op cit. Wikipedia article

[181] Friedrich Hayek, "The Pretence of Knowledge" lecture delivered to the Nobel Prize banquet, December 11, 1974 as reported on www.nobelprize.org, " the official website of the Nobel Prize" http://www.nobelprize.org/nobel_prizes/economics/laureates/1974/hayek-lecture.html/

45. Compact town in a hot climate

This is a design that cools the built community with breezes and shade. It represents a variation on a theme that architect Paolo Soleri calls "arcology," a word combining architecture and ecology and in his meaning, a town in a single structure. It also represents the highest degree of land and energy saving – a completely car free way of living with nature a short walk out the door.

CHAPTER 16

World Rescue

Chaos, holistic management, rescue

To many people "world rescue" sounds presumptuous, impossibly ambitious, maybe even embarrassing to be associated with. For some, seemingly far too top-down. Nip it in the bud before it gets started! Or, ignore it to death. It suffers all the problems and excuses of the effort to change cities but more so. "Cities are so big how can I get a handle on changing them?" As someone who has been promoting changing cities into ecocities for more than 40 years I'm used to it, though. I need only extend ambition for my species a little more to imagine rescuing the world. Plus, the right sort of city is a long step in that direction anyway. Why shouldn't everyone be doing something to rescue those in trouble?

People dreaming of peace after the shock and horror of the Second World War came up with various ideas of some sort of world government but were brought up short in no short order by the great majority. Despite the disaster of that nation-against-nation conflagration, the United Nations was and still is eternally suspect in the eyes of many people in every country fearful of other countries and any foreign authorities that threaten any aspect of what is thought to be traditional national sovereignty; any attempt at *anything* that tries to unite human action for *any end* is gravely suspect.

But if we acknowledge our big environmental and geopolitical problems and that we need a rescue of some sort we will have to admit we need a different type of world initiative than those tried before and I'd suggest one more on the order of a chaos of independent efforts united around the goals of social, political, economic and ecological sustainability.

Chaos and order of this sort, like any other of my "dimensional pairs" with its freedom of movement and possibility structure around a good notion of what makes sense to do – and not just thinking it but doing it – is, I believe, the key. Like many dimensional pairs, this one, chaos and order united, might just produce a new reality in the way new levels of evolution, even new phenomena dealt with in physics, are "emergent" out of things and forces, principles and particulars from which the emergent mass/energy thing, condition or even new law could never have been predicted.

I've described physics emerging out of subatomic particles and the "strong force" as stars formed and chemistry emerging from the heavier than hydrogen and helium elements when these elements were sprayed out from exploding stars to form next generation stars and planets. Chemical and electromagnetic attraction take over from merely gravitational attraction and on the scale of the geological and biological while dark matter continues with gravity to give emergence to the pattern of stars compacting into clusters called galaxies while dark energy scatters strings of galaxies spreading out through the universe, this studied in physics, math and cosmology.[182] Emergence seems to be the only constant throughout the whole pattern from "The Creation" through creative processes at work all the time to "eventually," the infinitely small to the infinitely large in scale. I've called "emergence happens" as the closest we will ever come to a formula describing the most comprehensive general field phenomenon in the universe.

This sounds like a stretch but brings us to the idea that the political agreement for how to rescue the world might itself emerge if we prepare the ground well, as something unknown and unknowable in its fullness, but vaguely suggested by the elements of what's needed for survival and thriving. We can help set the stage, but ourselves and the forces of nature and those forces and things we have unleashed here on our Third Planet are the actors writing the endlessly rewritten script as we go. If that swarm of events on stage happens to be something to which we can give a core and direction, a vision for progress, if not a clear set of goals that have to be accepted by all, perhaps some real progress can be made and an emergent civilization headed toward surviving and thriving will not escape our grasp on a planet heating up and in a biosphere withering away.

---

[182] Robert B. Laughlin's book *A different Universe – reinventing physics from the bottom down*, Basic Books, New York, 2005, follows the phenomenon of emergence of unpredictable things, processes and even natural laws starting as early as the Big Bang and small as subatomic particles then moving deep into the future. He maintains the emergence pattern is all-pervasive. I'd include it in the realms ecoevolution, society of politics, human invention and building ecocities.

As suggested earlier, education is the key to preparing for the emergent institutions and actions that might rescue us yet. And patient toil, as Gandhi reminded us, inescapable for results. In actuality that chaos of people and institutions tuned generally to one another producing an emergent reality, though a cumulatively very destructive reality in terms of nature, resources and the planet's limits today, is modeled in general pattern by neoliberal corporate globalism itself. The agreements of goals and operations are accepted, therein, by many even ferocious competitors as the game board that defines an enormous amount of the economic and societal action but for maximum gain and growth (as best one can win it) rather than for health for the whole planet (as best we can all insure it, that is, make it sustainable).

Both game boards can be designed and a world rescue strategy is one that might be characterized as for the infinite game, the open-ended game, the game of rules evolving and changing with the universe and our evolving selves and society itself. The amazing little book *Finite and Infinite Games* by James Carse[183] lays out many aspects of the difference between the games that are defined into existence with set rules written by people, such as attempted by economists seeking final answers in their formulas, rules posited as unchanging for the particular game, as compared to the game of life living and changing. The objective of the finite game is to win when it comes to an end – add up your victory or subtract your loss. The objective of the infinite game in the real conditions of life is to keep playing and keep it changing as the world itself keeps changing. *Finite and Infinite games* is as close to a scientific proof that economists' if-then games stand separate from and in their type, as happenstance as to whether they have relevance or not. With more relevant education and clear notions of proportions and priorities there is no reason the infinite game can't overtake the finite game, maximum health over maximum gain. If not exactly in my terminology, the Six Big Ones financed by the Three Golden Sacred Cows, bearing any other name but meaning the same, it is a most promising means.

Another way to put it is that we need a new kind of education, an education game in action whose objective *is* large action, that is, taking the sort of ideas we have in this book that serve as tools for heading in the right direction and getting on with such an education that builds with all possible care yet haste while learning, building, educating, learning, building, educating, learning, building, educating... round and round as the built world also educates while needing education to get built. Note where education is supposed to produce "educated" people, it's closer to the finite game, and where producing people always being educated, its closer to the infinite game. (It has always bothered me when people say they "were educated" at such and such a school, as if they shouldn't see themselves as *becoming* educated to the very end of life.) Institutions for education already exist, in any case, and can adopt the content suggested in this book. And, there are more forms of education

183 James P. Carse, *Finite and Infinite Games – A Vision of Life as Play and Possibility*, The Free Press, a division of Macmillan, Inc., 1986.

than schools: NGO's need to join the movement, the media can help, informal networks of family and friends can intentionally educate and new institutions can be founded, such as the Ecocity University and schools for peace and non-violence strategy like the Highlander Folk School in Tennessee.

To emphasize where the rubber hits the road – as a bicycling figure of speech, not car – leading educational institutions of all sorts need to emphasize location aware "green jobs." Which brings us to "holistic management" – a concept promoted by Allan Savory not just in his management of grasslands but for almost any project for healthy ends. On one hand we have people saying, "We will probably see some global heating but will adjust pretty well – don't panic!" They are influential enough that they have most people who are dealing with the problem talking about adaptation, which I think of as rolling over and playing dead. How are polar bears going to adapt to shrinking ice packs on the Arctic Ocean? They can't turn into fish so they can swim the greatly increasing distances between patches of ice or utilize their hunting strategy if all the ice disappears. Getting ready for and accommodating the disaster – investing your energy in planning and building dikes around costal population areas for example – while neglecting serious strenuous efforts to avoid the problem in the first place is avoiding hard work and is intellectually bankrupt in my opinion. Even the term "mitigation" as in, "Mitigate climate change by driving less and recycling more," for example, is used incorrectly. Mitigation means making something bad, less bad. For example, mitigation money for small waterway improvements I've been involved in, like planting native riparian vegetation, have been provided to "mitigate" the damage done by building a large parking lot that paves over a nearby creek and contributes to flood water runoff in heavy rains.

Concerning climate, to actually make things better we have to stop global heating (though admittedly it will take some time, how long we know not) and help the planet back to some semblance of the more slowly moving dynamic stability of climate. Because people don't dare to think such positive thoughts, the implications for hard work being so obvious, they try to use the word "mitigate" to look positive when it is only helping to make an enormously negative condition a little less negative.

To actually do the heavy lifting though, along comes holistic management, through the back door. What I mean by that is only my own experience with thinking through that notion after discovering the work of Allan Savory. I've always been a so-called "holistic" thinker back even into my teenage years. But Savory anchored the idea in a particularly powerful set of things to do that can be educated about and then turned into realities in sequestering CO2, enriching soil and restoring water tables and waterways lost to non-holistic management by people covering vast landscapes of this planet.

I think people tend to think best, in learning mode, in terms of very particular things they can visualize that fit well and clearly illustrate underlying principles. If those things can be cracks in the door to profound truths that lead ever deeper into actions that bring on solutions, we have something of a sequence that could help us all considerably. When I first read Allan Savory's work I thought it was brilliant in just this way. Not only do we just *see* the pattern of gathering large herds of grazing herbivores together that fertilize, seed, and plow with hooves vast landscapes like giant living agricultural machines, not only would the whole panorama become a beautifully clear and easily understood illustration of the way evolution works over time with the herbivores, carnivores, plants, seeds, soil, sun and water producing vast landscapes of fecundity sequestering CO2 and restoring soil fertility, aquifers and waterways, but the means becomes clear as exactly what Savory calls "holistic management".

Savory points out our traditional way of simplifying the world to attempt to manage it for our benefit appeared to work for a while – or at least we thought so – which was to posit a vision and mission for what it is we hope to accomplish, set up targets and timelines and then go for it. The problem is life on Earth isn't linear like that. Linear is a simplification for getting particular things done and coincides with the linear nature of language, one word after another in a pattern stringing through time to convey meaning. But reality is not just linear cause and effect but a pattern of networks of cross-influence among wholes in three-dimensional space. If you don't grasp the way that works you constantly get puzzling failures in larger environments. For example, the truism around the world is that when the land is damaged by over grazing or by fire, we should rest the land so that animals are excluded and you give the plants a chance to recover, as if all the animals did was damage plants.

Nonsense! The grass needs the animals for seed distribution and germination assistance inside their warm wet digestive tracts even if it is a draught outside the animals' skin. And you have heard some of this here before. The key is the whole systems perspective, which is just another way of confirming what ecology tells us.

To better understand what at first glance might look a bit overwhelmingly complex, Savory points out that you have to keep aware that there are only four major components interrelating that define these wholes and when you get used to them, the patterns are clear and then manageable in the holistic manner. They are sun, water, minerals and the biological community. And what is, as he calls it, the guiding element in it all, the "magnetic north?" A holistic goal. As Ken Schneider pointed out that urban planners in his time had no "ideal" to help direct their discipline, unlike the ideal of justice for law, beauty for the art, health for medicine and truth for the science, philosophy and theology, so we need a holistic goal for our actions on Earth that might seek to solve whole Earth problems or attain best results for all of us, which includes the other life forms too. That would be simply a holistic goal. Like myself with the words ecocity and miniplexion so with Allan Savory that he thinks it is important enough to try coining a new word to focus our effort to understand the significance therein and calls it our "holisticgoal." You might almost say it is the composite of those ideals just mentioned. It's where holistic management is headed, once managed by ecoevolution and now with human management – if we know what we are doing – now a partner with nature.

Understanding the above we can delve into the details some with enormously positive impact on the whole systems.

Meantime the more linear ideas about management – but mostly use of resources – prevails and could last a long, damaging time. A friend of mine is the son of the inventor of industrial diamonds. The inventor was Howard Tracy Hall. His son David is also an inventor and now with over 300 US patents to his name, most of them in drilling equipment and better industrial diamond technology for his company called Novatek out of Provo, Utah. He warns us that although the Peak Oil Paul Reveres are correct in that the oil and gas resources of the Earth are limited if large and that peak oil production and then decline to The End is inevitable, it might be much farther into the future than most people think.

New technology, some of it invented by David himself, is making horizontal drilling and fracking productive for vast reserves that only five to ten years ago looked unavailable or prohibitively expensive. Yes more expensive but as prices for fuel go up in the long term and if for automotropolis habits people insist on driving, driving, driving, not economically unavailable after all.

David proposes car-free cities with strips of mid density laid out in a pattern first proposed by Joseph Smith, founder of the Mormon religion. He imagines nodes of higher density community and commercial services at various corners. Between the strips, which are zero lot line row house style with high intensity rooftop gardens and greenhouses, he proposes intensive horticultural production and between the strips of built up infrastructure, wider strips of more intensive agricultural production, not necessarily all organic as he's an advocate of various complex emerging innovations in farming if the bottom line seems to be healthy. Such communities he sees as adjunct to existing cities more generalized in their production – industrial, commercial, finance, educational, etc. So we talk a lot about that and mull over the positive implications of car fee designs.

Meantime he's making drills that get purchased by oil and gas companies furthering fracking. We also talk about threatening climate change. So recently I asked him, "Do you sometime think about your karma?" "Every night," he said, "If we don't decide to just leave most of it in the ground, I'll have a lot to answer for." I thought that was a pretty interesting comment from an extraordinarily complex man. He clarified what he has been learning while inventing, activities he seems as unable to cease pursuing as I am the ideas I find fascinating in my own thinking and efforts to do various things. In an e-mail to me in February, 2013 he upped my education some:

"I attended some drilling technology meetings in Houston this last week and learned more about horizontal drilling and the effect that is having on the reserves of natural gas and oil. There are a few critical technology needs that the industry… including Novatek [David's company], are working on [for] solutions.

Crawlers, so that pipe is pulled rather than pushed so that the horizontal distance can be increased from 5 miles to 10 miles or more.

Along string vibrators to reduce the static friction on the pipe.

Along string electrical power so that more advanced tools and electronics can be used throughout the drill string [for sensing the geologic formations surrounding and their likelihood for hosting oil or gas]

Indexable [diamond] bits so that a new bitface can be presented to the formation without tripping in and out of the hole.

These solutions will reach the industry within the next 10 years and when fully implemented will open up even more vast reserves of oil and gas world wide."

Hall then suggests several changes consistent with much in this book to deal with the problems that are likely with these changes including restraining use and says, "And... at the same time... we need to move toward walkable cities so that the overall need for energy is substantially reduced."[184]

Daunting though solving the fossil fuels problem sounds given the economists' habit of calling for more ever more, bought into by the vast majority of all the rest of us, renewable energy systems are growing rapidly. Germany and Denmark are among the fastest growing, showing growth rates many times higher than average world population growth. In fact population is shrinking in a number of developed countries, real efficiencies are improving and if we used the vast amplifications revealed in biological leveraging and "holistic management" as suggested by Allan Savory, we could release enormous forces for positive change in the right direction. Add to that the immense savings of switching from cities for machines to ecocities for people and tapping into the wealth presently in the hoards of the very wealthy and the military and a possible solution, a goal for a world rescue, begins to emerge out of the fog of confusion and give-up "adaptation" depression of those *not* in denial. There is a way: let "can do" thrive.

There could be millions of jobs making money strategically directing nature's agents of change toward ever-higher carbon sequestration and biodiversity. The titans of present energy, suburb-building and transportation industries rail against most things solar, wind and organic saying they need to protect jobs. Ridiculous. There are many studies showing there are more jobs to be created in the transition to a sane future. We will need some conscientious planning and investment in transition training because the healthy things in evolution's miniplexion pattern are as complex or more than burning oil and dissolving cities out over the landscape.

From Plan B to World Rescue

Probably our best shot at an overall effective and uniting approach at this time has been modeled by Lester Brown's Plan B and the institute he founded called

[184] David Hall, personal e-mail to Richard Register, February 27, 3012

Earth Policy Institute with its crew of eight constantly tuning up his plan with updated statistics on practically every problem and solution imaginable. He's retiring and the organization is dissolving, but you will get the idea.

Major components of his plan:

- cut global carbon emissions 80% by 2020
- stabilize world population at no more than 8 billion by 2040
- eradicate poverty
- restore forests, soils, aquifers and fisheries.[185]

Well that's easy to say – but he has educated means he has spent his life learning about to apply. What is particularly interesting, he has taken up the economists' challenge and added capital numbers in the two major components of his budget to, essentially, rescue the planet:

- basic social goals, $75 billion a year (with a sampling of three line items):
    - universal primary education, $10 billion a year
    - aid to women, infants and pre-school children, $4 billion a year
    - reproductive health and family planning, $21 billion a year...
- Earth restoration goals, $110 billion a year (with a sampling):
    - planting trees, $23 billion
    - protecting top soil on cropland, $24 billion
    - protecting biological diversity,$31 billion
- Grand total: $185 billion a year.[186]

His many and detailed proposed policies and capital allocations were targeted to particular tasks to deliver particular services, which he explained.

Excellent. But leading and powerful as his approach has been, we need much more emphasis on the layout and structure of the city and a clear development of a set of prioritizations – many of the details of which he filled out quite beautifully – based on real world proportionalizing.

Knowing what to build, with the courage to build it

Remembering Gandhi's admonition that it will take education and toil opens us up to the deeper question of courage. This fits under "generosity" in my Six Big Ones. Remember also that courage is the master virtue since exercise of all

[185] Lester Brown, *World on the Edge – how to prevent environmental and economic collapse*, W.W. Norton and Company, Ltd., London, 2011, p. 16

[186] Ibid., p.199

the other virtues depends upon it. And in times that are bad or headed that way it will take a lot of courage.

Sometimes something deceptively small takes considerable courage – which probably means it's not so small after all. Take this case:

I was very involved in the General Plan review process in Berkeley, California about the year 2001. By then I'd spent more than 25 years in the city trying to see an integral neighborhood project built, get a pedestrian street created, open a creek in a case where a building would be removed with a willing seller deal to set a precedent and for opening a whole largely buried creek from spring to bay. For that and other ecocity changes, inserting into the General Plan an Ecocity Zoning Map would have been very helpful in guiding the future land use changes.

None of the above was successful. I had been important in successful efforts for smaller schemes like designing and building solar greenhouses, getting about 100 fruit trees planted along sidewalks, in front yards, at schools and youth activity centers and community gardens, getting two blocks of buried creeks opened up – daylighted was the "in" term – and planted in native species in separate parts of the city, designing and getting the city to build a "Slow Street" to give the advantage over cars to bicyclists, pedestrians and neighborhood residents. That last project was built and ran six blocks – not the 20+ blocks of the original aspiration. All these were accomplished with work by others as well as myself, with allied groups and the two organizations of which I was the founding President, both of them educational and research California non-profit organizations. They were Urban Ecology – 1974 to about 2007 when it became effectively inactive and Ecocity Builders, 1991, when I left Urban Ecology, to the present.

As a very active participant in the Berkeley General Plan process I attended more than half the various commission and neighborhood meetings around town. I was attempting to get elements of our ecocity program to be adopted by the various commissions and to gain public support for these so that the City Council would amend the General Plan and the zoning code to be supportive of rather than obstructive – the then and present condition – to many ecocity features in the city.

In the neighborhood meetings the typical response to any substantial change was hostile, with neighbors watching each other closely to make sure others on their block were equally opposed to any policy or regulation that might relate to basic building design and land use changes. Almost nothing of serious effect on the ecological impacts of the city could be approved. Bear in mind that virtually all citizens of Berkeley insist they are ardent environmentalists and are members of the Sierra Club, Friends of the Earth, Save the San Francisco Bay Association or other such organizations. The what-you-might-call first level punch line was this: After speaking out on one or another of our ecocity proposals, one of the neighbors who actually liked the idea would wait until the meeting was over and everyone was filing out. He or she would then come up to me and say something like this: "Thank God you said that. It was a good idea but I'd be scared to death to support anything like that – my neighbors would kill me." "My neighbors would kill me" *was* a quote said a couple times.

What's the problem here? I mention this because it is the stumbling block at the starting block. In dozens of interviews I'm asked what is the most formidable impediment to building ecocities or making progress with any other of my ideas for investing in the solutions I propose? I've often said that people need to learn a little about ecocity design, saying the seemingly self-serving, "Read my books." But for reasons deeper than lack of a basic language to make the territory at least somewhat familiar, people simply refuse to think. They refuse to get started. A big wall goes up. Even when clear about the benefits of the offerings – how useful or creative they might be, how practical the various approaches in terms of social and environmental health, job creation, long term profitability, even how beautiful many of the changes might be, how much their children would enjoy and learn from various changes including bringing creeks back – no approach seems to make much difference. And the more "educated" the people the worse the problem of even opening the subject seems to be.

Berkeley in the early 2000s – I don't know if it is still the case but expect that it is – was proud of the fact that it had more PhDs per capita than all but one other city in the country (number one being Ann Arbor, Michigan). I'd joke, "Ah-hah, the second smartest city in the country." But they didn't laugh. In Ithaca, New York, a city with not just one major school of higher learning, not just Cornell University but Ithaca College as well, the good burghers were adamant in stopping efforts by Ithaca Ecovillage co-founder Joan Bokaer when she tried to raise interest in linking the city center by streetcar with efforts to create a few more ecovillages in several outlying areas. (She was also the co-convener or our Third International Ecocity Conference in Senegal.) These have the potential for becoming larger pedestrian-oriented ecovillages. There is high agricultural production potential there and such villages could host graceful living a short distance from the town center and the two campuses while also producing food, as her ecovillage does. The town is proud of its very active and successful Farmers Market where fresh produce has proved the demand for local farm products. The issue: no one wanted to face the "problem" of losing a few parking spaces for their cars to make room for the streetcars. End of subject. Very few dared appear in the eyes of their neighbors to be giving the idea some credit, to open it up for discussion. The neighbors would object – vigorously. "If I supported that my neighbors would kill me."

We have in this fear of neighbors the first level of fear and loathing that closes minds so thoroughly that people refuse to even begin thinking about the difficult moves (that for me are just plain fun) that could lead more deeply into the ecocity transitions. This unwillingness to think at all is most essentially a lack of courage, a kind of moral laziness. If the issue is as important as the liberal energy efficient car buyers of Berkeley and Ithaca claim it is in regard to dealing seriously with climate change, Peak Oil, growing species extinctions and other impending crises, one's even tempted to call it cowardice in the face of a clear and present danger though bringing that up – the opposite of courage – won't fly politically. They even say we have a potential world catastrophe of unprecedented dimensions themselves yet they won't listen to the argument that streetcars and urban design or creek restoration with bicycle and pedestrian paths has a gigantic positive effect partially solving the problems they say they are worried about. I've had the debate with friends, "Is it outright evil or simply laziness born of comfort that causes the worst problems in the world?" Laziness allows the evil to grow and evil exploits the laziness that helps it grow. Then everyone blames the evil – in somebody else – ignoring the laziness wherever it falls.

In the economics context of this book again, remember Adam Smith was more interested in issues of morals and ethics than economics, as guides *for* economics, a higher order of ordering things.

So we are back to courage – courage to think as maybe the most basic of the virtues to make all other virtues possible.

46. Small plaza up against forest and field

This scene – schematic of course as I would not propose no railings for transparent architectural plastic bridges – features bridges, café, sculptural fish ladder, bicycle racks, small work vehicle, newspaper stand and path out into a natural environment.

A sampling of good ideas

In getting ready for the next emergent steps in healthy evolution, although its next stages are unpredictable and full of surprises, hopefully some very positive ones, it would pay to notice what things and actions make sense in preparation, which would be the essence of a world rescue approach. Several ideas loom large, good ideas consistent with what I've built up in this book's attempt at building an economics on what we build.

One of the more obvious is lending support to the United Nations. Fear of foreign governments and fear of revolution inside and chaos coming from outside attack is not without basis so some seem to think that a convocation of nations of which "ours" is one against all the others is the worst of all possible worlds. The idea itself of seeking peaceful relations through strategies assisted by law, policy and diplomacy would seem to benefit the great majority, that is all but those who like the heroics, power and honorifics of being conquerors or like identifying with such violent, inflated people, an idea that should be dated by now. A little home team sports boosterism OK, but jingoistic nationalism… Deeper than that we need a consciousness rising in the billions of people around the world who are worried about the future and see that we can build – literally build – a far healthier future than the one we seem to be careening toward today.

The UN may be ineffectual in a few ways but mostly that is understandable in the fact that its diplomats have no "deliberative powers." That can change. This notion is explained well in Cass Sunstein's book *The Second Bill of Rights – FDR's Unfinished Revolution and Why We need it More than Ever*, quoted earlier. He points out that in the formative days of the United States of America, between the Declaration of Independence and the adoption of the Constitution and the Bill of Rights, the Federalists were anxious to preserve as much power close to home in the states as possible. They initially favored giving the various state's Congressional representatives instructions to support or not this bill so that all of the particular state's interests would be served. The only problem was sometimes the state's interests would be in conflict with some of other state's interests. If all states would support only what they wanted, no matter what the other states wanted, few compromises would ensue and logjams would result blocking almost any kind of policy for the good of the Union. And what if one or a few of the states had an idea that was detrimental to the Union or even themselves but that they had not yet thought through well enough to discover the problem? Then if the representatives did not have a certain range of deliberative powers and representatives of other states convinced them of the errors in their earlier thinking, good new legislation would often be blocked and everyone would suffer.

Deliberation at the national level, the Constitutional Convention eventually decided, would be needed to come to the best arrangement for everyone. The representatives should bear in mind what their constituents wanted but at the same time might learn a thing or two in thinking through problems with their colleagues in Congress. Representatives, in other words, needed deliberative powers. If they antagonized some of their constituents on one issue, they could likely please them on others – just the game of being a politician in a system that tries to have the whole country as the highest beneficiary of their efforts. If they were good at their job they could also convince many of their constituents that he or she – and they – were learning something new and improved. The essence of the arrangement is that the states of the US gave up some sovereign powers to the nation as a whole.

This can happen in the international arena. But in the United Nations, the nations' representatives, the ambassadors, unlike members of the US Congress representing their states, have no deliberative powers. Many countries are too fearful of the others, or have mercantilist desires to best the others in the gamesmanship of self-interested economics to allow deliberation that might lead to agreements that might be contrary to "instructions" from home. At the General Assembly of the UN they have no common clear outside enemy that unites them against those outside the assembly – who would they be against as a collective? The Martians? Venusians? Mooneranians? Whereas inside any country, everyone outside the country is a potential enemy so the political subdivisions within a country can compromise on various things for the common defense and other goods, such as one might think, the economics of protective tariffs that their own workers might thrive. This is a dilemma around which only giving away some traditionally sovereign powers to the international agreement can be solved, as giving some deliberative powers to Congress Members is required for relatively harmonious running of democratic governments, whether of the winner-take all mold of the US or the parliamentary mode of most of its fellow democracies.

Coming to a point of trust sufficient to make progress here probably can only happen as part of Norbert Elias's overall civilizing process, in other words, a powerful consensus on the part of billions of people waking up to issues as powerfully and clearly understood as means to further healthy evolution in what we build and how we live. Naomi Klein's new book, *This Changes Everything*,[187] suggests climate change may be the issue to unite us all in a common effort to save much of what's left of life on Earth, and I would say yes – by way of understanding we now need to grant deliberative powers to our representatives when they appear to represent most of our interests but a little more importantly, can think clearly and responsibly on behalf of all life too, learn something along the way and teach us their constituents what they learn. I would add in addition, this body, representing governments representing peoples of nations (imperfectly of course, but a good try) has a far higher moral mandate than any body overseeing trade agreements, such as NAFTA or WTO.

What about the World Court that many countries simply write off, reserving the option to do their own occasional invasion, assassination, foreign regime change

[187] Naomi Klein, Op Cit.

by force or other terrorist activity? First of all remember that we have already started the process of backing off from war in that, as Pinker points out, violence in general has been in a very long term pattern of decline. We've given up as ridiculous dueling on the level of individuals at personal war and eschewed nuclear war at the extreme of really big, disgusting, stupid wars. We now have to apply the lessons from the extremes to the medium range violent conflicts carrying the civilizing process another step closer to Peace on Earth, Peace *with* Earth. In this civilizing process it is important to recognize and fine tune the "deliberative" process of those we select to represent us. And in countries like China that are centrally planned and do not have broad general elections, the leaders can grant to their ambassadors limited deliberative powers too – while contemplating a little more democracy at home. Countries like the United States could do well to do the same by closing the revolving door between government and profit oriented business and strictly limiting the influence of massive amounts of money in elections. Such egregious capitalism is so last decade!

Giving support to the United Nations helps, but there has to be an attitude shift among nation states to make serious progress there. For example, the current funding of United Nations activities comes from membership dues. Some countries disapproving of the UN's policies, such as the United States when the UN was unsupportive of the Bush Administration invasion of Iraq, withhold dues, causing another layer of disruption in the institution's ability to function properly. A partial fix might be this: Futurist economist Hazel Henderson has been promoting a 1% tax on stock market transactions to fund the United Nations since 1995, a doubly good idea that would help make the UN a little more independent of distorting influences from nations that don't want to cooperate, while creating a modest amount of breaks on speculation in the market.

Among those ideas I think national governments everywhere should take very seriously is the idea of a "Department of Peace" in each government of the world. On February 3, 2009 Congressman Dennis Kucinich introduced House of Representatives HR 808 to try to establish a Cabinet level department in the Administration of the United States government to be called the Department of Peace and Non-violence. As usual with most of the truly revolutionary, creative effective and conciliatory moves to solve larger than national or corporate problems this one was roundly ignored and sometimes ridiculed. Those getting wealthy and enjoying power from their mastery of exaggerated gamesmanship or international maneuvering for more money and power are very reluctant to embrace peace or support the threat thereof. Thus most of his congressional colleagues cast Representative Kucinich's proposal as hopelessly naïve, a non-starter. But it remains, separate from self-serving dogma of those believing in neoclassical economics and exaggerated gamesmanship, a very powerful idea for improvement.

The Department of Peace would attempt to serve non-violent resolution of conflicts internationally and within the United States. Perhaps more importantly it would facilitate creating the atmosphere and educational and institutional basis to prevent conflicts of a wide variety from arising in the first place. It would therefore support study of non-violence philosophy and strategy throughout history: Jesus, Tolstoy, Gandhi, Martin Luther King, Jr., Claudette Colvin... It would promote understanding through arts, sciences, anthropology and other cultural exchanges and study and promote "conflict resolution, non-violent intervention, mediation, peaceful resolution of conflict and structured mediation of conflict." In addition the legislation would create a Peace Academy modeled after the US military academies, also "providing a four year concentration in peace education. Graduates would be required to serve five years in public service in programs dedicated to domestic or international non-violent conflict resolution." [188] Needless to say Congress didn't pass the bill. Later for that step in the civilizing process. But… it's in fact getting later every day and things are changing.

Departments of Ecological Development could help. These would be governmental departments similar to the Office of Appropriate Technology under Governor Jerry Brown in his first two terms as California Governor, 1975 to 1983. The office researched and supported solar and wind energy, innovative architecture, better recycling, organic and urban agriculture and a range of environmentally benign and generally healthy technologies. Departments of Ecological Development would take several long steps beyond with much stronger powers serving to oversee and significantly influence and in some cases control what are now departments of energy, transportation, housing and urban and rural development and those aspects of the "interior" or "homeland" that have to do with preservation of natural areas and mineral, water and forest production, use and, as in the case of mines, habitat restoration after use. Bywords would be, "development yes, but ecologically healthy and socially equitable." As it is evident that cities can build soils and biodiversity, becoming net contributors to a healthy environment, so we need institutions that actually support, plan and build like that. This department would help guide, build pilot projects and allocate funds for projects to be constructed, but chief among them and as soon as possible, large pieces of the ecocity. These departments could exist on national, state and city level. Cities adopting ecocity zoning maps would receive resources from higher up – state or national – to help build projects accomplishing a shift in development toward "vitality centers:" downtowns, major district centers and neighborhood centers becoming ecocities, ecotowns and ecovillages in a landscape of natural and agricultural lands returning, and in the pattern of the ecotropolis described herein.

And, realizing that we are building ourselves as surely as we are building our buildings and whole civilizations we might thus, each of us, become instruments of a world rescue strategy, not as a rigidly structured, centrally planned enterprise like the Soviet Union's, but like chaos + educated order = rescue, all of us engaged in

[188] Both quotes above taken from his website: http://kucinich.house.gov/issues/issue/?IssueID=1564#Legislation%20to%20Create%20a%20Department%20of%20Peace

our own unique ways with some but not overbearing control from various centralized government agencies and business of a scale to build the large as well as the small.

Arcosanti, Auroville, Gaviotas, Curitiba, Vancouver, Tianjin Ecocity

To briefly note, as we approach the end of this book, there are some things "ecocity" to learn from each of the above towns committed in different ways to sustainability. From this short list of cities we have some good ideas to mull over as we go about thinking of designing the city of the future, creating jobs, solving problems, literally building a better economics.

Arcosanti, Arizona, Paolo Soleir's frankly experimental city in the high Arizona desert in Southwest USA is the community most specifically ecocity by intent. He even called it an "urban laboratory," enjoying the irony and thought provoking of so labeling a very small project (of very large ambition) way out in the middle of nowhere. Not that the lizards and cactuses would think of it as anything other than home, as somewhere. So do a smattering of people from around the world who have agreed to go there to help build a pedestrian town to exemplify everything one could try to learn from in the quest for a city healthy in the ecological and evolutionary trajectory of life on Earth. That's the purpose. The attempt struggles on with just a few dozen people keeping the faith as hundreds of students getting college credit, volunteers over the years and thousands of visitors a year puzzle their way through tours of what is now a graceful world of flowing concrete forms dressed out in olive trees and tall cypress, and soft yet severe desert views in green, yellow and tan all around. There's a touch of city in the country: café, gallery, multi-story apartments, a string of spare hotel rooms. To drop yourself down into the middle of the world quest for the city of the future self-consciously anchored in all of evolution's past moving fast forward, this is the place. Founded in 1970 it is the first direct attempt to self-consciously create the ecologically healthy city. I was there the founding day; of course I love the place.

The philosophical grounding here is in the notion that cities need to be complex, three-dimensional structures for pedestrians, frugal, lean, efficient. Then like the human brain it would have the physical structure to enable next steps in the evolution of social consciousness and evolution. Does Arcosanti hope to rescue the world? It is more like it wants to create a new world, next steps, but these by intention not random selection, in evolution. With us, Soleri believed, intention, child of complex thought, entered evolution. So from now on the way the universe evolves is our fault or to our credit. Does that seem strangely delusional for such a small effort so far from the complete small city or 5,000 to 7,000 citizens Paolo hoped to have built by now, still only about 5% "complete"? It all starts in the mind, but we need a place, a physical home to sit there, think there and dedicate effort to the goal. This one, with all its problems, is the place where that started. Whether history will recognize it as such, who knows.

Auroville, India, which I visited, toured for several days and where I gave a talk on ecocities once is the town of around 2,000 aspiring to be the international city of 30,000 in which all citizens are citizens of the world engaged in looking for and attempting to build a physical community to help humanity evolve toward an ever more highly evolved and healthy peaceful future, a container, it was hoped, for helping fulfill human personal and collective potential. It's founder was Mirra Alfassa, known there as The Mother, a follower of the Hindu revolutionary turned grounded mystic Sri Aurobindo, making Auroville the launch site for our inner spiritual and outer, expressed as city, exploration of an evolving universe. There's much striking modern architecture there, scattered about with weakly centered clusters of buildings laid out around an immense banyan tree, a magnificent shimmering 5/8ths dome spherical meditation building covered in gold disks, and a wide circular bowl like a 360 degree amphitheater. In the middle of that grand open space, an urn with soil from 124 countries was placed there in dedication to the city's mission at the town's founding in 1968, as mentioned earlier.

I can't help noting that many, I believe most of the homes and other buildings too, were surrounded by small concrete lined moats of water about a foot wide and a foot deep to keep out snakes and insects. There are several architecture studios there and production facilities for earthen building materials, thin cast concrete outhouses and sewage treatment system tanks and other regionally important products.

Gaviotas got the sustainable technologies and the community of peaceful, creative initiative right. Founded by the inspired and magnetically friendly, mechanically ingenious and socially dedicated Colombian Paolo Lugari far from the cities of his country, Gaviotas was another laboratory, less explicitly anchored in the quest for the city of the future as city design and structure than Arcosanti, but more developed in technological invention and production. The anchor there appears to be in a philosophy of peaceful, useful, affordable, innovative contribution to society through the making of imaginative new tools and products. What emerged from the remote and soggy flatlands with borderline poisonous soil – very high in aluminum content – was a steady stream of invention of water pumps, inexpensive solar and wind technologies, forest products and a message of peaceful contribution that, back to Bogota and other cities in Colombia, has been slowly changing the city, one or a thousand solar panels at a time toward at least some of the base technologies of the ecocity.

The most remarkable thing about Gaviotas from my perspective is the respect its contributions has gathered such that even in the wild outback of Colombia's violent battles between army, drug dealers and growers, left wing revolutionaries and right wing death squads, the pioneers there from around the world and the local farmers and indigenous people constitute a strangely quiet and peacefully busy production contributing so conspicuously to betterment it survives and thrives where no one would believe possible.

Lugari chose the site, he says, specifically because it was difficult approaching the impossible and if a creative, contributing community could be established in such an inhospitable if beautiful natural environment, perhaps a way could be discovered to live in that manner anywhere. The key, perhaps good luck windfall, was the suggestion of an early visitor that perhaps in the difficult soils of the site a tree called the Caribbean pine might flourish as it does in similarly severe conditions in Honduras. It did flourish, conditioning the soil and thereby seeding… with a little help from bird droppings and encroaching native animals headed north from the Amazon region after centuries of absence. The pines themselves turned out to have copious resin production that Gaviotans harvest for paints, dies and other products, while the accumulating newly conditioned soil provides year by year for an ever-expanding experiment in food production. Most impressive is the great almost universal respect for the project such that it can thrive in a hostile social environment, made less so by the presence of such an uplifting community of dedicated innovators and workers.

Vancouver announced in 2010 it was going to be the greenest city in the world. The bravado was based on early influences partially from our own 1990 First International Ecocity Conference held in Berkeley. The city decided long before not to slice through its center with freeways but instead create a powerfully pedestrian centered infrastructure. Just to look at it with cars everywhere you'd wonder exactly what that might mean but various details add up to an environment lively and pleasant enough that far more people commute outward – if they commute far at all – than in to the center. One reason is the relatively narrow band of development that constitutes the higher density central area and the decision to space the buildings far enough from one another that the bays and inlets and postcard perfect snow capped mountains in winter that embrace the town on all sides simply said create a beautiful environment accessible to all. In somewhat finer grain detail, many of the building downtown have platforms of two to four stories with plants, often including sizable trees, on these "pedestals." Then with towers set back from the street edge with trees on both street and terrace, the tall buildings recede into the unconscious and the impression on ground level is almost cozy small town – for the dwellers high in the air who, in another mood, get the expansive views of the town and the wild next door. A fair number of the tall building also have trees on top, some protected by windscreens. Lots of glass on the buildings reflects light down into the streets making them feel airy and anything but overwhelmed and oppressed by the actually quite large scale that reigns.

Another thing to learn from Vancouver: Bill Rees, the co-creator of the ecological footprint idea and terminology with his doctoral student Mathis Wakernagle points out that despite Vancouver's intent and generally "green" appearance and function in its beautiful environment, it's ecological footprint is actually relatively large. But the lesson here is that it is very had to make luxurious "green." Rich people who add to the average ecological footprint with their distant vacations, expensive product cashe, advance college studies and travels for their children and investments in active businesses around the world skew the footprint greatly toward the unsustainable. To truly understand our impacts it is required not only to understand the interrelations of parts in whole systems like living organisms and cities, but to disaggregate very different activities and investments from the basic forms and functions of the built environment. High consumption levels and sprawling cities are both big problems. There is the fact that the large single family home with triple garage is, as Ken Schneider suggested, a magnet that tends to attract excessive acquisition of not very important stuff with an important implication for unsustainability.

Curitiba? I've described some of its powerful contributions earlier but wanted to make sure all over again, that you remembered.

Out with Star Wars, in with Peace on Earth, Peace with Earth

Then there is Los Alamos, New Mexico, the Atomic City, Secret City shrouded in trees floating remote and high above the desert west of the Rio Grande. In 1965 I was 21 years old and disturbed by the rapidly growing American War on Vietnam. I started a loosely organize group called No War Toys. Growing up in the shadow of the mushroom cloud – living directly across the Rio Grande Valley from Los Alamos, New Mexico in my family's hobby ranch with one horse south of Santa Fe – I was wondering where all this violence and war came from. Where in the human psyche or our systems of teaching, learning and organizing human production and activity? Was there some kind of myth holding the pattern together going back to primordial days? Was there a kind of Darwinian survivalist gene, gone a little overboard, amplified by our cleverness building weapons and machines up to and including the B-29 bombers my father put through their paces in New Mexico before they were commissioned out over the Pacific to bomb Japan? These inventions for war, shortly after the war, included the hydrogen bombs my parents' friends were designing across the valley in the Los Alamos Mountains where the sun set every evening. Though I didn't hear the quote by J. Robert Oppenheimer, Scientific Director of the project to build the atomic bomb called the Manhattan Project until around 20 years later, I'd gotten the drift that hiding under grade school desks when a siren went off wasn't going to help much in a thermonuclear attack. Said Oppenheimer:

"I have been asked whether in the years to come it would be possible to kill 40 million Americans in the 20 largest American towns in a single night. I'm afraid that the answer to that question is yes… The only hope for our future safety must lie in a collaboration based on confidence and good faith with the other peoples of the world."[189] Talk about the high bar of the civilizing process! The world wasn't yet ready for it.

Oppenheimer used to puzzle people with ideas that seemed what we'd say today were "out of the box" and this idea of collaboration struck many as wildly naïve. A lot of them were busy building bomb shelters encouraged by the federal government. When facing foreign enemies across barriers of communication how are we to know they aren't in fact planning to attack us? But ideas are amazingly slippery things, able to slither around almost any barrier including national boarders. For example my idea to do something about war toys slipped through from the Soviet Union shortly after the alligator crawling boy, 4th of July, 1965, when an artist friend of a friend named Jack Zajac came back from there – an unusual trip to take in 1965 – and told me, "They don't have any toy weapons in Russia. They lost too many people in the Second World War and won't tolerate 'playing' around with pretending to kill anyone. War is serious, catastrophic. They didn't even have chocolate soldiers," he told me. Chocolate soldiers really hit me. Really?! But what affected him most was shortly after arriving home in Los Angeles, a little boy, a total stranger, pointed a toy gun at him and pretended to kill him just shortly off the airplane. "It really unnerved me," he said. Nuclear weapons if they haven't led to the coziest of collaboration among nations, do seem to have taken the steam out of world scale wars. As the civilizing process progresses there may come a day as ideas slide through razor wire boarder fences, between armed guards and intellectuals a little too comfortable, when ecocities get built and war is finally as unthinkable, even as *embarrassing* as dueling.

The day after the dinner with the returning artist I started wondering about what war toys might mean in society. Rather quickly I said to myself, "Maybe I can do something about this, learn something, change something." My notion at the time I started the grassroots campaign I called No War Toys was that as complex as the answer was no doubt, a lot of the training for acceptance of violence and even the idea that war is glorious and exciting must have come from that most excellent of educational environments and opportunities: the everyday home. Not only that but at a time when we are all very young and impressionable children. The little girls miss most of the propaganda, subtle and not so, since generally they are not given the toy weapons to pretend to kill one another for fun… or maybe practice? Remember the word "pretend" is pre + tend, to tend to do something before actually doing it, a kind of practice. So it was a male thing, between little boys and their big fathers. Then the little ones were released to do whatever they wanted with their toys and their similarly influenced friends.

Since my father heard a loud pop when he was sixteen only to immediately find his brother in the adjoining room shot by his own hand through his head, blood still flowing across the floor, I got no gun, toy or otherwise, when growing up. I didn't

[189] J. Robert Oppenheimer, as featured in the film documentary by Jon Else, *The Day After Trinity*, 1980

hear this story until No War Toys was five years old. My father took guns, real and fake, quite seriously, even had a powerful aversion to them and yet, as you noticed, commissioned the big planes to fly off and bomb the Japs. Maybe one of his planes was the Enola Gay. So I decided creating a debate around the issue would be my contribution to the anti-war movement. And it was fascinating, serious and fun. First, working with children and various types of toys was great. We constructed tree houses macho enough to make mothers nervous and beautiful giant sandcastles on beaches in California, Canada, Hawaii and Florida enjoyed by hundreds of people at a time, good means to publicity come education for the ideas involved. Then off to PTA meetings, alternative schools (always against The War) and radio and television shows (usually pro-war) to explore the subject with parents, teachers, psychologists, pro- and anti-war activists, even some military recruiters (in favor of the war) and returning vets (usually against the war, and by the way I never witnessed or even heard of anyone spitting on any vets; that was a fable circulated to make the anti-war protesters look bad. In fact most of us peaceniks felt profoundly sad that so many young men were tricked or forced into fighting, killing and dying – and kept ignorant of Vietnam history and the economics of the war that profited certain people greatly).

An interesting observation hit me immediately: No War Toys supporters appeared from all quarters, right and left, those supporting the war and those opposed. To my surprise some liberals considered withholding war toys from little boys to be a form a censorship. They thought boys needed them to understand what the truth of the larger society actually was, whereas I thought portraying war as fun was the Big Lie, perhaps as basic as one could get, at the foundation for jingoistic indoctrination. War isn't fun, except vicariously for safe and secure armchair observers, video game buffs and – for real – some dangerous people with a loose identity screw who just plain love violence. Some very conservative people, even ones in favor of the war, thought what I was doing was a very good thing because weapons are to be considered for their legitimate use in defending what we believe in and should not be played with in any way, so serious was the issue of defense: train your boys *that*. Give them lectures and only real guns. And I could respect that.

But most germane here are two things: the toy weapons definitely had something to do with building the myth of violence in our character from deep into the past and forever into the future. Remember the opening Star Wars "crawl": "A long time ago in a galaxy far, far away…" Are we stuck with that condition, a permanent feature of our deepest being, that we will always be violent and ever so well organized for war? Or is it a myth conditional on many factors that is not necessarily utterly deterministic? Or is it one myth battling another myth we might cast as "Star Wars" vs. "Peace on Earth, Peace *with* Earth?" That competition or "battle" could come out in a number of very different ways, undoubtedly all healthier than taking war to its ultimate conclusion, which we see over and over in movies as whole planets are blown to vapor. In this debate I tend to agree with Bertrand Russell, who I remember said something like, "The only thing certain about human nature is its infinite malleability." Thus as we need to look at our bizarrely gigantic artifact list these days with an eye to dropping many items on it that range from absurd to wildly destructive or just a waste of our lives' precious time, we need also design and build ourselves to be peace makers and builders.

Now, getting a little late in my life, I agree with my earlier incarnation as an impressionable youth – the set of No War Toys issues was worth paying attention to. At the most benign, pretending to kill your friends in fun armed mayhem was a waste of time when otherwise the child could be learning all sorts of creative skills, cultivating interest in art, science, nature, garden, other people in other places and societies, actual history instead of dreams of conquest acted out physically and thus reinforced somatically: body and mind mutually reinforcing. Such activity amounts to the theme I've brought up a few times here, that we design ourselves by what we commit ourselves to in practice, and that the building of one's self has a great deal to do with literally building, and *that* intimately connected with our economics.

But most important on the economics theme, the culture pattern model describes a whole psychological and sociological ecology of interlinked causes and effects and networks of cross influences, all very complex but with patterns. These patterns are essentially "ecological." I'm reminded of a dozen billboards Greenpeace activists mounted in their founding early days in Vancouver: "Ecology? – Look it up! You're involved."[190] About then, in the days building toward Earth Day 1970, the whole notion of ecology was just beginning to build up, a key not just to environmental issues but a way of looking at whole systems and the complex events and simpler comprehensive patterns within them.

These large and pervasive cultural patterns have enormous easily dismissed implications, that is, they often suggest real work is required to solve some inherent problem – easier to latch on to a simple detail and pretend you are doing something worthwhile solving a short-term piece of the problem instead of the problem itself. You can generally get things right or very wrong in assessing one of these large whole systems patterns, and they exist among people in society as culture pattern models of some serious consistency. One of the key criteria in determining whether you are right or wrong in your assessment is gaining a correct sense of the proportions of things, the large and the most important, and prioritizing accordingly, dealing with them first. By now this is familiar to you as one of the recurring themes in these pages. To get hung up on a little detail within the whole you are likely to fix the car in Los Angeles, fail to fix the city, create a massively wrong set of assumptions about cities and then heat up and wreck the climate system of a whole planet. As said earlier this isn't a theory – it happened.

[190] This great quote can be found in *Greenpeace – how a group of ecologists, journalists, and visionaries changed the world*, by Rex Weyler, Rodale and Raincoast Books, Vancouver, British Columbia, Canada, 2004. Said Wyler, "...the word 'ecology' was not well known at the end of the 1960s. Few colleges offered ecology courses..." p. 52. "On his own initiative, at a cost of $4,000, [Ben] Metcalf placed twelve billboards around the city." p 54.

This principle of right assessment of whole systems, requiring that one knows something of the related components and the basic patterns within the whole system, describes complex living organisms such as yourself, dear reader, the way languages work, the general patterns of ecoevolution that create (cause to "emerge") new forms and functions. These occur in the miniplexion pattern that suggests that cities be compact, basically three-dimensional and ordered in particular ways that help cause the fair-price setting marketplace. That also emerges as another case of what appears to be a self-organizing system. Thus we see correct assessment of important things evident in whole systems despite their fuzzy edges – just like ecological niches in their larger bioregions and those bioregions in their larger or even continental environments or ocean zones called "large marine environments" or LMEs in the oceanographers' trade.

What all this implies is that the whole systems understanding, despite its fuzzy edges, minor inaccuracies and the unpredictable nature of what could be called "products of emergence" is more dependable than the if-then games of the economists in which the "ifs" are dubious or outright absurd. It also suggests that whole cultures drift rather massively in general directions according the changing ideas and values within and therefore each of us in our small ways is intimately connected to what could be changes toward either the ecocity civilization I have in mind here or in other directions. It also suggests, as I noticed in working in the No War Toys effort that a crucial component in the upward momentum would have to be a notion of the importance of disciplined non-violence, a major theme that needs to strengthen many times over in society if we are to solve our ecological and hence evolutionary problems. As the elephant is a keystone species in its ecology, the strong presence of a movement toward non-violent solution of our problems, based on the sanctity of life, human and other, is a keystone species in the culture pattern model that sees a healthy future coming, rather than Jane Jacobs' *Dark Age Coming*. One direction of drift in the whole cultural sense could be toward whatever it takes to just consciously declare and specifically work toward a world rescue effort – it is not something that can't be contemplated, and in the contemplating, helped along. And its essence is an economics of non-violence.

On to real solutions

So what would be the core of a world rescue campaign? We don't have to describe too much beyond the general roles for different sectors. If the basics are understood – that we need to study, try out promising solutions, experience and learn, which was FDR's mode of operation, if we gain a sense for the overall principles and the conditions that prevail now and have a sense of direction for an evolving healthy cultural pattern model, which is to also say when seen in the environmental context, we begin to manage things holistically – then many things will fall into place.

If we know something about healthy kinds of agriculture and cities, if we grasp the implication of nature-overwhelming numbers of people and if we see markets for both their creative possibilities and their needs to be fair for all engaged in exchange, monetized or not, many solutions will appear. There is plenty of creativity in us collectively if we can summons the can-do spirit.

An outline for a world rescue campaign would grow from the soil of education – institutionalized and self-organized both. Alignment is a key concept here. In different roles of government, business, NGOs, and as individuals we have an infinite variety of very healthy options: pass good laws, run green and socially conscientious businesses, work with and strengthen NGOs that support sustainability. Help shape all these while shaping ourselves in our lifestyles with the cultural pattern of many mutually complementary activities and an awareness that a lot of things on today's artifact list are genuinely not aligned with a healthy future or are a waste of our lives' precious time. With some of the principles in this book that constitute something of a theory for economics and evolution/ecology all at the same time, we can fill in and improvise into a future where the positive may well materialize out of – emerge from – those positive efforts that today so often seem overwhelmed by business as usual, unhealthy habits and, in some people, real pathologically greedy and power hungry states of mind.

Dismantle the empire? What will the violent folk do? (And the workers at the defense plants?) We need to provide jobs for everyone in building the ecocity civilization as we disempower organized violence. We can't dismantle the empire all at once because security is a real need in an armed world, but we can take the warnings of Chalmers Johnson to heart and we can further the conditions that make it possible if we have a little of Gandhi's patience and willingness to toil for that kind of education.

In the traditional economics realm there is the straight-forward economic admonishment that helps defuse the exaggerated gamesmanship. Contrary to Alan Greenspan's belief system up to the financial crisis of 2008, the evidence is that the market geared for highest levels of gambling for maximum and unjustifiable return from the "real economy" is not designed to limit corruption and promote market health; the exact reverse is the case. That means bring back Glass Steagall and re-erect that "firewall" between community banks and the gambling houses on Wall Street. That means get rid of the "revolving door" and place some of the regulators in charge of Treasury and the Fed instead of those who were, in an earlier role, and likely to return to, in charge of exactly those institutions that need regulation. Keep the roles clear to avoid Jane Jacob's "rancid hybrids."

Then there is disempowering the priesthood of economics in which a dramatic and powerfully meaningful early step would be to remove the Nobel name from the Swedish National Bank's prize in economics. Why not the "Swedish National Bank Prize in Economics?" Let the finite games continue, with all the bogus "if-thens" they like, but don't let such prizes pretend they are supporting the discovery of profound laws of the universe or shedding light on the infinite game of life in its thriving.

Support graduated income tax – celebrate philanthropists who give their money back to the world that helped them or their parents make their money in ways that make it a healthier world. Make them heroes even if you think they may be just trying to look good. Put positive pressure on them to be good guys. They are in many cases in fact helping and often genuinely care a great deal. And acknowledge that businesses can be and often are extremely creative, creating valuable products, services and jobs, contributing enormously to society – there is nothing wrong with decent capitalism. There will always be swings in valuation in the market place seeking fair prices and there will be bubbles but make the swings mild swings instead of wild swings that destroy investments like Warren Buffett's labeled "economic weapons of mass destruction."

Then there is: stop subsidizing oil and coal companies and highways. In fact, get rid of your car at the first opportunity. The biggest "driver" of destructive change may in fact be the driver. You may have to move your residence if you abandon your car by the wayside of your road to semi-enlightenment. You may have to plan way ahead and support zoning to provide the mixed uses that make car free city living possible. That's good! Protect and expand social security investments and benefits. Access those Three Sacred Golden Cows for the capital to build a better future before it's too late.

Personally, recycle assiduously. Conserve energy at home. Bike don't drive and all those good things environmentalists have been talking about for many decades now. Kick stupid things off your artifact list: sell them, give them away, dismantle them and recycle their components, comment on how out of style they are, turn them in for melting down, compost them. Travel less, stay longer, get to know the cultures you visit… So many good things to do. If you are personally serious about confronting the problems of the gigantic corporations, that have bought our lawmakers and elected leaders, boycott all nationally advertised products – buy local. A more refined version of this is to subscribe to boycott and buy lists to vote with your money as well as your votes.

Then a particular idea from this book: build the ecocity university – or several of them – quick.

Those are just a sampling of actions consistent with building healthy economics, infrastructure and sustainable ways of life. You will have to pull some more order out of all the many possible preparations for the next emergence into something actually healthy. C+O=S: Chaos plus order equals solutions. I believe this book supplies many ideas and tools to make that possible, to "shrink for prosperity," shrink in the mass/energy realm and prosper in the realm of satisfaction in our lives. I'll end with a kind of recap of what I think are the most consequential ideas to encapsulate important concepts to help us along our way:

1.) Nature's mass/energy chlorophyll based economics – you're involved.

2.) Transitioning into human economics most massively through what we literally build (human economics) – again, you can help.

3.) The best from capitalism and socialism can supply us with many good and workable ideas.

4.) Getting rid of exaggerated gamesmanship that inflates competition into violence – really crucial.

5.) The ecological imperative of our times requiring proper proportionalizing and prioritizing – a major consciousness shift and discipline in attaining the competence to act for a healthy future.

6.) Adopt the Six Big Ones prioritization framework for thinking all this through – it clarifies a lot: in the physical realm: #1 population, #2 agriculture/diet, #3 built environment (ecocities), #4 natural carbon sequestration; and in the mental, psychological, spiritual realm: #5 generosity and #6 education.

7.) Paying for a full-employment transition to the ecocity civilization via accessing the capital of the Three Sacred Cows: #1 the very wealthy, #2 the military, and #3 the waste in the automobile/sprawl infrastructure recycled into the ecocity civilization's physical infrastructure – that's were the rubber of capital meets the road of a revived Progress with a capital "P."

8.) Then spread the word – which is a rather conventional idea embracing educational communications of all kinds from word of mouth among "the people in the street," emerging "social media" and everyday entertainment to the public media of radio and television and established traditional schools from nursery to university – but aligned with a world rescue strategy concept.

9.) "Shrink for Prosperity" is a pretty good slogan and directive in generally waking people up to the possibilities…

10.) …and "Life, liberty and the experience of happiness for all" – not a bad motto for happy future building.

11.) All the above while working for the positive surprises of emergence into a more compassionate and creative ecoevolution.

That's the best I can do for the most important basics to remember. The whole book is the best I can offer for the details. Now it's your turn.

Idea Glossary

There are a number of ideas in this book that I think are helped greatly if we try to find the right words for them. Ancient Chinese saying: The beginning of wisdom is calling things by their right names. Here's my attempt at that. I offer some new concepts and names – part of the emergence of our self-organizing times – but also in this book bring attention to what I think are key ideas from others concerned with the state of our world. I'll simply list them below, my unique contributions first (to the best of my knowledge) and those from other sources I think especially important, second.

Ideas and terms I'm contributing, with approximate dates of origin, most ideas and terms dated 2010 and later were thought up while working on this book.

The Artifact list 1997
Cooling the Earth, a goal, if contemplated, potentially powerful for solving problems 2000
Correct proportionalizing, then, prioritizing 2010
Department of Ecological Development 1982
Dimensional pairs, 2005
Ecocity, 1979
Ecotropolis, 2011
Evoecolution, 2012
Evolution theory's cooperative half of the dimensional pair (Endosymbiosis (Lynn Margulis)*) to pair with the competitive half illuminated by Darwin and Wallace 2012*
Exaggerated Gamesmanship, 2014
Life, Liberty and the Experience of Happiness for All, motto for a world rescue campaign 20014
Location aware green jobs, 2007
Miniplexion, 1972
The mention that dismisses, 2005
Natural carbon sequestration 2013
Nature's economics linked to human's economics chiefly through what we build, 2010
Peace on Earth, Peace with *earth, 1989*
Proportionalizing and prioritizing as strategic first step, 2011

The Rust factor, 1998
Shrink for Prosperity, 2004
The Six Big Ones, 2013
The Three Sacred Golden Cows, 2008
Unseen guiding hand as a self-organizing emergent phenomenon, 2012

Good ideas and terms I feature by others, generally not mainstream
Arcology (Paolo Soleri)
Barter society never existed; first economics was gifting (Marcel Mauss)
The civilizing process (Norbert Elias championed by Stephen Pinker)
The culture pattern model, CPM (1960s child psychologists)
Decent capitalism and developmentalism put up against industrial Communism under dictatorships (liberals after World War II)
Deficit spending for future return (John Maynard Keynes)
Degrowth economics (a whole movement of people from John Ruskin through E.F. Schumacher to contemporary degrowth/ ecological economists)
Ecocity fractal (Paul Downton)
Emergent phenomena (Robert Laughlin and others)
Endosymbiosis (Lynn Margulis)
Experiment, learn, be flexible (Franklin Roosevelt's approach)
Firewall separation between community banks and big finance gambling (Glass Steagall Act and Franklin Roosevelt initiatives)
Holistic management (Allan Savory)
Invisible guiding hand – price fixing market as emerging self-organizing system, though he didn't put it quite that way (Adam Smith)
The Jevons Paradox (William Stanley Jevons)
Nobel Prize in Economics should be Bank of Sweden Prize (Hazel Henderson, Thomas Berry, Peter Nobel)
One percent transaction on stock market trades to fund the United Nations, mildly regulate high finance investment gambling (Hazel Henderson)
Plan B (Lester Brown)
Role of cities in evolution (Paolo Soleri)
Satyagraha, "truth force," approximately (M.K. Gandhi)
Self-organizing, emergent things, processes, systems, laws (chaos theorcticians and others including Robert Laughlin)
Takers and traders syndrome (Jane Jacobs)
Tax high, spend on building right (Franklin Roosevelt, continued under Truman and Eisenhower, reversed under Johnson, made extreme reverse under Reagan)
Technostructure, (John Kenneth Galbraith)

World rescue strategy campaign idea – my version being a revision of Lester Browns "Plan-B" and Al Gore's "Global Marshall Plan"

Acknowledgements

It is so nice to have a few good friends and believe me their help was crucial in writing this book. As usual in my attempts to be a writer, or at least someone saying something I think is ultimately friendly and helpful and getting it down in words and some imagery, best on paper, it's been years on this now in you hands. Or maybe on your screen. But at publication time, we haven't worked that out quite yet.

Those who just helped sustain the faith over all these years and up to the moment, architect Bill Mastin, artist Susan Felter and technical writer and general polymath with an incredible memory, Ray Bruman – he took the picture of me for my first book: *Another Beginning,* 1978 – thanks most sincerely. Then friends like Nancy Lieblich and Sylvia McLaughlin have radiated the warmth and appreciation that in the cold, hard times make so much difference. Those bridging friendship and "really solid influence" on my ecocity thinking: Paul Downton and Cherie Hoyle who organized our Second International Ecocity Conference, in Australia, and Joan Boaker who also organized one, the Third International Ecocity Conference in Senegal, Wang Rusong from China who organized the yet another conference in our series, held in China and Kirstin Miller, yet one more working with me to produce a great one in San Francisco in 2008, plus being the focus of much of the rest of my life for about 14 years – all inspired and sustained while I was trying to tune up the material you see here in this book. You can see my friends and work mates are quite entwined.

Sliding into the comrades in arms, not as close but so important: Earnest "Chick" Callenbach and Paolo Soleri, both of whom, and Rusong too, are no longer with us and who I miss very sorely. They had an enormous amount to do with my thinking and doggedness, which as you know everyone needs to have to write a book. That or a no-visible-means-of-support lifeline that lets them float into the job – which is definitely not my case. Rusong was also my heartfelt patron in that he invited me to China for the first dozen or more of my 23 trips there, to speak at conferences, many of which he organized himself as Director of the Research Center for Ecological and Environmental Sciences at the Chinese Academy of Science.

My relatively new-found friends at C&P Architecture with offices in several cities in China have been an enormous help in the last three years, providing for about another ten trips to many different cities in China. In particular, President

Fan Bin there and head of the Tianjin and Beijing offices has been a true and extraordinarily helpful friend during the last four years I've been working off and on with this book, and I've had the ever so helpful assistance of Ruby Yangxue and fine translation of Ma Jia in more than 15 conference and seminars in almost as many cities, some of which they set up for me themselves.

In a particular location Lin Xuefeng and Victor Liu at Tianjin Eco-city have been extraordinarily helpful hosting my five trips there and giving me the keys to the new city and lots of targeted tours. Qiu Baoxing recent Vice Minister of Housing and Urban-Rural Development for the country, who took my book *Ecocities* to the leadership of China resulting in the country adopting many of the ideas and terminology from the book – if not all obviously – has also been extraordinarily helpful both in cultivation of the all important ideas at the roots of the subject and in connecting with Chinese urban design and development.

It has also been a delight also to work with Latha Chhetri, Chief Urban Planner in Bhutan at the Ministry of Works and Human Settlement and her colleague, the country's Sr. Urban Designer, Tshering Dorji. And I'd like to honor in a rather diffuse way the interest I've enjoyed in my work leading to my talks in by now over 34 countries around the world: Thank you Korea, Nepal, Australia, Italy, Austria, Brazil, Colombia, Turkey and Canada, all of you there with a strong interest in my work, enough to bring me to your beautiful lands several times each, and source of inspiration and the connections that lead to policy or building or some of both, plus generate the kind of material at the foundation of this book, I owe you all enormous thanks. Right up to the moment, I'll mention my invitation to present at a conference organized by the World Academy of Art and Science, from the organization's president, Garry Jacobs – I'm a Fellow of the Academy – which was held in Baku, Azerbaijan this spring on building trust in a region under enormous pressure right now – Middle East, poor Africa and Eastern Europe – an experience shaping my last minute thoughts going into polishing my efforts here in this book.

As to people who have helped most directly with the writing in that they have read or lent material support – money or travel to gather more experiences and ideas – these would include, for some advice after reading various drafts, some rather different from what you see here, Rick Smith at Wayne State University, Detroit, Rick Pruetz, past Planning Director of Burbank, California and currently a member of the Board of Directors of Ecocity Builders. Special thanks to one who made the most thorough read and comment appraisal, my friend from Arcata and Humboldt State University, Stacy Becker, an administrator of various student and community projects there.

I've had financial support in the earliest days of beginning to work on this book from the Foundation for Sustainability and Innovation and its mainspring, Ron Chilcote. Also similar help from inventor industrialist David Hall of the company mentioned in the text called Novatek in Provo, Utah. He and Ron got me to Nepal, Bhutan, Detroit and Washington D.C., and David, once to China with himself, his wife and others from Novetek for meet with Rusong and the Mayor and head planners of a city of 2,000,000 there. Joell Jones, who grew up in New Orleans sent me to that disaster zone three months after Hurricane Katrina for my suggestions on what ecocity insights might lend to recovery and rethinking there, "getting me into" my campaigns to revive the ancient strategy of dealing with rising waters by building compact, pedestrian ecocity design on artificial mounds of everyday local earth. One such initiative is so new I don't even have it in this book. It's called the Bigger Bay Ecotropolis and hopes to influence the San Francisco Bay with the ideas Joell got me into.

Very helpful buying me time to write through money raised in a Kickstarter campaign my thanks to: Thierry delmarcelle, Ian Douglas, Jane Engle, Arinna Grittani, Mario Hotchkiss, Gerd Junne, Ralph Kratz, Peter McCrea. Bill Rees, Laura Srewop, Michelle Stucky, Cassio Taniguchi, Ray Tomalty, Marc Vangelisti, David Van Setters.

Most recently David Eifler, who has off and on given some very helpful financial as well as very warm moral assistance and encouragement has also most recently helped pay for this publication and is currently planning, as Librarian of the University of California at Berkeley Environmental Design Library, a display of my books, drawing and perhaps models starting in the fall of 2016. This is to be a celebration of the 30th anniversary of publication of my book *Ecocity Berkeley – Building Cities for a Healthy Future*. And throughout the whole time I've been writing toward, organizing and trying to tune up this work, going back to about 2006, my non-profit organization, Ecocity Builders has been the beneficiary of crucial support from the Mazer Foundation and one of our Board of Director Members, Steve Bercu. Recent past and current Board Members Tong Yen Ho from Singapore and recent CEO of the Tianjin Eco-city project and Jeff Stein, President of the Cosanti Foundation building Arcosanti, thanks for your help and encouragement too.

That brings me up to date, background and assistance to writing this book.

By the way, a few people have commented my writing is a bit breezy for the serious content, with a title sounding a bit grandiose. About the latter complaint I can only say it's not my idea! Al Gore and Lester Brown lead the way, with all due credit given herein, and besides, we should all try to "improve reality" as Farley cartoonist for the San Francisco Chronicle cartoonist Phil Frank put it. About my somewhat informal style in serious topics – some have suggested I should make up my mind to be more serious or do a book that doesn't try to effect serious change. But I beg to differ and try out something maybe a little unique: jump into the movement to improve things with some levity. In fact I've learned to enjoy writing whereas it use to be such a chore. The difference is the notion I've heard attributed to Ema Goldman, an anarchist, which I'm not, but she said something like, "If I can't dance I don't want to be in your revolution."

Well we have a revolution here and I can't think of anything more pleasurable to do. So let's dance.

Index

About the Author

Richard Register grew up in New Mexico under the shadow of the mushroom cloud, knowing some designers of the hydrogen bombs, the end of the world. So naturally he has been concerned with how to turn *that* around. He built sculpture for the sense of touch (maybe we could get back "in touch"), started a peace group called No War Toys (wondering what the influence of encouraging little boys to pretend to kill their friends for fun might have on human propensity to war).

Later he decided to focus on ecologically healthy cities because, after all, they are big. The biggest most environmentally consequential things we build in fact. So we better build them right. Doing so begins to define a new economics and new relationship to ecology and evolution. So it seems he's something of a fanatic for trying to shape us up to rescue the world. If we can strive to understand the universe and dream of life everlasting, either for individuals or for life itself collectively, why not? That's what he thinks. So his profession evolved to suggestion for means of survival and thriving. He lives in Oakland, California, writes, draws and travels internationally to talk about all this and to try to keep learning.

53525064R00233

Made in the USA
San Bernardino, CA
19 September 2017